Prize for the brave is there,
    Rest for the weary thrall,
When ever everywhere
    God shall be all in all.

From *O quanta qualia sunt illa sabbata*
Peter Abelard (1079–1142)
Translated by Gerard Moultrie

The

Abelard Hymnal

Medieval Christian Songs
Translated Into English

✝

EDITED BY

RYAN B. JAWAD

Deus in omnibus

MMXX

Library of Congress Cataloging-in-Publication Data
The Abelard Hymnal: Medieval Christian Songs Translated Into English / edited by Ryan B. Jawad
    English
    ISBN 978-1-7349443-0-3

A special thanks to Bärenreiter-Verlag for giving permission to use the hymn melodies. Thanks also to the forum members of Stack-Exchange, Gregorio Users Google Group, and MusicaSacra for help with computer code, translations, and liturgical terminology.

This book was typeset in TeXShop 4.44 using Gregorio 5.2.1.

Visit Deusinomnibus.com for new orders.

Contents

Introduction

This hymnal is a collection of early Christian poems translated into English and set to melodies from the medieval period. The 56 poems are selected from *One Hundred Latin Hymns: Ambrose to Aquinas* (*OHLH*), edited by Peter G. Walsh and Christopher Husch. *OHLH* is number 18 in the Dumbarton Oaks Medieval Library series and is a critical edition of early Christian poems written between the 4th and 13th centuries. The 183 melodies for the poems are taken from *Die mittelalterlichen Hymnenmelodien des Abendlandes* (*HA*), volume 1 in Bärenreiter's Monumenta Monodica Medii Aevi series. *HA*, written by Bruno Stäblein, is a catalogue of hymns from medieval Europe and contains well over 1000 different melodies. The melodies that I selected come from manuscripts that date between the 11th and 15th centuries. The translations for the poems are taken from a variety of sources, though most are from 19th-century England. For criteria used in selecting the translations and other methodology, see "Further Information on the Hymnal".

I should mention here that any particular poem was often associated with more than one melody. Stäblein records, for example, that the hymn *Iam lucis orto sidere* was used with more than 25 different melodies, many of which are from the same time and same place. Moreover, the same melody was often used for multiple poems. Melody 142 in *HA*, for example, was used with at least 10 different poems. For these reasons, I use the word "hymn" only when referring to a particular poem / melody combination. 183 of the 187 hymns in this hymnal have unique melodies.

In most cases, I chose a poem from *OHLH* based on whether I could find a corresponding melody in *HA* and a suitable translation. Some may wonder, for example, why I did not include the well-known hymn *Adore devote, latens veritas*, even though it appears in *OHLH*. In fact, *Adore devote* does not have a single melody in *HA*. I was surprised, also, to find that it is not listed in any of the 12 databases of medieval manuscripts in the Cantus Index Network (Koláček).

The two earliest hymnals with directly transcribable notes are from Kempten and Moissac (Caldwell). Their respective archives are Zürich, Zentralbibliothek, Rh 83, dated around the year 1000, and Roma, Biblioteca Apostolica Vaticana Ross. 205, also dated around 1000. 18 of the hymns that I selected for this hymnal come from these two archives, both of which are catalogued in *HA*.

Layout

The hymns appear in chronological order, sorted first by poem date and then by melody date. The following information is included on the first page of each hymn: the title, the rubric, the place and date of the melody, the range of the melody, the author and date of the poem, the translator, which stanzas are translated (if not all of them), any melodic alterations between stanzas, possible selections or divisions, and, if applicable, the processional stanza pattern.

The title of each hymn is in Latin. The Latin name is simply the first few words of the poem, so in most cases, the meaning of the title can be understood by looking at the opening lyrics. Each hymn has a unique number and is prefixed with a cross (e.g. †104: Ave, Maris Stella). For help pronouncing the Latin, see "Pronouncing the Titles".

Stäblein includes rubrics found in the manuscripts for many of the hymns. I translated these and included them underneath the titles on the lefthand side. For some hymns, the rubrics may be less relevant today, while others may have no rubrics at all. For recommendations on when to sing each hymn, see "Rubrics for the Poems and Hymns" and "Liturgical Themes".

Underneath the title on the righthand side is the place of the melody, followed by the date: that is, the place associated with the archive in which the hymn is found, followed by the date of the archive. Most of this information is given in *HA*. The composers of the melodies are not listed because they are all anonymous.

Each hymn begins with a large first letter called the initial. The space above the initial is typically reserved for the mode of the piece. However, some of the hymns begin in one mode and end in another, while others do not seem to be in a mode at all. For this reason, I decided instead to use this space for the range of the melody. The range assumes that Do is C and Fa is F. For more information on the clefs and music notation, see "Reading Square Notation".

The author of the poem is given on the bottom left. This is followed by the date of the poem. The date is the most specific that I could find for the poem. Rarely, it is an exact year; more often, it is the birth and death dates of the author. In most cases, though, the date given is only a general time frame like 9th–10th century. Below the author is the translator. If not all stanzas are translated, a set of numbers is listed such as "2–5, 9 / 10". This means that stanzas 2–5 and 9 are translated out of 10 total stanzas.

Generally speaking, each hymn repeats its melody every stanza. However, manuscripts occasionally indicate slight melodic alterations between stanzas. These alterations are detailed in the "Kritischer Bericht" of *HA*, and with a few exceptions, I included them in the scores. This information is placed in a footnote on the righthand side. An example of such a footnote is "(1) iii:3–4, iv:3, (2) iv:3". The numbers in parentheses refer to the stanzas that contain the alterations, the lowercase roman numerals refer to the lines in the stanza, and the numbers after the colon refer to the syllables. In the example above, there are alterations to the melody in stanza 1 on line 3 at the 3rd and 4th syllables. In the same stanza, there is an alteration in the 4th line at the 3rd syllable. In stanza 2, there is an alteration on line 4 at the 3rd syllable. Note that stanzas in the scores are separated by a double bar, while poem lines are separated by a single bar; a partial bar is used for poems with longer lines and divides each line roughly in half.

For some poems, particularly the longer ones, certain selections or divisions were commonly made. This information is given on the bottom right. "Selection" and "division" are abbreviated "sel" and "div", respectively. An example is "div: 1–7; 8–9, 11, 13", indicating that the hymn was often divided into two separate hymns: stanzas 1–7 were sung as one hymn, while stanzas 8–9, 11, and 13 were sung as another. A few of the hymns are classified as "Processionals" in *HA*. These hymns differ from the others in that they have a refrain. The refrain is repeated between each stanza, though sometimes it is also repeated halfway through each stanza. Such details are also listed on the bottom right and are prefixed with a "P".

Additional Remarks

The translations appear in this hymnal as they do in the sources. Punctuation, capitalization, and spelling are left unaltered, including archaic spellings such as "burthen" and "pretious". In some cases, the pronunciation of words may need to be adjusted slightly to fit with the music. Typically, this means combining two syllables into one. "Heaven", for example, may need to be sung as one syllable: "Heav'n". Other examples are "glo-ri-ous" sung as "glo-rious", "ra-di-ant" as "ra-diant", and "par-don-ing" as "par-d'ning". The contractions are often but not always written in by the translators.

If combining two syllables into one makes a group of notes awkward to sing, the singer may want to experiment with assigning the first syllable to the first notes in the group and the second syllable to the remaining notes. If the two syllables are set to only a single note, the singer may consider adding another note at the same pitch. Both techniques are frequently seen in manuscripts when a line of a poem contains too many syllables. See *Aeterna Christi munera* on page 60 of *HA* for an example containing both of these techniques.

Some manuscripts append "Amen" cadences to the hymns. If they are listed in *HA*, I added them to the scores accordingly. Flat signs, too, are included as they appear in *HA*. The flat sign was only used with the note B (assuming Do is C and Fa is F), and it only carried for the length of the word. Manuscripts do not always agree on whether a note should be flat. Stäblein writes that the flats he indicates are on the reserved side and that many of the Bs were probably sung as B-flats (xv). Singers may want to experiment with adding additional B-flats.

The lists on the following pages highlight different aspects of the hymnal. For a more detailed report, including citations for dates, archives, and translations, see "Notes on the Poems and Melodies".

This hymnal is named in honor of Peter Abelard (1079–1142), who wrote the beautiful hymn *O quanta qualia sunt illa sabbata*, †184. I had hoped to include more of his hymns, but unfortunately, all of the original melodies for the others have been lost.

Ryan B. Jawad

Authors and Dates of the Poems

Ambrose of Milan (ca. 334–397)

> Aeterne rerum conditor | Deus, creator omnium | Hic est dies verus Dei | Iam surgit hora tertia | Illuminans altissimus | Intende, qui regis Israel | Splendor paternae gloriae

Prudentius (348–410)

> Ales diei nuntius | Nox et tenebrae et nubila

Sedulius (fl. 425–450)

> A solis ortus cardine

Venantius Fortunatus (ca. 535–610)

> Crux benedicta nitet (ca. 567) | Pange, lingua (ca. 567) | Vexilla regis prodeunt (ca. 567)

Theodulf of Orléans (ca. 750–821)

> Gloria, laus, et honor (ca. 818)

Peter Abelard (1079–1142)

> O quanta qualia sunt illa sabbata (ca. 1131)

Thomas Aquinas (1225–1274)

> Verbum supernum prodiens (1264)

Anonymous

> (390–423)
>> Aeterna Christi munera

(475–525)

Mediae noctis tempus est

(8th c.)

Iam lucis orto sidere | Rector potens, verax Deus |
Te lucis ante terminum

(8th–9th c.)

Aurora lucis rutilat | Dei fide, qua vivimus

(ca. 803–869)

Consors paterni luminis | O lux beata Trinitas |
Somno refectis artubus | Summae Deus clementiae |
Tu, Trinitatis unitas

(9th c.)

Aeterne rex altissime | Audi, benigne conditor |
Ave, maris stella | Beata nobis gaudia |
Nunc, sancte nobis Spiritus

(9th–10th c.)

Aeterna caeli gloria | Caeli Deus sanctissime |
Christe, redemptor omnium | Conditor alme siderum |
Deus, tuorum militum | Ex more docti mystico |
Iam Christus astra ascenderat | Iesu, corona virginum |
Iesu, nostra redemptio | Iesu, redemptor omnium |
Immense caeli conditor | Lucis creator optime |
Magnae Deus potentiae | Primo dierum omnium |
Quem terra pontus aethera | Rerum Deus tenax vigor |
Rex gloriose martyrum | Telluris ingens conditor

(999)

Agnoscat omne saeculum

(ca. 1026)

A Patre unigenitus

(1000–1075)

Iam, Christe, sol iustitiae | Qua Christus hora sitiit

(11th c.)

Optatus votis omnium

Times and Places of the Melodies

Austria (12th–15th c.): 24 melodies
> Dürnstein | Heiligenkreuz | Klosterneuburg |
> Sankt Florian | Sankt Lambrecht | Vorau

Czech Republic (14th c.): 1 melody
> Prague

England (12th–13th c.): 15 melodies
> Worcester | [unspecified]

France (11th–15th c.): 56 melodies
> Angers | Bayeux | Châlons-en-Champagne |
> Clermont-Ferránd | Fécamp | Laon | Le Mans | Limoges |
> Moissac | Nevers | Normandy | Paris

Germany (11th–15th c.): 22 melodies
> Fritzlar | Hegau | Kempten | Lehel | Regensburg |
> Rüdnitz | Schäftlarn

Italy (11th–14th c.): 46 melodies
> Ascoli Piceno | Benevento | Gaeta | Milan | Piacenza |
> Ravenna | Rome | Verona | [unspecified]

Poland (15th c.): 1 melody
> Środa Śląska

Switzerland (12th–15th c.): 22 melodies
> Einsiedeln | Engelberg | Fribourg | Lausanne | Rheinau

Archives for the Melodies

Angers, Bibliothèque de la Ville 113 (105) (14th–15th c.)

Bari, San Nicola s. n. (13th c.)

Benevento, Biblioteca Capitolare VI 38 (11th c.)

Berlin, Staatsbibliothek Hamilton 688 (ca. 1267)

———, Staatsbibliothek Mus. ms. 40612 (1300–1350)

Clermont-Ferránd, Bibliothèque Municipale et Universitaire 74 (14th c.)

Einsiedeln, Stiftsbibliothek 336 (1100–1150, 1225–1275)

Engelberg, Stiftsbibliothek 8 (ca. 1400)

———, Stiftsbibliothek 314 (1372)

Freiburg (Schweiz), Kantons- und Universitätsbibliothek L 322 (14th c.)

Graz, Universitätsbibliothek 387 (1350–1400)

Heiligenkreuz, Stiftsbibliothek 20 (12th–13th c.)

Karlsruhe, St. Blasien 77 (1439–1442)

Kassel, Landesbibliothek theol. 2° 96 (1334)

Klosterneuburg, Stiftsbibliothek 1000 (1336)

Laon, Bibliothèque Com. 263 (1100–1150)

Lausanne, Bibliothèque Cantonale et Universitaire V 1184 (13th c.)

London, British Museum Add. 34209 (12th c.)

München, Bayerische Staatsbibliothek Clm 17009 (1462)

———, Fransician abbey of St. Anna s. n. (1227–1235)

Oxford, Corpus Christi College N. 134 (12th–13th c.)

Padova, Biblioteca Capitolare A 47 (12th c.)

Paris, Bibliothèque de l' Arsenal 114 (1471)

———, Bibliothèque de l' Arsenal 279 (ca. 1234)

———, Bibliothèque Mazarine 344 (1350–1400)

———, Bibliothèque Nationale lat. 777 (11th c.)

———, Bibliothèque Nationale lat. 1269 (1309)

———, Bibliothèque Nationale n. a. lat. 1235 (12th c.)

———, Bibliothèque Sainte-Geneviève 112 (1450–1500)

———, Bibliothèque Sainte-Geneviève 113 (14th–15th c.)

Piacenza, Biblioteca Capitolare 65 (ca. 1200)

Praha, Knihovna pražské metropolitní kapituly, Sveti Vid
  Cim. 7 (1325–1375)

———, Univerzitní knihovna XII E 15c (1300–1350)

Regensburg, Staatliche und Kreisbibliothek Lit. 19 (14th c.)

Roma, Biblioteca Apostolica Vaticana Regin. lat. 2050
  (13th–14th c.)

———, Biblioteca Apostolica Vaticana Ross. 205 (ca. 1000)

———, Biblioteca Capitolare San Pietro B 79 (1200–1250)

———, Biblioteca Casanatense 1574 (12th c.)

———, Biblioteca Casanatense 1695 (12th–13th c.)

———, Santa Sabina, Archivum Generale Ordinis
  Predicatorum s. n. (ca. 1255)

Rouen, Bibliothèque de la Ville 248 (12th–13th c.)

Sankt Florian, Stiftsbibliothek XI 407 (15th c.)

———, Stiftsbibliothek XI 410 (15th c.)

Verona, Biblioteca Capitolare CIX (102) (11th c.)

Vorau, Stiftsbibliothek 252 (ca. 1458)

Worcester, Cathedral Library F 160 (ca. 1230)

Wrocław, Biblioteka Kapitulna, Cod. 58 (15th c.)

Zürich, Zentralbibliothek, Rh 18 (12th c.)

———, Zentralbibliothek, Rh 21 and 22 (1459)

———, Zentralbibliothek, Rh 83 (ca. 1000)

Translators

Baker, Henry Williams (1821–1877)
> Christe, redemptor omnium

Blew, William John (1808–1894)
> Ex more docti mystico | Iesu, redemptor omnium

Bridges, Robert Seymour (1844–1930)
> Splendor paternae gloriae

Caswall, Edward (1814–1878)
> Consors paterni luminis | Mediae noctis tempus est |
> Rerum Deus tenax vigor

Chambers, John David (1805–1893)
> Beata nobis gaudia | Dei fide, qua vivimus |
> Deus, creator omnium | Deus, tuorum militum |
> Iam, Christe, sol iustitiae | Primo dierum omnium |
> Qua Christus hora sitiit | Rector potens, verax Deus |
> Rex gloriose martyrum | Summae Deus clementiae |
> Tu, Trinitatis unitas

Charles, Elizabeth Rundle (1828–1896)
> Optatus votis omnium | Vexilla regis prodeunt

Copeland, William John (1804–1885)
> Iam surgit hora tertia | Illuminans altissimus

Dearmer, Percy (1867–1936)
> Quem terra pontus aethera

Drummond, William (1585–1649)
> O lux beata Trinitas

Duffield, Samuel Willoughby (1843–1887)
> Telluris ingens conditor

Edersheim, Alfred (1825–1889)
> Conditor alme siderum

Hewett, John William (1824–1886)
> Te lucis ante terminum

Housman, Laurence (1865–1959)
> Aeterne rex altissime

Kynaston, Herbert (1809–1878)
> Aeterne rerum conditor

Lacey, Thomas Alexander (1853–1931)
> Audi, benigne conditor

MacGill, Hamilton Montgomerie (1807–1880)
> Pange, lingua

McDougall, Alan Gordon (1895–1964)
> Iam lucis orto sidere

Moultrie, Gerard (1829–1885)
> O quanta qualia sunt illa sabbata

Neale, John Mason (1818–1866)
> A Patre unigenitus | A solis ortus cardine | Aeterna caeli gloria | Aeterna Christi munera | Aeterne rex altissime | Agnoscat omne saeculum | Aurora lucis rutilat | Caeli Deus sanctissime | Crux benedicta nitet | Gloria, laus, et honor | Iesu, corona virginum | Iesu, nostra redemptio | Immense caeli conditor | Intende, qui regis Israel | Lucis creator optime | Magnae Deus potentiae | Quem terra pontus aethera

Newman, John Henry (1801-1890)
 Nunc, sancte nobis Spiritus

Pope, Robert Martin (1865-1944)
 Ales diei nuntius | Nox et tenebrae et nubila

Riley, John Athelstan Laurie (1858–1945)
 Ave, maris stella

Wackerbarth, Athanasius Diedrich (1813–1884)
 Verbum supernum prodiens

Wallace, John (1838–1896)
 Iam Christus astra ascenderat | Somno refectis artubus

Woodward, George Ratcliffe (1848–1934)
 Hic est dies verus Dei

Musica!

†1: Aeterne rerum conditor

At Lauds.

Germany: Kempten (ca. 1000)

D–C

E - ternal God, Thy Word was light, Ere sun

and moon ruled day or night, The drowsy race of

life to time With sweet vi-cissi-tude of chime.

2) Hark! morning's herald winds his horn, To wake

the world ere day is born; Night's latest watch with

timely blast To sound, or e'er the night is past.

Ambrose of Milan (ca. 334–397)
tr. Herbert Kynaston

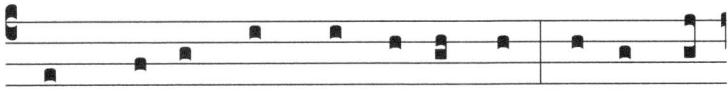

3) Lured by that voice the daystar flies To part the

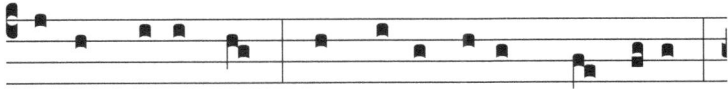

curtain of the skies; And sinful vi-sions flee a-way,

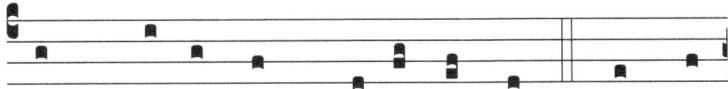

Chased by the breath of coming day. 4) That cry

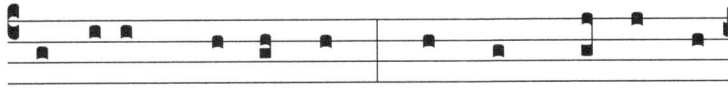

the anchor'd seaman cheers Who wish'd for day, till

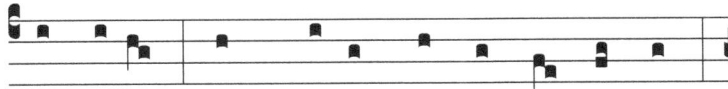

day appears, Smote Pe-ter's sin, ere morning grew,

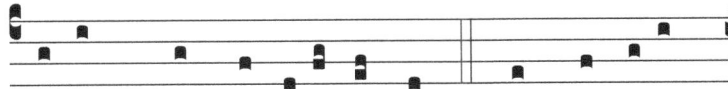

Dissolved with peni- tential dew. 5) Sleepers a-wake!

the cockcrow's sounds Twice call the day to duty's

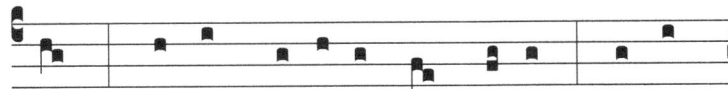

rounds; To warn us of our plighted troth, To wake,

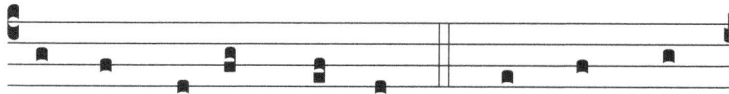

and then to chide our sloth. 6) That voice day's

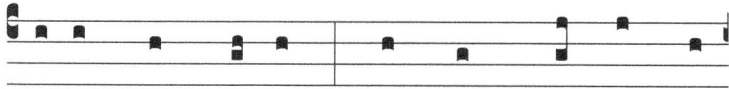

earliest hope be- stows, And warms the soul ere

morning glows; Night's spoiler sheaths his death-

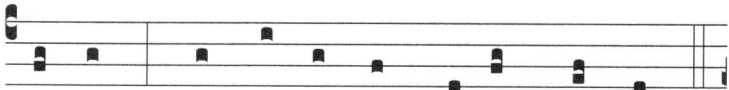

ful sword, And lapsing faith re- gains the Lord.

7) Turn, Lord, and look! Thy loving eyes, Turn'd once,

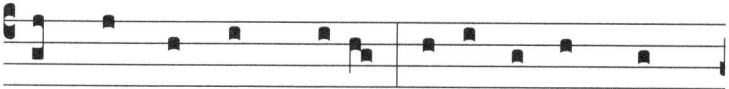

turn him who thrice denies; To softest dews night's

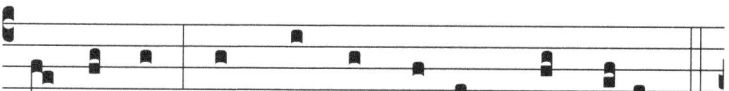

darkest sins Melt, ere Thy pardon's day begins.

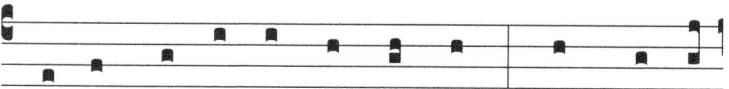

8) Daystar within, ere morning break, Make all my

heart to Thee a-wake; Let prayer outstrip the dawn-

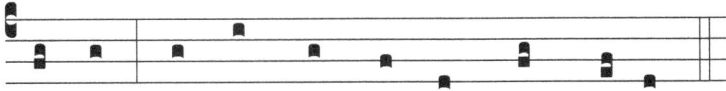

ing rays, And life's first whisper'd notes be praise!

†2: Aeterne rerum conditor

At Lauds.

Italy: Verona (11th c.)

B–G

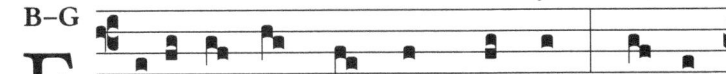

E - ternal God, Thy Word was light, Ere sun

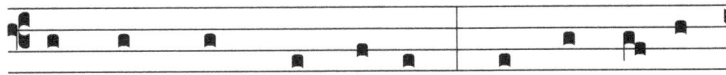

and moon ruled day or night, The drowsy race

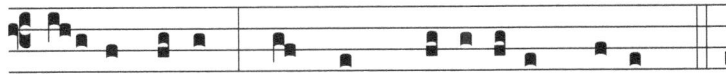

of life to time With sweet vi-cissi-tude of chime.

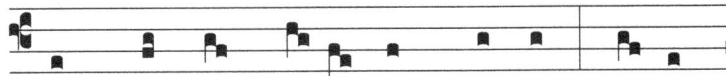

2) Hark! morning's herald winds his horn, To wake

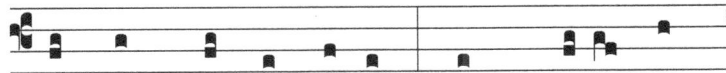

the world ere day is born; Night's latest watch

Ambrose of Milan (ca. 334–397) (1) ii:3,5, iii:2, (2) i:7
tr. Herbert Kynaston

with timely blast To sound, or e'er the night is

past. 3) Lured by that voice the daystar flies To

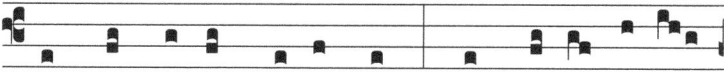

part the curtain of the skies; And sinful vi-sions

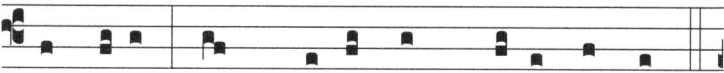

flee a-way, Chased by the breath of coming day.

4) That cry the an-chor'd seaman cheers Who wish'd

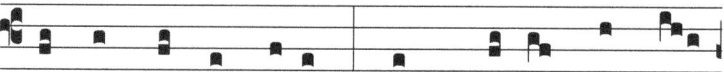

for day, till day appears, Smote Pe-ter's sin, ere

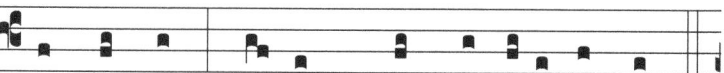

morning grew, Dis-solved with peni- tential dew.

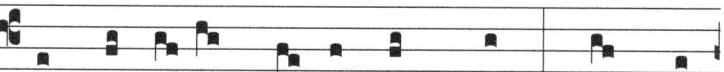

5) Sleepers a- wake! the cockcrow's sounds Twice call

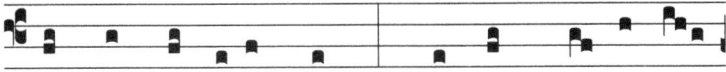

the day to duty's rounds; To warn us of our

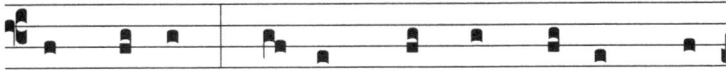

plighted troth, To wake, and then to chide our

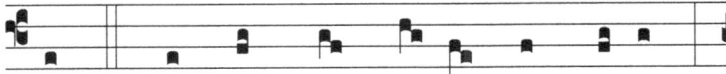

sloth. 6) That voice day's ear-liest hope be-stows,

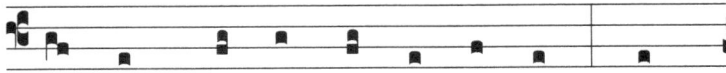

And warms the soul ere morning glows; Night's

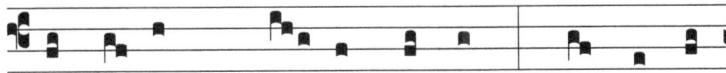

spoiler sheaths his deathful sword, And lapsing

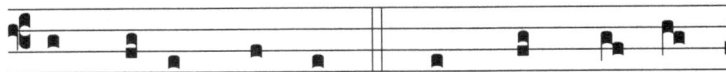

faith re-gains the Lord. 7) Turn, Lord, and look!

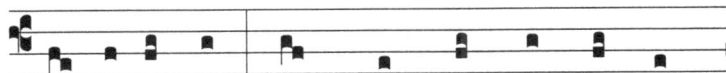

Thy loving eyes, Turn'd once, turn him who thrice

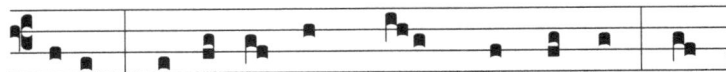

denies; To softest dews night's darkest sins Melt,

8

ere Thy pardon's day begins. 8) Daystar within, ere

morning break, Make all my heart to Thee a-wake;

Let prayer outstrip the dawning rays, And life's

first whisper'd notes be praise! A- men.

†3: Aeterne rerum conditor

Switzerland: Rheinau (1459)

E–D

E - ternal God, Thy Word was light, Ere sun

and moon ruled day or night, The drowsy race of

life to time With sweet vi-cissi-tude of chime.

Ambrose of Milan (ca. 334–397)
tr. Herbert Kynaston

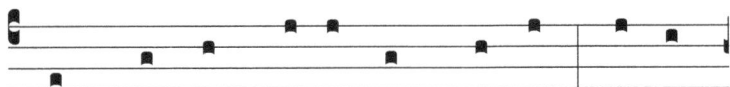

2) Hark! morning's herald winds his horn, To wake

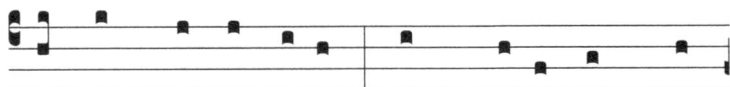

the world ere day is born; Night's latest watch with

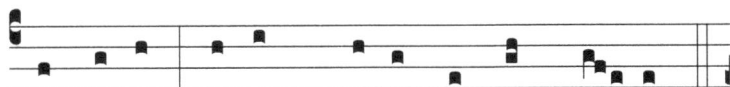

timely blast To sound, or e'er the night is   past.

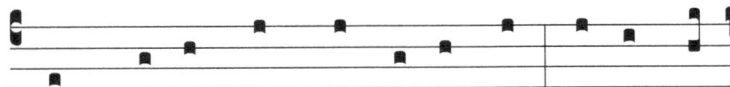

3) Lured by that voice the daystar flies To part the

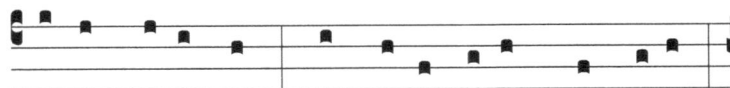

curtain of the skies; And sinful vi-sions flee a-way,

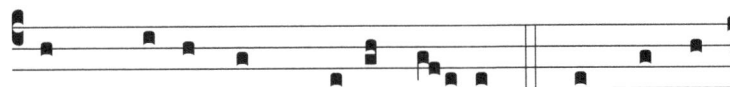

Chased by the breath of coming day. 4) That cry the

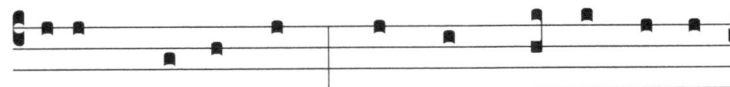

anchor'd seaman cheers Who wish'd for day, till day

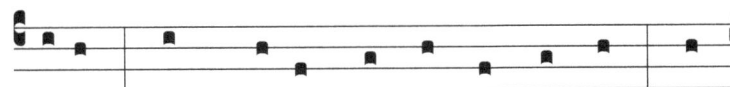

appears, Smote Pe-ter's sin, ere morning grew, Dis-

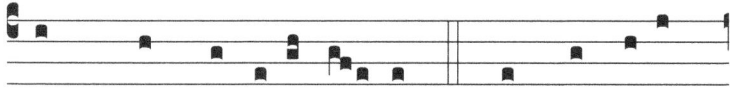

solved with peni- tential dew. 5) Sleepers a-wake!

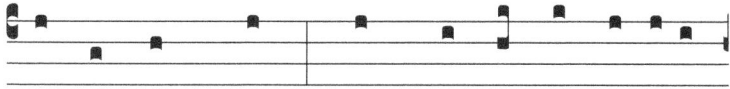

the cockcrow's sounds Twice call the day to duty's

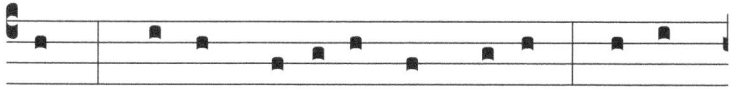

rounds; To warn us of our plighted troth, To wake,

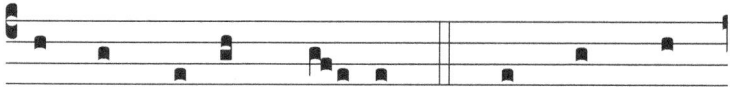

and then to chide our sloth. 6) That voice day's

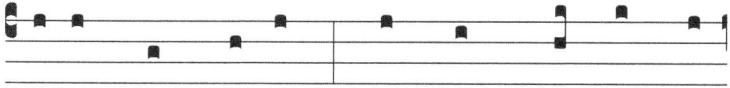

earliest hope be- stows, And warms the soul ere

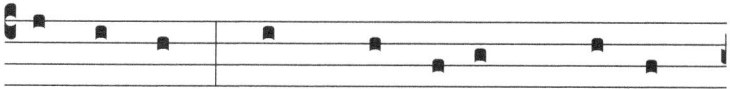

morning glows; Night's spoiler sheaths his death-

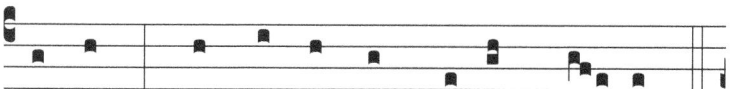

ful sword, And lapsing faith re-gains the Lord.

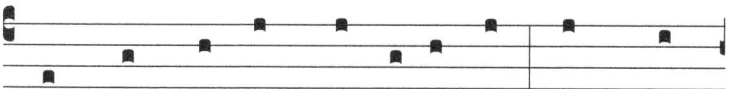

7) Turn, Lord, and look! Thy loving eyes, Turn'd once,

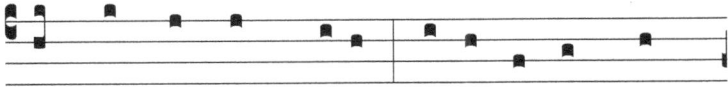

turn him who thrice denies; To softest dews night's

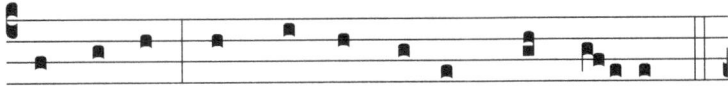

darkest sins Melt, ere Thy pardon's day be- gins.

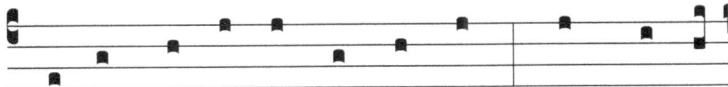

8) Daystar within, ere morning break, Make all my

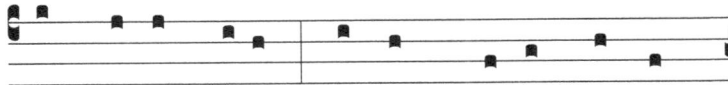

heart to Thee a-wake; Let prayer outstrip the dawn-

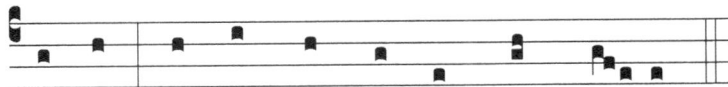

ing rays, And life's first whisper'd notes be praise!

†4: Deus, creator omnium

Saturdays at Vespers.

Germany: Kempten (ca. 1000)

C–C

M ak-er of all things! God Most High! Great

Ambrose of Milan (ca. 334–397)
tr. John David Chambers

Ruler of the starry sky! Who, robing day with

beauteous light, Hast clothed in soft re-pose the

Night, 2) That sleep may wearied limbs re- store,

And fit for toil and use once more; May gently

sooth the careworn breast, And lull our anx- ious

griefs to rest; 3) We thank Thee for the day that's

gone, We pray Thee now the night comes on; O

help us sinners as we raise To Thee our vo- tive

hymn of praise! 4) To Thee our hearts their mu-

sic bring, Thee our u-nit- ed voices sing, To Thee

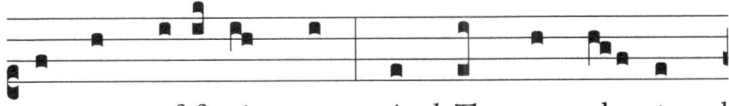

our rapt af-fections soar, And Thee our chas-tened

souls a- dore. 5) So when the parting beams of

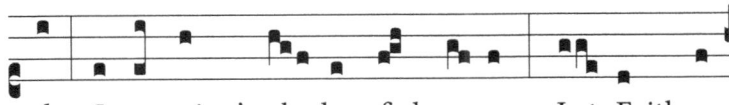

day In evening's shadow fade a- way, Let Faith no

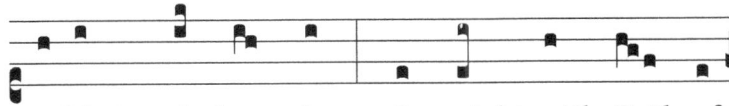

wildering darkness know But night with Faith ef-

ful-gent glow. 6) O sleepless ever keep the mind!

But guilt in last-ing slumber bind; Let Faith our pu-

ri-ty re-new, And temper sleep's le-thargic dew.

7) From eve-ry carnal passion free, O may our hearts

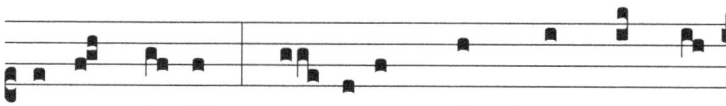

re-pose in Thee; Nor envious fiend with harmful

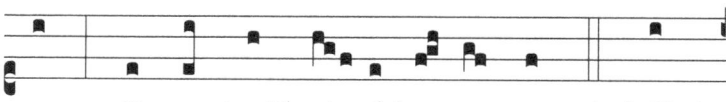

snare, Our rest with sin- ful ter-rors scare! 8) Christ

with The Fa-ther ev-er One! Spirit! of Fa- ther and

of Son, God o-ver all, of mighty sway, Shield us

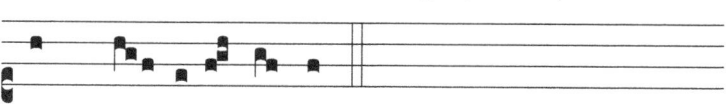

Great Trin-i- ty! we pray.

†5: Deus, creator omnium

Italy: Verona (11th c.)

F–E

M aker of all things! God Most High! Great

Rul- er of the starry sky! Who, robing day with

beauteous light, Hast clothed in soft re- pose the

Night, 2) That sleep may wearied limbs re- store,

And fit   for toil and use once more; May gently

sooth the careworn breast, And lull our anxious

griefs to rest; 3) We thank Thee for the day that's

Ambrose of Milan (ca. 334–397)   (1) ii:2,6, iv:2
tr. John David Chambers

gone, We pray Thee now the night comes on; O

help us sin-ners as we raise To Thee our vo-tive

hymn of praise! 4) To Thee our hearts their mu-

sic bring, Thee our u- nit-ed voic-es sing, To Thee

our rapt af- fections soar, And Thee our chastened

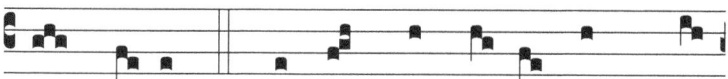

souls a- dore. 5) So when the parting beams of

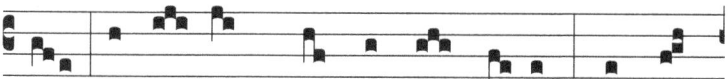

day In eve-ning's shadow fade a- way, Let Faith

no wildering darkness know But night with Faith ef-

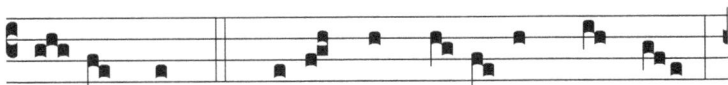

ful-gent glow. 6) O sleepless ev-er keep the mind!

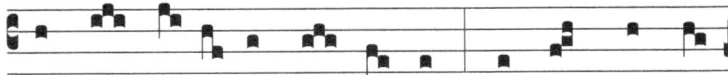

But guilt in lasting slumber bind; Let Faith our pu-

ri- ty re-new, And temper sleep's le-thar-gic dew.

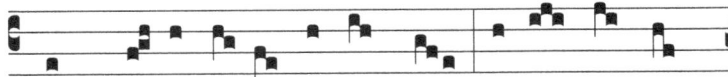

7) From every carnal passion free, O may our hearts

re-pose in Thee; Nor en-vious fiend with harmful

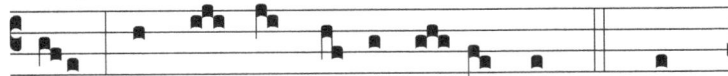

snare, Our rest with sin-ful ter-rors scare! 8) Christ

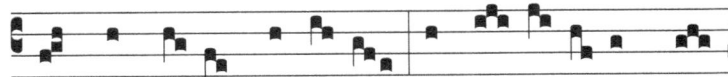

with The Fa-ther ev-er One! Spirit! of Fa-ther and

of Son, God o- ver all, of mighty sway, Shield us

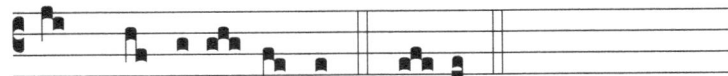

Great Trini- ty! we pray. A- men.

†6: Deus, creator omnium

Saturday in the octave of Pentecost.

France: Laon (1100–1150)

D–B

Maker of all things! God Most High! Great Ruler of the starry sky! Who, robing day with beauteous light, Hast clothed in soft re-pose the Night, 2) That sleep may wearied limbs re- store, And fit for toil and use once more; May gently sooth the careworn breast, And lull our anxious

Ambrose of Milan (ca. 334–397)
tr. John David Chambers

griefs to   rest; 3) We thank Thee for the day that's

gone, We pray Thee now the night comes on; O

help us sin-ners as we raise To Thee our vo-tive

hymn of   praise! 4) To Thee our hearts their mu-

sic bring, Thee our u-nit-ed voices sing, To Thee

our rapt af-fections soar, And Thee our chastened

souls a-   dore. 5) So when the parting beams of

day In evening's shadow fade a- way, Let Faith no

wildering darkness know But night with Faith ef-

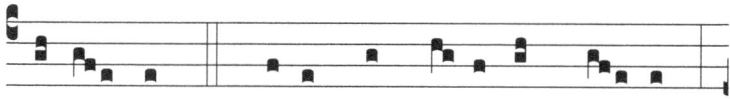

fulgent glow. 6) O sleepless ev-er keep the mind!

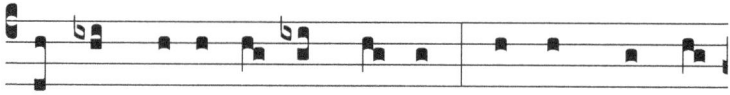

But guilt in lasting slumber bind; Let Faith our pu-

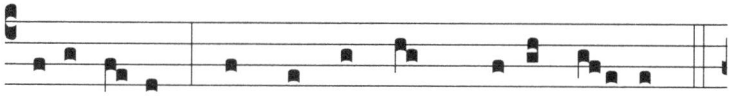

ri-ty re-new, And temper sleep's le-thargic dew.

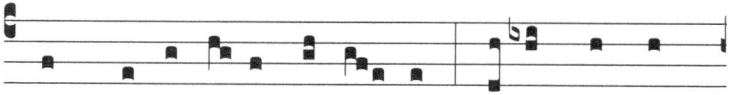

7) From every carnal passion free, O may our hearts

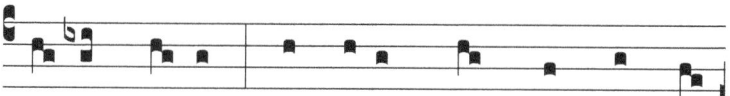

re- pose in Thee; Nor envious fiend with harmful

snare, Our rest with sin-ful terrors scare! 8) Christ

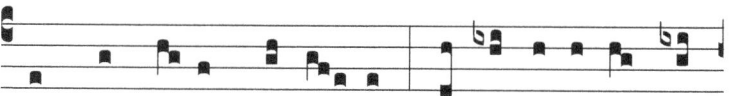

with The Fa-ther ev-er   One! Spirit! of Fa-ther and

of Son, God o-ver all, of mighty sway, Shield us

Great Trini- ty! we pray.

†7: Deus, creator omnium

At Vespers.

Austria: Heiligenkreuz (12th–13th c.)

F–C

Maker of all things! God Most High! Great

Ruler of the starry sky! Who, robing day with beau-

teous light, Hast clothed in soft re-pose the Night,

2) That sleep may wearied limbs re-store, And fit for

Ambrose of Milan (ca. 334–397)
tr. John David Chambers

[musical notation]

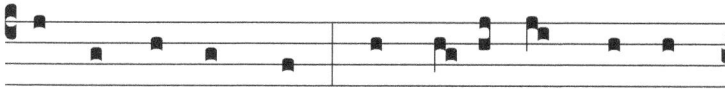

toil and use once more; May gently sooth the care-

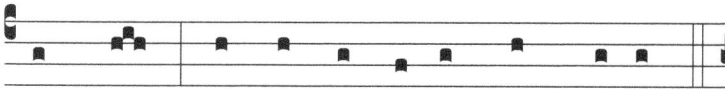

[musical notation]

worn breast, And lull our anxious griefs to rest;

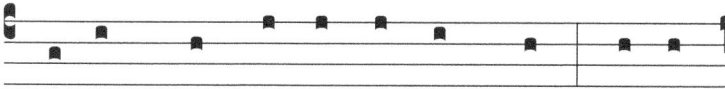

[musical notation]

3) We thank Thee for the day that's gone, We pray

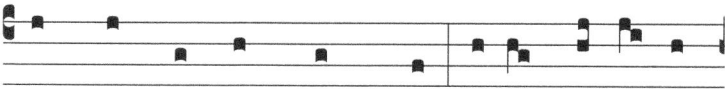

[musical notation]

Thee now the night comes on; O help us sin-ners

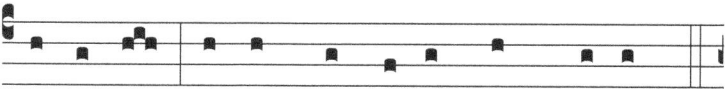

[musical notation]

as we raise To Thee our vo-tive hymn of praise!

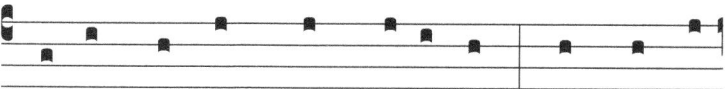

[musical notation]

4) To Thee our hearts their music bring, Thee our u-

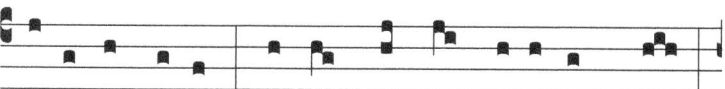

[musical notation]

nited voices sing, To Thee our rapt af-fections soar,

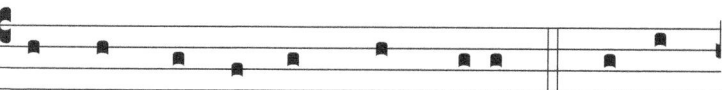

[musical notation]

And Thee our chastened souls a- dore. 5) So when

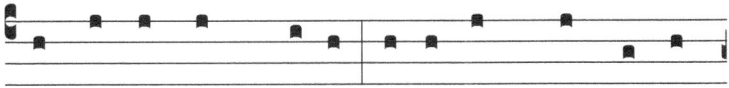

the parting beams of day In evening's shadow fade

a-way, Let Faith no wildering darkness know But

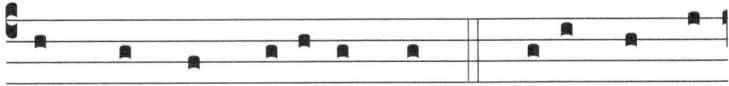

night with Faith ef-fulgent glow. 6) O sleepless ev-

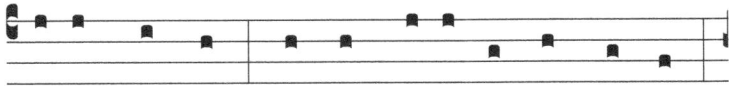

er keep the mind! But guilt in lasting slumber bind;

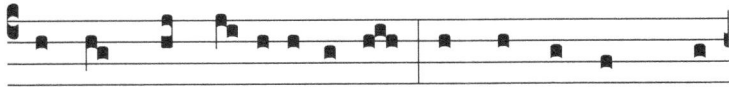

Let Faith our pu-ri-ty re-new, And temper sleep's le-

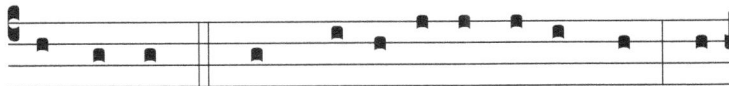

thargic dew. 7) From every carnal passion free, O

may our hearts re-pose in Thee; Nor en-vious fiend

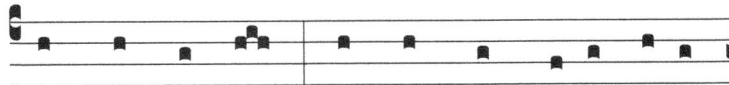

with harmful snare, Our rest with sinful terrors

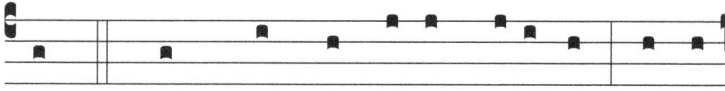

scare! 8) Christ with The Fa-ther ever One! Spirit!

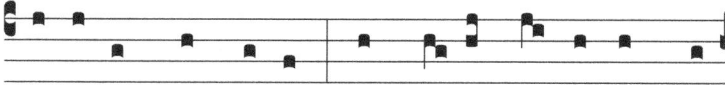

of Fa-ther and of Son, God o- ver all, of mighty

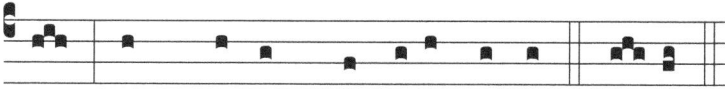

sway, Shield us Great Trini- ty! we pray. A- men.

†8: Deus, creator omnium

Saturdays at Vespers.

Austria: Klosterneuburg (1336)

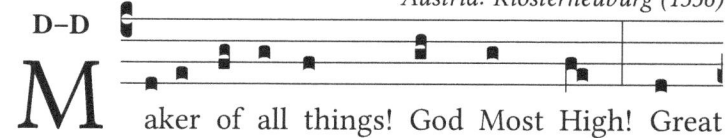

D–D

Maker of all things! God Most High! Great

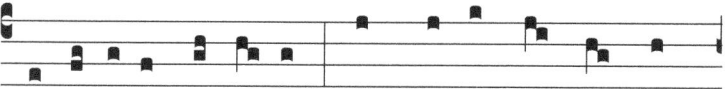

Ruler of the starry sky! Who, robing day with beau-

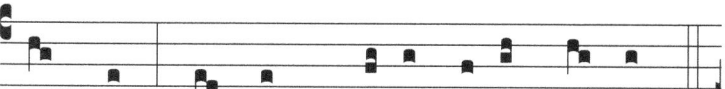

teous light, Hast clothed in soft re-pose the Night,

Ambrose of Milan (ca. 334–397)
tr. John David Chambers

2) That sleep may wearied limbs re-store, And fit for

toil and use once more; May gently sooth the care-

worn breast, And lull our anxious griefs to rest;

3) We thank Thee for the day that's gone, We pray

Thee now the night comes on; O help us sin-ners

as we raise To Thee our vo-tive hymn of praise!

4) To Thee our hearts their music bring, Thee our u-

nited voices sing, To Thee our rapt af- fections soar,

And Thee our chastened souls a- dore. 5) So when

the parting beams of day In evening's shadow fade

a- way, Let Faith no wildering darkness know But

night with Faith ef-fulgent glow. 6) O sleepless ever

keep the mind! But guilt in lasting slumber bind;

Let Faith our pu-ri- ty re-new, And temper sleep's

le-thargic dew. 7) From every carnal passion free,

O may our hearts re-pose in Thee; Nor envious fiend

with harmful snare, Our rest with sinful terrors

scare! 8) Christ with The Fa-ther ever One! Spirit!

of Fa-ther and of Son, God o-ver all, of mighty

sway, Shield us Great Trini- ty! we pray. A- men.

†9: Hic est dies verus Dei

On the Resurrection of the Lord.

Italy: Gaeta (12th c.)

D–C

This is the day the Lord hath made, In unbe-

clouded lights ar-ray'd; His sa-cred Blood who free-

Ambrose of Milan (ca. 334–397)
tr. George Ratcliffe Woodward

ly spilt, To wash the world from stains of guilt.

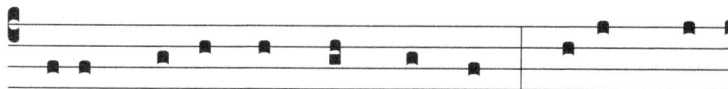

2) Regain, ye faithless, faith and sight! A-wake, and

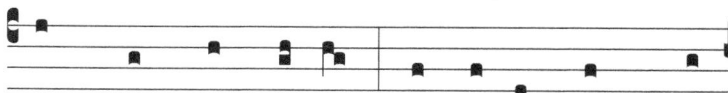

Christ shall give ye light: Lo! he that shrove the

dy-ing thief Shall ease the burthen of your grief.

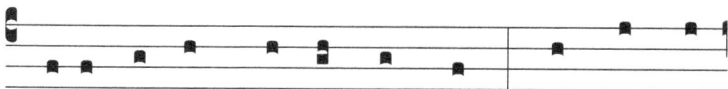

3) O wonder-faith! ere sun went down, Who bore the

cross, soon wore the crown: Saints many win the

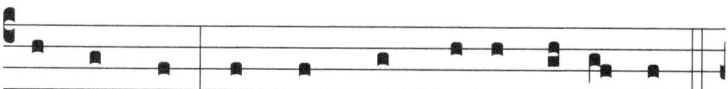

heav'nly hall; That some-time sinner outran all.

4) Yea, Angels stand in mute a-maze, As on that bod-

y rack'd they gaze, Whose soul, that unto Christ

doth cleave, Shall gift of endless life re-ceive. 5) O

mystery deep! set was his mind To cleanse the taint

of human-kind; To free from bonds a guilty race,

Man must the sins of man ef-face. 6) What more

sublime can be than this, That very sin should end

in bliss! Yea, perfect love out-casteth fear; By Je-su's

death new life is here. 7) Gorge, hungry Death, bait,

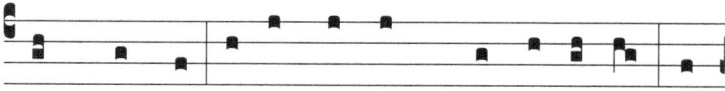

hook, and all! In net, out-spread for other, fall! The

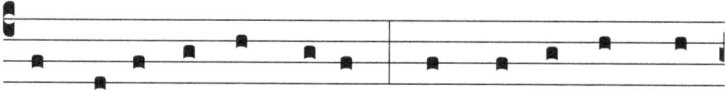

Life of all mankind is slain, That all mankind may

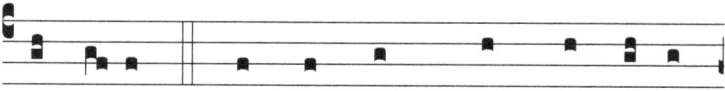

life re-gain. 8) And what though death o'er all hath

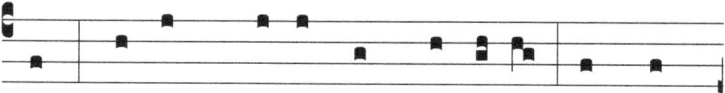

past? Up-spring to life shall all at last: 'Tis Death

shall perish, Death a-lone, By his own weapons o-

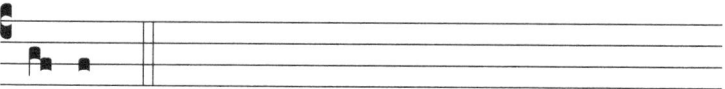

ver-thrown.

†10: Hic est dies verus Dei

On Pascha until the Ascension
except on holy feasts.

Austria: Heiligenkreuz (12th–13th c.)

This is the day the Lord hath made, In unbe-

clouded lights ar-ray'd; His sa-cred Blood who free-

ly spilt, To wash the world from stains of guilt.

2) Regain, ye faithless, faith and sight! A-wake, and

Christ shall give ye light: Lo! he that shrove the

dy-ing thief Shall ease the burthen of your grief.

3) O wonder-faith! ere sun went down, Who bore the

Ambrose of Milan (ca. 334–397)
tr. George Ratcliffe Woodward

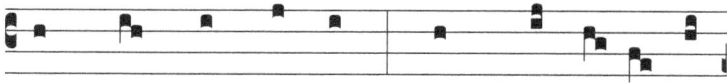

cross, soon wore the crown: Saints many   win the

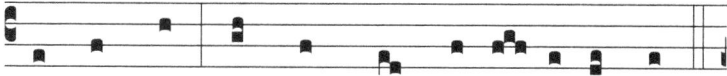

heav'nly hall; That some-time sinner outran all.

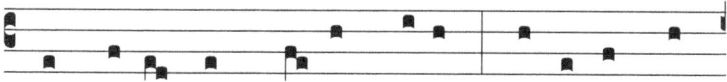

4) Yea, Angels stand in mute a-maze, As on that bod-

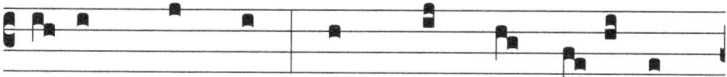

y   rack'd they gaze, Whose soul, that un-to Christ

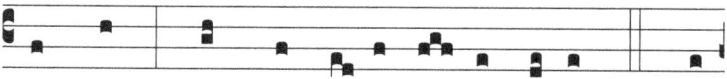

doth cleave, Shall gift of endless life re-ceive. 5) O

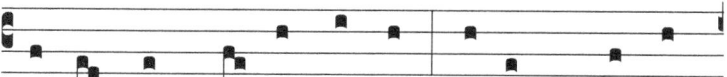

mystery deep! set was his mind To cleanse the taint

of human-kind; To free from bonds a guilty race,

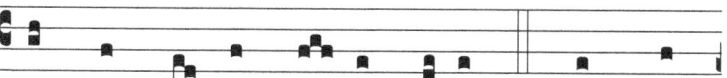

Man must the sins of   man ef-face. 6) What more

sublime can be than this, That very sin should end

in bliss! Yea, perfect love out-casteth fear; By Je-su's

death new life is here. 7) Gorge, hungry Death, bait,

hook, and all! In net, out-spread for other, fall! The

Life of all mankind is slain, That all mankind may

life re-gain. 8) And what though death o'er all hath

past? Up-spring to life shall all at last: 'Tis Death

shall per-ish, Death a- lone, By his own weapons

o-verthrown. A- men.

†11: Hic est dies verus Dei

Switzerland: Einsiedeln (1225–1275)

A–G

This is the day the Lord hath made, In unbe-

clouded lights ar-ray'd; His sa-cred Blood who free-

ly spilt, To wash the world from stains of guilt.

2) Regain, ye faithless, faith and sight! A-wake, and

Christ shall give ye light: Lo! he that shrove the

dy-ing thief Shall ease the burthen of your grief.

3) O wonder-faith! ere sun went down, Who bore the

Ambrose of Milan (ca. 334–397)
tr. George Ratcliffe Woodward

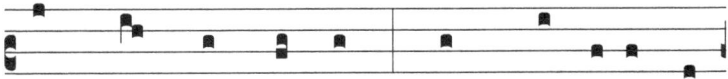

cross, soon wore the crown: Saints many win the

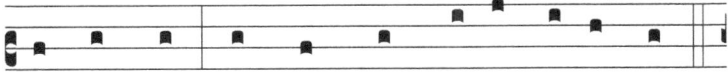

heav'nly hall; That some-time sinner outran all.

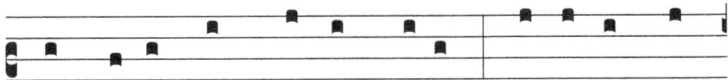

4) Yea, Angels stand in mute a-maze, As on that bod-

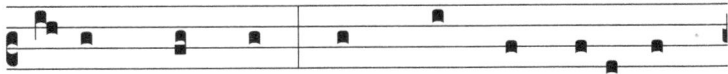

y rack'd they gaze, Whose soul, that unto Christ

doth cleave, Shall gift of endless life re-ceive. 5) O

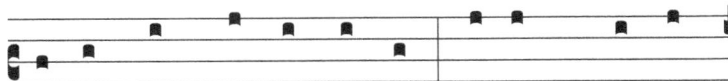

mystery deep! set was his mind To cleanse the taint

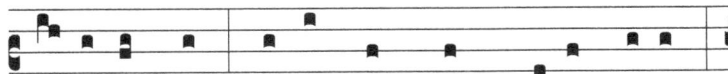

of human-kind; To free from bonds a guilty race,

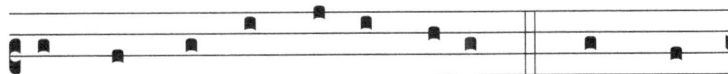

Man must the sins of man ef-face. 6) What more

sublime can be than this, That very sin should end

in bliss! Yea, perfect love out-casteth fear; By Je-

su's death new life is here. 7) Gorge, hungry Death,

bait, hook, and all! In net, out-spread for other, fall!

The Life of all mankind is slain, That all mankind

may life re-gain. 8) And what though death o'er all

hath past? Up-spring to life shall all at last: 'Tis

Death shall perish, Death a- lone, By his own weap-

ons o-verthrown.

†12: Iam surgit hora tertia

At Terce
during the whole week.

Austria: Heiligenkreuz (12th–13th c.)

B–A

'T is the third hour, the ho-ly time, When

Christ the bitter Cross did climb, Fix'd be the soul

in-tent in prayer, No thought unhallow'd harbour'd

there. 2) Who in his heart would Christ enshrine,

Unstain'd must keep his soul within, With vows

unceasing must se-cure The Holy Spirit's Presence

pure. 3) This is the hour which clos'd a-main Ac-

Ambrose of Milan (ca. 334–397) (8) ii:5
tr. William John Copeland

cursed guilt's le-thargic reign, The empire loos'd

of death and hell,   And cancell'd sin's primaeval

spell. 4) Hence by the grace of Christ began Those

blessed times to ru-in'd man, When one pure Truth

the Churches fill'd   One Faith through every bos-

om thrill'd. 5) From summit of His Triumph high,

He thus be-spake His Mother nigh, 'Mother,' He

said, 'Behold thy son,' 'Behold thy Mother, faithful

one.' 6) In mystery deep He thus implied Th' es-

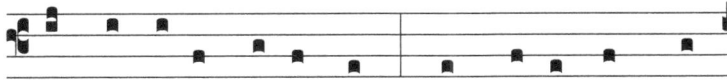

pousals of the Virgin Bride, Nor, Virgin-born, im-

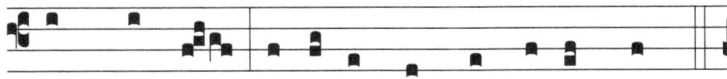

pair'd the claim Of Virgin-Mother's sa-cred name.

7) Deep mystery, which to faith re-veal'd With heav-

enly wonders Je-sus seal'd, Yet would not faith-

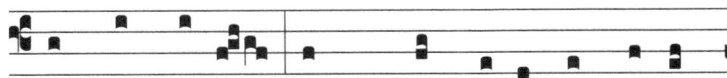

less man be-lieve, Though who be-lieveth, he shall

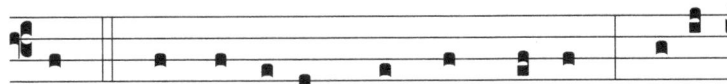

live. 8) Yea we be-lieve God born on earth, A ho-

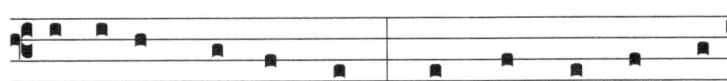

ly Virgin's spotless Birth, Who bare the sins of

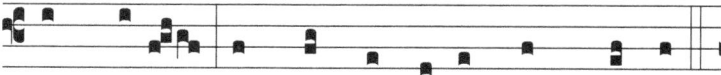

earth a-way, Now with the Fa-ther reigns for aye.

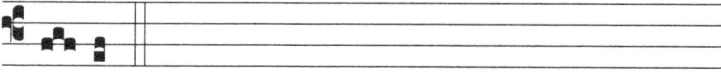

A- men.

†13: Illuminans altissimus

At Lauds.

Italy: Verona (11th c.)

F–F

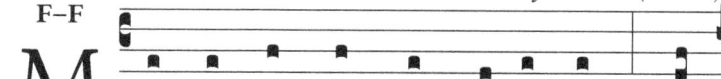

Most Highest, Who dost kindle bright Yon

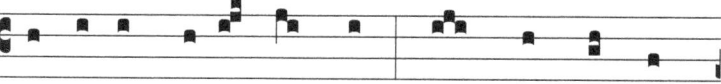

starry orbs of sparkling light, Peace, Life, and Light,

and Truth, look down, Je- su, from Heaven Thy sup-

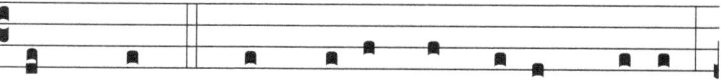

pliants own. 2) Whether this day, as twice of old,

The streams of Jordan backward roll'd, When there

Ambrose of Milan (ca. 334–397)
tr. William John Copeland

(5,7) i:3–4,7

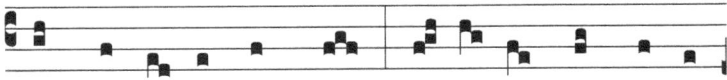

Thy mystic Presence stood To hal-low Thy Baptis-

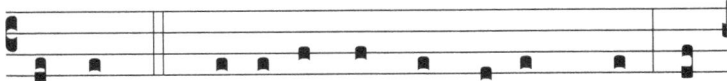

mal flood. 3) Or in the sky Thy glittering star Thy

Virgin-Birth proclaim'd a- far, And on this morn

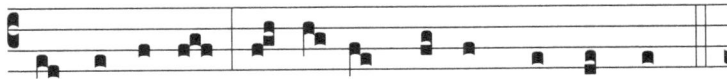

the sages led To worship at Thy manger bed.

4) Or in the urns with water fill'd Thy power the lus-

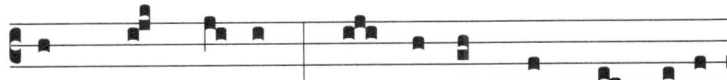

cious wine dis-till'd, And he that bare the water

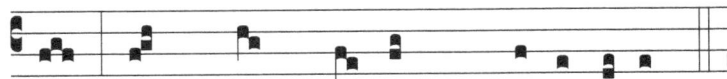

knew Whence sprang the draughts he never drew.

5) Beheld the waves with crimson dyed, Tranc'd in-to

wine the crystal tide, The very el-e- ment a-ghast

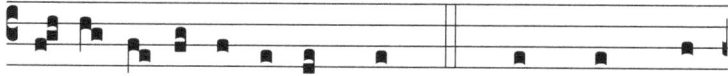

In- to an-other na-ture pass'd. 6) Thus when Thy

hand five thousand fed With those five loaves of

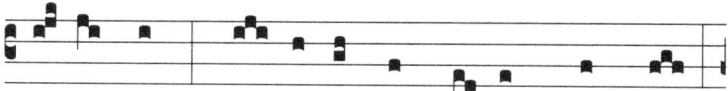

broken bread, e'er in the lips of them that ate

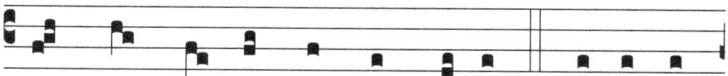

Thou didst the growing meal create. 7) By its own

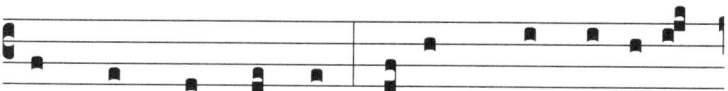

waste th' exhaustless store In-creas'd and multi-plied

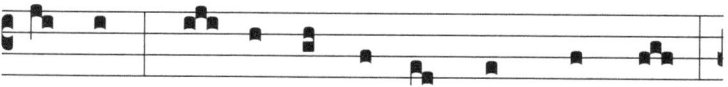

the more, Nor wonder ye, such sight who view,

These springs should flow exhaustless too. 8) Bread

through the hands that break it pours, Streams out

like Heaven's sponta-neous showers, Fragments un-

broke, un-touch'd supplies A- round them like the

waters rise. A- men.

†14: Illuminans altissimus

*On the Epiphany
of the Lord.*

Austria: Heiligenkreuz (12th–13th c.)

G–D

M
ost Highest, Who dost kindle bright Yon

starry orbs of sparkling light, Peace, Life, and Light,

Ambrose of Milan (ca. 334–397)
tr. William John Copeland

(7) i:1

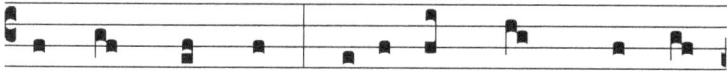

and Truth, look down, Je-su, from Heaven Thy sup-

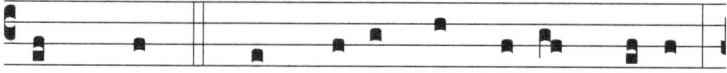

pliants own. 2) Whether this day, as twice of old,

The streams of Jordan backward roll'd, When there

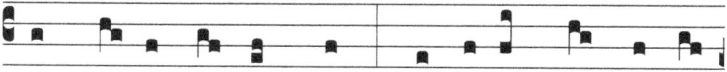

Thy mystic Presence stood To hallow Thy Baptis-

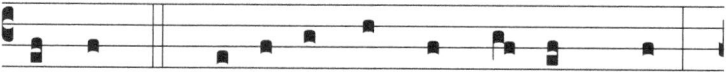

mal flood. 3) Or in the sky Thy glit-tering star

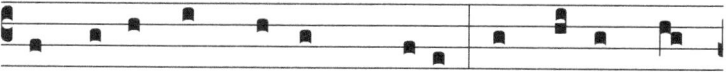

Thy Virgin-Birth proclaim'd a- far, And on this morn

the sages led To worship at Thy manger bed.

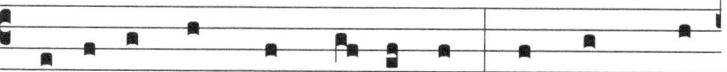

4) Or in the urns with wa-ter fill'd Thy power the

luscious wine distill'd, And he that bare the wa-ter

knew Whence sprang the draughts he never drew.

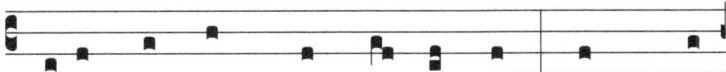

5) Beheld the waves with crimson dyed, Tranc'd in-

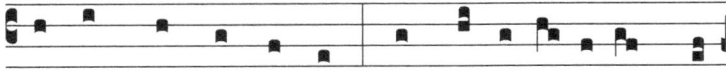

to wine the crystal tide, The very el- e-ment a-

ghast In-to another na-ture pass'd. 6) Thus when

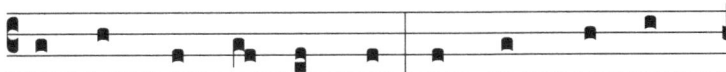

Thy hand five thousand fed With those five loaves

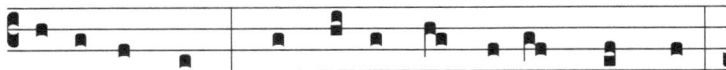

of broken bread, e'er in the lips of them that ate

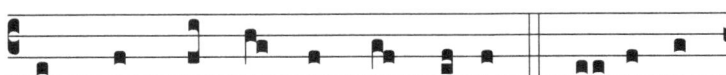

Thou didst the growing meal create. 7) By its own

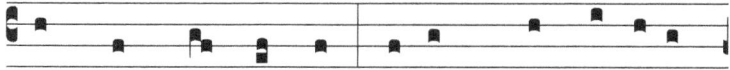

waste th' exhaustless store In-creas'd and multi-plied

the more, Nor wonder ye, such sight who view,

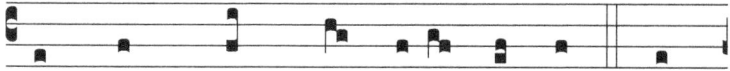

These springs should flow exhaustless too. 8) Bread

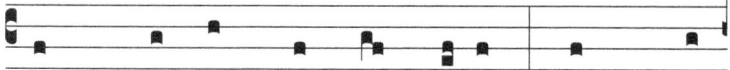

through the hands that break it pours, Streams out

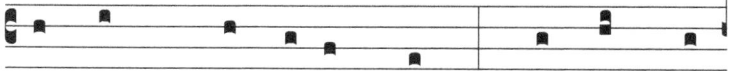

like Heaven's sponta-neous showers, Fragments un-

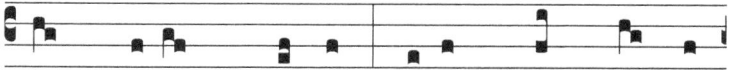

broke, untouch'd supplies A- round them like the

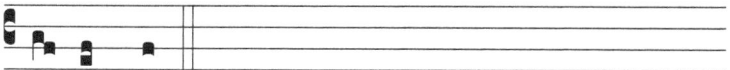

wa-ters rise.

†15: Intende, qui regis Israel

On the Nativity of the Lord at Vespers.

France: Nevers (12th c.)

D–C

Come, Thou Redeemer of the earth, Come,

testi-fy Thy Virgin-birth: All lands ad-mire,—all

times ap-plaud; Such is the birth that fits a God.

3) Begot- ten of no hu-man will, But of the Spirit,

mystic still, The Word of God, in flesh ar- ray'd,

The promised fruit to man display'd. 4) The Vir-

Ambrose of Milan (ca. 334–397)
tr. John Mason Neale: 2–8 / 8

(3) i:2

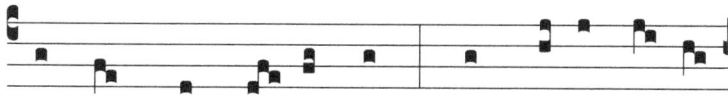

gin womb that bur-den gain'd With Virgin honour

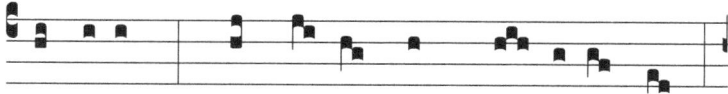

all unstain'd: The banners there of   virtue glow:

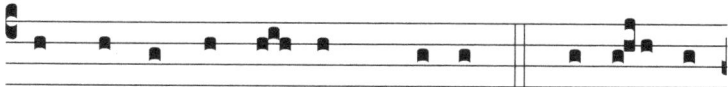

God in His temple   dwells be-low. 5) Proceed-ing

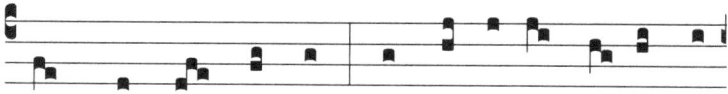

from His Chamber free, The royal hall of chasti-

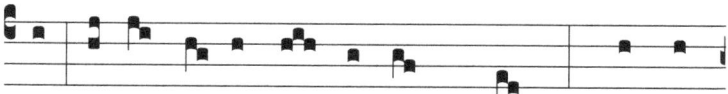

ty, Gi-ant of twofold substance, straight His des-

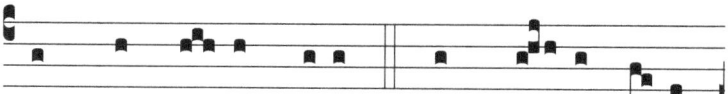

tined way He runs e- late. 6) From God the Fa-ther

He proceeds: To God the Fa-ther back He speeds:

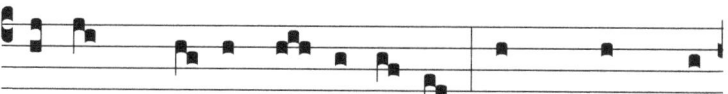

Proceeds,—as far as   very   hell; Speeds back,—to

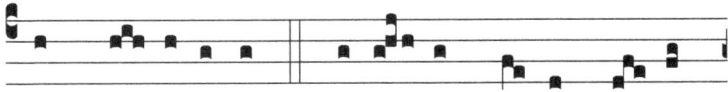

light in- ef-fa-ble. 7) O E- qual to Thy Fa- ther,

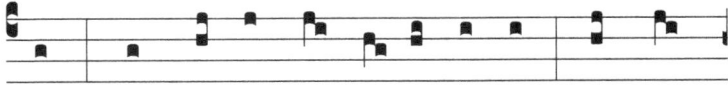

Thou! Gird on Thy fleshly mantle now: The weak-

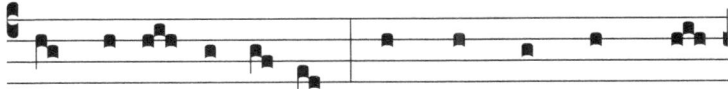

ness of our mortal state With deathless might in-

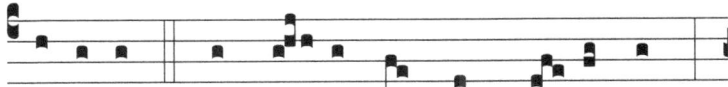

vigor-ate. 8) Thy cra- dle here shall glit-ter bright,

And darkness breathe a newer light: Where end-

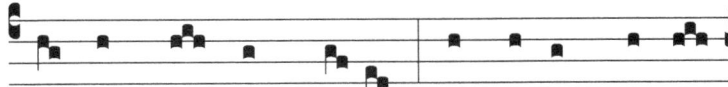

less faith shall shine se- rene, And twilight never

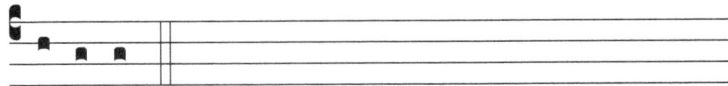

in-tervene.

50

†16: Intende, qui regis Israel

Switzerland: Einsiedeln (1225–1275)

C–A

Come, Thou Re- deemer of the earth, Come,

testi- fy Thy Virgin- birth: All lands admire,—all

times ap-plaud; Such is the birth that fits a God.

3) Begotten of no human will, But of the Spirit, mys-

tic still, The Word of God, in flesh ar- ray'd, The

promised fruit to man display'd. 4) The Virgin

womb that burden gain'd With Virgin honour all

Ambrose of Milan (ca. 334–397)
tr. John Mason Neale: 2–8 / 8

unstain'd: The banners there of virtue glow: God

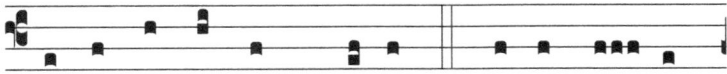

in His temple dwells be-low. 5) Proceeding   from

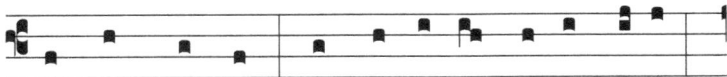

His Chamber free, The royal hall of chasti-ty,

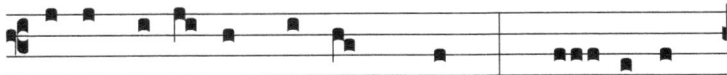

Gi-ant of twofold substance, straight His   destined

way He runs e- late. 6) From God the Fa-ther He

proceeds: To God the Fa-ther back He speeds: Pro-

ceeds,—as far as very   hell; Speeds back,—to light

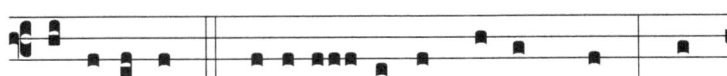

in-ef-fa-ble. 7) O E-qual to Thy Fa-ther, Thou! Gird

on Thy fleshly mantle now: The weakness of our

mortal state With deathless might in-vigor-ate.

8) Thy cradle   here shall glitter bright, And darkness

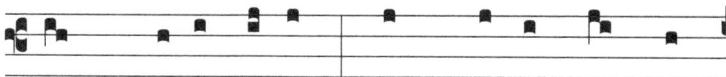

breathe a newer light: Where endless faith shall

shine se-rene, And twilight never in-tervene.

†17: Intende, qui regis Israel

Vigil of the Nativity at Vespers.

England: Worcester (ca. 1230)

D–D

C ome, Thou Redeemer of the earth, Come, tes-

Ambrose of Milan (ca. 334–397)
tr. John Mason Neale: 2–8 / 8

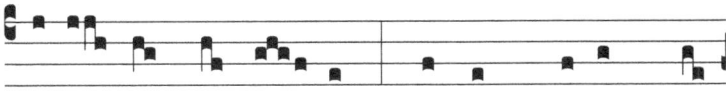

ti- fy Thy Vir- gin- birth: All lands admire,—all

times ap- plaud; Such is the birth that fits a

God. 3) Begot- ten of no human will, But of the

Spir- it, mystic still, The Word of God, in flesh

ar- ray'd, The promised fruit to man dis- play'd.

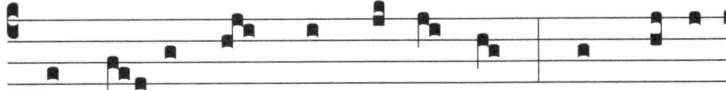

4) The Vir- gin womb that burden gain'd With Virgin

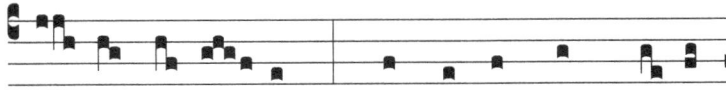

hon-our all un- stain'd: The banners there of vir-

tue glow: God in His tem-ple dwells be- low.

5) Proceed- ing from His Chamber free, The royal

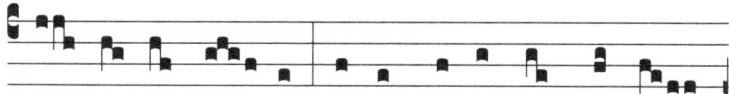

hall of chasti-   ty, Gi- ant of twofold substance,

straight His des-tined way He   runs e-   late.

6) From God the Fa- ther He proceeds: To God the

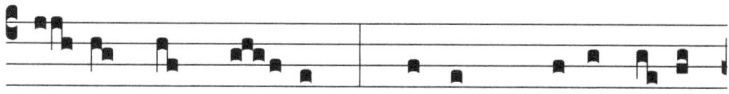

Fa- ther back He   speeds: Proceeds,—as far as ver-

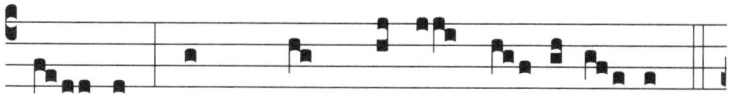

y   hell; Speeds back,—to light in- ef-fa- ble.

7) O E-   qual to Thy Fa-ther, Thou! Gird on Thy

fleshly mantle   now: The weakness of our mortal   state With deathless might in- vigor- ate.

8) Thy cra- dle here shall glitter bright, And darkness

breathe a   newer   light: Where endless faith shall

shine se-   rene, And twilight nev-er   in-ter- vene.

†18: Intende, qui regis Israel

Austria: Dürnstein (15th c.)

C–G

Come, Thou Redeemer of the earth, Come,

testi-fy Thy Virgin-birth: All lands ad-mire,—all

Ambrose of Milan (ca. 334–397)
tr. John Mason Neale: 2–8 / 8

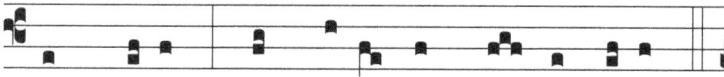

times applaud; Such is the birth that fits a God.

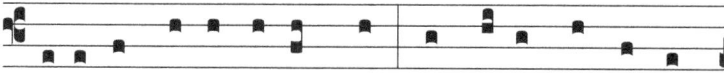

3) Begotten of no human will, But of the Spirit, mys-

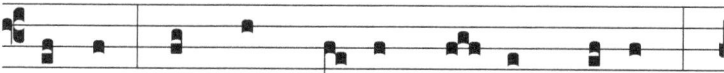

tic still, The Word of God, in   flesh ar- ray'd,

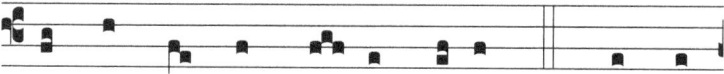

The promised fruit to   man display'd. 4) The Vir-

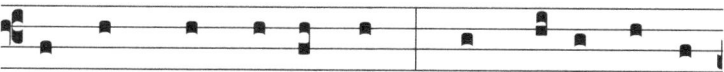

gin womb that burden gain'd With Virgin honour

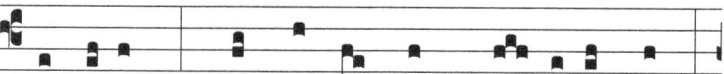

all unstain'd: The banners there of   virtue glow:

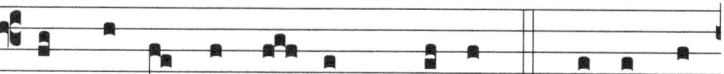

God in His temple   dwells be- low. 5) Proceeding

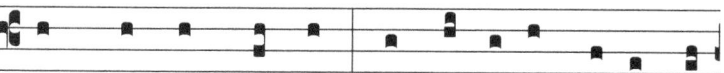

from His Chamber free, The royal hall of chasti-

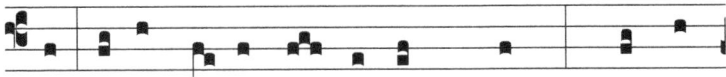

ty, Gi-ant of twofold substance, straight His des-

tined way He runs e- late. 6) From God the Fa-ther

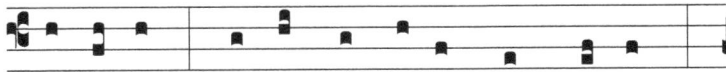

He proceeds: To God the Fa-ther back He speeds:

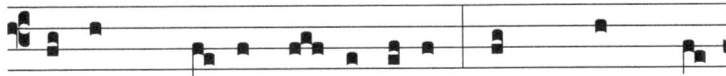

Proceeds,—as far as very hell; Speeds back,—to

light in- ef-fa- ble. 7) O E- qual to Thy Fa- ther,

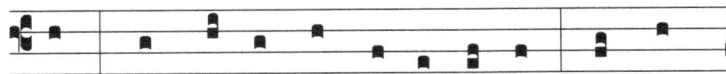

Thou! Gird on Thy fleshly mantle now: The weak-

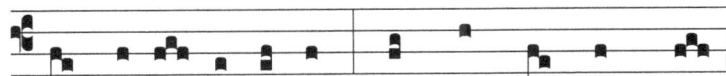

ness of our mortal state With deathless might in-

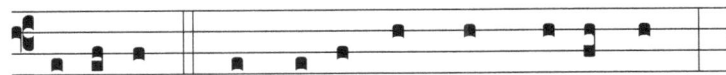

vigor- ate. 8) Thy cradle here shall glitter bright,

And darkness breathe a newer light: Where end-

less faith shall shine se-rene, And twilight never

in-tervene.

†19: Splendor paternae gloriae

At Lauds.

Germany: Kempten (ca. 1000)

C–A

O splendour of God's glory bright, O Thou

that bringest light from light, O Light of light,

light's living spring, O day all days il-lumining.

2) O Thou true sun on us thy glance Let fall in roy-

Ambrose of Milan (ca. 334–397)
tr. Robert Seymour Bridges

al ra-di-ance, The Spirit's sancti-fy-ing beam Up-

on our earthly senses stream. 3) The Fa-ther too

our prayers implore, Fa-ther of glory evermore,

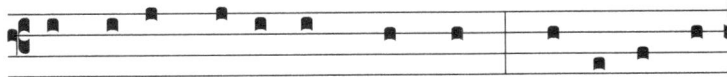

The Fa-ther of all grace and might, To banish sin

from our de-light: 4) To guide whate'er we nobly

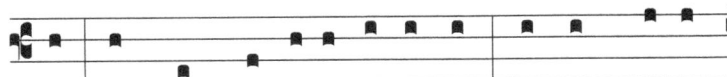

do, With love all envy to subdue, To make ill-for-

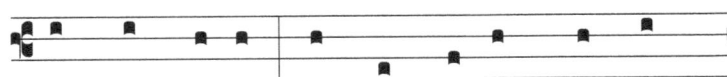

tune turn to fair, And give us grace our wrongs

to bear. 5) Our mind be in his keeping placed,

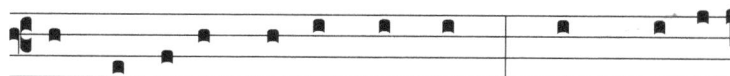

Our body true to him and chaste, Where on-ly

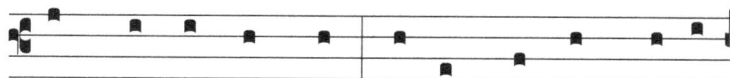

Faith her fire shall feed To burn the tares of Sa-

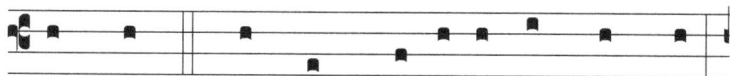

tan's seed. 6) And Christ to us for food shall be,

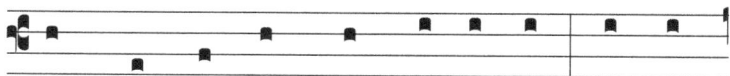

From him our drink that welleth free, The Spir-

it's wine, that maketh whole, And mocking not, ex-

alts the soul. 7) Re-joicing may this day go hence,

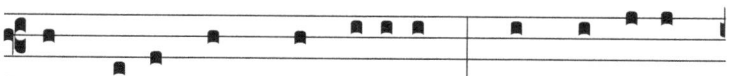

Like virgin dawn our innocence, Like fiery noon

our faith appear, Nor know the gloom of twilight

drear. 8) Morn in her rosy car is borne; Let Him

come forth our perfect Morn, The Word in God the

Fa-ther one, The Fa-ther perfect in the Son.

†20: Splendor paternae gloriae

At Lauds.

Austria: Heiligenkreuz (12th–13th c.)

C–G

O splendour of God's glory bright, O Thou

that bringest light from light, O Light of light,

light's living spring, O day all days il- lumining.

2) O Thou true sun on us thy glance Let fall in roy-

Ambrose of Milan (ca. 334–397)
tr. Robert Seymour Bridges

al ra-di-ance, The Spirit's sancti-fy-ing beam Up-

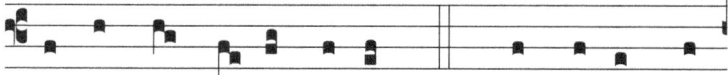

on our earthly senses stream. 3) The Fa-ther too

our prayers implore, Fa-ther of glory evermore,

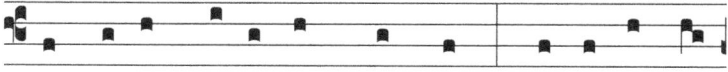

The Fa-ther of all grace and might, To banish sin

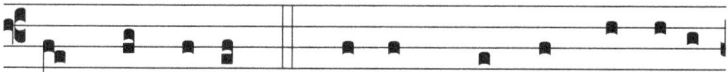

from our de-light: 4) To guide whate'er we nobly

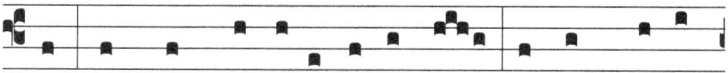

do, With love all envy to subdue, To make ill-for-

tune turn to fair, And give us grace our wrongs

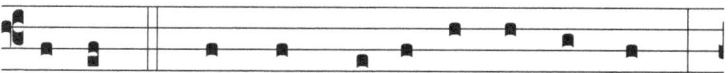

to bear. 5) Our mind be in his keeping placed,

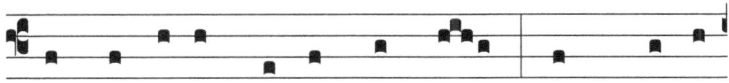

Our body true to him and chaste, Where on-ly

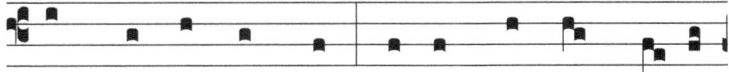

Faith her fire shall feed To burn the tares of Sa-

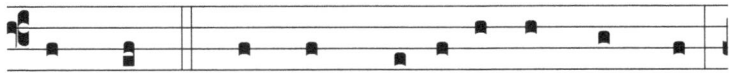

tan's seed. 6) And Christ to us for food shall be,

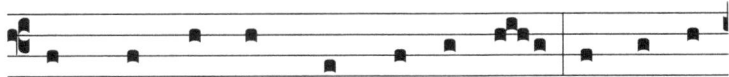

From him our drink that welleth free, The Spirit's

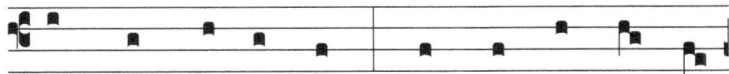

wine, that maketh whole, And mocking not, ex-

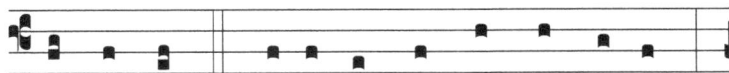

alts the soul. 7) Re-joicing may this day go hence,

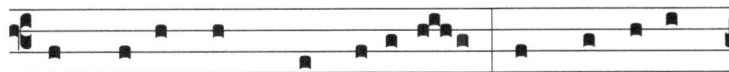

Like virgin dawn our innocence, Like fiery noon

our faith appear, Nor know the gloom of twilight

drear. 8) Morn in her rosy car is borne; Let Him

come forth our perfect Morn, The Word in God the

Fa-ther one, The Fa-ther per-fect in the Son.

†21: Splendor paternae gloriae

At Lauds.

Germany: Lehel (1227–1235)

F–A

O splendour of God's glory bright, O Thou

that bringest light from light, O Light of light,

light's living spring, O day all days il-lumining.

2) O Thou true sun on us thy glance Let fall in royal

Ambrose of Milan (ca. 334–397)
tr. Robert Seymour Bridges

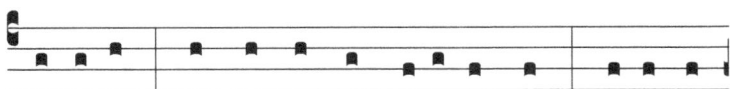

ra-di-ance, The Spirit's sancti-fy-ing beam Upon our

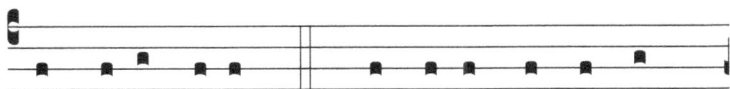

earthly senses stream. 3) The Fa-ther too our prayers

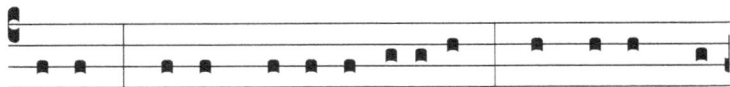

implore, Fa-ther of glory evermore, The Fa-ther of

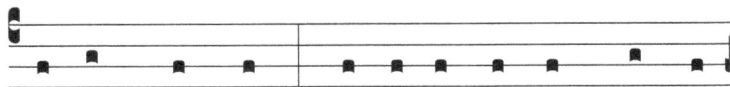

all grace and might, To banish sin from our de-

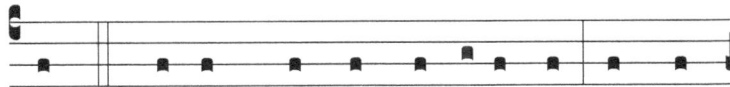

light: 4) To guide whate'er we nobly do, With love

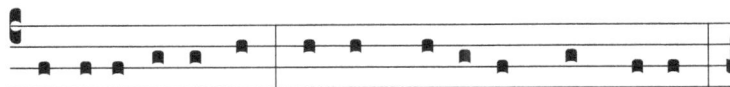

all envy to subdue, To make ill-fortune turn to fair,

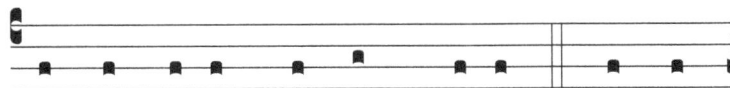

And give us grace our wrongs to bear. 5) Our mind

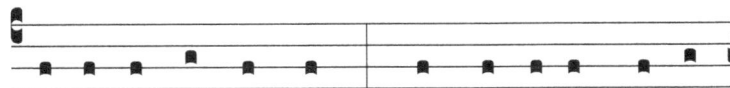

be in his keeping placed, Our body true to him

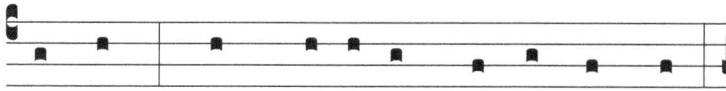

and chaste, Where on-ly Faith her fire shall feed

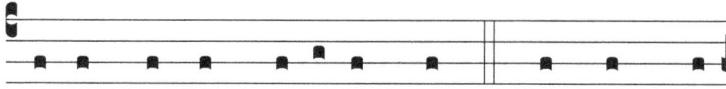

To burn the tares of Sa-tan's seed. 6) And Christ to

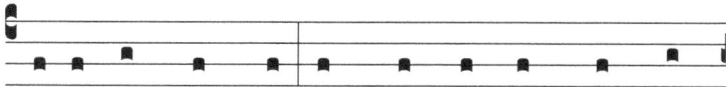

us for food shall be, From him our drink that well-

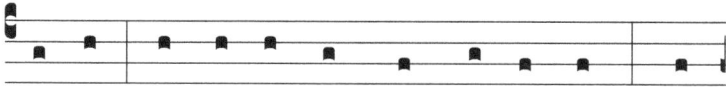

eth free, The Spirit's wine, that maketh whole, And

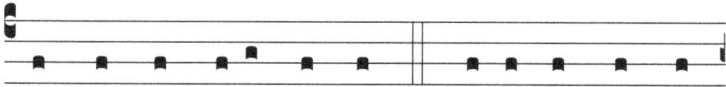

mocking not, exalts the soul. 7) Re-joicing may this

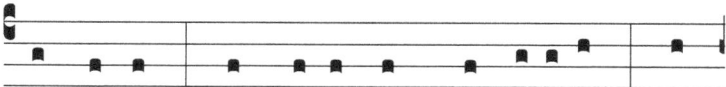

day go hence, Like virgin dawn our innocence, Like

fiery noon our faith appear, Nor know the gloom

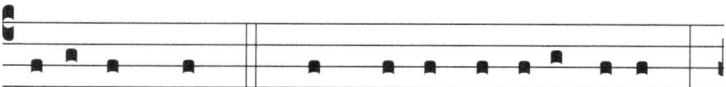

of twilight drear. 8) Morn in her rosy car is borne;

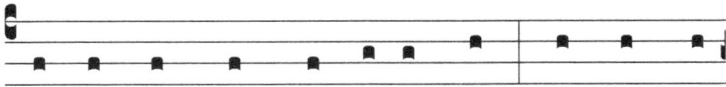

Let Him come forth our perfect Morn, The Word in

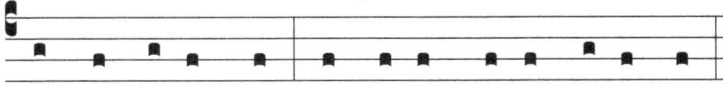

God the Fa-ther one, The Fa-ther perfect in the Son.

†22: Splendor paternae gloriae

Feria 2 at Lauds.

France: Le Mans (1450–1500)

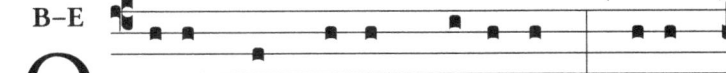

B–E

O splendour of God's glory bright, O Thou

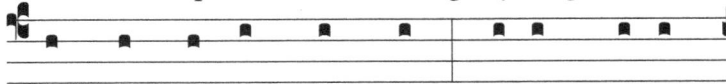

that bringest light from light, O Light of light,

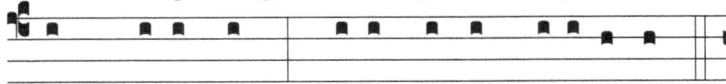

light's living spring, O day all days il-lumining.

2) O Thou true sun on us thy glance Let fall in roy-

al ra-di-ance, The Spirit's sancti-fy-ing beam Up-

Ambrose of Milan (ca. 334–397)
tr. Robert Seymour Bridges

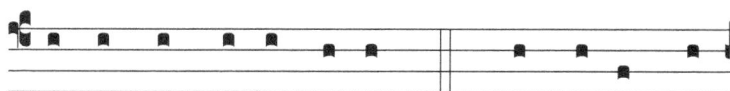

on our earthly senses stream. 3) The Fa-ther too

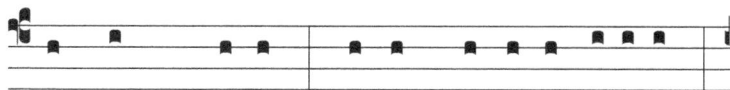

our prayers implore, Fa-ther of glory evermore,

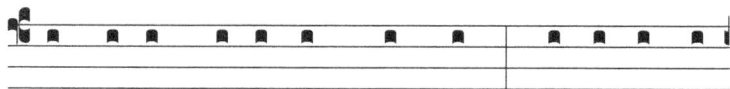

The Fa-ther of all grace and might, To banish sin

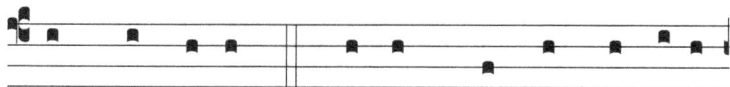

from our de-light: 4) To guide whate'er we nobly

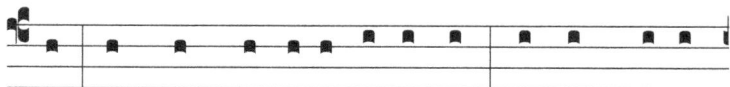

do, With love all envy to subdue, To make ill-for-

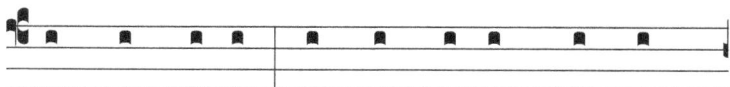

tune turn to fair, And give us grace our wrongs

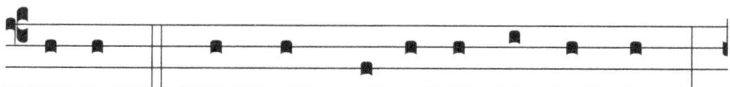

to bear. 5) Our mind be in his keeping placed,

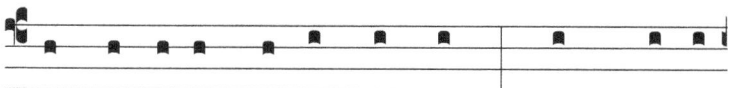

Our body true to him and chaste, Where on-ly

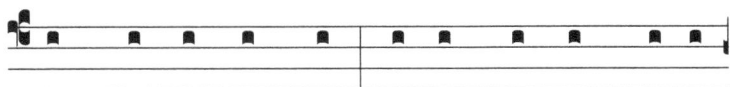

Faith her fire shall feed To burn the tares of Sa-

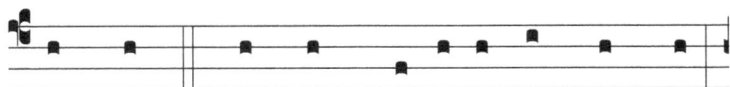

tan's seed. 6) And Christ to us for food shall be,

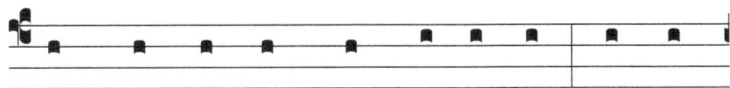

From him our drink that welleth free, The Spir-

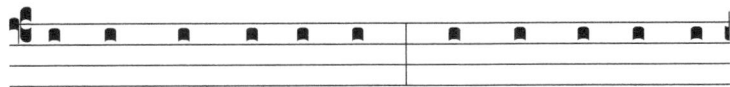

it's wine, that maketh whole, And mocking not, ex-

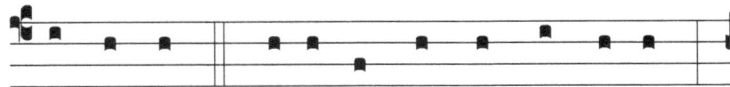

alts the soul. 7) Re-joicing may this day go hence,

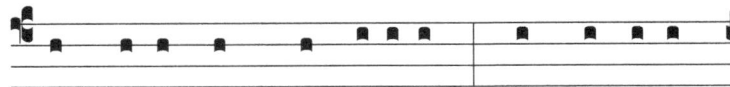

Like virgin dawn our innocence, Like fiery noon

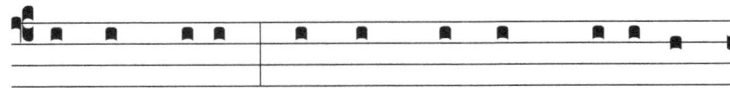

our faith appear, Nor know the gloom of twilight

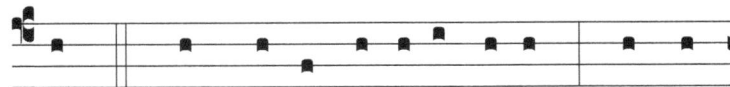

drear. 8) Morn in her rosy car is borne; Let Him

come forth our perfect Morn, The Word in God the

Fa-ther one, The Fa-ther perfect in the Son.

†23: **Ales diei nuntius**

At Lauds.

Italy: Verona (11th c.)

D–B

A - wake! the shining day is born! The herald

cock proclaims the morn: And Christ, the soul's A-

wakener, cries, Bidding us back to life a- rise. 2) A-

way the sluggard's bed! a-way The slumber of the

soul's de-cay! Ye chaste and just and temperate,

Prudentius (348–410)
tr. Robert Martin Pope

sel: 1–2, 21, 25

Watch! I am standing at the gate. 3) Af-ter the sun

hath risen red 'Tis late for men to scorn their bed,

Unless a portion of the night They seize for la-bours

of the light. 4) Mark ye, what time the dawn draws

nigh, How 'neath the eaves the swallows cry? Know

that by true si-mili- tude Their notes our Judge-

's voice prelude. 5) When hid by shades of dark

malign On beds of softness we re-cline, They call

us forth with music clear Warning us that the day

is near. 6) When breezes bright of o- rient morn

With rosy hues the heavens a- dorn, They cheer with

hope of gladdening light The hearts that spend in

toil their might. 7) Though sleep be but a passing

guest 'Tis type of death's perpetual rest: Our sins

are as a ghastly night, And seal with slumbers deep

our sight. 8) But from the wide roof of the sky

Christ's voice peals forth with ur- gent cry, Call-

ing our sleep-bound hearts to rise   And greet the

dawn with wakeful eyes. 9) He bids us fear lest sen-

sual ease Unto life's end the spirit seize And in

the tomb of shame us bind, Till we are to the true

light blind. 10) 'Tis said that baleful spirits roam

A-broad beneath the dark's vast dome; But, when

the cock crows, take their flight Sudden dispersed

in sore af-fright. 11) For the foul vo-taries of the

night Abhor the coming of the light, And shamed

be-fore salva-tion's grace The hosts of darkness hide

their face. 12) They know the cock doth prophe- sy

Of Hope's long-promised morning sky, When comes

the Majes-ty Di-vine Upon a-wakened worlds to

shine. 13) The Lord to Pe-ter once foretold What

meaning that shrill strain should hold, How he be-

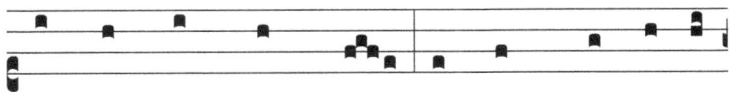

fore cock-crow would lie   And thrice his Master

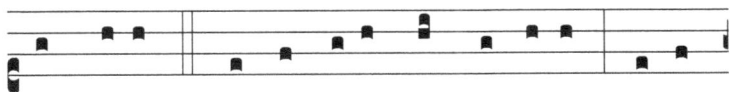

dear deny. 14) For 'tis a law that sin is done Be-fore

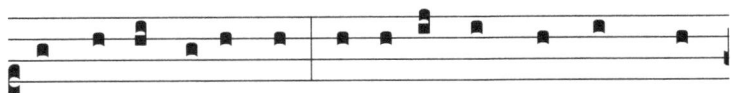

the herald of the sun To humankind the dawn pro-

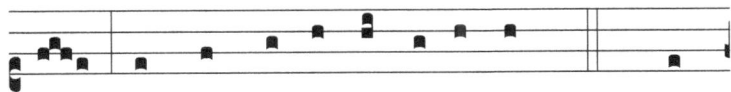

claims And with his cry the sinner shames. 15) Then

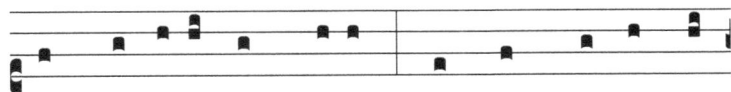

wept he bitter tears a-ghast That from his lips the

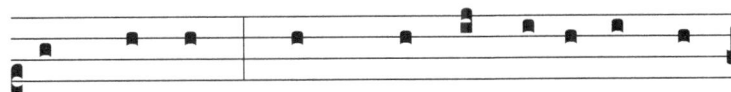

words had passed, Though guileless he his soul pos-

sessed And faith still reigned within his breast.

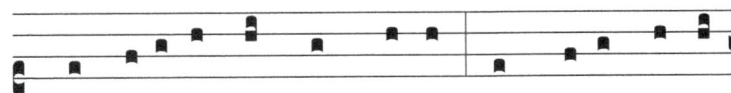

16) Nor ever reckless word he said Thereaf-ter, by his

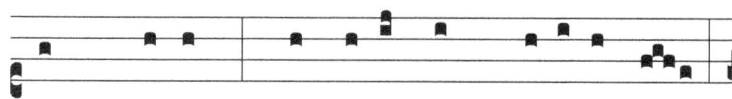

tongue be-trayed, But at the cock's familiar cry

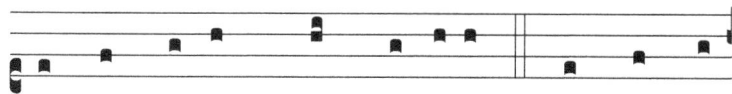

Humbled he turned from vani- ty. 17) Therefore it

is we hold to-day That, as the world in stillness

lay, What hour the cock doth greet the skies,

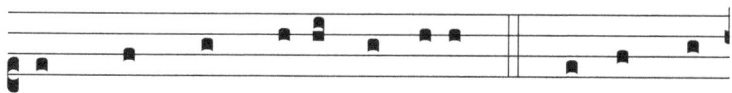

Christ from deep Hades did a- rise. 18) Lo! then the

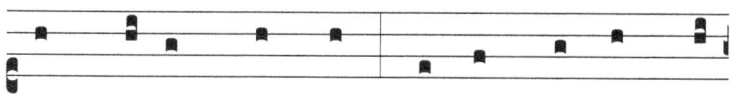

bands of death were burst, Shattered the sway of

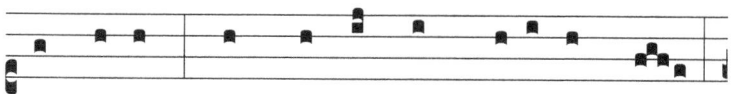

hell ac-curst: Then did the Day's supe-rior might

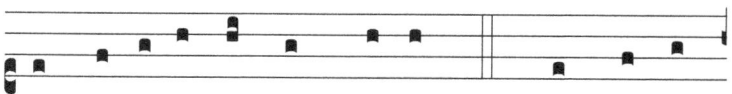

Swiftly dispel the hosts of Night. 19) Now let base

deeds to si-lence fall, Black thoughts be stilled be-

yond re-call: Now let sin's o-piate spell re-tire   To

that deep sleep it doth in-spire. 20) For all the hours

that still remain Until the dark his goal at-tain,

A-lert for duty's stern command Let every soul a

sentry stand. 21) With sober prayer on Je-sus call;

Let tears with our strong crying fall; Sleep cannot

on the pure soul steal That supplicates with fervent

zeal. 22) Too long did dull o-blivion cloud Our mo-

tions and our senses shroud: Lulled by her numbing

touch, we stray In dreamland's in-ef-fectual way.

23) Bound by the dazzling world's soft chain 'Tis false

and fleeting gauds we gain, Like those who in deep

slumbers lie:— Let us a-wake! the truth is nigh.

24) Gold, honours, pleasure, wealth and ease, And all

the joys that mortals please, Joys with a fa-tal

glamour fraught— When morning comes, lo! all are

nought. 25) But thou, O Christ, put sleep to flight

And break the i- ron bands of night, Free us from

burden of past sin   And shed Thy morning rays

within. A- men.

†24: Nox et tenebrae et nubila

Switzerland: Einsiedeln (1225–1275)

C–C

Ye   clouds and darkness, hosts of night That

breed confu- sion and af- fright, Begone! o'erhead

Prudentius (348–410)
tr. Robert Martin Pope

sel: 1–3, 13, 15

the dawn shines clear, The light breaks in and

Christ is here. 2) Earth's gloom flees broken and dis-

persed, By the sun's piercing shafts coerced: The

daystar's eyes rain in-fluence bright And co-lours

glimmer back to sight. 3) So shall our guilty

midnight fade, The sin-stained heart's gross dusk-

y shade: So shall the King's All-ra-diant Face

Sudden un-veil our deep disgrace. 4) No longer

then may we disguise Our dark in-tents from those

clear eyes: Yea, at the dayspring's advent blest

Our inmost thoughts will stand confest. 5) The thief

his hidden traffic plies Unmarked be-fore the dawn

doth rise: But light, the foe of guile concealed,

Lets no ill craft lie un-re-vealed. 6) Fraud and De-

ceit love on-ly night, Their wiles they practise out

of sight; Curtained by dark, A-dultery too   Doth

his foul treacher-y   pursue, 7) But slinks a-bashed

and shamed a-way Soon as the sun re-kindles day,

For none can damning light re-sist   And 'neath

its rays in sin persist. 8) Who doth not blush o'er-

took by morn And his long night's ca-rousal scorn?

For day subdues the lustful soul,   And doth all

foul de-sires control. 9) Now each to earnest life a-

wakes, Now each his wanton sport forsakes; Now

foolish things are put a- way   And gravi- ty re-

sumes her sway. 10) It   is   the hour for du-ty's

deeds, The path to which our la-bour leads, Be it the

fo-rum, army, sea,   The mart or field or fac-to-

ry. 11) One seeks the plaudits of the bar, One the

stern trumpet calls to war: Those bent on trade and

husbandry   At greed's be-hest for lu-cre sigh.

12) Mine is no rhetor- i- cian's fame, No petty u- su-

ry I claim; Nor am I skilled to face the foe:

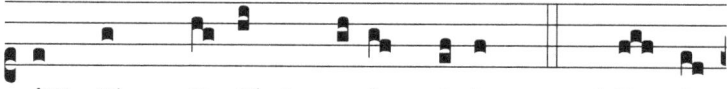

'Tis Thou, O Christ, a- lone I know. 13) Yea, I

have learnt to wait on Thee With heart and lips

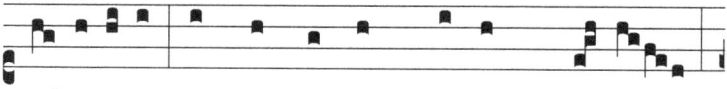

of puri-ty, Humbly my knees in prayer to bend,

And tears with songs of praise to blend. 14) These

are the gains I hold in view And these the arts

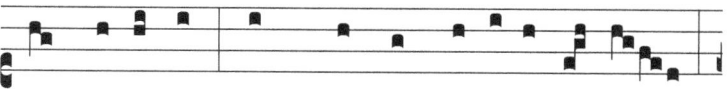

that I pursue: These are the of-fices I ply

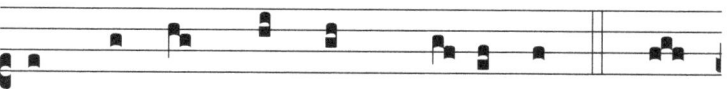

When the bright sun mounts up the sky. 15) Prove

Thou my heart, my every thought, Search in-to

all that I have wrought: Though I be stained with

blots within, Thy quickening rays shall purge

my sin. 16) O may I ever spotless be As when

my stains were cleansed by Thee, Who bad'st me

'neath the Jordan's wave Of yore my soiled spirit

lave. 17) If e'er since then the world's gross night

Hath cast its curtain o'er my sight, Dispel the cloud,

O King of grace, Star of the East! with thy pure

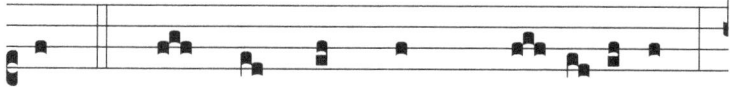

face. 18) Since Thou canst change, O ho-ly Light,

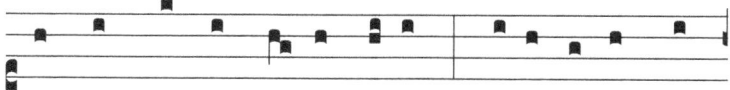

The blackest hue to milky white, Ebon to clearness

crystal-line, Wash my foul stains and make me

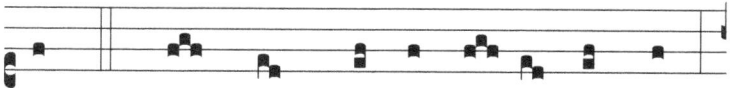

clean. 19) 'Twas 'neath the lonely star-blue night

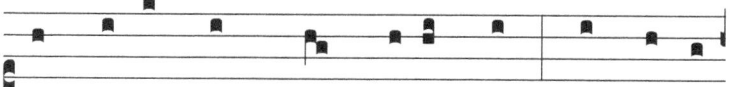

That Ja-cob waged the une-qual fight, Stoutly he

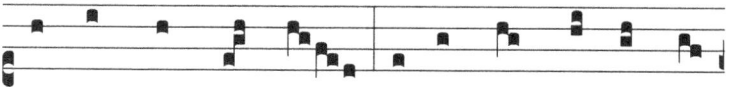

wrestled with the Man In darkness, till the day

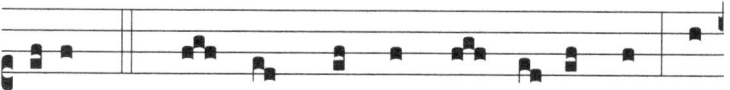

began. 20) And when the sun rose in the sky He

halted on his shrivelled thigh: His natural might

had ebbed a- way, Vanquished in that tremen-

dous fray. 21) Not wounded he in nobler part

Nor smitten in life's fount, the heart: But lust was

shaken from his throne And his foul empire o- ver-

thrown. 22) Whereby we clearly learn a- right That

man is whelmed by deadly night, Unless he own

God conqueror And strive a- gainst His will no

more. 23) Yet happier he whom ris-ing morn Shall

find of na-ture's strength forlorn, Whose warring

flesh hath shrunk a- way,   Palsied by virtue's puis-

sant sway. 24) And then at length let darkness flee,

Which all too long held us in fee, 'Mid wildering

shadows made us stray   And led in devious tracks

our way. 25) We pray Thee, Rising Light se-rene,

e'er as Thyself our hearts make clean: Let no de-ceit

our lips de-file　Nor let our souls be vexed by

guile. 26) O　keep us, as the hours proceed, From

ly-ing word and e-vil deed, Our roving eyes from

sin set free,　Our body　from impu-ri-ty. 27) For

thou dost from a-　bove survey The converse of

each fleeting day: Thou dost foresee from morning

light　Our every deed, until the night. 28) Jus-tice

and judgment dwell with Thee, Whatever is, Thine

eye doth see: Thou know'st what human hearts con-

ceive   And none Thy wisdom may de-ceive.

†25: Nox et tenebrae et nubila

On the Nativity of the Lord
at Nocturns.

Switzerland: Engelberg (ca. 1400)

D–D

Ye clouds and darkness, hosts of night That

breed confu-sion and af-fright, Be-gone! o'erhead

the dawn shines clear, The light breaks in and

Christ is here. 2) Earth's gloom flees broken and

Prudentius (348–410)   sel: 1–3, 13, 15
tr. Robert Martin Pope

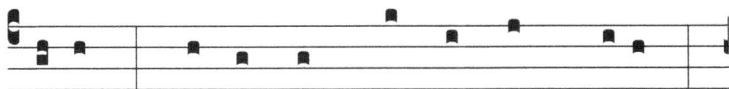

dispersed, By the sun's piercing shafts coerced:

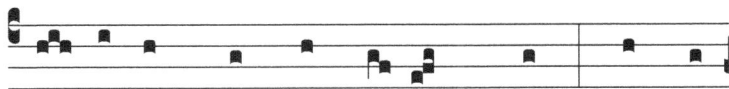

The daystar's eyes rain in- fluence bright And co-

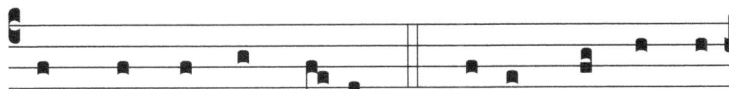

lours glimmer back to sight. 3) So shall our guilty

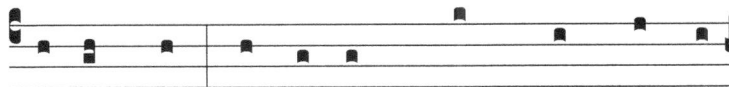

midnight fade, The sin-stained heart's gross dusky

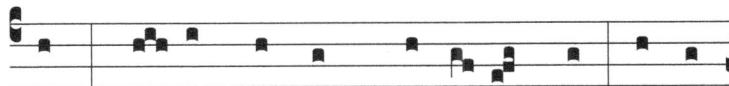

shade: So shall the King's All-ra-diant Face Sudden

unveil our deep dis-grace. 4) No longer then may we

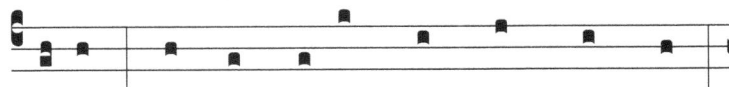

disguise Our dark in-tents from those clear eyes:

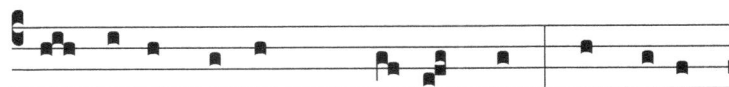

Yea, at the dayspring's ad-vent blest Our inmost

thoughts will stand confest. 5) The thief his hidden

traffic plies Unmarked be-fore the dawn doth rise:

But light, the foe of guile concealed, Lets no ill

craft lie unre-vealed. 6) Fraud and Deceit love on-

ly night, Their wiles they practise out of sight; Cur-

tained by dark, A-dul-tery too Doth his foul treach-

er-y pursue, 7) But slinks a-bashed and shamed a-

way Soon as the sun re-kindles day, For none can

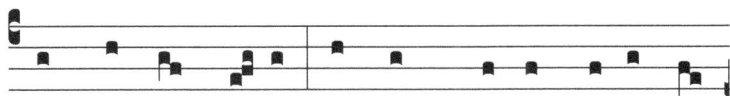

damning light re-sist And 'neath its rays in sin per-

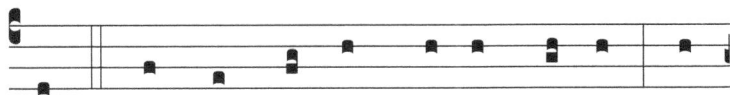

sist. 8) Who doth not blush o'ertook by morn And

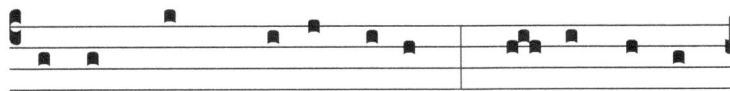

his long night's ca-rousal scorn? For day subdues

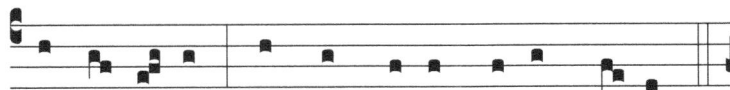

the lustful soul, And doth all foul de-sires control.

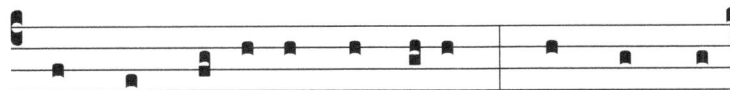

9) Now each to earnest life a-wakes, Now each his

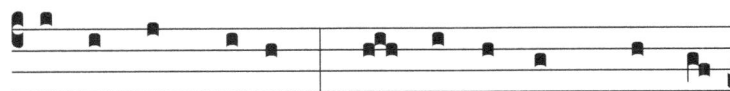

wanton sport forsakes; Now foolish things are put

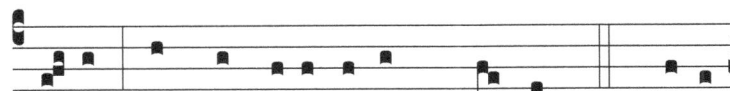

a- way And gravi- ty re-sumes her sway. 10) It is

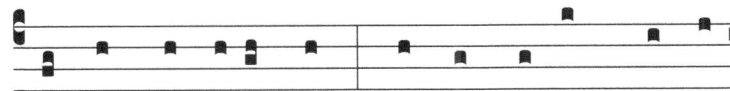

the hour for duty's deeds, The path to which our la-

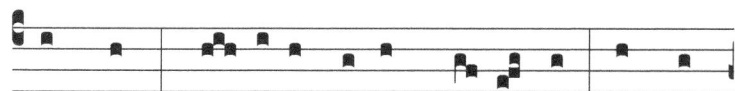

bour leads, Be it the fo-rum, ar-my, sea, The mart

or field or facto-ry. 11) One seeks the plaudits of the

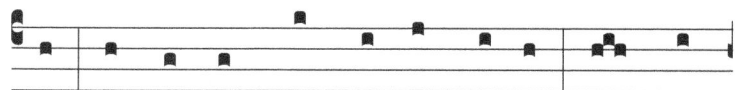

bar, One the stern trumpet calls to war: Those bent

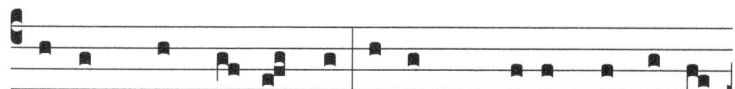

on trade and husbandry At greed's behest for lu-cre

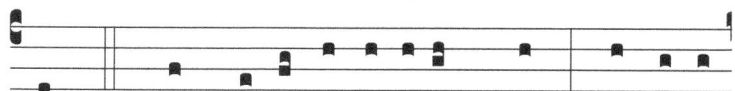

sigh. 12) Mine is no rhetori- cian's fame, No petty

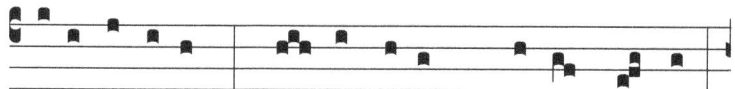

u-su-ry I claim; Nor am I skilled to face the foe:

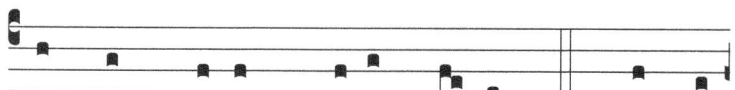

'Tis Thou, O Christ, a- lone I know. 13) Yea, I

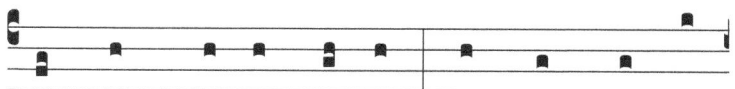

have learnt to wait on Thee With heart and lips

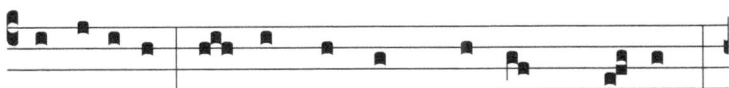

of puri-ty, Humbly my knees in prayer to bend,

And tears with songs of praise to blend. 14) These

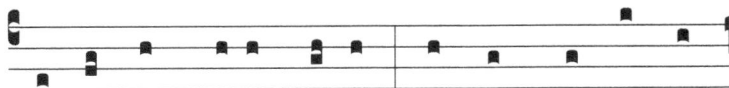

are the gains I hold in view And these the arts that

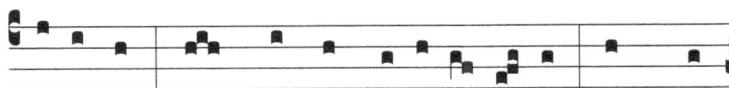

I pursue: These are the of-fices I ply When the

bright sun mounts up the sky. 15) Prove Thou my

heart, my every thought, Search in-to all that I have

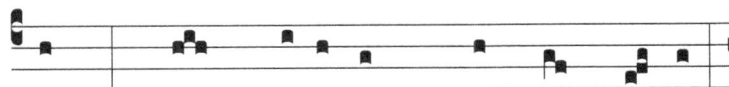

wrought: Though I be stained with blots within,

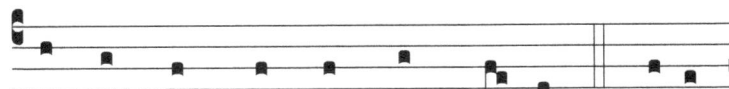

Thy quickening rays shall purge my sin. 16) O may

I ever spotless be As when my stains were cleansed

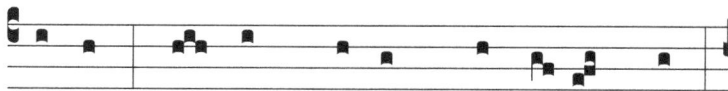

by Thee, Who bad'st me 'neath the Jordan's wave

Of yore my soiled spirit lave. 17) If e'er since then

the world's gross night Hath cast its curtain o'er my

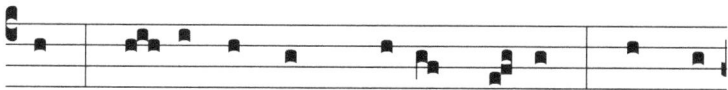

sight, Dis-pel the cloud, O King of grace, Star of

the East! with thy pure face. 18) Since Thou canst

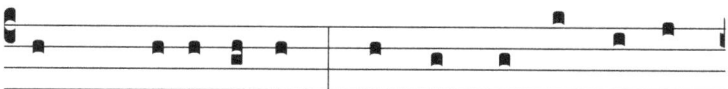

change, O ho-ly Light, The blackest hue to milk-

y white, Eb- on to clearness crystal-line, Wash my

foul stains and make me clean. 19) 'Twas 'neath the

lonely star-blue night That Ja-cob waged the un-

e-qual fight, Stoutly he wrestled with the Man In

darkness, till the day be-gan. 20) And when the sun

rose in the sky He halted on his shrivelled thigh:

His natural might had ebbed a- way, Vanquished

in that tremendous fray. 21) Not wounded he in

nobler part Nor smitten in life's fount, the heart:

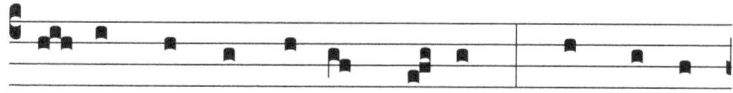

But lust was shaken from his throne And his foul

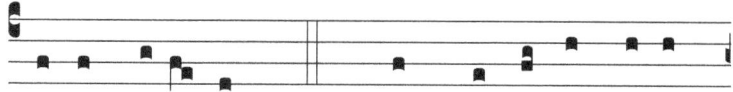

empire o-ver-thrown. 22) Whereby we clearly learn

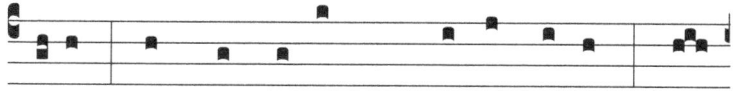

a-right That man is whelmed by deadly night, Un-

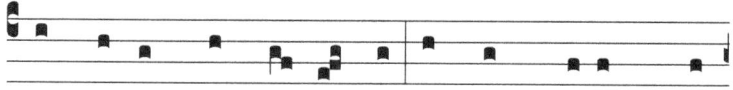

less he own God conqueror And strive a-gainst His

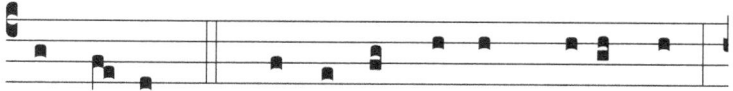

will no more. 23) Yet happier he whom rising morn

Shall find of na-ture's strength forlorn, Whose war-

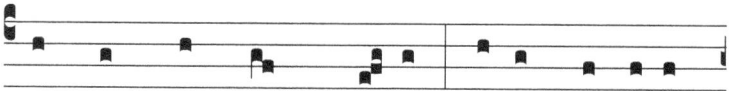

ring flesh hath shrunk a- way, Palsied by virtue's

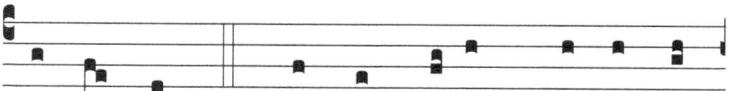

puissant sway. 24) And then at length let darkness

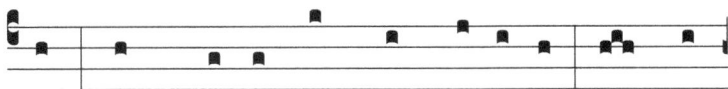

flee, Which all too long held us in fee, 'Mid wil-

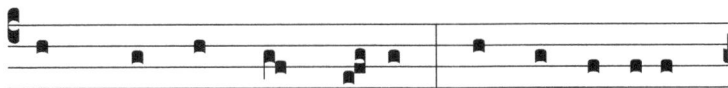

dering shadows made us stray And led in devious

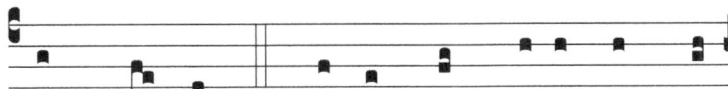

tracks our way. 25) We pray Thee, Rising Light se-

rene, e'er as Thyself our hearts make clean: Let

no de-ceit our lips de-file Nor let our souls be

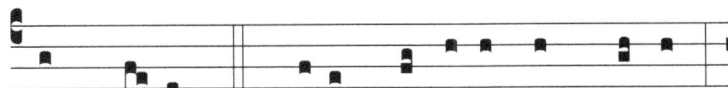

vexed by guile. 26) O keep us, as the hours proceed,

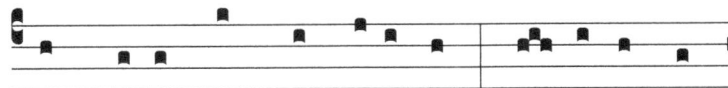

From ly-ing word and e-vil deed, Our roving eyes

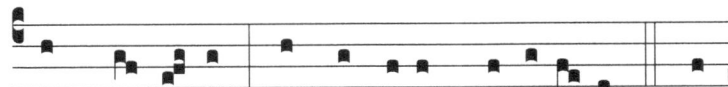

from sin set free, Our body from impuri- ty. 27) For

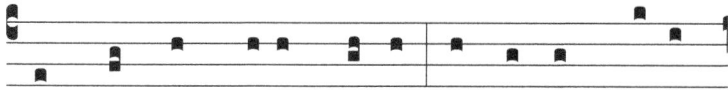

thou dost from a-bove survey The converse of each

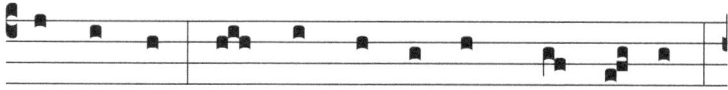

fleeting day: Thou dost foresee from morning light

Our every deed, until the night. 28) Justice and judg-

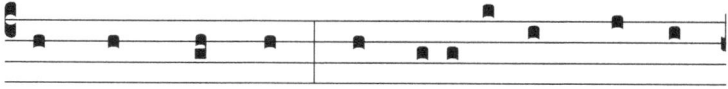

ment dwell with Thee, Whatever is, Thine eye doth

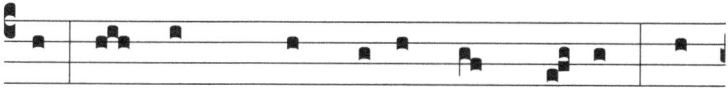

see: Thou know'st what human hearts conceive And

none Thy wisdom may de-ceive.

†26: Aeterna Christi munera

On the nativity of apostles.

France: Moissac (ca. 1000)

D–C

The eternal gifts of Christ the King, The Mar-

tyrs' glorious deeds, we sing: And while due hymns

of praise we pay, Our thankful hearts cast grief a-

way. 2) The Church in these her princes boasts,

These victor chiefs of war-rior hosts: The soldiers

of the heavenly hall, The lights that rose on earth

Anonymous (390–423)
tr. John Mason Neale

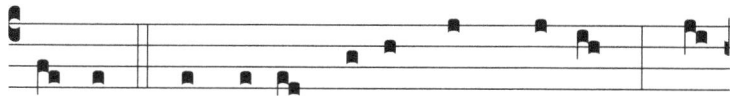

for all. 3) The terrors of the world de-spised, The

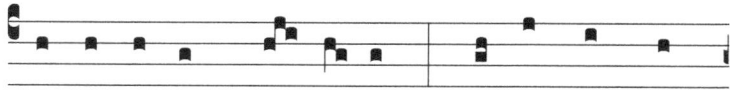

body's torments lightly prized, By one brief space

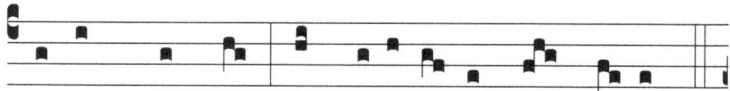

of death and pain Life ever-lasting they ob-tain.

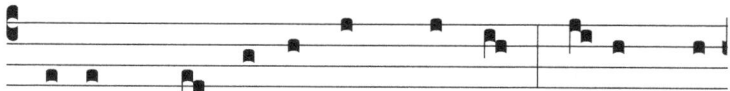

4) To flames the Martyr Saints are hal'd: By teeth of

savage beasts as-sail'd: A-gainst them, arm'd with

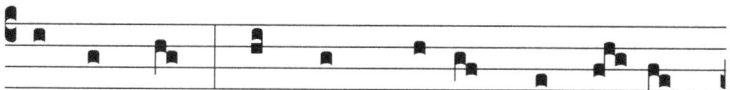

ruthless brand And hooks of steel, the tor-turers

stand. 5) The mangled frame is tortur'd sore: The

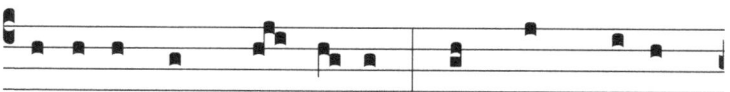

ho-ly life-drops freshly pour: They stand unmov'd

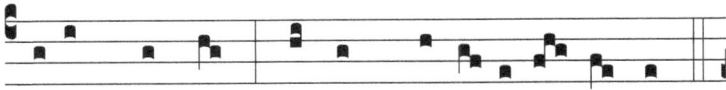

a-midst the strife, By grace of ev-er-last-ing life.

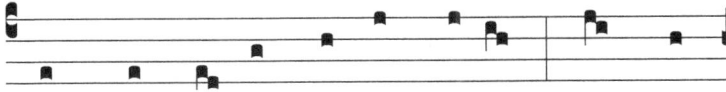

6) 'Twas thus the yearning faith of Saints, The uncon-

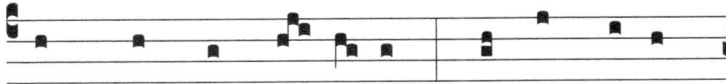

quer'd hope that nev-er faints, The love of Christ

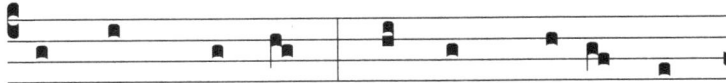

that knows not shame, The Prince of this world

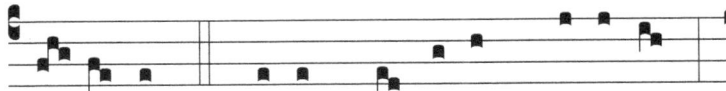

o- ver-came. 7) In these the Fa-ther's glory shone,

In these the will of God the Son: In these exults

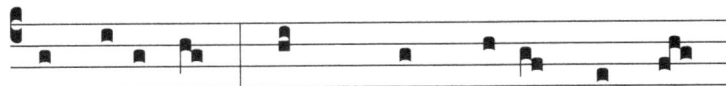

the Holy Ghost, Through these re-joice the Heav-

enly host. 8) Redeemer, hear us of Thy love, That,

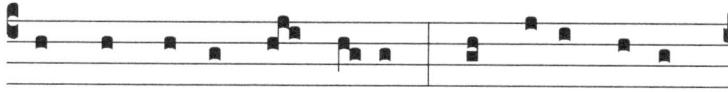

with the Martyr Host a- bove, Hereaf-ter, of Thine

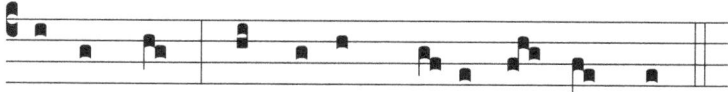

endless grace, Thy servants al- so may have place.

†27: Aeterna Christi munera

At a Nocturn.

Italy: Verona (11th c.)

B–A

The eternal gifts of Christ the King, The

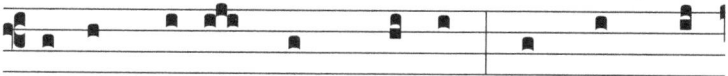

Martyrs' glorious deeds, we sing: And while due

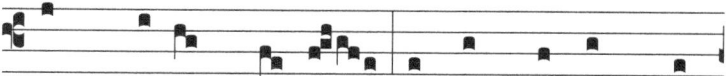

hymns of praise we pay, Our thankful hearts cast

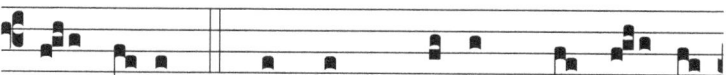

grief a- way. 2) The Church in these her princes

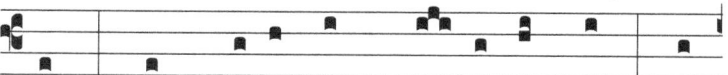

boasts, These victor chiefs of warrior hosts: The

Anonymous (390–423)   (4) i:5
tr. John Mason Neale

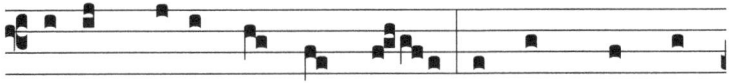

soldiers of the heavenly hall, The lights that rose

on earth for all. 3) The terrors of the world de-

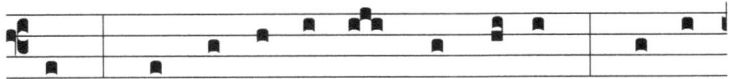

spised, The body's torments lightly prized, By one

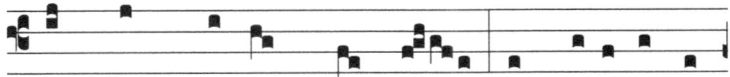

brief space of death and pain Life ever-lasting

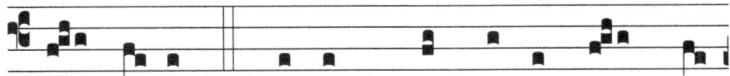

they ob-tain. 4) To flames the Martyr Saints are

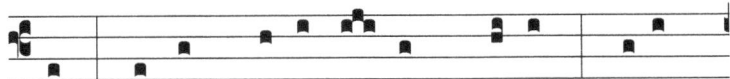

hal'd: By teeth of savage beasts as-sail'd: A-gainst

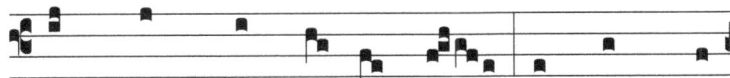

them, arm'd with ruthless brand And hooks of

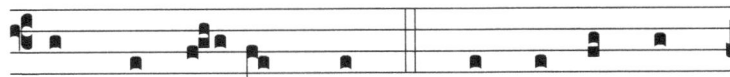

steel, the tor- turers stand. 5) The mangled frame

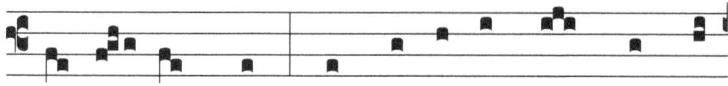

is   tor- tur'd sore: The ho- ly life- drops freshly

pour: They stand unmov'd a-midst the strife, By

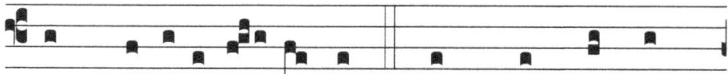

grace of ever-last-ing life. 6) 'Twas thus the yearn-

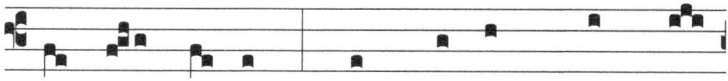

ing faith of Saints, The unconquer'd hope that

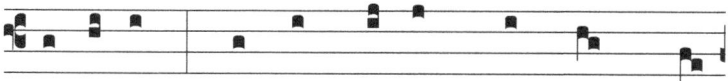

never faints, The love of Christ that knows not

shame, The Prince of this world o-   ver- came.

7) In these the Fa-ther's glo- ry shone, In these the

will of   God the Son: In these exults the Ho-ly

Ghost, Through these re-joice the Heavenly host.

8) Redeemer, hear us of Thy love, That, with the

Martyr Host a- bove, Hereaf-ter, of Thine endless

grace, Thy servants al-so may have place. A- men.

†28: A solis ortus cardine

On the Epiphany.

Germany: Kempten (ca. 1000)

D–D

From lands that see the sun a- rise, To earth's

remotest bounda- ries, The Virgin-born to-day we

sing, The Son of Mary, Christ the King. 2) Blest Au-

Sedulius (fl. 425–450)
tr. John Mason Neale: 1–9, 11, 13 / 23

div: 1–7; 8–9, 11, 13

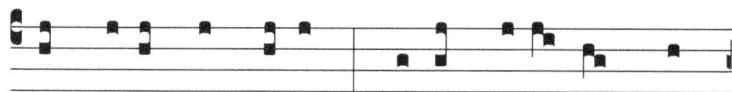

thor of this earthly frame, To take a ser-vant's form

He came, That liber-at-ing flesh by flesh, Whom He

had made might live a- fresh. 3) In that chaste par-

ent's ho-ly womb Ce-lestial grace hath found its

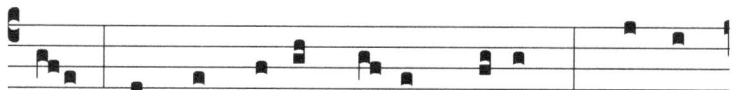

home: And she, as earthly bride unknown, Yet calls

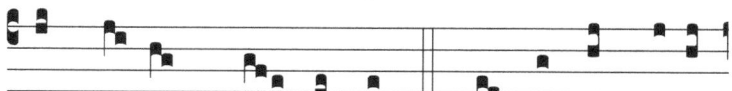

that Off-spring blest her own. 4) The mansion of the

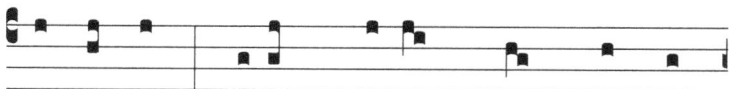

modest breast Becomes a shrine where God shall

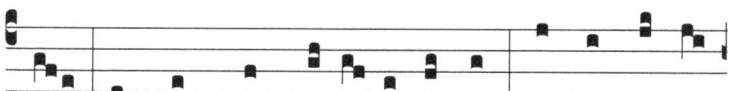

rest: The pure and unde-fil-ed one Conceived in

her womb The Son. 5) That Son, that Royal Son she

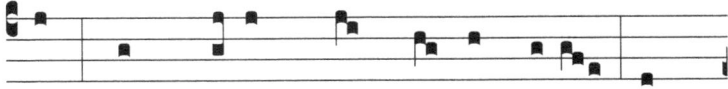

bore, Whom Gabriel's voice had told a- fore: Whom,

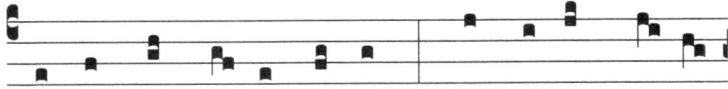

in His Mother yet conceal'd, The In- fant Baptist

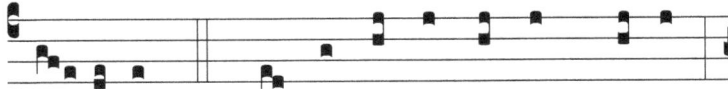

had re-veal'd. 6) The manger and the straw He bore,

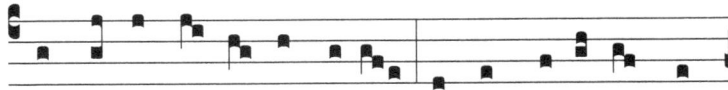

The cradle did He not abhor: By milk in in-fant por-

tions fed, Who gives e'en fowls their dai- ly bread.

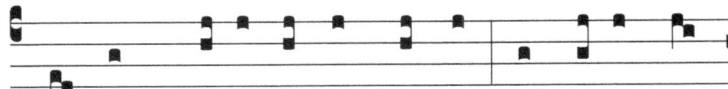

7) The Heavenly chorus fill'd the sky, The Angels sang

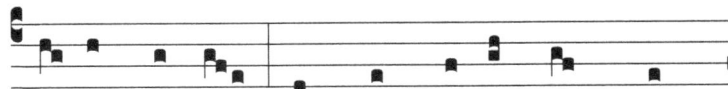

to God on high, What time to shepherds, watch-

ing lone, They made Crea- tion's Shepherd known.

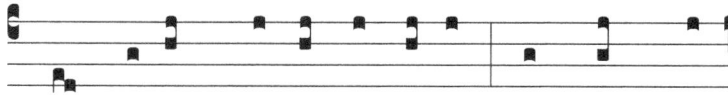

8) Why, impious Herod, vainly fear, That Christ the

Saviour cometh here? He takes not earthly realms

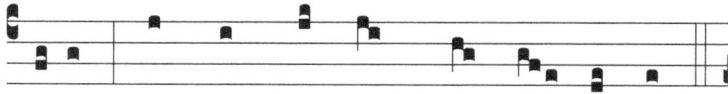

a-way, Who gives the crown that lasts for aye.

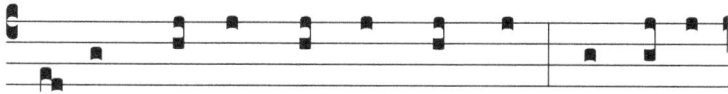

9) To greet His birth the wise men went, Led by the

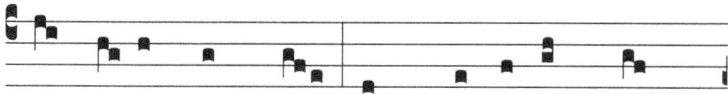

star be-fore them sent: Called on by light, towards

Light they press'd, And by their gifts their God con-

fess'd. 11) In ho-ly Jordan's purest wave The heav-

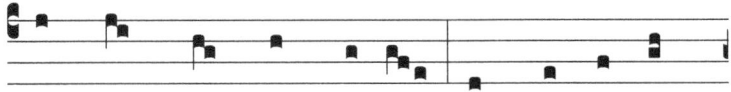

'nly Lamb vouchsaf'd to lave: That He, to Whom

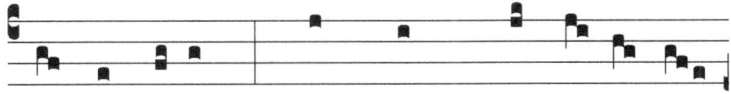

was sin unknown, Might cleanse his people from

their own. 13) New mira- cle of Power Di-vine!

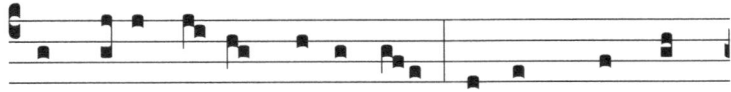

The water reddens in-to wine: He spake the word;

and pour'd the wave In other streams than na- ture

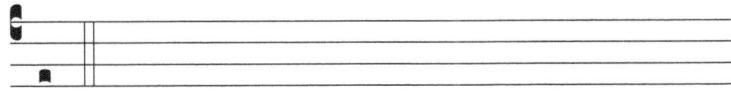

gave.

†29: A solis ortus cardine

On the vigil of
the Nativity of the Lord.

France: Laon (1100–1150)

D–D

From lands that see the sun a- rise, To earth's

remotest bounda- ries, The Vir- gin- born to- day

we sing, The Son of Mary, Christ the King. 2) Blest

Author of this earthly frame, To take a ser-vant's

form He came, That lib- er-at- ing flesh by flesh,

Whom He had made might live a- fresh. 3) In that

Sedulius (fl. 425–450) (1,8) ii:6, iii:4–5
tr. John Mason Neale: 1–9, 11, 13 / 23 div: 1–7; 8–9, 11, 13

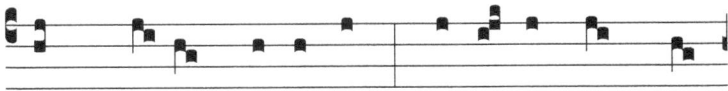

chaste parent's ho-ly womb Ce-les-tial grace hath

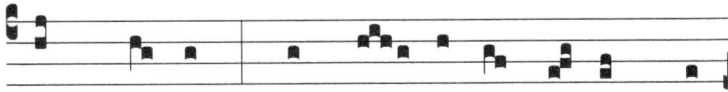

found its home: And she, as earthly bride un-

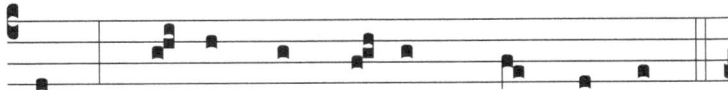

known, Yet calls that Off-spring blest her own.

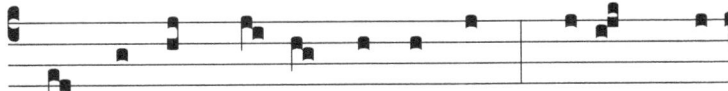

4) The mansion of the modest breast Becomes a

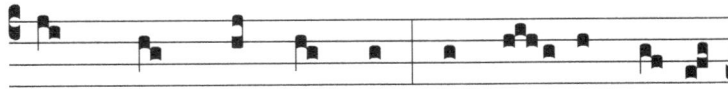

shrine where God shall rest: The pure and un-de-

fil-ed one Conceived in her womb The Son. 5) That

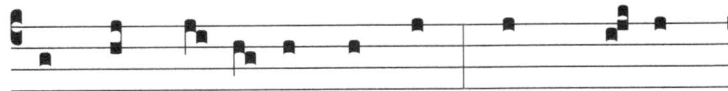

Son, that Royal Son she bore, Whom Ga-briel's

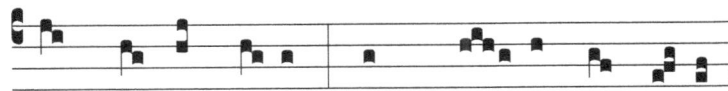

voice had told a- fore: Whom, in His Mother yet

conceal'd, The In-fant Baptist had re-veal'd. 6) The

manger and the straw He bore, The cradle did He

not ab-hor: By milk in in-fant portions fed, Who

gives e'en fowls their dai-ly bread. 7) The Heaven-

ly chorus fill'd the sky, The An-gels sang to God

on high, What time to shepherds, watching lone,

They made Crea- tion's Shepherd known. 8) Why,

impious Herod, vainly fear, That Christ the Saviour

cometh here? He takes not earthly realms a-way,

Who gives the crown that lasts for aye. 9) To greet

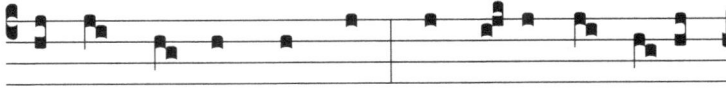

His birth the wise men went, Led by the star be-fore

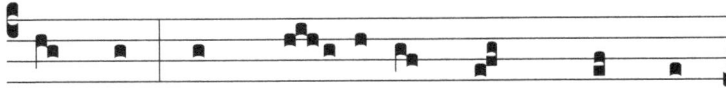

them sent: Called on   by light, towards Light they

press'd, And by their gifts their God confess'd.

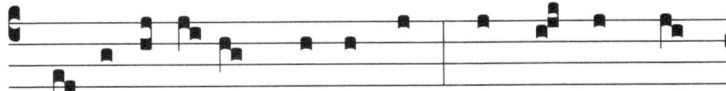

11) In ho-ly Jordan's purest wave The heav'nly Lamb

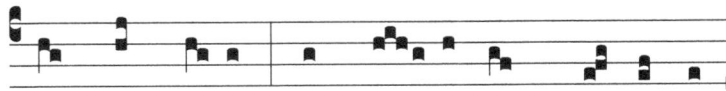

vouchsaf'd to lave: That He,   to Whom was sin un-

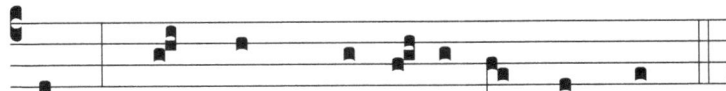

known, Might cleanse his people from their own.

13) New mira- cle of Power Di-vine! The wa-ter red-

dens in-to wine: He spake the word; and pour'd the

wave In other streams than na-ture gave.

†30: A solis ortus cardine

Switzerland: Einsiedeln (1100–1150)

C–B

From lands that see the sun a- rise, To earth's

re-motest bounda- ries, The Vir-gin-born to- day we

sing, The Son of Mary, Christ the King. 2) Blest Au-

thor of this earthly frame, To take a servant's form

Sedulius (fl. 425–450)　　　　　　　　　div: 1–7; 8–9, 11, 13
tr. John Mason Neale: 1–9, 11, 13 / 23

He came, That lib-er-at-ing flesh by flesh, Whom

He had made might live a- fresh. 3) In that chaste

parent's ho-ly womb Ce-lestial grace hath found

its home: And she, as earthly bride unknown, Yet

calls that Off-spring blest her own. 4) The mansion

of the modest breast Becomes a shrine where God

shall rest: The pure and unde- fil-ed one Conceived

in her womb The Son. 5) That Son, that Royal Son

she bore, Whom Gabriel's voice had told a- fore:

Whom, in His Mother   yet conceal'd, The In-fant

Baptist had re-veal'd. 6) The manger and the straw

He bore, The cradle did He not abhor: By milk in

in-fant portions fed, Who gives e'en fowls their dai-

ly bread. 7) The Heavenly chorus fill'd the sky, The

Angels sang to God on high, What time to shep-

herds, watching lone, They made Crea- tion's Shep-

herd known. 8) Why, impious Herod, vainly fear,

That Christ the Saviour cometh here? He takes not

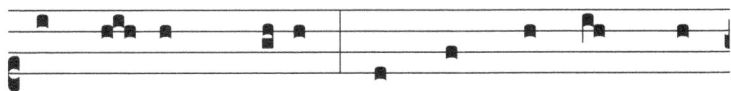

earthly realms a-way, Who gives the crown that

lasts for aye. 9) To greet His birth the wise men

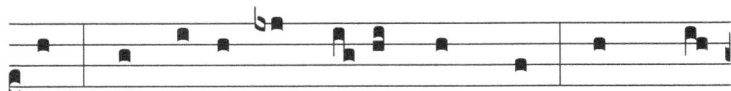

went, Led by the star be-fore them sent: Called on

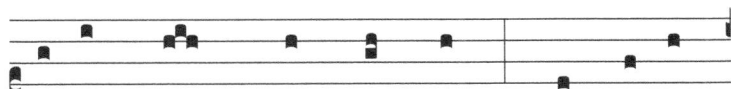

by light, towards Light they press'd, And by their

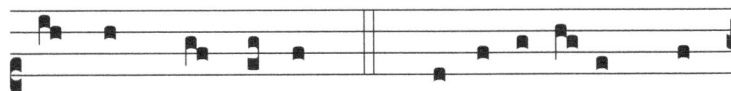

gifts their God confess'd. 11) In ho-ly Jordan's pur-

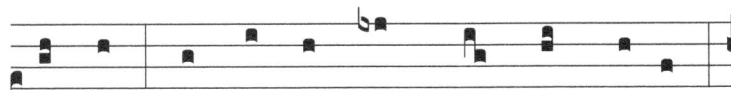

est wave The heav'nly Lamb vouchsaf'd to lave:

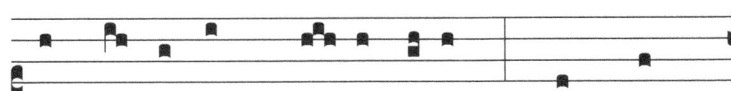

That He, to Whom was sin unknown, Might cleanse

his people from their own. 13) New mira- cle of

Power Di- vine! The water reddens in- to wine:

He spake the word; and pour'd the wave In other

streams than na-ture gave.

†31: A solis ortus cardine

At Lauds.

Italy: Gaeta (12th c.)

E–E

From lands that see the sun a- rise, To earth's

remotest bounda- ries, The Virgin-born to-day we

sing, The Son of Mary, Christ the King. 2) Blest Au-

Sedulius (fl. 425–450)
tr. John Mason Neale: 1–9, 11, 13 / 23

div: 1–7; 8–9, 11, 13

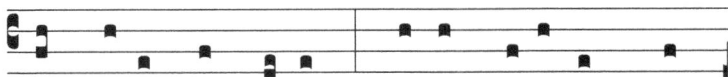

thor of this earthly frame, To take a servant's form

He came, That liber-at-ing flesh by flesh, Whom He

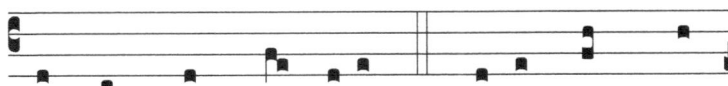

had made might live a- fresh. 3) In that chaste par-

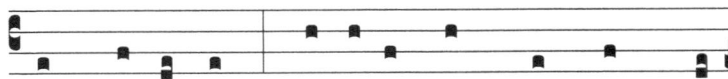

ent's ho-ly womb Ce-lestial grace hath found its

home: And she, as earthly bride un-known, Yet calls

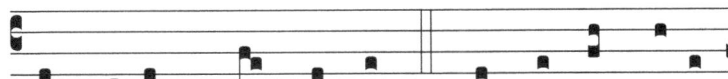

that Offspring blest her own. 4) The mansion of the

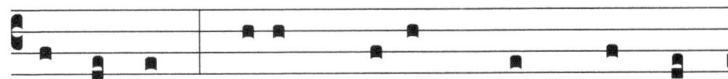

modest breast Becomes a shrine where God shall

rest: The pure and unde- fil-ed one Conceived in

her womb The Son. 5) That Son, that Royal Son she

bore, Whom Gabriel's voice had told a- fore: Whom,

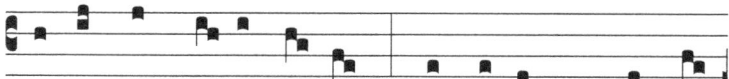

in His Mother yet conceal'd, The In-fant Baptist had

re- veal'd. 6) The manger and the straw He bore,

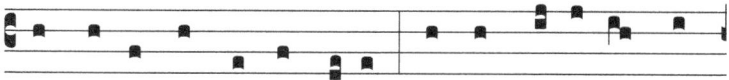

The cradle did He not abhor: By milk in in-fant por-

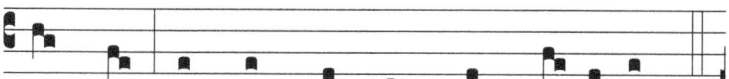

tions fed, Who gives e'en fowls their dai-ly bread.

7) The Heavenly chorus fill'd the sky, The Angels sang

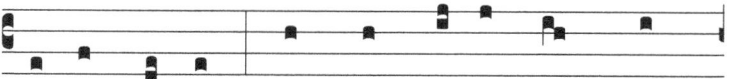

to God on high, What time to shepherds, watch-

ing lone, They made Crea- tion's Shepherd known.

8) Why, impious Herod, vainly fear, That Christ the

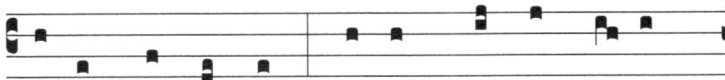

Saviour cometh here? He takes not earthly realms

a- way, Who gives the crown that lasts for aye.

9) To greet His birth the wise men went, Led by the

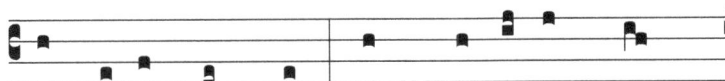

star be-fore them sent: Called on by light, towards

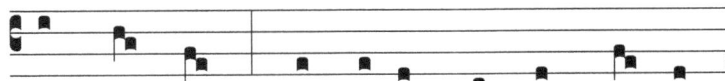

Light they press'd, And by their gifts their God con-

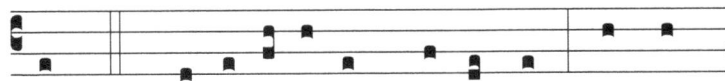

fess'd. 11) In ho-ly Jordan's purest wave The heav-

'nly Lamb vouchsaf'd to lave: That He, to Whom

was sin un-known, Might cleanse his people from

their own. 13) New mira- cle of Power Di-vine! The

water reddens in-to wine: He spake the word; and

pour'd the wave In other streams than na-ture gave.

†32: A solis ortus cardine

At Lauds.

Italy: Gaeta (12th c.)

F–E

From lands that see the sun a- rise, To earth's

remotest bounda- ries, The Virgin-born to-day we

Sedulius (fl. 425–450) div: 1–7; 8–9, 11, 13
tr. John Mason Neale: 1–9, 11, 13 / 23

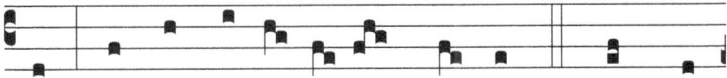

sing, The Son of Mary, Christ the King. 2) Blest Au-

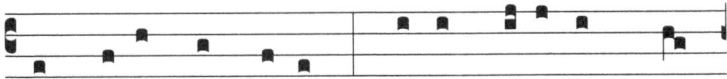

thor of this earthly frame, To take a servant's form

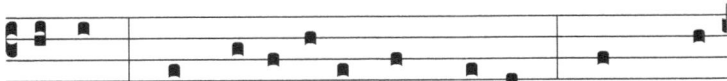

He came, That liber-at-ing flesh by flesh, Whom He

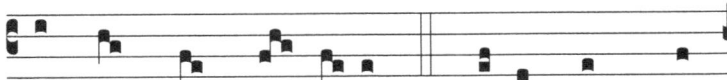

had made might live a- fresh. 3) In that chaste par-

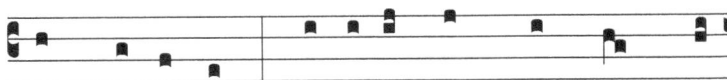

ent's ho-ly womb Ce-lestial grace hath found its

home: And she, as earthly bride unknown, Yet calls

that Off-spring blest her own. 4) The mansion of the

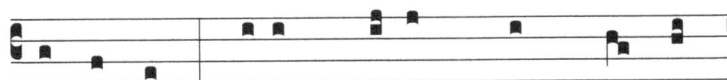

modest breast Becomes a shrine where God shall

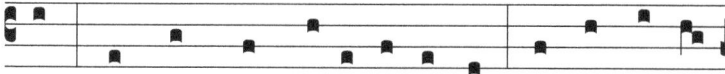

rest: The pure and unde-fil-ed one Conceived in

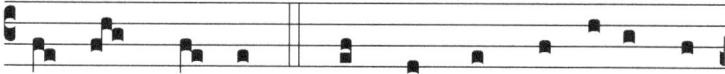

her womb The Son. 5) That Son, that Royal Son she

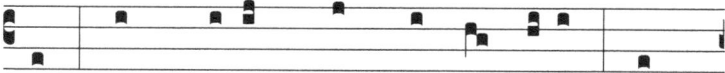

bore, Whom Gabriel's voice had told a- fore: Whom,

in His Mother yet conceal'd, The In-fant Baptist

had re-veal'd. 6) The manger and the straw He bore,

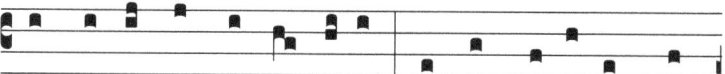

The cradle did He not abhor: By milk in in-fant por-

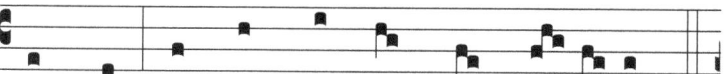

tions fed, Who gives e'en fowls their dai- ly bread.

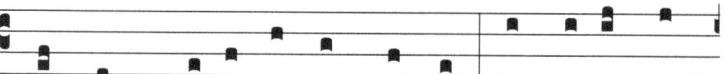

7) The Heavenly chorus fill'd the sky, The Angels sang

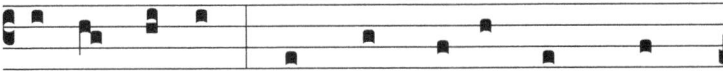

to God on high, What time to shepherds, watch-

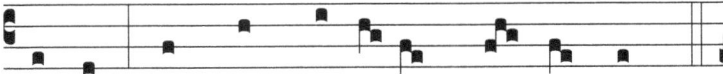

ing lone, They made Crea- tion's Shepherd known.

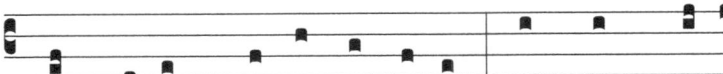

8) Why, impious Herod, vainly fear, That Christ the

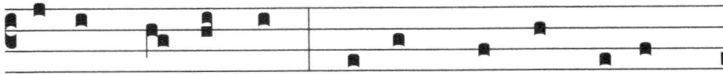

Saviour cometh here? He takes not earthly realms

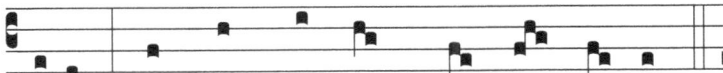

a-way, Who gives the crown that lasts for aye.

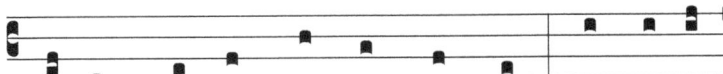

9) To greet His birth the wise men went, Led by the

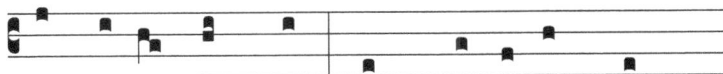

star be-fore them sent: Called on by light, towards

Light they press'd, And by their gifts their God con-

fess'd. 11) In ho-ly Jordan's purest wave The heav-

'nly Lamb vouchsaf'd to lave: That He, to Whom

was sin unknown, Might cleanse his people from

their own. 13) New mira- cle of Power Di-vine! The

water reddens in-to wine: He spake the word; and

pour'd the wave In other streams than na- ture gave.

†33: A solis ortus cardine

Within the octave of the Epiphany
with three lessons.

England: Worcester (ca. 1230)

F rom lands that see the sun a- rise, To earth's

remotest bounda- ries, The Vir-gin-born to-day we

sing, The Son of Mary, Christ the King. 2) Blest Au-

thor of this earth-ly frame, To take a ser-vant's

form He came, That lib-er-at-ing flesh by flesh,

Whom He had made might live a- fresh. 3) In that

chaste parent's ho- ly womb Ce-lestial grace hath

Sedulius (fl. 425–450)
tr. John Mason Neale: 1–9, 11, 13 / 23

div: 1–7; 8–9, 11, 13

found its home: And she, as earthly bride unknown,

Yet calls that Off-spring blest her own. 4) The man-

sion of the mod- est breast Becomes a shrine where

God shall rest: The pure and unde-fil-ed one Con-

ceived in her womb The Son. 5) That Son, that Roy-

al Son she bore, Whom Gabriel's voice had told

a- fore: Whom, in His Mother yet conceal'd, The

In- fant Baptist had re- veal'd. 6) The manger and

the straw He bore, The cradle did He not ab-hor:

By milk in in-fant portions fed, Who gives e'en

fowls their dai-ly bread. 7) The Heavenly chorus

fill'd the sky, The Angels sang to God on high,

What time to shepherds, watching lone, They made

Crea- tion's Shepherd known. 8) Why, impious Her-

od, vain-ly fear, That Christ the Saviour com-eth

here? He takes not earthly realms a-way, Who gives

the crown that lasts for aye. 9) To greet His birth

the wise men went, Led by the star be-fore them

sent: Called on by light, towards Light they press'd,

And by their gifts their God confess'd. 11) In ho-ly

Jordan's pur- est wave The heav'nly Lamb vouch-

saf'd to lave: That He, to Whom was sin unknown,

Might cleanse his people from their own. 13) New

mira- cle of Power Di-vine! The water reddens into wine: He spake the word; and pour'd the wave

In other streams than na-ture gave.

†34: A solis ortus cardine

France: Clermont-Ferránd (14th c.)

D–C

From lands that see the sun a- rise, To earth's

remotest bounda- ries, The Virgin-born to-day we

sing, The Son of Mary, Christ the King. 2) Blest Au-

thor of this earthly frame, To take a ser-vant's

Sedulius (fl. 425–450) div: 1–7; 8–9, 11, 13
tr. John Mason Neale: 1–9, 11, 13 / 23

form He came, That liber-at-ing flesh by flesh,

Whom He had made might live a- fresh. 3) In that

chaste parent's ho-ly womb Ce-lestial grace hath

found its home: And she, as earthly bride unknown,

Yet calls that Offspring blest her own. 4) The man-

sion of the modest breast Becomes a shrine where

God shall rest: The pure and unde-fil-ed one Con-

ceived in her womb The Son. 5) That Son, that Roy-

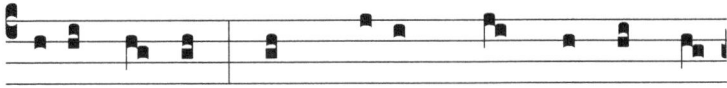

al Son she bore, Whom Gabriel's voice had told a-

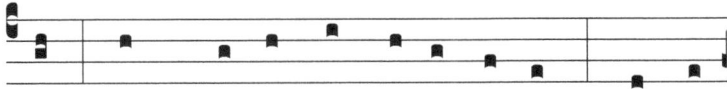

fore: Whom, in His Mother yet conceal'd, The In-

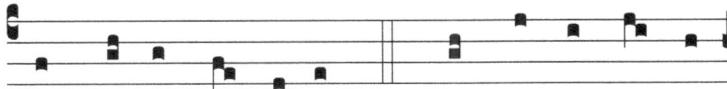

fant Baptist had re-veal'd. 6) The manger and the

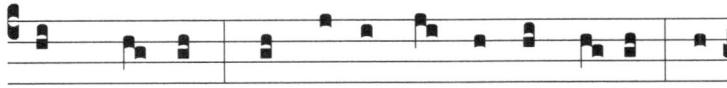

straw He bore, The cradle did He not ab-hor: By

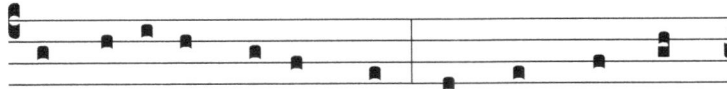

milk in in-fant portions fed, Who gives e'en fowls

their dai-ly bread. 7) The Heavenly chorus fill'd the

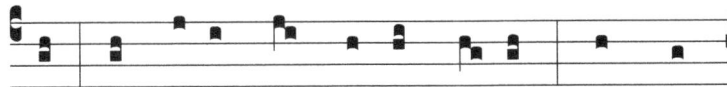

sky, The Angels sang to God on high, What time

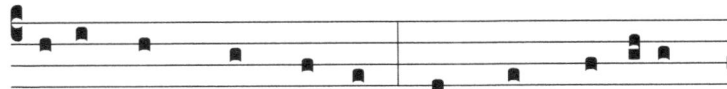

to shepherds, watching lone, They made Crea- tion's

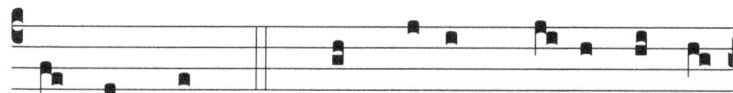

Shepherd known. 8) Why, impious Herod, vainly

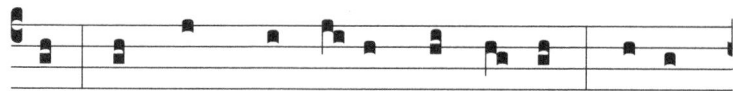

fear, That Christ the Saviour cometh here? He takes

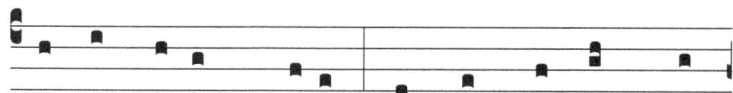

not earthly realms a-way, Who gives the crown that

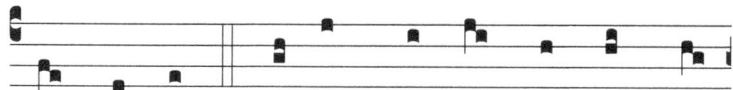

lasts for aye. 9) To greet His birth the wise men

went, Led by the star be-fore them sent: Called on

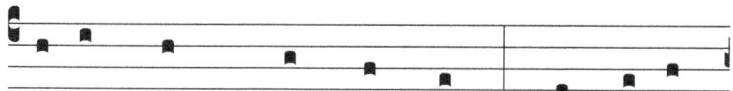

by light, towards Light they press'd, And by their

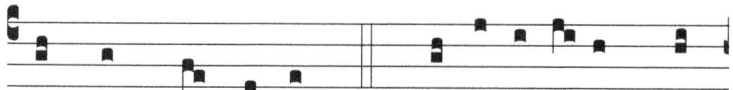

gifts their God confess'd. 11) In ho-ly Jordan's pur-

est wave The heav'nly Lamb vouchsaf'd to lave:

That He, to Whom was sin unknown, Might cleanse

his people from their own. 13) New mira- cle of

Power Di- vine! The water reddens in- to wine:

He spake the word; and pour'd the wave In other

streams than na- ture gave.

†35: Mediae noctis tempus est

Third and fourth Sundays in Lent
at Nocturns.

Central or southern Italy (ca. 1267)

C–A

'Tis the solemn midnight hour;— With the

Anonymous (475–525)
tr. Edward Caswall

sel: 1–6, 13

Psalmist let us sing,   To the Lord of grace and

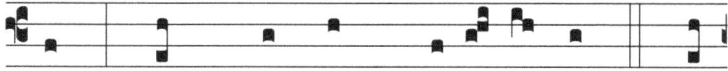

power, Heav'n and earth's triu- nal King; 2) Fa-

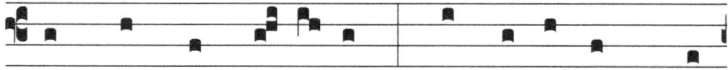

ther, Son, and Ho-ly Ghost, One in Substance ev-

ermore,   Whom the bright Angel-ic host, Bent

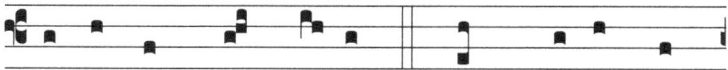

in prostrate awe, a- dore. 3) 'Twas at this same

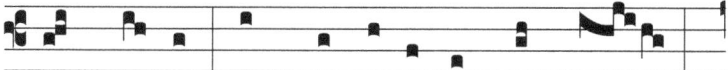

hour of old, Smit by a de-stroying breath,

E-gypt's first-born sons grew cold In the sudden

sleep of death. 4) This same hour on Is-rael's race

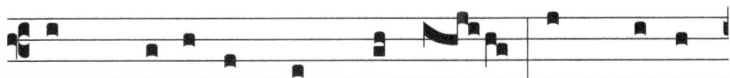

Pour'd salva-tion from on high; When be-fore

the sign of grace, Harmless pass'd th' Avenger

by. 5) Whence to all the sons of light Still it tells

of peace and rest; Breeding sadness and af-

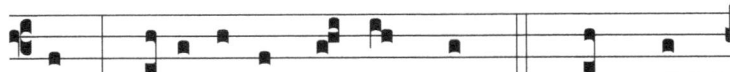

fright Only in the sin-ner's breast. 6) Lord, thine

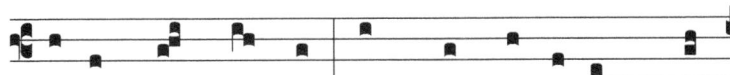

Is- rael true are we; Thou our confi- dence and

aid; Foes of every foe of Thee, Who shall make

our heart a- fraid? 7) This a- gain is that same

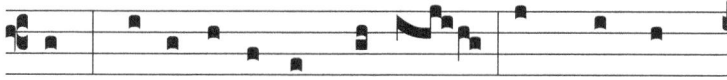

hour, As in ho-ly writ we learn,   When the Bride-

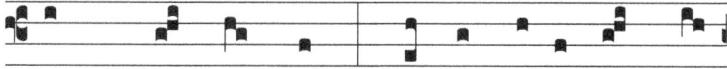

groom, girt with power, In His glory shall re-

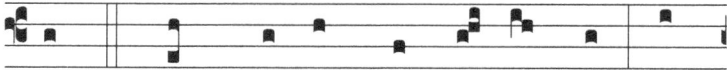

turn. 8) Whom to meet, the Vir-gins wise Bear-

ing lamps of purest light,   Joy and gladness in

their eyes, Forth shall go in snowy white. 9) While

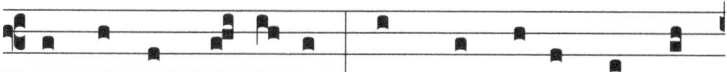

the foolish, all in vain Knocking at the heavenly

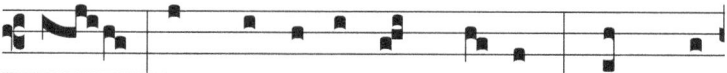

door,   Must in outer night re-main, There to

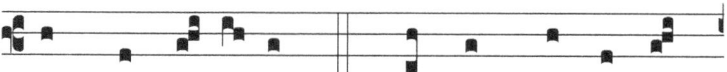

weep for ev-er-more. 10) Ah! then, let us watch

and pray; So that, ever on our guard,   Come the

Lord whene'er He may, He may find us well pre-

pared. 11) At the midnight hour a- gain, Singing to

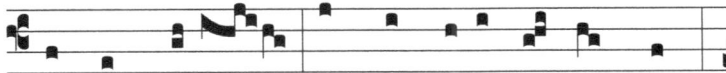

the Lord a- loud,   Paul and Si-las felt their chain

Melt be-fore the might of God. 12) Lord! from earth,

our prison-house, Unto Thee we lift our prayer;

Loose the sins that fet-ter us, And Thy true Be-

lievers spare. 13) Make us worthy, glo-rious King,

Of Thy Kingdom and of Thee; So may we Thy

glo-ries sing Through a glad E- ter-ni- ty! 14) Hon-

our, glory, blessing, praise, To the Fa-ther, and the

Son, With the Spirit, through all days, While

e- ternal ag-es run.

†36: Crux benedicta nitet

On the Exaltation of the Holy Cross.

Italy: Ravenna (12th c.)

D–C

That blest Cross is displayed, where the Lord

in the flesh was suspended, And, by His blood, from

Venantius Fortunatus (ca. 567) P: 1, 1, 2a, 1, 2b, 1, 3a, 1, 3b, etc.
tr. John Mason Neale

their wounds cleansed and re-deemed His e- lect:

2) Where for us men, through His love, be-come the

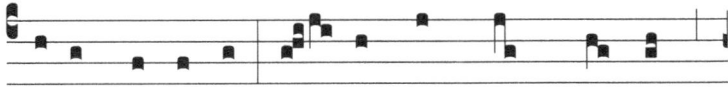

victim of mercy, He,   the Blest Lamb, His sheep

saved from the fangs of the wolf: 3) Where by His

palms transpierced He re-deemed the world from its

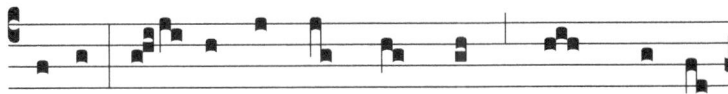

ru-in, And by His own dear Death closed up the

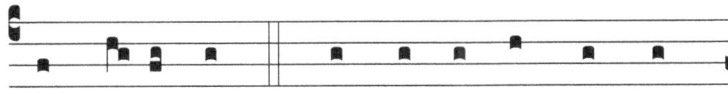

path of the grave. 4) This was the hand that, trans-

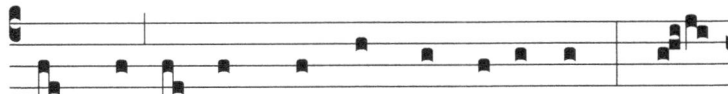

fixed by the nails, and bleeding of old times, Paul

from the depth of his crime ran-somed, and Pe-ter

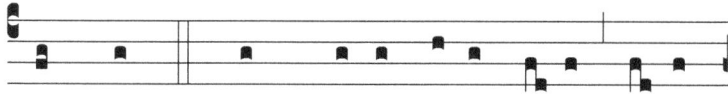

from death. 5) Strong in thy fertile ar-ray, O Tree

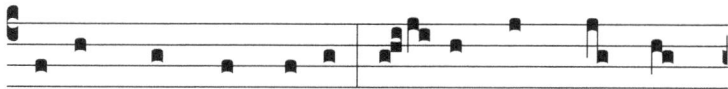

of sweetness and glory. Bear-ing such new-found

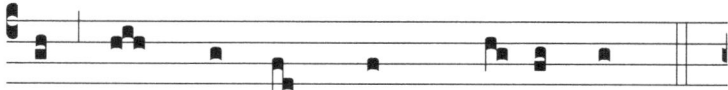

fruit 'midst the green wreaths of thy boughs:

6) Thou by thy sa-vour of life the dead from their

slumbers re-storest, Ren- dering sight to the eyes

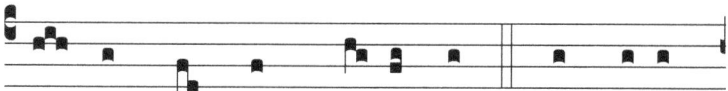

that have been closed to the day. 7) Heat is there

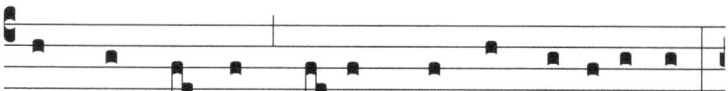

none that can burn be-neath thy shadowy covert:

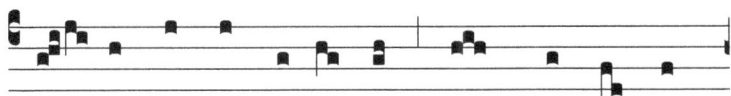

Nor   can the sun in the noon strike, nor the moon

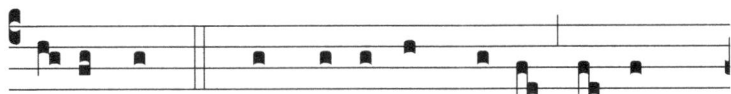

in the night. 8) Planted art thou be-side the streams

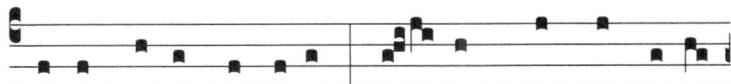

of the rivers of waters: Fo-   liage and loveli- est

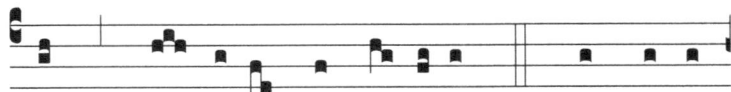

flowers scat-tering widely a- broad. 9) Fast in thy

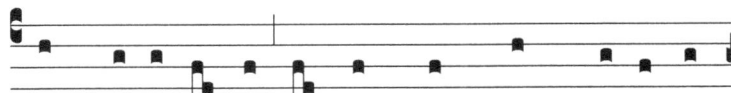

arms is en-folded the Vine; from whom in its ful-

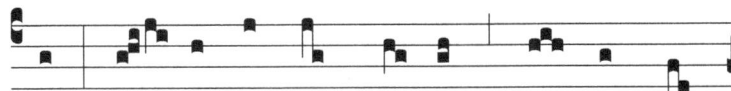

ness, Flow-eth the blood-red juice, wine that gives

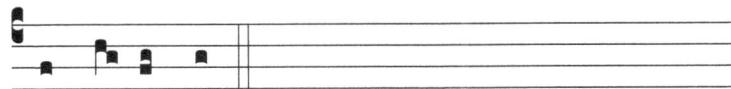

life to the soul.

†37: Pange, lingua

For the Passion of the Lord.

France: Moissac (ca. 1000)

D–C

Sing the Cross! the conflict telling Crown'd

with glory more than woe; Sing the battle and the

triumph, Tell its fame to all be-low, How by death

the world's Redeemer O-verthrew and bound His

foe. 2) Touch'd with pity for the ru-in Of our first-

made fa-ther's fall, When the fa-tal fruit he tasted,

On one mouthful staking all; God mark'd out the

Venantius Fortunatus (ca. 567)
tr. Hamilton Montgomerie MacGill

div: 1–4, 6; 7–10

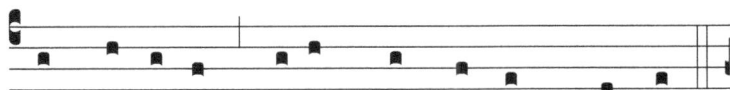

tree of Calvary, E- den's tree to match withal.

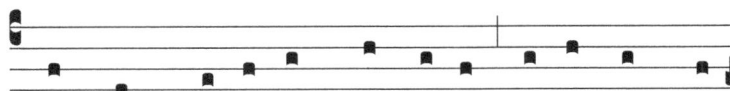

3) Law could on-ly yield our rescue As the fruit of

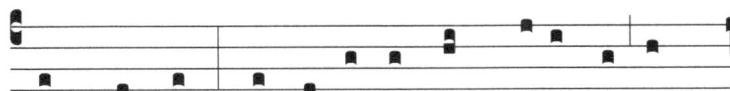

pains and toils; Art by art the great Restorer Foiled,

and took the Traitor's spoils; Thus His healing balm

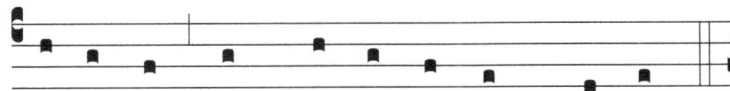

He gathered Where the foe had spread his wiles.

4) At the time a- fore appointed, Coming in His Fa-

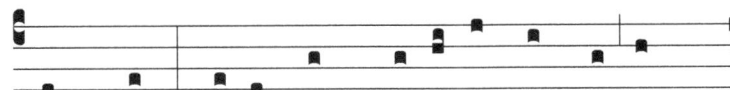

ther's name, In the womb of Virgin Mother Clothed

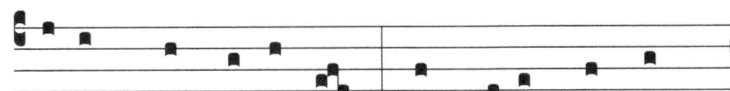

in flesh, with feeble frame; Born a man, the world's

Crea- tor From the throne of glory came. 5) Hark!

the cry of In-fant wailing In the manger, meanly

laid; Child all lowly, God all ho-ly! Not in robes of

light ar-ray'd; But in swaddling bands en-folded

By that blessed Mother-Maid. 6) Thirty winters has

He number'd Here on earth in quest of me; Yea, my

soul! thy great Redeemer Ago-nizing on the tree,

As the Lamb of God, up-lifted, Bleeds, and bows the

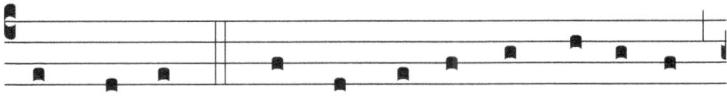

head for thee. 7) Fainting, lo! the gall He tasteth;

See the thorns, the nails, the spear, From His ebbing

life are drawing Crimson blood and water clear!

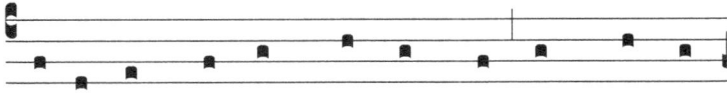

Fit for cleansing souls, and cleansing Earth, and sea,

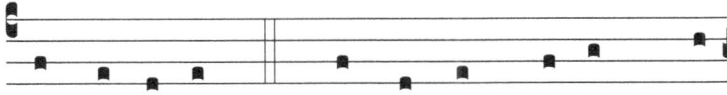

and starry sphere. 8) Faithful Cross of Christ, we

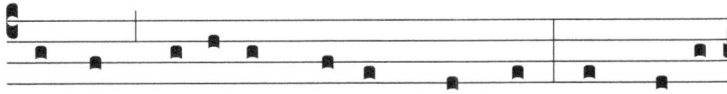

hail thee; Of all trees on earth most fair! None in all

the forest yieldeth Leaf, or flower, or fruit so rare.

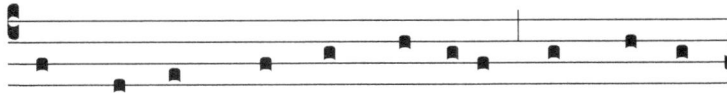

Sweetest wood! yea, sweetest i- ron! Sweetest bur-

den, fit to bear. 9) Tree of awful beauty, bend thee,

Bend; thy stubborn branches bring Softly round the

Form thou bearest; O'er His head thy shadow fling;

Gently in thine arms uphold Him, For of glory He

is King. 10) Worthy Thou to bear the ransom Of a

shipwreck'd world art found, And to be our Ark of

safety, For ce-lestial harbour bound; Sa-cred, hence,

that blood has made thee, As it flowed and wrapt

thee round.

†38: Pange, lingua

France: Moissac (ca. 1000)

Sing the Cross! the conflict telling Crown'd

with glory more than woe; Sing the bat-tle and the

triumph, Tell its fame to all be-low, How by death

the world's Redeemer O-verthrew and bound His

foe. 2) Touch'd with pity for the ru-in Of our first-

made fa-ther's fall, When the fa-tal fruit he tasted,

On one mouthful staking all; God mark'd out the

Venantius Fortunatus (ca. 567)   div: 1–4, 6; 7–10
tr. Hamilton Montgomerie MacGill

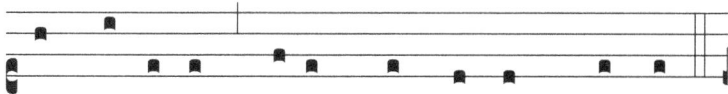

tree of Calvary, E-den's tree to match withal.

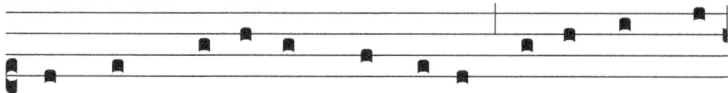

3) Law could on-ly yield our rescue As the fruit of

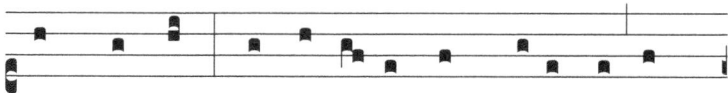

pains and toils; Art by art the great Restorer Foiled,

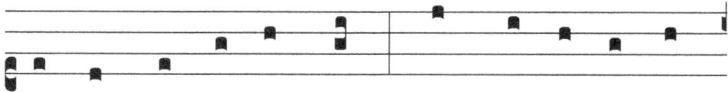

and took the Traitor's spoils; Thus His healing balm

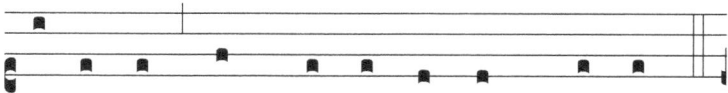

He gathered Where the foe had spread his wiles.

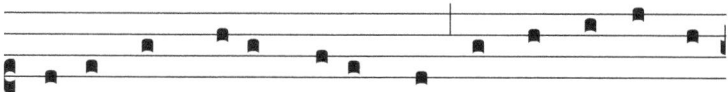

4) At the time a-fore appointed, Coming in His Fa-

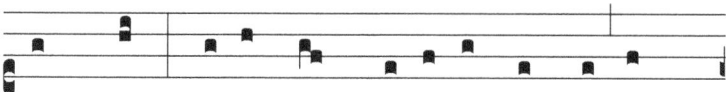

ther's name, In the womb of Virgin Mother Clothed

in flesh, with feeble frame; Born a man, the world's

Crea- tor From the throne of glory came. 5) Hark!

the cry of In-fant wailing In the manger, meanly

laid; Child all lowly, God all ho-ly! Not in robes of

light ar-ray'd; But in swaddling bands en-folded

By that blessed Mother-Maid. 6) Thirty winters has

He number'd Here on earth in quest of me; Yea, my

soul! thy great Redeemer Ago-nizing on the tree,

As the Lamb of God, up-lifted, Bleeds, and bows the

head for thee. 7) Fainting, lo! the gall He tasteth; See

the thorns, the nails, the spear, From His ebbing life

are drawing Crimson blood and water clear! Fit for

cleansing souls, and cleansing Earth, and sea, and

starry sphere. 8) Faithful Cross of Christ, we hail

thee; Of all trees on earth most fair! None in all

the forest yieldeth Leaf, or flower, or fruit so rare.

Sweetest wood! yea, sweetest i- ron! Sweetest bur-

den, fit to bear. 9) Tree of awful beauty, bend thee,

Bend; thy stubborn branches bring Softly round the

Form thou bearest; O'er His head thy shadow fling;

Gently in thine arms uphold Him, For of glory He

is King. 10) Worthy Thou to bear the ransom Of a

shipwreck'd world art found, And to be our Ark of

safety, For ce-lestial harbour bound; Sa-cred, hence,

that blood has made thee, As it flowed and wrapt

thee round.

†39: Pange, lingua

At a Nocturn.

Italy: Verona (11th c.)

C–C

S ing the Cross! the conflict tell-ing Crown'd

with glory more than woe; Sing the battle and

the tri- umph, Tell its fame to all be- low, How

by death the world's Redeemer O-verthrew and

bound His foe. 2) Touch'd with pity for the ru-in

Of our first-made fa-ther's fall, When the fa-tal

fruit he tasted, On one mouthful staking all; God

Venantius Fortunatus (ca. 567)
tr. Hamilton Montgomerie MacGill

div: 1–4, 6; 7–10

mark'd out the tree of Calvary, E-den's tree to

match withal. 3) Law could on-ly yield our res-cue

As the fruit of pains and toils; Art by art the great

Restorer Foiled, and took the Traitor's spoils; Thus

His healing balm He gathered Where the foe had

spread his wiles. 4) At the time a- fore appointed,

Coming in His Fa-ther's name, In the womb of

Virgin Mother Clothed in flesh, with feeble frame;

Born a man, the world's Crea- tor From the throne

of glory came. 5) Hark! the cry of In-fant wail-

ing In the manger, meanly laid; Child all lowly,

God all ho-ly! Not in robes of light ar-ray'd; But

in swaddling bands en-folded By that blessed

Mother-Maid. 6) Thirty winters has He number'd

Here on earth in quest of me; Yea, my soul! thy

great Redeemer Ago- nizing on the tree, As the

Lamb of God, up-lift-ed, Bleeds, and bows the head

for thee. 7) Fainting, lo! the gall He tasteth; See

the thorns, the nails, the spear, From His ebbing

life are drawing Crimson blood and water clear!

Fit for cleansing souls, and cleansing Earth, and

sea, and starry sphere. 8) Faithful Cross of Christ,

we hail thee; Of all trees on earth most fair! None

in all the forest yieldeth Leaf, or flower, or fruit so

rare. Sweetest wood! yea, sweetest i- ron! Sweet-

est burden, fit to bear. 9) Tree of awful beauty,

bend thee, Bend; thy stubborn branches bring Soft-

ly round the Form thou bearest; O'er His head thy

shadow fling; Gently in thine arms uphold Him,

For of glory He is King. 10) Worthy Thou to bear

the ransom Of a shipwreck'd world art found,

And to be our Ark of safety, For ce-lestial harbour

bound; Sa-cred, hence, that blood has made thee,

As it flowed and wrapt thee round. A- men.

†40: Pange, lingua

Sunday on the Passion of the Lord
at Vespers and at Nocturns.

Italy: Gaeta (12th c.)

E–C

S ing the Cross! the conflict telling Crown'd

with glory more than woe; Sing the battle and the

triumph, Tell its fame to all be-low, How by death

the world's Redeemer O-verthrew and bound His

Venantius Fortunatus (ca. 567)   div: 1–4, 6; 7–10
tr. Hamilton Montgomerie MacGill

foe. 2) Touch'd with pity for the ru-in Of our first-

made fa-ther's fall, When the fa-tal fruit he tasted,

On one mouthful staking all; God mark'd out the

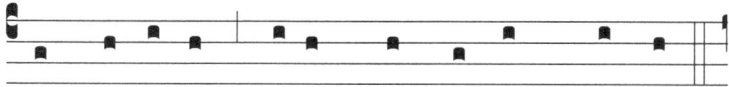

tree of Calvary, E- den's tree to match withal.

3) Law could on-ly yield our rescue As the fruit of

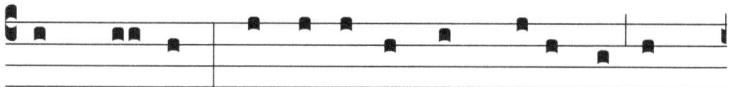

pains and toils; Art by art the great Restorer Foiled,

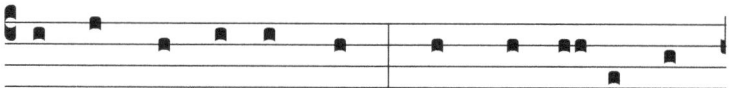

and took the Traitor's spoils; Thus His healing balm

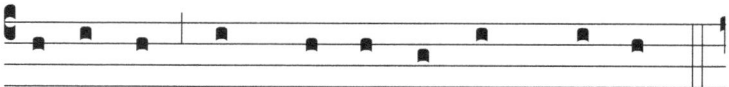

He gathered Where the foe had spread his wiles.

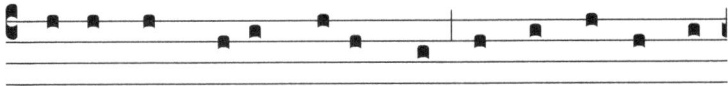

4) At the time a- fore appointed, Coming in His Fa-

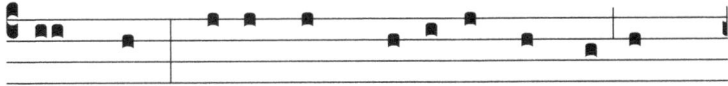

ther's name, In the womb of Virgin Mother Clothed

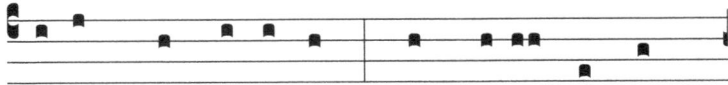

in flesh, with feeble frame; Born a man, the world's

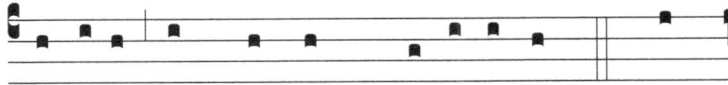

Crea- tor From the throne of glory came. 5) Hark!

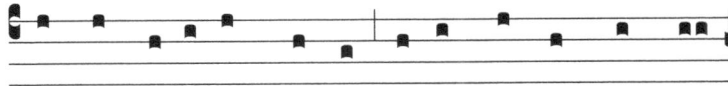

the cry of In-fant wailing In the manger, meanly

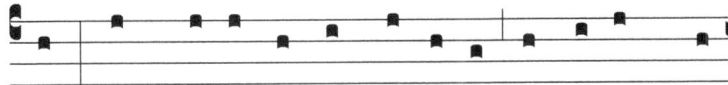

laid; Child all lowly, God all ho-ly! Not in robes of

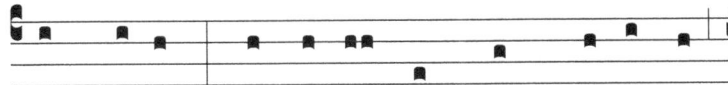

light ar-ray'd; But in swaddling bands en-folded

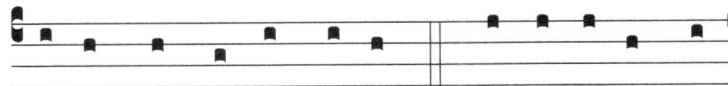

By that blessed Mother-Maid. 6) Thirty winters has

He number'd Here on earth in quest of me; Yea, my

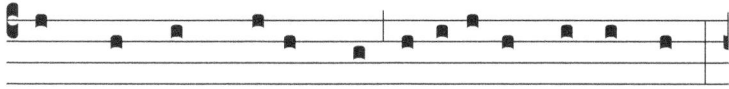

soul! thy great Redeemer Ago-nizing on the tree,

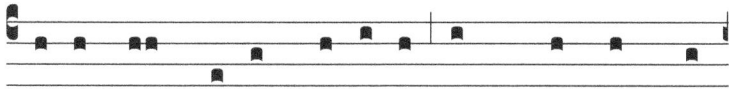

As the Lamb of God, up-lifted, Bleeds, and bows the

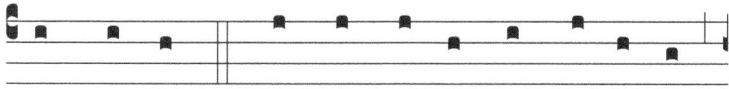

head for thee. 7) Fainting, lo! the gall He tasteth;

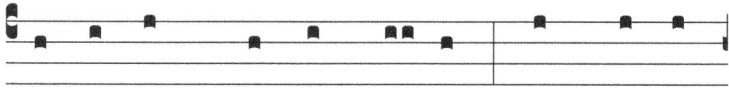

See the thorns, the nails, the spear, From His ebb-

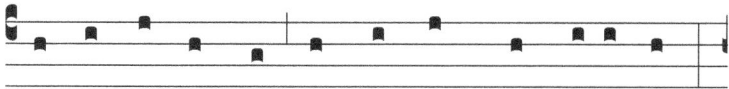

ing life are drawing Crimson blood and water clear!

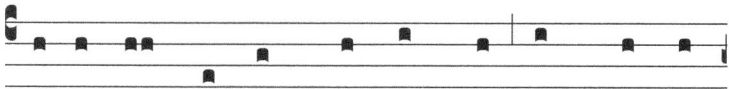

Fit for cleansing souls, and cleansing Earth, and sea,

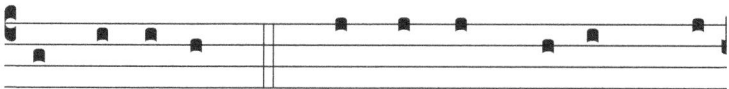

and starry sphere. 8) Faithful Cross of Christ, we

hail thee; Of all trees on earth most fair! None in all

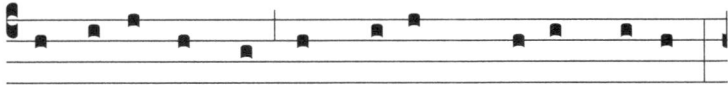

the forest yieldeth Leaf, or flower, or fruit so rare.

Sweetest wood! yea, sweetest i- ron! Sweetest bur-

den, fit to bear. 9) Tree of awful beauty, bend thee,

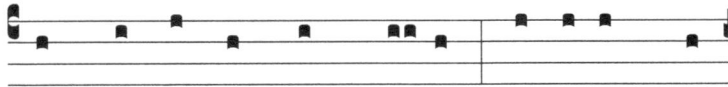

Bend; thy stubborn branches bring Softly round the

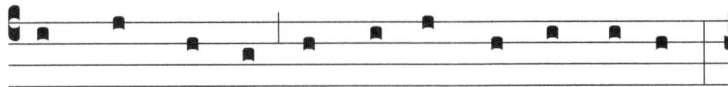

Form thou bearest; O'er His head thy shadow fling;

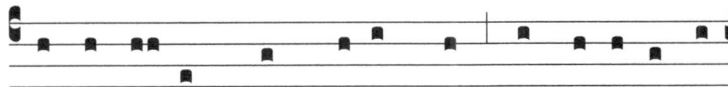

Gently in thine arms uphold Him, For of glory He

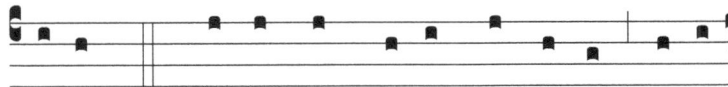

is King. 10) Worthy Thou to bear the ransom Of a

shipwreck'd world art found, And to be our Ark of

safety, For ce-lestial harbour bound; Sa-cred, hence,

that blood has made thee, As it flowed and wrapt

thee round.

†41: Pange, lingua

France: Paris (12th–13th c.)

C–E

S ing the Cross! the conflict tell-ing Crown'd

with glory more than woe; Sing the battle and the

Venantius Fortunatus (ca. 567)   P: 8, 1, 8, 2, 8, 3, etc., omit 5
tr. Hamilton Montgomerie MacGill

triumph, Tell its fame to all be-low, How by

death the world's Re-deemer O-verthrew and

bound His foe. 2) Touch'd with pity for the ru-

in Of our first-made fa-ther's fall, When the fa-tal

fruit he tasted, On one mouthful staking all;

God mark'd out the tree of Calvary, E-den's tree

to match withal. 3) Law could on-ly yield our res-

cue As the fruit of pains and toils; Art by art

the great Re- storer   Foiled, and took the Trai-

tor's spoils; Thus His healing balm He gathered

Where the foe had spread his wiles. 4) At the time

a- fore appointed, Coming in His Fa-ther's name,

In the womb of Virgin Mother   Clothed in flesh,

with feeble frame; Born a   man, the world's Crea-

tor   From the throne of   glory came. 5) Hark! the

cry of In-fant wailing In   the manger, meanly laid;

Child all   lowly, God all   ho-ly!   Not in robes

of   light ar-ray'd; But in   swaddling bands en-fold-

ed   By that blessed Mother-Maid. 6) Thirty win-

ters has He number'd Here on earth in   quest of

me; Yea, my   soul! thy great Re- deemer   Ago-

niz-ing on the tree, As the Lamb of God, up-lift-

ed,   Bleeds, and bows the head for thee. 7) Faint-

ing, lo! the gall He tasteth; See the thorns, the nails,

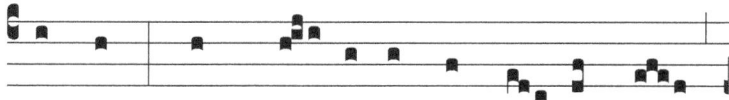

the spear, From His ebbing life are drawing

Crimson blood and water clear! Fit for cleansing

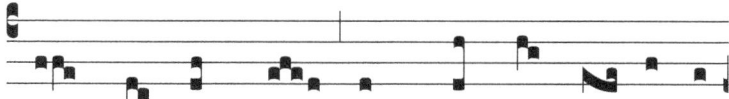

souls, and cleansing   Earth, and sea, and starry

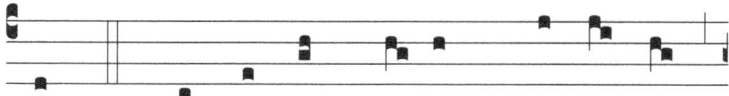

sphere. 8) Faithful Cross of Christ, we hail thee;

Of all trees on earth most fair! None in   all the

forest yieldeth   Leaf, or flower, or   fruit so rare.

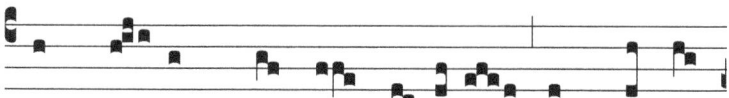

Sweetest wood! yea, sweetest i- ron! Sweetest bur-

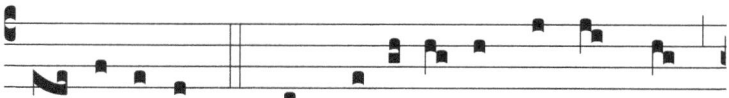

den, fit to bear. 9) Tree of awful beauty, bend thee,

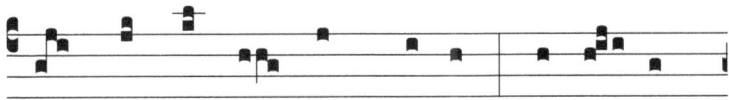

Bend; thy stubborn branches bring Softly   round

the Form thou bearest;   O'er His head thy shadow

fling; Gently   in thine arms up-hold Him,   For of

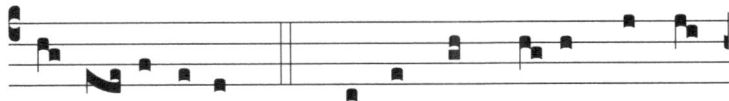

glo-ry He is King. 10) Worthy Thou to bear the ran-

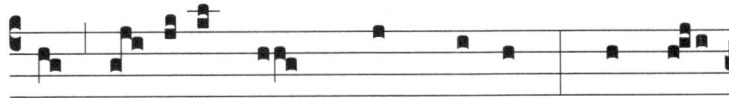

som Of a shipwreck'd world art found, And to

be our Ark of   safety,   For ce-les-tial harbour

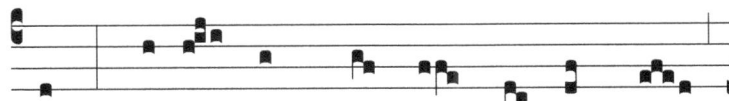

bound; Sa-cred, hence, that blood has made thee,

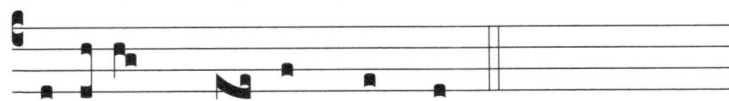

As it flowed and wrapt thee round.

†42: Pange, lingua

Saturday on the Passion of the Lord
at Lauds.

Southern Italy (13th c.)

A–F

S ing the Cross! the conflict tell- ing

Crown'd with glory more than woe; Sing the

battle and the tri- umph, Tell its fame to all

be- low, How by death the world's Redeem-er

O-ver-threw and bound His foe. 2) Touch'd with

pity for the ru- in Of our first-made fa-

ther's fall, When the fa-tal fruit he tast-

Venantius Fortunatus (ca. 567)
tr. Hamilton Montgomerie MacGill

div: 1–4, 6; 7–10

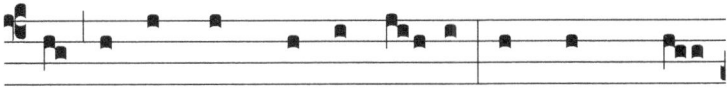

ed, On one mouthful staking all; God mark'd out

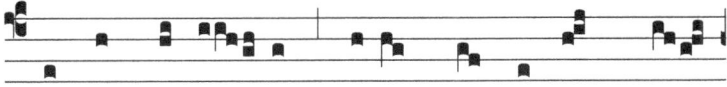

the tree of Cal- vary, E-den's tree to match with-

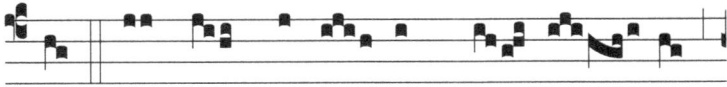

al. 3) Law could on-ly yield our res- cue

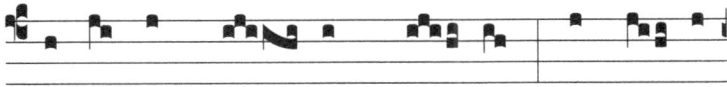

As the fruit of pains and toils; Art by art

the great Re- stor- er Foiled, and took the

Traitor's spoils; Thus His heal-ing balm He gath-

ered Where the foe had spread his wiles. 4) At

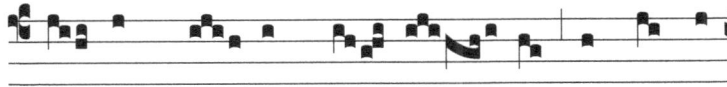

the time a- fore ap- point- ed, Coming in

His   Fa-ther's name, In the womb of   Virgin

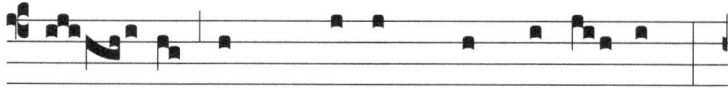

Moth-   er   Clothed in flesh, with feeble   frame;

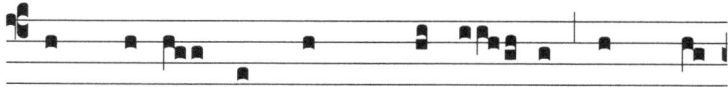

Born   a   man,   the   world's   Crea-   tor   From   the

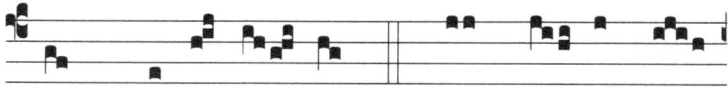

throne of glo-ry   came. 5) Hark! the   cry   of

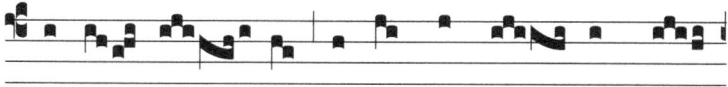

In-fant wail-   ing   In   the   manger,   meanly

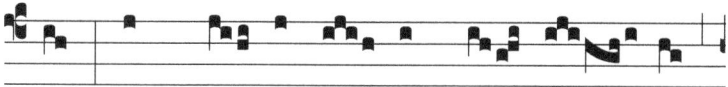

laid; Child all   lowly,   God   all   ho-   ly!

Not   in robes   of   light ar-   ray'd; But in swaddling

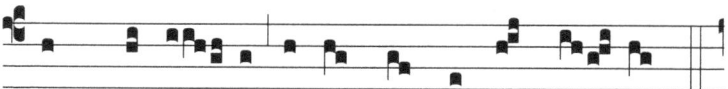

bands en-fold- ed By that blessed Mother-   Maid.

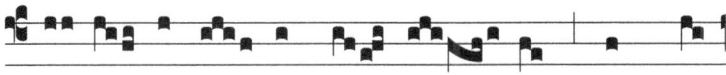

6) Thirty   winters   has   He   num-   ber'd   Here   on

earth   in   quest   of   me;   Yea,   my   soul!   thy

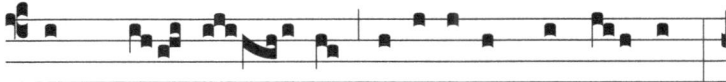

great   Re-   deem-   er   Ago- nizing   on   the   tree,

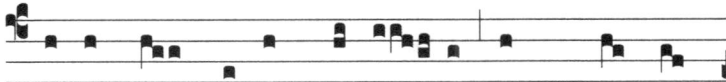

As the Lamb of God, up-lift- ed, Bleeds, and bows

the head for   thee. 7) Fainting, lo! the   gall He

tast-   eth; See   the   thorns,   the   nails,   the

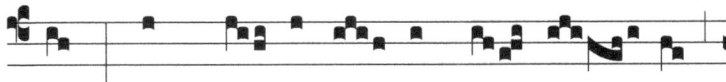

spear, From His ebbing   life   are   draw-   ing

Crimson blood and water   clear! Fit for cleansing

souls, and cleansing Earth, and sea, and starry

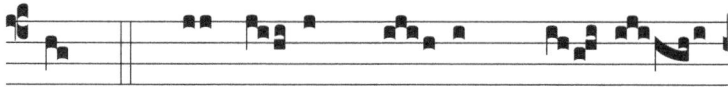

sphere. 8) Faithful Cross of   Christ, we   hail

thee; Of all trees on   earth most fair! None in

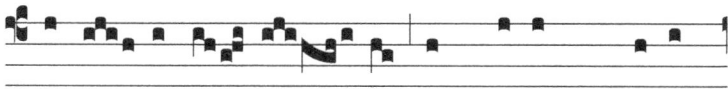

all the   forest   yield-   eth Leaf, or flower, or fruit

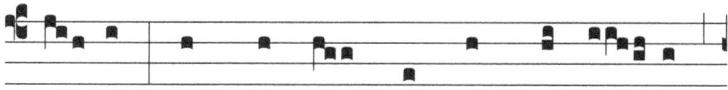

so   rare. Sweetest wood! yea, sweetest i-   ron!

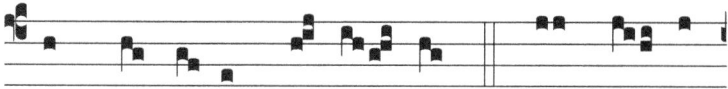

Sweetest burden, fit to   bear. 9) Tree of   aw-

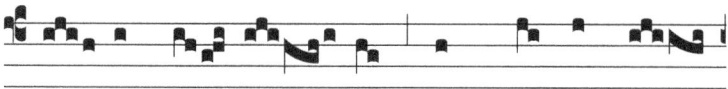

ful   beauty,   bend   thee, Bend; thy stubborn

branches   bring Softly   round the   Form thou

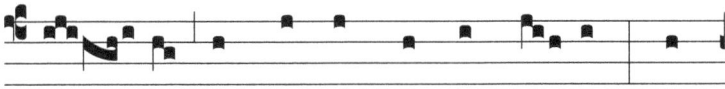

bear- est; O'er His head thy shadow fling; Gen-

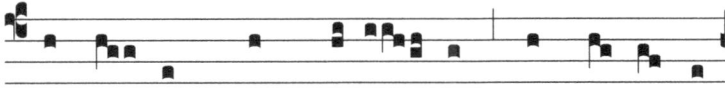

tly in thine arms uphold Him, For of glo-ry

He is King. 10) Wor-thy Thou to bear the

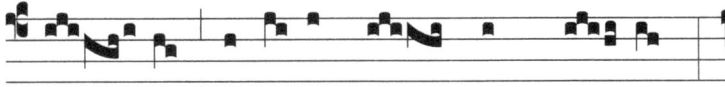

ran- som Of a shipwreck'd world art found,

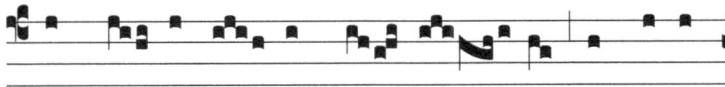

And to be our Ark of safe- ty, For ce-les-

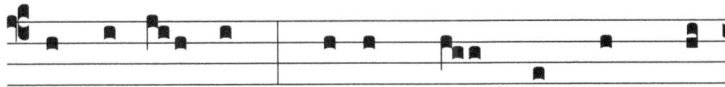

tial harbour bound; Sa-cred, hence, that blood has

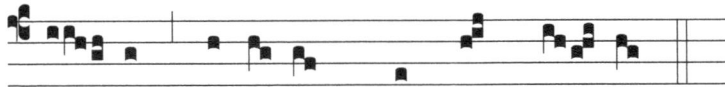

made thee, As it flowed and wrapt thee round.

†43: Pange, lingua

On the Passion of the Lord
at a Nocturn.

Germany: Rüdnitz (1325–1375)

C–B

S ing the Cross! the conflict tell-ing Crown'd

with glory more than woe; Sing the bat-tle and

the tri- umph, Tell its fame to all be- low, How

by death the world's Redeemer O-verthrew and

bound His foe. 2) Touch'd with pit-y for the ru-

in Of our first-made fa-ther's fall, When the fa-

tal fruit he tast-ed, On one mouthful staking all;

Venantius Fortunatus (ca. 567)
tr. Hamilton Montgomerie MacGill

div: 1–4, 6; 7–10

God mark'd out the tree of Calvary, E-den's tree

to match withal. 3) Law could on-ly yield our res-

cue As the fruit of pains and toils; Art by art

the great Restor-er Foiled, and took the Traitor's

spoils; Thus His healing balm He gathered Where

the foe had spread his wiles. 4) At the time a-

fore appointed, Coming in His Fa-ther's name, In

the womb of Virgin Mother Clothed in flesh, with

feeble frame; Born a man, the world's Crea- tor

From the throne of glory came. 5) Hark! the cry

of In-fant wail-ing In the manger, meanly laid;

Child all lowly, God all ho- ly! Not in robes of

light ar- ray'd; But in swaddling bands en-folded

By that blessed Mother-Maid. 6) Thirty winters has

He number'd Here on earth in quest of me; Yea,

my soul! thy great Redeemer Ago- nizing on the

tree, As the Lamb of God, up-lifted, Bleeds, and

bows the head for thee. 7) Fainting, lo! the gall He

tast-eth; See the thorns, the nails, the spear, From

His ebbing life are drawing Crimson blood and wa-

ter clear! Fit for cleansing souls, and cleansing

Earth, and sea, and starry sphere. 8) Faithful Cross

of Christ, we hail thee; Of all trees on earth most

fair! None in all the forest yieldeth Leaf, or flower,

or fruit so rare. Sweetest wood! yea, sweetest i-

ron! Sweetest burden, fit to bear. 9) Tree of aw-

ful beauty, bend thee, Bend; thy stubborn branch-

es bring Softly round the Form thou bearest; O'er

His head thy shadow fling; Gently in thine arms

uphold Him, For of glory He is King. 10) Worthy

Thou to bear the ran-som Of a shipwreck'd world

art found, And to be our Ark of safe-ty, For ce-lestial harbour bound; Sa-cred, hence, that blood

has made thee, As it flowed and wrapt thee round.

†44: Pange, lingua

At a Nocturn.

Austria: Klosterneuburg (1336)

B–A

Sing the Cross! the conflict telling Crown'd

with glory more than woe; Sing the battle and the

tri-umph, Tell its fame to all be-low, How by death

the world's Redeemer O-verthrew and bound His

foe. 2) Touch'd with pity   for the ru- in Of our

Venantius Fortunatus (ca. 567)   div: 1–4, 6; 7–10
tr. Hamilton Montgomerie MacGill

first-made fa-ther's fall, When the fa-tal fruit he

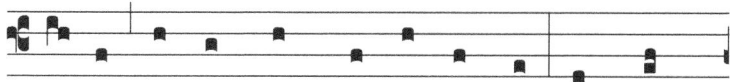

tasted, On one mouthful staking all; God mark'd

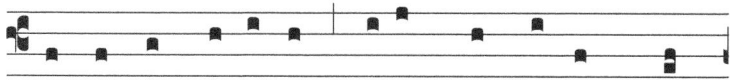

out the tree of Calvary, E-den's tree to match with-

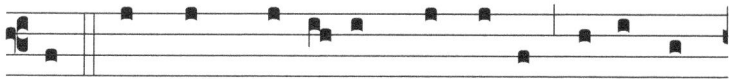

al. 3) Law could on-ly yield our rescue As the fruit

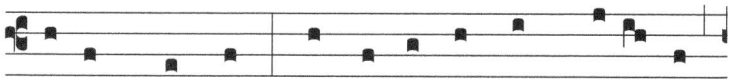

of pains and toils; Art by art the great Restorer

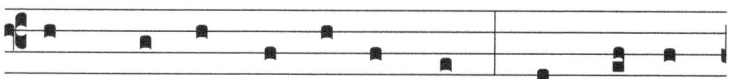

Foiled, and took the Traitor's spoils; Thus His heal-

ing balm He gathered Where the foe had spread

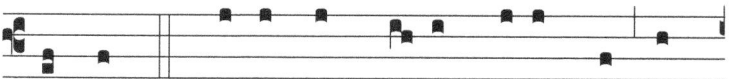

his wiles. 4) At the time a- fore appointed, Com-

ing in His Fa-ther's name, In the womb of Vir-

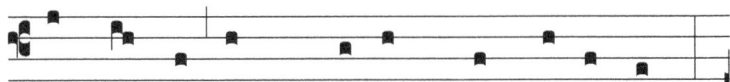

gin Mother Clothed in flesh, with feeble frame;

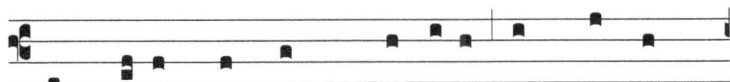

Born a man, the world's Crea- tor From the throne

of glory came. 5) Hark! the cry of In-fant wailing

In the manger, meanly laid; Child all lowly, God

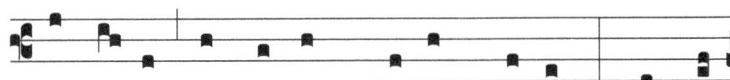

all ho- ly! Not in robes of light ar- ray'd; But in

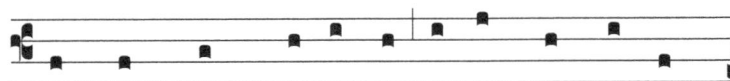

swaddling bands en-folded By that blessed Moth-

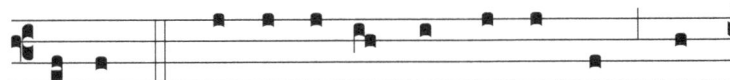

er-Maid. 6) Thirty winters has He number'd Here

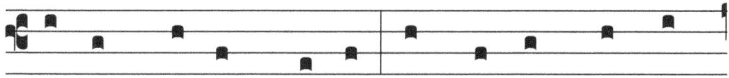

on earth in quest of me; Yea, my soul! thy great

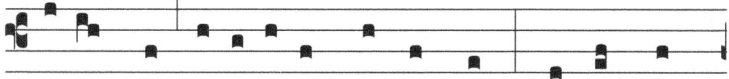

Redeemer Ago- nizing on the tree, As the Lamb

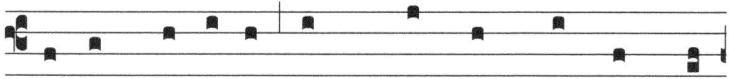

of God, up- lifted, Bleeds, and bows the head for

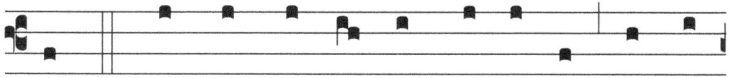

thee. 7) Fainting, lo! the gall He tasteth; See the

thorns, the nails, the spear, From His ebbing life

are drawing Crimson blood and water clear! Fit for

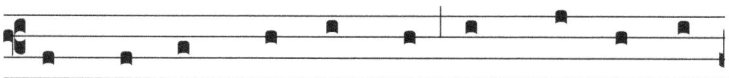

cleansing souls, and cleansing Earth, and sea, and

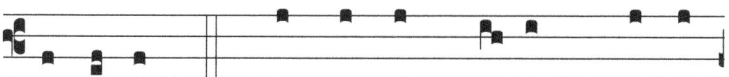

starry sphere. 8) Faithful Cross of Christ, we hail

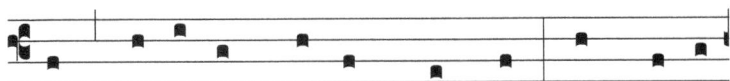

thee; Of all trees on earth most fair! None in all

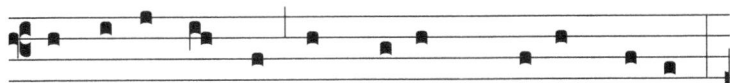

the forest yieldeth Leaf, or flower, or fruit so rare.

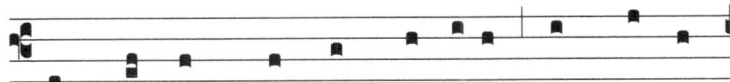

Sweetest wood! yea, sweetest i- ron! Sweetest bur-

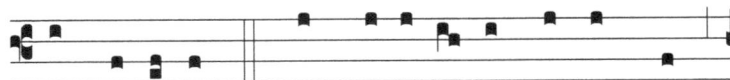

den, fit to bear. 9) Tree of awful beauty, bend thee,

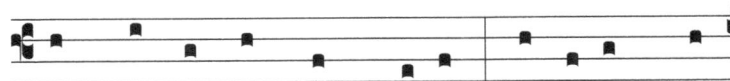

Bend; thy stubborn branches bring Softly round the

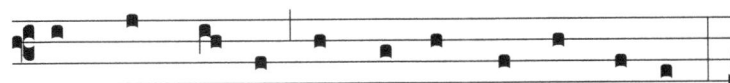

Form thou bearest; O'er His head thy shadow fling;

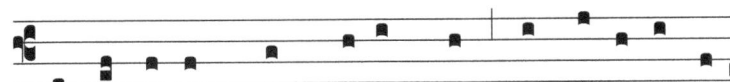

Gently in thine arms uphold Him, For of glory He

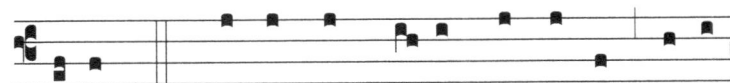

is King. 10) Worthy Thou to bear the ransom Of a

shipwreck'd world art found, And to be our Ark of

safety, For ce-lestial harbour bound; Sa-cred, hence,

that blood has made thee, As it flowed and wrapt

thee round. A-   men.

†45: Vexilla regis prodeunt

For the Passion of the Lord.

Germany: Kempten (ca. 1000)

C–B

The Banner of the King goes forth, The

Cross, the ra- diant myster-y, Where, in a frame

of human birth, Man's Mak- er suf- fers on the

Venantius Fortunatus (ca. 567)   sel: 1, 3, 5–6, 8
tr. Elizabeth Rundle Charles

Tree. 2) Fix'd with the fa- tal nails to death, With

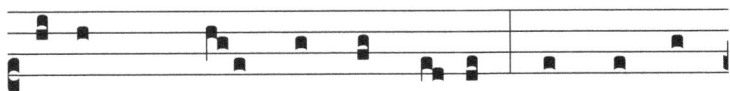

outstretch'd hands and pierced feet; Here the pure

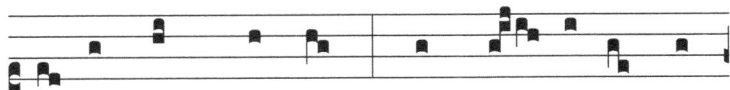

Vic- tim yields His breath, That our re- demption

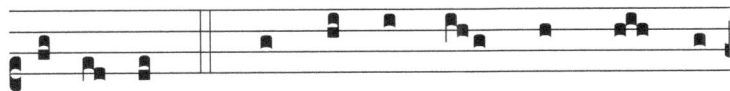

be complete. 3) And ere had closed that mournful

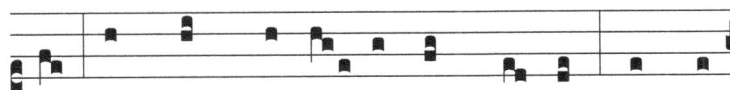

day, They wounded with the spear His side: That he

might wash our sins a-way, His blood pour'd forth

its crimson tide! 4) The truth that Da- vid learn'd

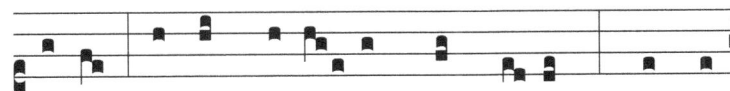

to sing, Its deep fulfil- ment here at- tains: "Tell all

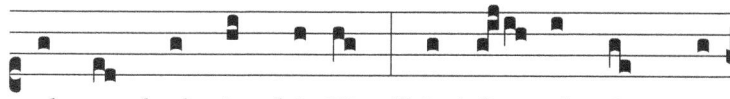

the earth the Lord is King!" Lo! from the Cross, a

King He reigns. 5) O most e- lect and pleasant Tree,

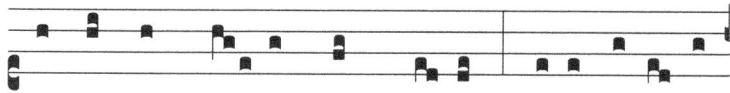

Chosen such sa- cred limbs to bear, A royal purple

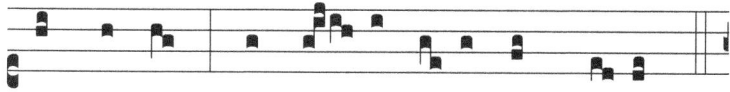

clotheth thee— The pur- ple of His blood is there!

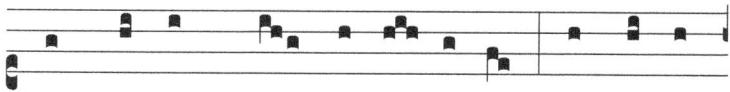

6) Blest on whose arms, in woe sublime, The Ransom

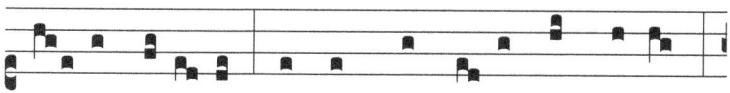

of the ages lay, Outweighing all the sins of Time,

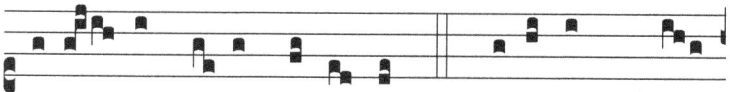

Despoil-ing Sa-tan of his prey. 7) A fragrance from

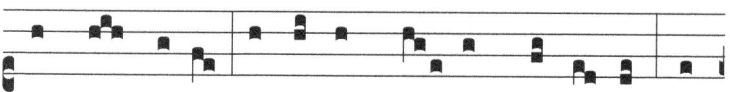

thy bark distils Surpassing heavenly nectar far; The

noblest fruit thy branches fills, Weapon of the vic-

to-rious war. 8) Hail al-tar, Vic- tim hail once more!

That glorious Pas- sion be a- dored! Since death the

Life Himself thus bore, And by that death our life

re- stored!

†46: Iam lucis orto sidere

France: Limoges (11th c.)

D–C

Now in the sun's new dawning ray, Lowly

of heart, our God we pray That He from harm may

Anonymous (8th c.)
tr. Alan Gordon McDougall

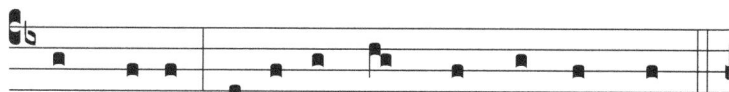

keep us free In all the deeds this day shall see.

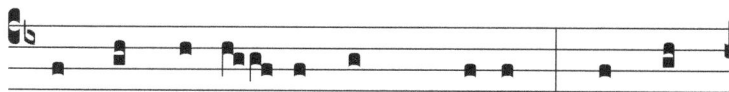

2) May fear of Him our tongues re-strain, Lest strife

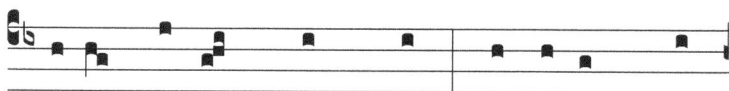

unguarded speech should stain: His fa-voring care

our guardian be, Lest our eyes feed on vani- ty.

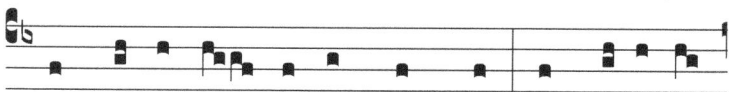

3) May every heart be pure from sin, And folly find

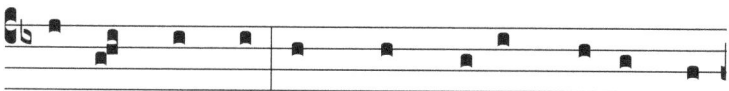

no place therein: Scant meed of food, ex-cess de-

nied, Wear down in us the body's pride. 4) That

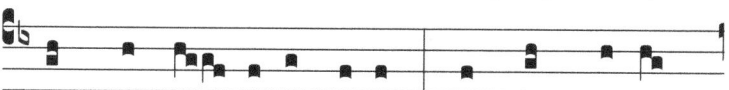

when the light of day is gone, And night in course

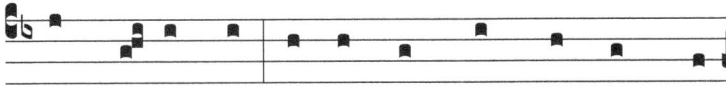

shall fol-low on, We, free from cares the world af-

fords, May chant the praise that is our Lord's.

†47: Iam lucis orto sidere

Switzerland: Einsiedeln (1100–1150)

D–D

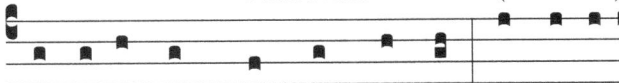

Now in the sun's new dawning ray, Lowly of

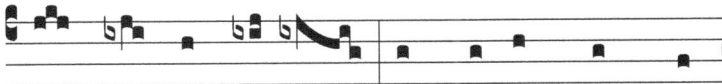

heart, our God we pray That He from harm may

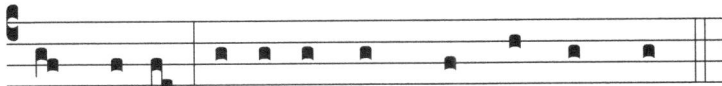

keep us free In all the deeds this day shall see.

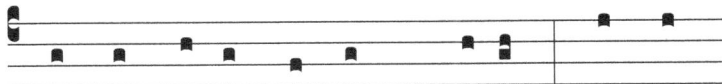

2) May fear of Him our tongues re-strain, Lest strife

Anonymous (8th c.)
tr. Alan Gordon McDougall

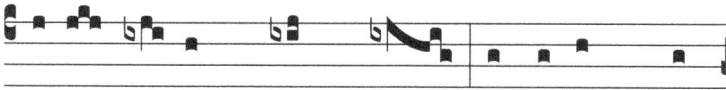

unguarded speech should stain: His fa-voring care

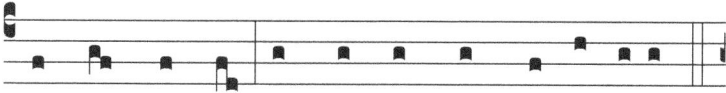

our guardian be, Lest our eyes feed on vani- ty.

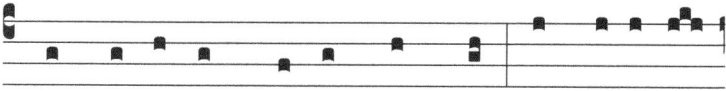

3) May every heart be pure from sin, And folly find

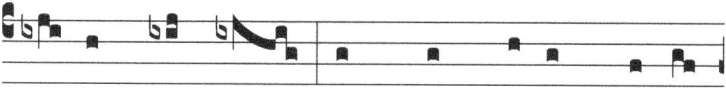

no place therein: Scant meed of food, ex-cess

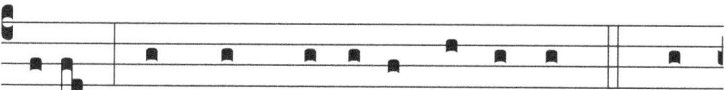

denied, Wear down in us the body's pride. 4) That

when the light of day is gone, And night in course

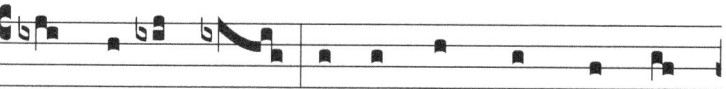

shall fol-low on,   We, free from cares the world

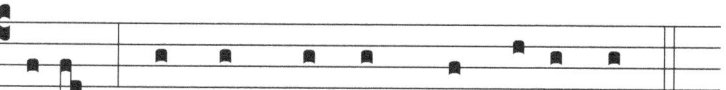

af-fords, May chant the praise that is our Lord's.

†48: Iam lucis orto sidere

On the vigil of the Epiphany
at Prime.

France: Laon (1100–1150)

E–F

Now in the sun's new dawning ray, Lowly

of heart, our God we pray That He from harm may

keep us free In all the deeds this day shall see.

2) May fear of Him our tongues re-strain, Lest strife

unguarded speech should stain: His fa-voring care

our guardian be, Lest our eyes feed on vani- ty.

3) May every heart be pure from sin, And fol-ly find

Anonymous (8th c.)
tr. Alan Gordon McDougall

no place therein: Scant meed of food, ex-cess de-

nied, Wear down in us the body's pride. 4) That

when the light of day is gone, And night in course

shall fol-low on, We, free from cares the world af-

fords, May chant the praise that is our Lord's.

†49: Iam lucis orto sidere

On the Epiphany at Prime.

France: Laon (1100–1150)

C–D

Now in the sun's new dawning ray, Lowly

Anonymous (8th c.)
tr. Alan Gordon McDougall

of heart, our God we pray That He from harm may

keep us free In all the deeds this day shall see.

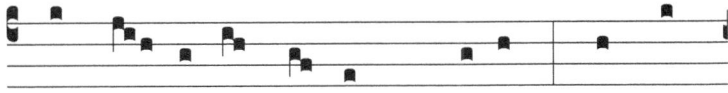

2) May fear of Him our tongues re-strain, Lest strife

unguarded speech should stain: His fa-voring care

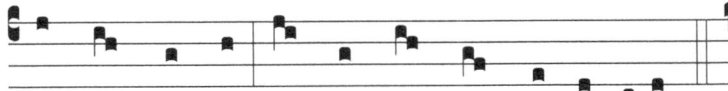

our guardian be, Lest our eyes feed on vani- ty.

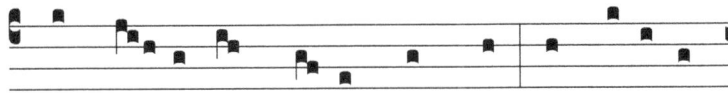

3) May eve-ry heart be pure from sin, And folly find

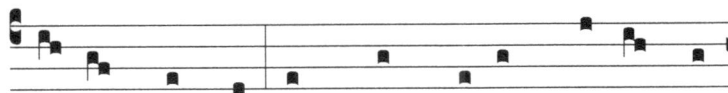

no place therein: Scant meed of food, ex-cess de-

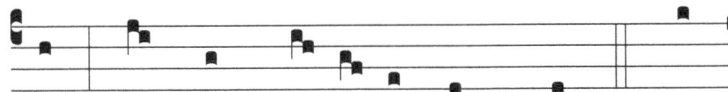

nied, Wear down in us the body's pride. 4) That

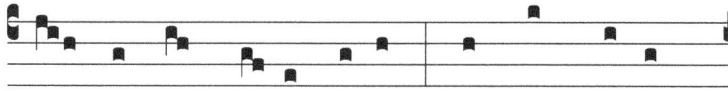

when the light of day is gone, And night in course

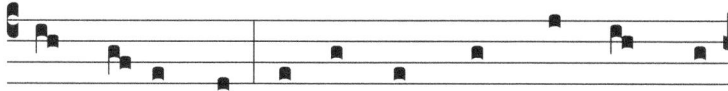

shall fol-low on, We, free from cares the world af-

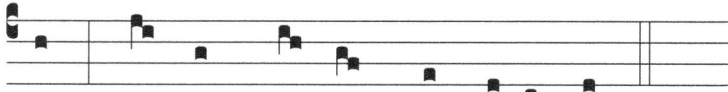

fords, May chant the praise that is our Lord's.

†50: Iam lucis orto sidere

Switzerland: Einsiedeln (1100–1150)

G–E

Now in the sun's new dawning ray, Lowly

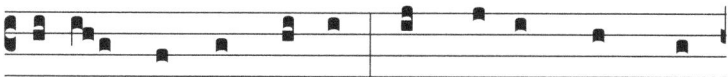

of heart, our God we pray That He from harm may

keep us free In all the deeds this day shall see.

Anonymous (8th c.)
tr. Alan Gordon McDougall

2) May fear of Him our tongues re- strain, Lest strife

unguarded speech should stain: His fa-voring care

our guardian be, Lest our eyes feed on van-i- ty.

3) May every heart be pure from sin, And folly find

no place therein: Scant meed of food, ex-cess de-

nied, Wear down in us the bod-y's pride. 4) That

when the light of day is gone, And night in course

shall follow on, We, free from cares the world af-

fords, May chant the praise that is our Lord's.

†51: Iam lucis orto sidere

At Prime.

France: Nevers (12th c.)

C–C

Now in the sun's new dawning ray, Lowly

of heart, our God we pray That He from harm may

keep us free In all the deeds this day shall see.

2) May fear of Him our tongues re-strain, Lest strife

unguarded speech should stain: His fa-voring care

our guardian be, Lest our eyes feed on van- i-

ty. 3) May every heart be pure from sin, And folly

Anonymous (8th c.)
tr. Alan Gordon McDougall

find no place therein: Scant meed of food, ex-cess

de-nied, Wear down in us the bod- y's pride.

4) That when the light of day is gone, And night in

course shall fol-low on, We, free from cares the

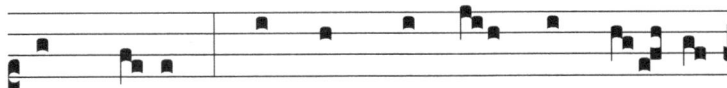

world af- fords, May chant the praise that is our

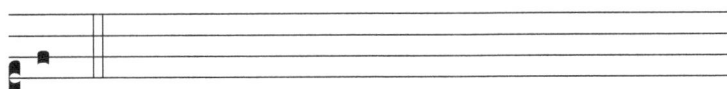

Lord's.

†52: Iam lucis orto sidere

At Prime.

France: Nevers (12th c.)

C–A

ow in the sun's new dawning ray, Low-

ly of heart, our God we pray   That He from harm

may keep us free   In all the deeds   this

day shall see. 2) May fear of Him our tongues re-

strain, Lest strife unguarded speech should stain:

His fa-voring care our guardian be,   Lest

our eyes feed   on vani- ty. 3) May every heart

Anonymous (8th c.)
tr. Alan Gordon McDougall

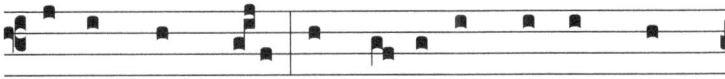

be pure from sin, And fol-ly find no place there-

in: Scant meed of food, ex-cess de-nied,

Wear down in us the body's pride. 4) That

when the light of day is gone, And night in course

shall follow on, We, free from cares the world

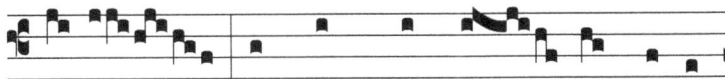

af- fords, May chant the praise that is our

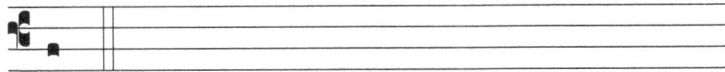

Lord's.

†53: Iam lucis orto sidere

At Prime.

France: Nevers (12th c.)

B–A

N ow   in the sun's new dawning ray, Lowly

of heart, our God we pray That He from harm may

keep us free In all the deeds this day shall see.

2) May fear of Him our tongues re-strain, Lest strife

unguarded speech should stain: His fa-voring care

our guardian be, Lest our eyes feed on vani- ty.

3) May every heart be pure from sin, And fol-ly find

Anonymous (8th c.)
tr. Alan Gordon McDougall

no place therein: Scant meed of food, ex-cess de-

nied, Wear down in us   the body's pride. 4) That

when the light of day is gone, And night in course

shall follow on, We, free from cares the world af-

fords, May chant the praise that is our Lord's.

†54: Iam lucis orto sidere

At Prime.

France: Nevers (12th c.)

A–F

Now in the sun's new dawning ray, Lowly

of heart, our God we pray That He from harm may

Anonymous (8th c.)
tr. Alan Gordon McDougall

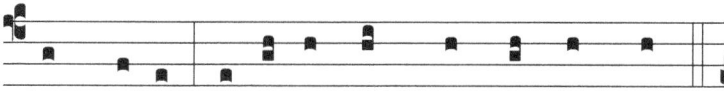

keep us free In all the deeds this day shall see.

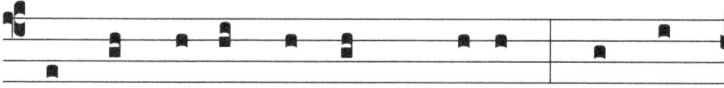

2) May fear of Him our tongues re-strain, Lest strife

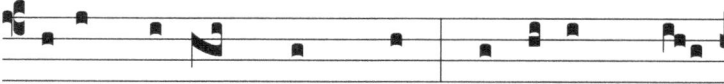

unguarded speech should stain: His fa-voring care

our guardian be, Lest our eyes feed on vani- ty.

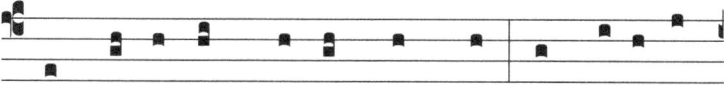

3) May every heart be pure from sin, And folly find

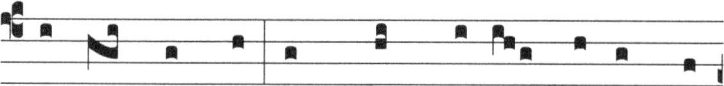

no place therein: Scant meed of food, ex-cess de-

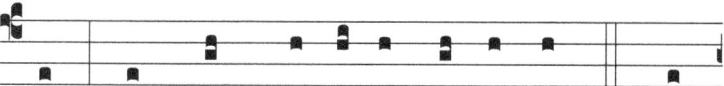

nied, Wear down in us the body's pride. 4) That

when the light of day is gone, And night in course

shall fol-low on, We, free from cares the world af-

fords, May chant the praise that is our Lord's.

†55: Iam lucis orto sidere

At Prime.

France: Nevers (12th c.)

C–B

Now in the sun's new dawning ray, Lowly

of heart, our God we pray That He from harm may

keep us free In all the deeds this day shall see.

2) May fear of Him our tongues re-strain, Lest strife

unguarded speech should stain: His fa-voring care

Anonymous (8th c.)
tr. Alan Gordon McDougall

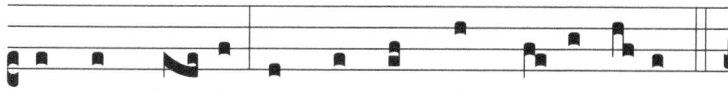

our guardian be, Lest our eyes feed on vani- ty.

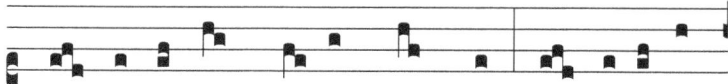

3) May every heart be pure from sin, And folly find

no place therein: Scant meed of food, ex-cess de-

nied, Wear down in us the body's pride. 4) That

when the light of day is gone, And night in course

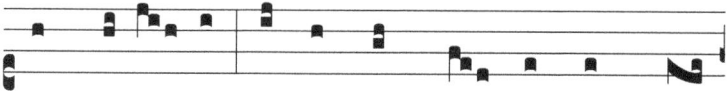

shall follow on, We, free from cares the world af-

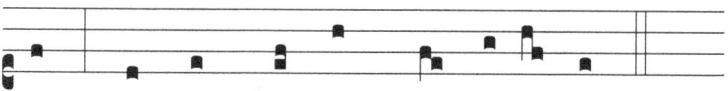

fords, May chant the praise that is our Lord's.

†56: Iam lucis orto sidere

At Prime.

France: Fécamp (12th–13th c.)

C–C

Now in the sun's new dawning ray, Lowly

of heart, our God we pray That He from harm may

keep us free In all the deeds this day shall see.

2) May fear of Him our tongues re-strain, Lest strife

unguarded speech should stain: His fa-voring care

our guardian be, Lest our eyes feed on vani- ty.

3) May every heart be pure from sin, And folly find

Anonymous (8th c.)
tr. Alan Gordon McDougall

no place therein: Scant meed of food, ex-cess de-

nied, Wear down in us the body's pride. 4) That

when the light of day is gone, And night in course

shall follow on, We, free from cares the world af-

fords, May chant the praise that is our Lord's.

†57: Iam lucis orto sidere

France: Fécamp (12th–13th c.)

C–B

Now in the sun's new dawning ray, Lowly

of heart, our God we pray That He from harm may

keep us free In all the deeds this day shall see.

2) May fear of Him our tongues re-strain, Lest strife

unguarded speech should stain: His fa-voring care

our guardian be, Lest our eyes feed on vani- ty.

3) May every heart be pure from sin, And folly find

Anonymous (8th c.)
tr. Alan Gordon McDougall

no place therein: Scant meed of food, ex-cess de-

nied, Wear down in us the body's pride. 4) That

when the light of day is gone, And night in course

shall fol- low on, We, free from cares the world af-

fords, May chant the praise that is our Lord's.

†58: Iam lucis orto sidere

At Prime.

Southern Italy (13th c.)

F–G

Now in the sun's new dawning ray, Low-

ly of heart, our God we pray That He from harm

Anonymous (8th c.)
tr. Alan Gordon McDougall

may keep us free In all the deeds this day

shall see. 2) May fear of Him our tongues re-strain,

Lest strife unguarded speech should stain: His fa-

voring care our guard- ian be, Lest our eyes feed

on van- i- ty. 3) May eve-ry heart be pure from

sin, And fol-ly find no place therein: Scant meed

of food, ex- cess denied, Wear down in us the

bod- y's pride. 4) That when the light of day is

gone, And night in course shall fol- low on, We,

free from cares the world af-fords, May chant the

praise that is our Lord's.

†59: Iam lucis orto sidere

Sundays in Advent at Prime, and on the day of
Saint Paul the apostle.

England: Worcester (ca. 1230)

D–D

Now in the sun's new dawning ray, Lowly

of heart, our God we pray That He from harm may

keep us free In all the deeds this day shall see.

Anonymous (8th c.)
tr. Alan Gordon McDougall

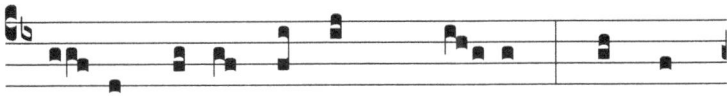

2) May fear of Him our tongues re- strain, Lest strife

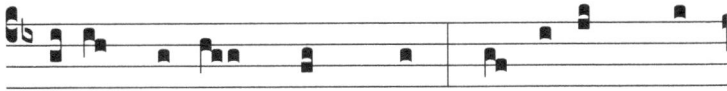

unguarded speech should stain: His fa-voring care

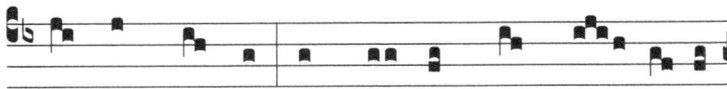

our guardian be, Lest our eyes feed on vani-

ty. 3) May every heart be pure from sin, And fol-

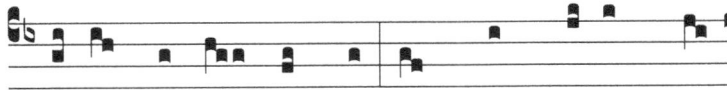

ly find no place therein: Scant meed of food, ex-

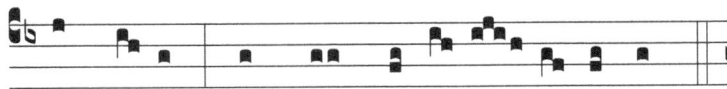

cess de-nied, Wear down in us the body's pride.

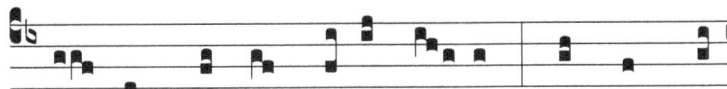

4) That when the light of day is gone, And night in

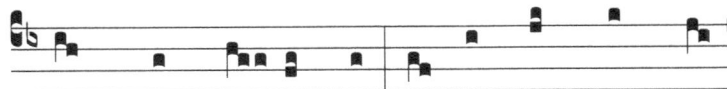

course shall fol- low on, We, free from cares the

world af- fords, May chant the praise that is our

Lord's.

†60: Iam lucis orto sidere

England: Worcester (ca. 1230)

G–E

Now in the sun's new dawning ray, Lowly

of heart, our God we pray That He from harm

may keep us free In all the deeds this day shall

see. 2) May fear of Him our tongues re-strain,

Lest strife unguarded speech should stain: His fa-

Anonymous (8th c.)
tr. Alan Gordon McDougall

voring care our guardian be, Lest our eyes feed

on vani- ty. 3) May every heart be pure from

sin, And folly find no place therein: Scant meed

of food, ex-cess denied, Wear down in us the bod-

y's pride. 4) That when the light of day is gone,

And night in course shall follow on, We, free from

cares the world af-fords, May chant the praise that

is our Lord's.

†61: Iam lucis orto sidere

First Sunday after the octave of the Epiphany
at Prime.

France: Paris (ca. 1255)

C–D

Now in the sun's new dawning ray, Lowly

of heart, our God we pray That He from harm may

keep us free   In all the deeds this day shall see.

2) May fear of Him our tongues re-strain, Lest strife

unguarded speech should stain: His fa-voring care

our guardian be,   Lest our eyes feed on vani- ty.

Anonymous (8th c.)
tr. Alan Gordon McDougall

3) May every heart be pure from sin, And fol-ly find

no place therein: Scant meed of food, ex-cess de-

nied, Wear down in us the body's pride. 4) That

when the light of day is gone, And night in course

shall follow on,   We, free from cares the world af-

fords, May chant the praise that is our Lord's.

†62: Iam lucis orto sidere

On feasts with nine lessons.

France: Angers (14th–15th c.)

C–B

Now in the sun's new dawning ray, Low-ly of heart, our God we pray That He from harm may keep us free   In all the deeds this day shall see. 2) May fear of Him our tongues re-strain, Lest strife unguarded speech should stain: His fa-voring care our guardian be,   Lest our eyes feed on van-i- ty. 3) May every heart be pure from sin, And fol-

Anonymous (8th c.)
tr. Alan Gordon McDougall

ly find no place therein: Scant meed of food, ex-cess

denied, Wear down in us the bod-y's pride. 4) That

when the light of day is gone, And night in course

shall follow on, We, free from cares the world af-

fords, May chant the praise that is our Lord's.

222

†63: Iam lucis orto sidere

At Prime.

Austria: Klosterneuburg (1336)

Now in the sun's new dawning ray, Lowly

of heart, our God we pray That He from harm may

keep us free In all the deeds this day shall see.

2) May fear of Him our tongues re- strain, Lest strife

unguarded speech should stain: His fa-voring care

our guardian be, Lest our eyes feed on van-i-

ty. 3) May every heart be pure from sin, And fol-

Anonymous (8th c.)
tr. Alan Gordon McDougall

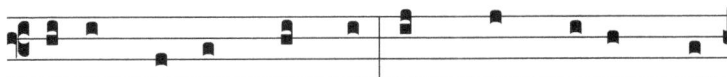

ly find no place therein: Scant meed of food, ex-

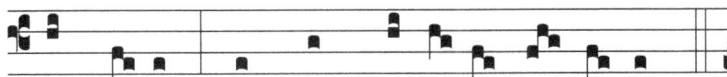

cess de-nied, Wear down in us the bod-y's pride.

4) That when the light of day is gone, And night

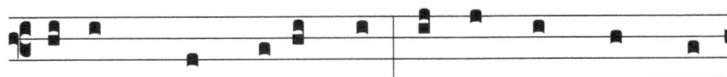

in course shall follow on, We, free from cares the

world af- fords, May chant the praise that is our

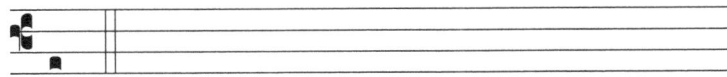

Lord's.

224

†64: Rector potens, verax Deus

At Sext.

France: Angers (14th–15th c.)

A–D

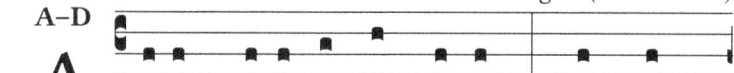

Al-mighty Ruler! God of Truth! Who guid'st

the changing scenes of Day, With golden beams il-

luming Morn, And kindling Noon with fiery ray;

2) O quench the baneful flames of strife, Bid every

hurtful passion cease, Vouchsafe unto our bodies

health, And keep our hearts in perfect peace.

Anonymous (8th c.)
tr. John David Chambers

†65: Rector potens, verax Deus

At Sext on thirds
and all doubles.

France: Châlons-en-Champagne (1309)

Al-mighty Ruler! God of Truth! Who guid'st

the changing scenes of Day, With golden beams il-

luming Morn, And kindling Noon with fiery ray;

2) O quench the baneful flames of strife, Bid every

hurtful passion cease, Vouchsafe unto our bodies

health, And keep our hearts in perfect peace.

Anonymous (8th c.)
tr. John David Chambers

†66: Rector potens, verax Deus

France: Paris (1350–1400)

C–B

A
l-mighty Ruler! God of Truth! Who guid'st

the changing scenes of Day, With golden beams il-

luming Morn, And kindling Noon with fiery ray;

2) O quench the baneful flames of strife, Bid every

hurtful passion cease, Vouchsafe unto our bodies

health, And keep our hearts in perfect peace.

Anonymous (8th c.)
tr. John David Chambers

†67: Rector potens, verax Deus

At Sext.

Switzerland: Engelberg (ca. 1400)

F–C

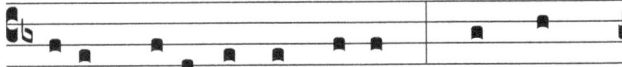

Al-mighty Ruler! God of Truth! Who guid'st

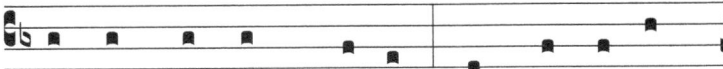

the changing scenes of Day, With golden beams

il-luming Morn, And kindling Noon with fiery

ray; 2) O quench the baneful flames of strife, Bid

every hurtful passion cease, Vouchsafe unto our

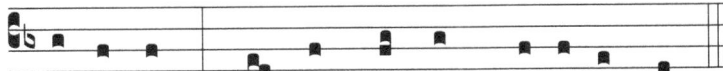

bodies health, And keep our hearts in perfect peace.

Anonymous (8th c.)
tr. John David Chambers

†68: Rector potens, verax Deus

France: Paris (1471)

C–C

A l-mighty Ruler! God of Truth! Who guid'st

the changing scenes of Day, With golden beams il-

luming Morn, And kindling Noon with fiery ray;

2) O quench the baneful flames of strife, Bid every

hurtful passion cease, Vouchsafe unto our bodies

health, And keep our hearts in perfect peace.

Anonymous (8th c.)
tr. John David Chambers

†69: Te lucis ante terminum

At Compline.

Germany: Kempten (ca. 1000)

C–A

Ere now the daylight fades a-way, Crea- tor

of the world, we pray, That Thou this night with

wonted love, Would'st shield Thy servants from a-

bove. 2) Let dreams and vi-sions all take flight, And

guilty phantoms of the night; And do Thou, Lord,

re-strain our Foe, Lest he should work us sin and

woe.

Anonymous (8th c.)
tr. John William Hewett

†70: Te lucis ante terminum

Switzerland: Einsiedeln (1100–1150)

E re now the daylight fades a-way, Crea-tor

of the world, we pray, That Thou this night with

wont-ed love, Would'st shield Thy ser-vants from

a-bove. 2) Let dreams and vi-sions all take flight,

And guilty phantoms of the night; And do Thou,

Lord, re-strain our Foe, Lest he should work us sin

and woe.

Anonymous (8th c.)
tr. John William Hewett

†71: Te lucis ante terminum

At Compline.

France: Nevers (12th c.)

Ere now the daylight fades a-way, Crea- tor

of the world, we pray, That Thou this night with

wonted love, Would'st shield Thy servants from a-

bove. 2) Let dreams and vi-sions all take flight, And

guilty phantoms of the night; And do Thou, Lord,

re-strain our Foe, Lest he should work us sin and

woe.

Anonymous (8th c.)
tr. John William Hewett

†72: Te lucis ante terminum

At Compline.

France: Nevers (12th c.)

Ere now the daylight fades a-way, Crea-tor of

the world, we pray, That Thou this night with wont-

ed love, Would'st shield Thy servants from a-bove.

2) Let dreams and vi-sions all take flight, And guilty

phantoms of the night; And do Thou, Lord, re-strain

our Foe, Lest he should work us sin and woe.

Anonymous (8th c.)
tr. John William Hewett

(2) i:1,4, ii:2

†73: Te lucis ante terminum

*Ordinary days
at Compline.*

Austria: Heiligenkreuz (12th–13th c.)

E–D

Ere now the daylight fades a-way, Crea- tor of

the world, we pray, That Thou this night with wont-

ed love, Would'st shield Thy servants from a- bove.

2) Let dreams and vi-sions all take flight, And guilty

phantoms of the night; And do Thou, Lord, re-strain

our Foe, Lest he should work us sin and woe.

A- men.

Anonymous (8th c.)
tr. John William Hewett

†74: Te lucis ante terminum

At Compline.

Italy: Rome (1200–1250)

F–E

E re now the day-light fades a-way, Crea- tor

of the world, we pray, That Thou this night with

wonted love, Would'st shield Thy ser- vants from a-

bove. 2) Let dreams and vi- sions all take flight,

And guilty phantoms of the night; And do Thou,

Lord, re-strain our Foe, Lest he should work us

sin and woe. A- men.

Anonymous (8th c.)
tr. John William Hewett

(1) ii:1, (2) i:6

†75: Te lucis ante terminum

Saturdays at Compline.

Germany: Rüdnitz (1325–1375)

C–G

E re now the daylight fades a-way, Crea- tor

of the world, we pray, That Thou this night with

wonted love, Would'st shield Thy servants from a-

bove. 2) Let dreams and vi-sions all take flight, And

guilty phantoms of the night; And do Thou, Lord,

re-strain our Foe, Lest he should work us sin and

woe.

Anonymous (8th c.)
tr. John William Hewett

†76: Te lucis ante terminum

For Saint Lambert.

Austria: Sankt Lambrecht (1350–1400)

Ere now the day-light fades a-way, Crea-tor of the world, we pray, That Thou this night with wonted love, Would'st shield Thy ser-vants from a- bove. 2) Let dreams and vi- sions all take flight, And guilty phantoms of the night; And do Thou, Lord, re-strain our Foe, Lest he should work us sin and woe.

Anonymous (8th c.)
tr. John William Hewett

†77: Te lucis ante terminum

Austria: Vorau (ca. 1458)

F–B

E re now the daylight fades a-way, Crea- tor of

the world, we pray, That Thou this night with wont-

ed love, Would'st shield Thy servants from a-bove.

2) Let dreams and vi-sions all take flight, And guilty

phantoms of the night; And do Thou, Lord, re-strain

our Foe, Lest he should work us sin and woe.

Anonymous (8th c.)
tr. John William Hewett

†78: Aurora lucis rutilat

Switzerland: Einsiedeln (1100–1150)

F–E

Light's glittering morn bedecks the sky,

Heav'n thunders forth its victor-cry; The glad earth

shouts its triumph high, And groaning Hell makes

wild re-ply. 2) While He, the King of glorious might,

Treads down Death's strength in Death's de-spite,

And trampling Hell by victor's right, Brings forth

His sleeping Saints to light. 3) Fast barr'd beneath

Anonymous (8th–9th c.)   sel: 1–4
tr. John Mason Neale

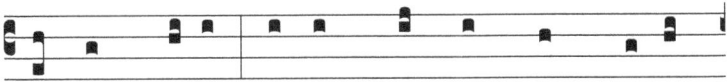

the stone of late, In watch and ward where soldiers

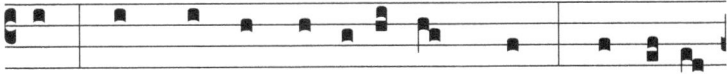

wait, Now shining in triumphant state, He rises

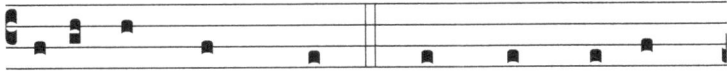

victor from death's gate. 4) Hell's pains are loos'd,

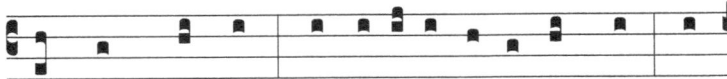

and tears are fled; Captivi- ty is captive led; The

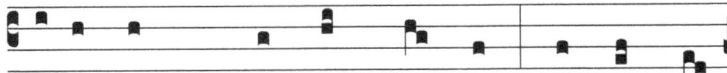

Angel, crowned with light, hath said, 'The Lord is

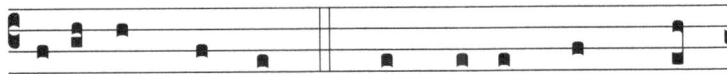

risen from the dead.' 5) The Apostles' hearts were

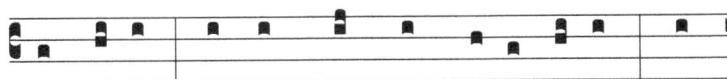

full of pain, For their dear Lord so lately slain, That

Lord His servants' wicked train With bitter scorn

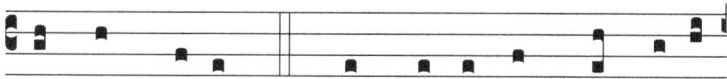

had dar'd ar-raign. 6) With gentle voice the Angel

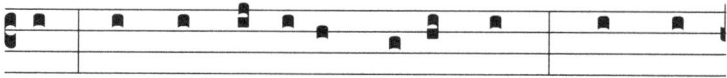

gave The women tidings at the Grave; 'Forthwith

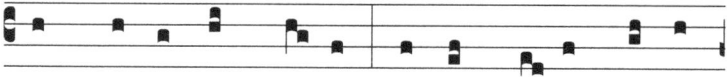

your Master shall ye see: He goes be-fore to Gal-

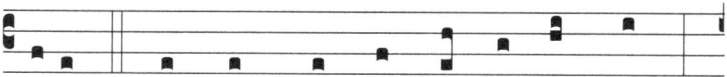

i- lee.' 7) And while with fear and joy they pressed

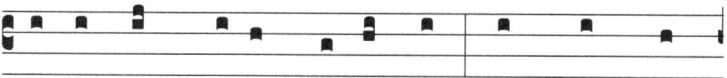

To tell these tidings to the rest, Their Lord, their

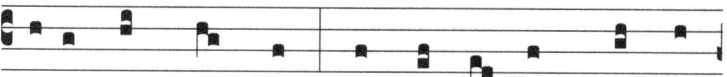

living Lord, they meet, And see His Form, and kiss

His Feet. 8) Th' Eleven, when they hear, with speed

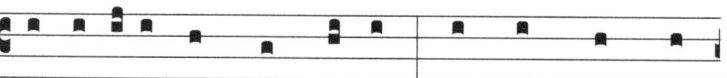

To Gali- lee forthwith proceed; That there they may

behold once more The Lord's dear Face, as oft a-

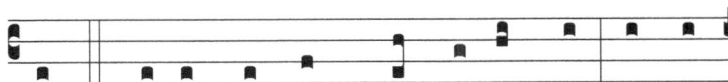

fore. 9) In this our bright and Paschal day The sun

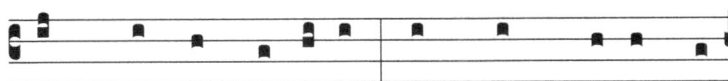

shines out with purer ray: When Christ, to earthly

sight made plain, The glad A- postles see a-gain.

10) The Wounds, the riven Wounds He shows In that

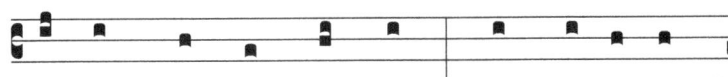

His Flesh with light that glows, With public voice,

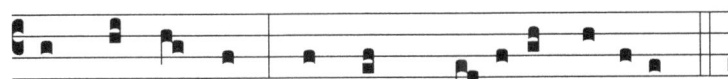

both far and nigh, The Lord's a- rising testi-fy.

11) O Christ, the King Who lov'st to bless, Do Thou

our hearts and souls possess; To Thee our praise

that we may pay, To Whom our laud is due, for aye.

†79: Aurora lucis rutilat

At Lauds.

Italy: Gaeta (12th c.)

D–C

Light's glittering morn bedecks the sky,

Heav'n thunders forth its victor-cry; The glad earth

shouts its triumph high, And groaning Hell makes

wild re- ply. 2) While He, the King of glorious

might, Treads down Death's strength in Death's de-

Anonymous (8th–9th c.)
tr. John Mason Neale

sel: 1–4

spite, And trampling Hell by victor's right, Brings

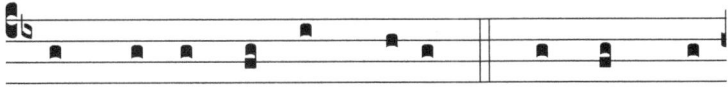

forth His sleeping Saints to light. 3) Fast barr'd be-

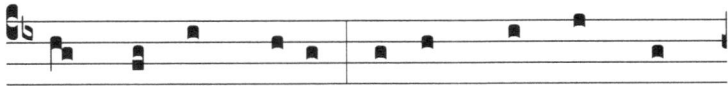

neath the stone of late, In watch and ward where

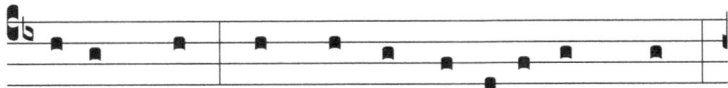

soldiers wait, Now shining in triumphant state,

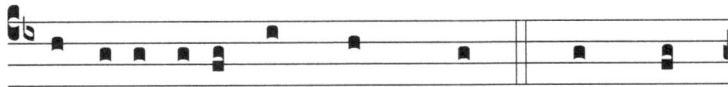

He rises victor from death's gate. 4) Hell's pains

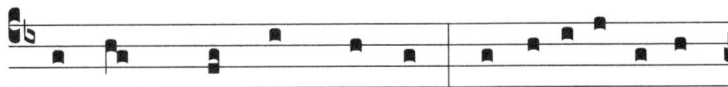

are loos'd, and tears are fled; Captivi- ty is cap-

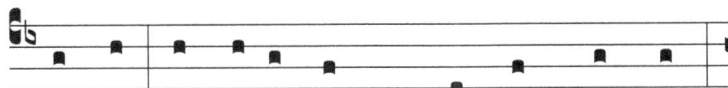

tive led; The Angel, crowned with light, hath said,

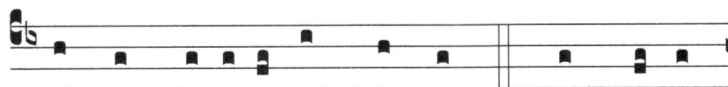

'The Lord is risen from the dead.' 5) The Apostles'

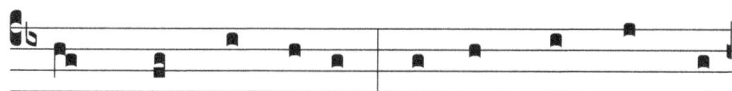

hearts were full of pain, For their dear Lord so

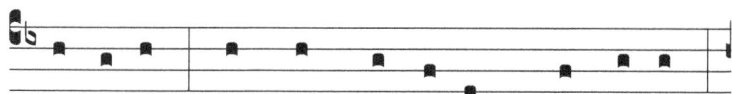

lately slain, That Lord His servants' wicked train

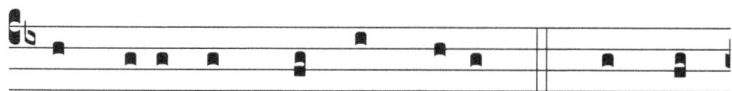

With bitter scorn had dar'd ar-raign. 6) With gen-

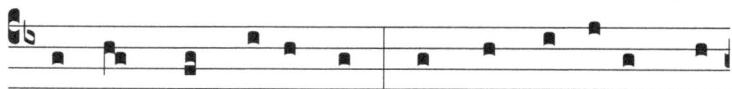

tle voice the Angel gave The women tidings at

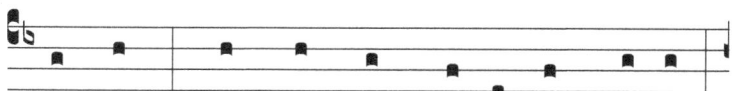

the Grave; 'Forthwith your Master shall ye see:

He goes be-fore to Gali- lee.' 7) And while with

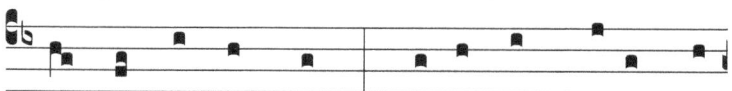

fear and joy they pressed To tell these tidings to

the rest, Their Lord, their living Lord, they meet,

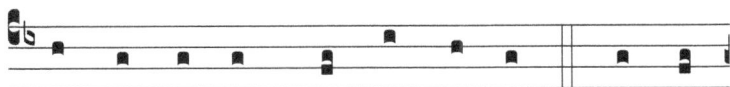

And see His Form, and kiss His Feet. 8) Th' Elev-

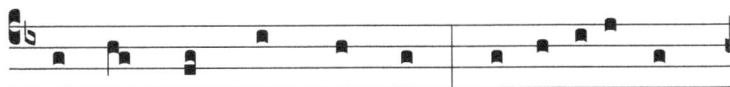

en, when they hear, with speed To Gali- lee forth-

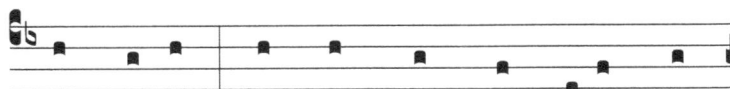

with proceed; That there they may behold once

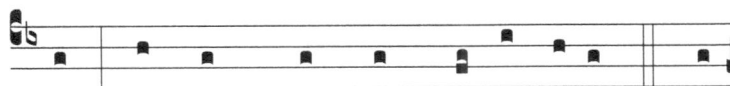

more The Lord's dear Face, as oft a- fore. 9) In

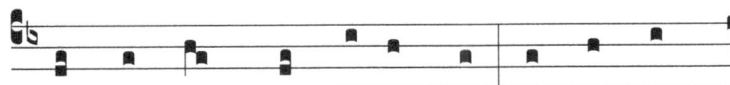

this our bright and Paschal day The sun shines

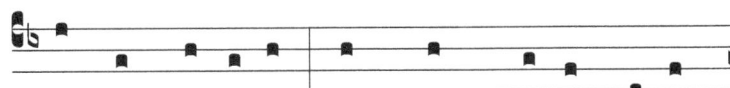

out with purer ray: When Christ, to earthly sight

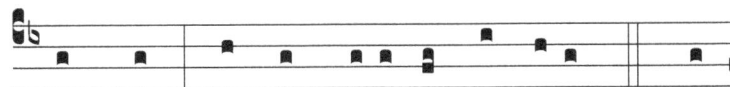

made plain, The glad A-postles see a-gain. 10) The

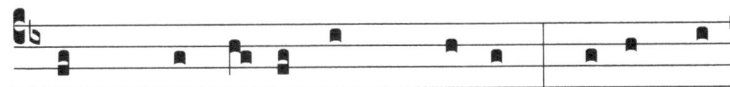

Wounds, the riv-en Wounds He shows In that His

Flesh with light that glows, With public voice, both

far and nigh, The Lord's a- rising testi-fy. 11) O

Christ, the King Who lov'st to bless, Do Thou our

hearts and souls possess; To Thee our praise that

we may pay, To Whom our laud is due, for aye.

†80: Aurora lucis rutilat

On Sundays at Lauds.

Central or southern Italy (ca. 1267)

D–B

Light's glittering morn bedecks the sky,

Heav'n thunders forth its victor-cry; The glad earth

Anonymous (8th–9th c.)
tr. John Mason Neale

sel: 1–4

shouts its triumph high, And groaning Hell makes

wild re-ply. 2) While He, the King of glorious might,

Treads down Death's strength in Death's de-spite,

And trampling Hell by victor's right, Brings forth

His sleeping Saints to light. 3) Fast barr'd beneath

the stone of late, In watch and ward where soldiers

wait, Now shining in triumphant state, He rises vic-

tor from death's gate. 4) Hell's pains are loos'd, and

tears are fled; Captivi- ty is captive led; The An-

gel, crowned with light, hath said, 'The Lord is ris-

en from the dead.' 5) The Apostles' hearts were full

of pain, For their dear Lord so lately slain, That

Lord His servants' wicked train With bitter scorn

had dar'd ar- raign. 6) With gentle voice the Angel

gave The women tidings at the Grave; 'Forthwith

your Master shall ye see: He goes be-fore to Gali- lee.' 7) And while with fear and joy they pressed

To tell these tidings to the rest, Their Lord, their

living Lord, they meet, And see His Form, and kiss

His Feet. 8) Th' Eleven, when they hear, with speed

To Gali- lee forthwith proceed; That there they may

behold once more The Lord's dear Face, as oft a-

fore. 9) In this our bright and Paschal day The sun

shines out with purer ray: When Christ, to earthly

sight made plain, The glad A-postles see a- gain.

10) The Wounds, the riven Wounds He shows In that

His Flesh with light that glows, With public voice,

both far and nigh, The Lord's a- rising testi- fy.

11) O Christ, the King Who lov'st to bless, Do Thou

our hearts and souls possess; To Thee our praise

that we may pay, To Whom our laud is due, for aye.

†81: Aurora lucis rutilat

At First Nocturn.

Switzerland: Lausanne (13th c.)

C–A

Light's glittering morn bedecks the sky,

Heav'n thunders forth its victor-cry; The glad earth

shouts its triumph high, And groaning Hell makes

wild re-ply. 2) While He, the King of glorious

might, Treads down Death's strength in Death's de-

spite, And trampling Hell by victor's right, Brings

forth His sleeping Saints to light. 3) Fast barr'd be-

Anonymous (8th–9th c.)
tr. John Mason Neale

sel: 1–4

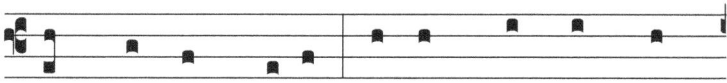

neath the stone of late, In watch and ward where

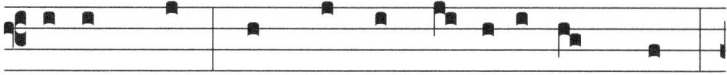

soldiers wait, Now shining in triumphant state,

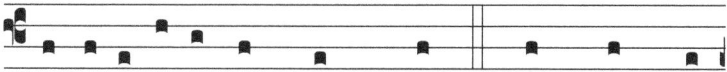

He rises victor from death's gate. 4) Hell's pains are

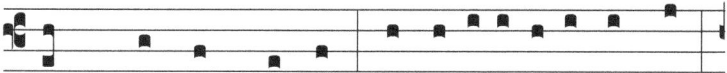

loos'd, and tears are fled; Captivi- ty is captive led;

The Angel, crowned with light, hath said, 'The Lord

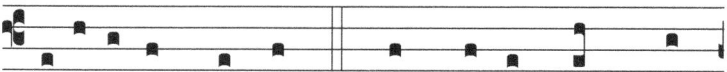

is risen from the dead.' 5) The Apostles' hearts were

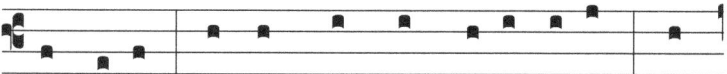

full of pain, For their dear Lord so lately slain, That

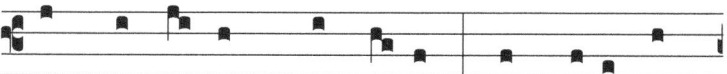

Lord His ser-vants' wicked train With bitter scorn

had dar'd ar-raign. 6) With gentle voice the Angel

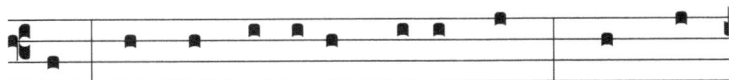

gave The women tidings at the Grave; 'Forthwith

your Master shall ye see: He goes be-fore to Gali-

lee.' 7) And while with fear and joy they pressed

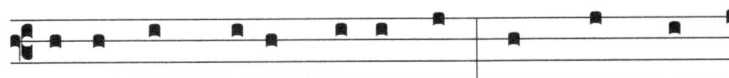

To tell these tidings to the rest, Their Lord, their

liv-ing Lord, they meet, And see His Form, and kiss

His Feet. 8) Th' Eleven, when they hear, with speed

To Gali- lee forthwith proceed; That there they may

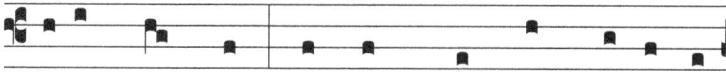

behold once more The Lord's dear Face, as oft a-

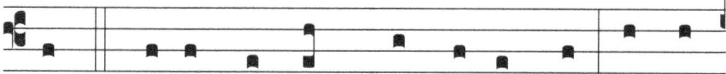

fore. 9) In this our bright and Paschal day The sun

shines out with purer ray: When Christ, to earthly

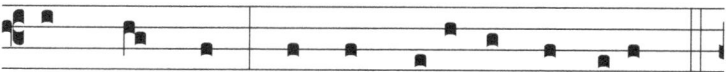

sight made plain, The glad A-postles see a-gain.

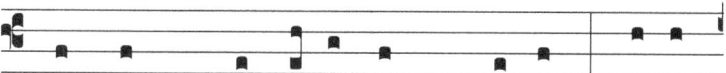

10) The Wounds, the riven Wounds He shows In that

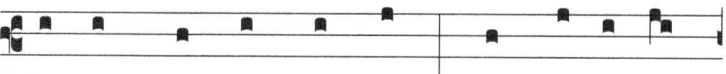

His Flesh with light that glows, With public voice,

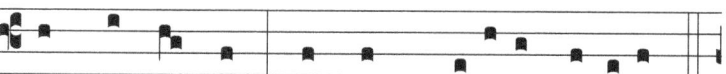

both far and nigh, The Lord's a-rising testi-fy.

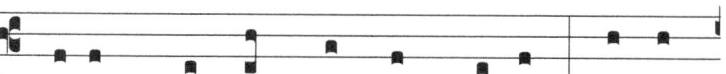

11) O Christ, the King Who lov'st to bless, Do Thou

our hearts and souls possess; To Thee our praise

that we may pay, To Whom our laud is due, for

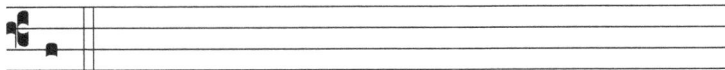

aye.

†82: Aurora lucis rutilat

Saturday in the octave of Pascha
at Lauds.

Southern Italy (13th c.)

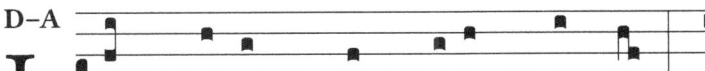

D–A

Light's glittering morn bedecks the sky,

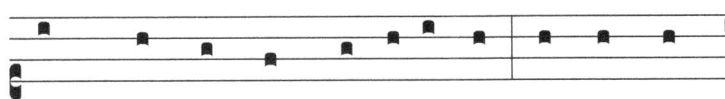

Heav'n thunders forth its victor-cry; The glad earth

shouts its triumph high, And groaning Hell makes

Anonymous (8th–9th c.)
tr. John Mason Neale

sel: 1–4

wild re-ply. 2) While He, the King of glorious might,

Treads down Death's strength in Death's de-spite,

And trampling Hell by victor's right, Brings forth

His sleeping Saints to light. 3) Fast barr'd beneath

the stone of late, In watch and ward where soldiers

wait, Now shining in triumphant state, He rises vic-

tor from death's gate. 4) Hell's pains are loos'd, and

tears are fled; Captivi- ty is captive led; The Angel, crowned with light, hath said, 'The Lord is ris-

en from the dead.' 5) The Apostles' hearts were full

of pain, For their dear Lord so lately slain, That

Lord His servants' wicked train With bitter scorn

had dar'd ar-raign. 6) With gentle voice the Angel

gave The women tidings at the Grave; 'Forthwith

your Master shall ye see: He goes be-fore to Gal-

i- lee.' 7) And while with fear and joy they pressed

To tell these tidings to the rest, Their Lord, their

living Lord, they meet, And see His Form, and kiss

His Feet. 8) Th' Eleven, when they hear, with speed

To Gali- lee forthwith proceed; That there they may

behold once more The Lord's dear Face, as oft a-

fore. 9) In this our bright and Paschal day The sun

shines out with purer ray: When Christ, to earthly

sight made plain, The glad A-postles see a- gain.

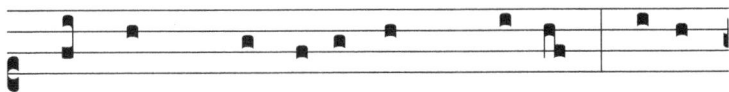

10) The Wounds, the riven Wounds He shows In that

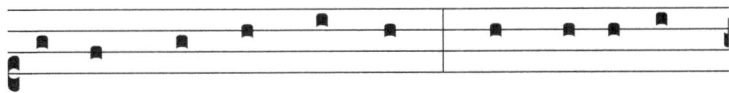

His Flesh with light that glows, With public voice,

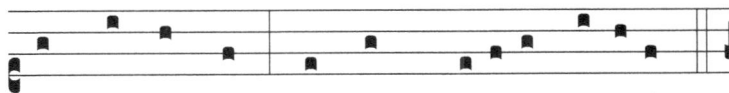

both far and nigh, The Lord's a- rising testi-fy.

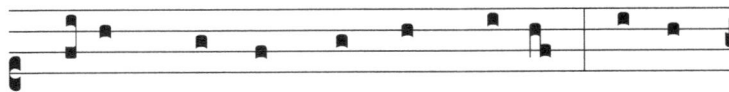

11) O Christ, the King Who lov'st to bless, Do Thou

our hearts and souls possess; To Thee our praise

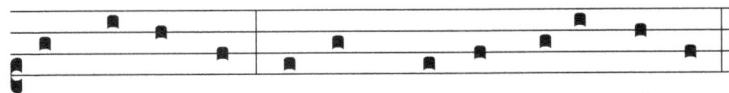

that we may pay, To Whom our laud is due, for aye.

†83: Aurora lucis rutilat

Switzerland: Engelberg (1372)

B–G

Light's glittering morn bedecks the sky,

Heav'n thunders forth its victor-cry; The glad earth

shouts its triumph high, And groaning Hell makes

wild re-ply. 2) While He, the King of glorious might,

Treads down Death's strength in Death's de-spite,

And trampling Hell by victor's right, Brings forth

His sleeping Saints to light. 3) Fast barr'd beneath

Anonymous (8th–9th c.)
tr. John Mason Neale

sel: 1–4

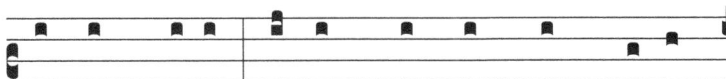

the stone of late, In watch and ward where soldiers

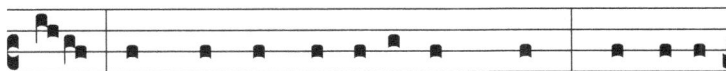

wait, Now shining in triumphant state, He rises

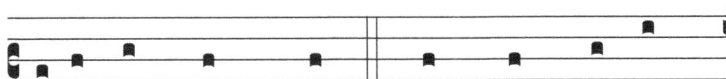

victor from death's gate. 4) Hell's pains are loos'd,

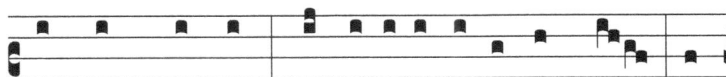

and tears are fled; Captivi- ty is captive led; The

Angel, crowned with light, hath said, 'The Lord is

risen from the dead.' 5) The Apostles' hearts were

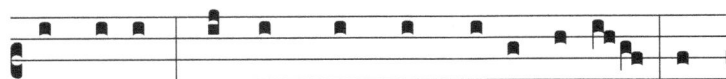

full of pain, For their dear Lord so lately slain, That

Lord His servants' wicked train With bitter scorn

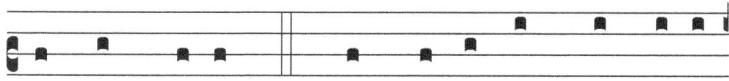

had dar'd ar-raign. 6) With gentle voice the Angel

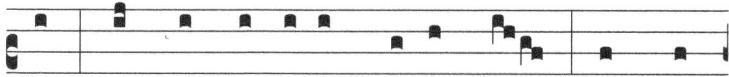

gave The women tidings at the Grave; 'Forthwith

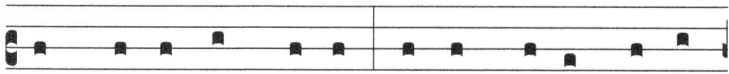

your Master shall ye see: He goes be-fore to Gal-

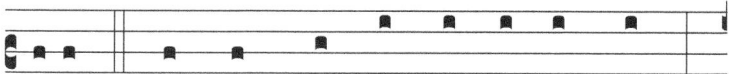

i- lee.' 7) And while with fear and joy they pressed

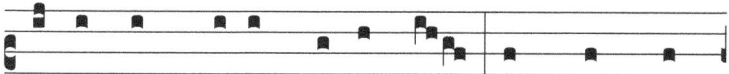

To tell these tidings to the rest, Their Lord, their

living Lord, they meet, And see His Form, and kiss

His Feet. 8) Th' Eleven, when they hear, with speed

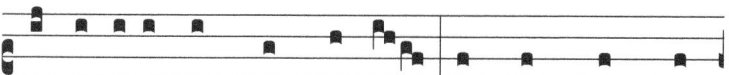

To Gali- lee forthwith proceed; That there they may

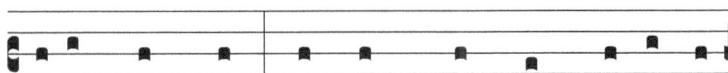

behold once more The Lord's dear Face, as oft a-

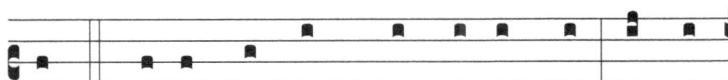

fore. 9) In this our bright and Paschal day The sun

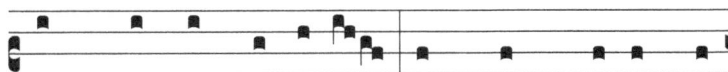

shines out with purer ray: When Christ, to earthly

sight made plain, The glad A-postles see a-gain.

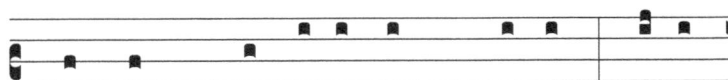

10) The Wounds, the riven Wounds He shows In that

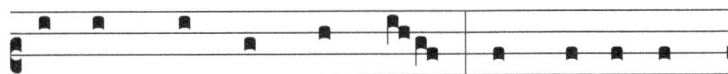

His Flesh with light that glows, With public voice,

both far and nigh, The Lord's a-rising testi-fy.

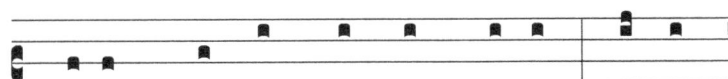

11) O Christ, the King Who lov'st to bless, Do Thou

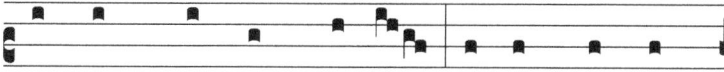

our hearts and souls possess; To Thee our praise

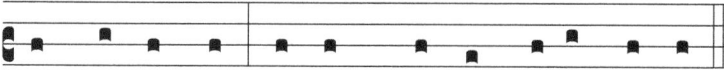

that we may pay, To Whom our laud is due, for aye.

†84: Dei fide, qua vivimus

At Terce.

Italy: Verona (11th c.)

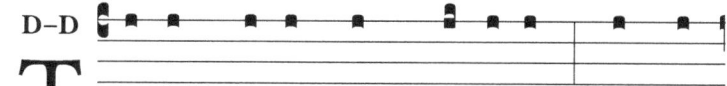

D–D

The Faith of God which we re-ceive, The eter-

nal Hope which we be-lieve, For all His Chari- ty

and Grace, Christ in His Glory let us praise! 2) Who

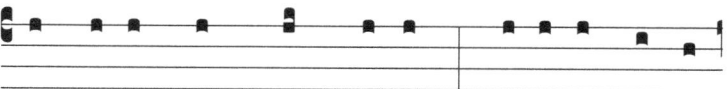

was at this Third Hour of dread, A Victim to His

Anonymous (8th–9th c.)
tr. John David Chambers

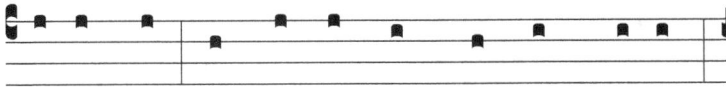

Passion led; And bearing meek The Cross of Pain,

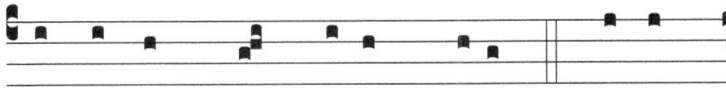

His wandering sheep re-stored a-gain. 3) We there-

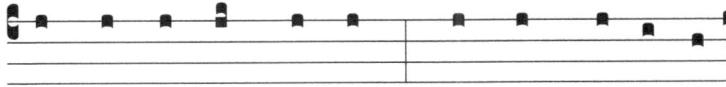

fore humbly make our prayer, That freed by His re-

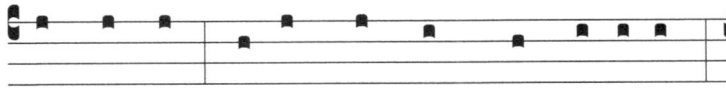

deeming care, He from this world may us de-liver,

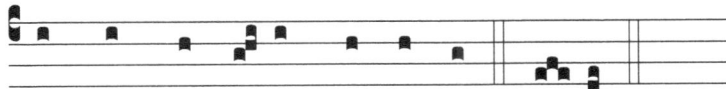

Who blots the re-cord out for ever! A- men.

†85: Dei fide, qua vivimus

During Lent.

France: Clermont-Ferránd (14th c.)

D–F

T he Faith of God which we re-ceive, The e-

Anonymous (8th–9th c.)
tr. John David Chambers

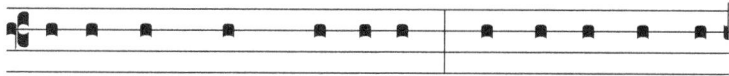

ternal Hope which we be-lieve, For all His Chari-

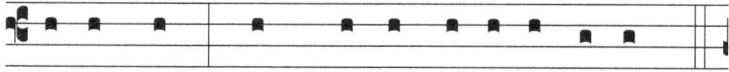

ty and Grace, Christ in His Glory let us praise!

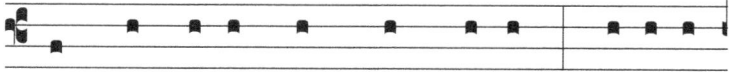

2) Who was at this Third Hour of dread, A Victim

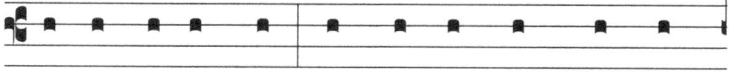

to His Passion led; And bearing meek The Cross

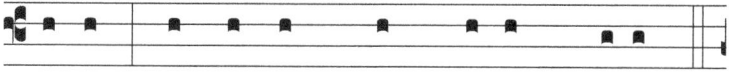

of Pain, His wandering sheep re-stored a- gain.

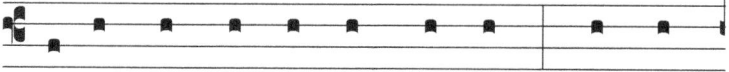

3) We therefore humbly make our prayer, That freed

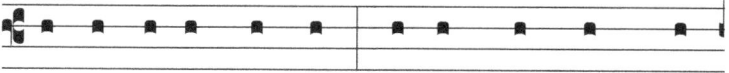

by His re-deeming care, He from this world may

us de-liver, Who blots the re-cord out for ever!

†86: Gloria, laus, et honor

The verses composed in praise of Christ by the presbyter Juvencus [sic].
*They are sung when they have returned and are approaching the main
doors of the church.*

Italy: Benevento (11th c.)

A–G

Glo-ry, and honour, and laud be to Thee, King

Christ the Redeemer! Children be-fore Whose steps

raised their Ho-sannas of praise. 2) Is-ra-el's Mon-

arch art Thou, and the glo- rious off-spring of Da-

vid, Thou That approachest a King blessed in the

Name of the Lord. 3) Glory to Thee in the high-est

the heav- en-ly ar-mies are singing: Glory to Thee

Theodulf of Orléans (ca. 818)   P: 1, 1, 2, 1, 3, 1, 4, 1, etc.
tr. John Mason Neale: 1–7 / 39

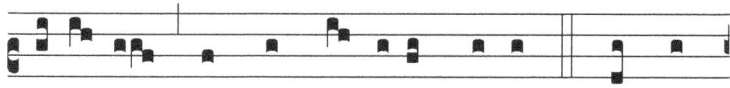

upon earth man and cre-a- tion re-ply. 4) Met Thee

with Palms in their hands that day the folk of the

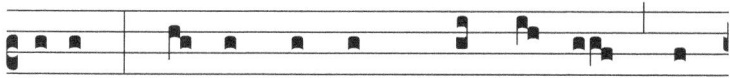

Hebrews: We with our prayers and our hymns now

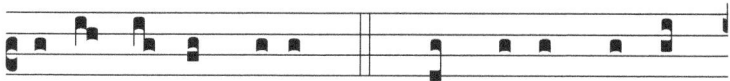

to Thy presence approach. 5) They to Thee proffered

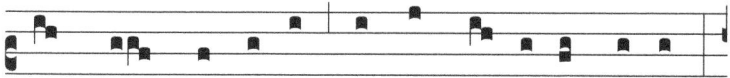

their praise for to her- ald Thy dol-or-ous Passion,

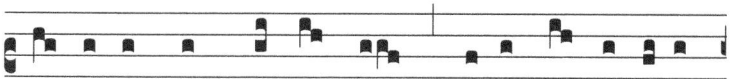

We to the King on His Throne ut-ter the ju-bi-lant

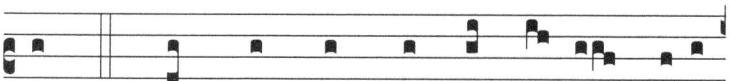

hymn. 6) They were then pleasing to Thee, unto

Thee our devo-tion be pleasing: Merci-ful King, kind

King, Who in all goodness art pleas'd. 7) They in

their pride of de-scent were right- ly the children

of Hebrews: He-brews are we, whom the Lord's

Passo-ver maketh the same.

†87: Gloria, laus, et honor

At the station.

Germany: Regensburg (14th c.)

C–D

Glo- ry, and honour, and laud be to Thee,

King Christ the Redeemer! Children be- fore Whose

steps raised their Ho-sannas of praise. 2) Is-ra-el's

Theodulf of Orléans (ca. 818)
tr. John Mason Neale: 1–7 / 23

P: 1, 2, 1, 3, 1b, 4, 1, 5, 1b, 6, 1

Monarch art Thou, and the glorious offspring of Da-

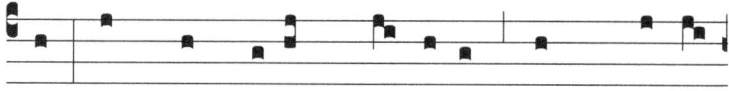

vid, Thou That approachest a King blessed in the

Name of the Lord. 3) Glory to Thee in the highest

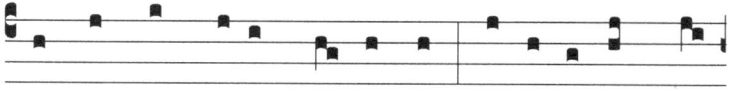

the heavenly armies are singing: Glory to Thee up-

on earth man and cre-a- tion re-ply. 4) Met Thee

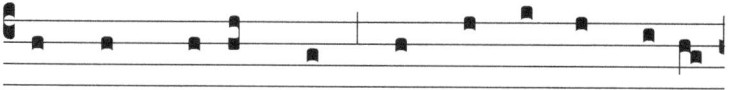

with Palms in their hands that day the folk of the

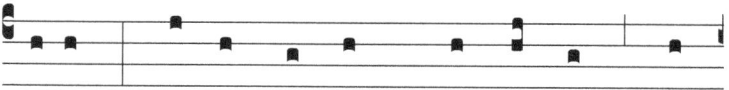

Hebrews: We with our prayers and our hymns now

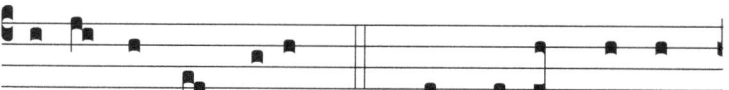

to Thy presence approach. 5) They to Thee proffered

their praise for to herald Thy dolor-ous Passion,

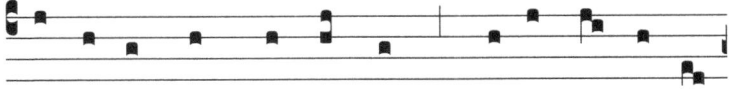

We to the King on His Throne ut-ter the ju-bi-

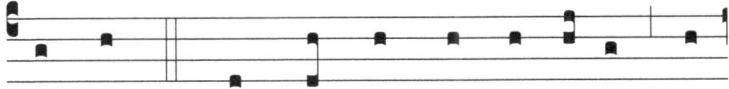

lant hymn. 6) They were then pleasing to Thee, un-

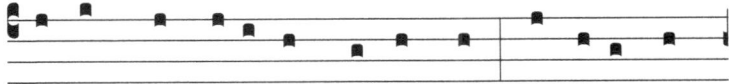

to Thee our devo-tion be pleasing: Merci-ful King,

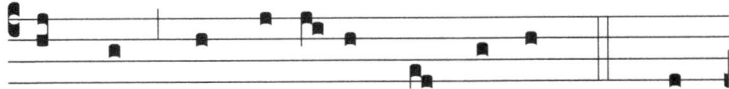

kind King, Who in all goodness art pleas'd. 7) They

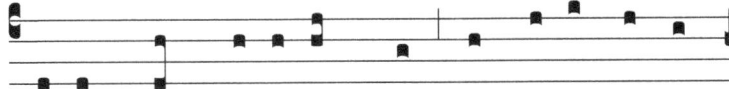

in their pride of de-scent were rightly the children

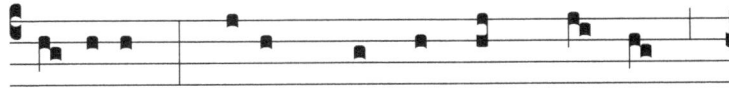

of Hebrews: Hebrews are we, whom the Lord's

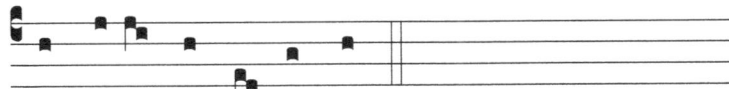

Passo-ver maketh the same.

†88: Consors paterni luminis

Feria 3 at Nocturns.

Germany: Kempten (ca. 1000)

D–A

Pure Light of light! e- ternal day; Who dost

the Fa-ther's brightness share; Our chant the mid-

night si- lence breaks;— Be nigh, and hearken to

our prayer. 2) Scatter the darkness of our minds,

And turn the hosts of hell to flight; Let not our

souls in sloth re-pose, And sleeping sink in end-

less night. 3) O Christ! for thy dear mercy's sake,

Anonymous (ca. 803–869)
tr. Edward Caswall

Spare us, who put our trust in Thee; Nor let our

early hymn as-cend In vain to thy pure Majes-ty.

4) Fa-ther of mercies! hear our cry; Hear us, O sole-

begotten Son! Who, with the Holy Ghost most high,

Reignest while endless ages run.

†89: O lux beata Trinitas

At Vespers.

Germany: Kempten (ca. 1000)

D–C

O Trini- ty, O blessed light, O U-ni-ty, most

princi-pal! The fiery sun now leaves our sight,

Anonymous (ca. 803–869)
tr. William Drummond

Cause in our hearts thy beams to fall. 2) Let us

with songs of praise di-vine, At morn and evening

thee implore, And let our glory bow'd to thine,

Thee glori-fy for evermore.

†90: O lux beata Trinitas

Switzerland: Einsiedeln (1100–1150)

C–A

O Trini- ty, O blessed light, O U-ni-ty,

most princi- pal! The fiery sun now leaves our

sight, Cause in our hearts thy beams to fall.

Anonymous (ca. 803–869)
tr. William Drummond

2) Let us with songs of praise di- vine, At morn and

evening thee im-plore, And let our glory bow'd to

thine, Thee glori-fy for ever- more.

†91: Somno refectis artubus

Feria 2 at Matins.

France: Le Mans (1450–1500)

A–C

Now that our limbs, re-freshed by sleep, New

vigour gain, let us a- rise; O Heavenly Fa-ther, deign

to keep Thine Ear at-tentive to our cries. 2) Thine

be the Name our tongue shall sing, And let our

Anonymous (ca. 803–869)
tr. John Wallace

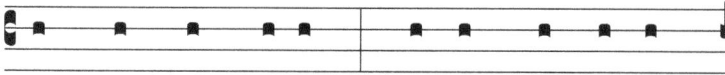

mind with Thee discourse; Be Thou our Sovereign

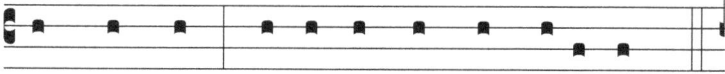

Lord and King, Of all our acts the Holy Source.

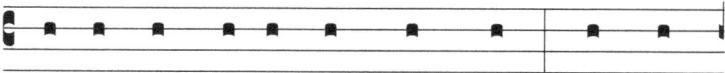

3) As darkness to the light gives place, And night

gives way be-fore the sun, So may the light of heav-

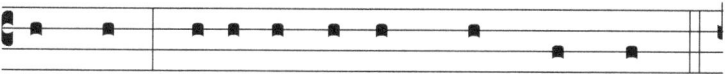

enly grace Undo the ill which night hath done.

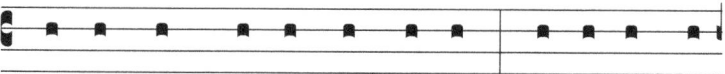

4) We beg Thee, on our bended knee, To pardon all

our guilty crime, That we who sing our hymns to

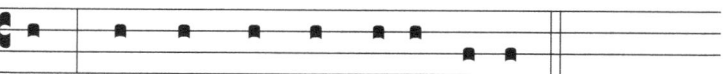

Thee, May sing Thy praises for all time.

†92: Summae Deus clementiae

Saturday at Nocturns.

Italy: Verona (11th c.)

C–B

Great God of boundless mercy hear! Thou

Framer of this earthly sphere! One, in e- terni-ty of

might! In Whom the immortal Three u- nite! 2) O

listen to our thankful lays Of mingled peni- tence

and praise; And set our hearts from er- ror free,

More amply to re-joice in Thee! 3) Our reins and

hearts in pity heal, And with Thy chastening fires

Anonymous (ca. 803–869)
tr. John David Chambers

(1) i:1–4, (2,4) i:4–5

anneal; Gird Thou our loins, each passion quell, And

every worldly lust expel. 4) Now as our anthems,

upward borne, A-wake the si-lence of the morn,

En-rich us with Thy gifts of Grace, From Heaven

Thy blissful dwelling-place! A- men.

†93: Tu, Trinitatis unitas

Feria 6 at Nocturns.

Italy: Verona (11th c.)

C–B

Thou Trini- ty of U-ni-ty! Great Ruler of

the World! To Thee We chant our canti-cles of

Anonymous (ca. 803–869)
tr. John David Chambers

(1) i:1–4, (5) i:4–5

praise; O listen to our early lays! 2) Now joyful

from the couch we rise, Though darkness veils the

si-lent skies; O make our mental failings whole,

Thou great Physi- cian of the soul! 3) If aught of

sin this night de-filed The soul, by Sa-tan's arts be-

guiled; Re-gard from Heaven Thy dwelling-place,

And cleanse it by Thy special grace. 4) Let pureness

every frame possess, No laggard sloth our hearts

oppress; Nor Sin's cold lepro- sy with ill The fer-

vour of our spirits chill. 5) Redeemer! in Thy sav-

ing might, Il-lume us with Thy healthful light; That

in our walk, from day to day, From Thee we never

more may stray. A- men.

†94: Aeterne rex altissime

At Lauds.

Italy: Verona (11th c.)

F–D

E - ter- nal Monarch, King most high, Whose

Blood hath brought re- demption nigh, By whom

Anonymous (9th c.)
tr. Neale & Housman: 1–4 & 5–7 / 7

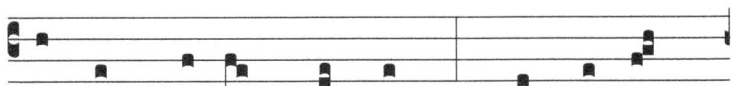

the death of Death was wrought, And conquering

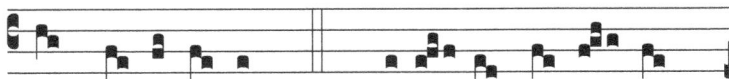

Grace's battle fought: 2) Ascending to the throne

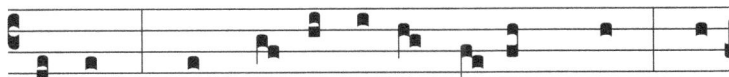

of might, And seated at the Fa- ther's right, All

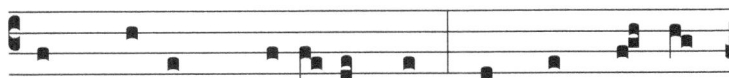

power in heaven is Je- su's own, That here his man-

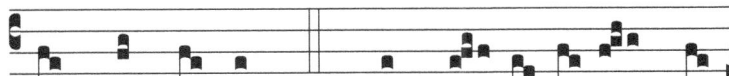

hood had not known. 3) That so, in na- ture's tri-

ple frame, Each heavenly and each earthly name,

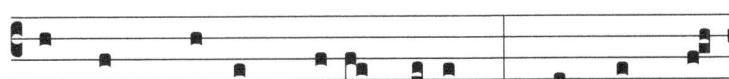

And things in Hell's a- byss abhorred, May bend the

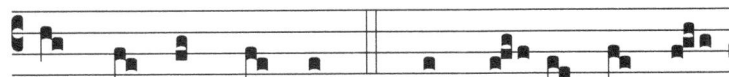

knee and own him Lord. 4) Yea, An- gels tremble

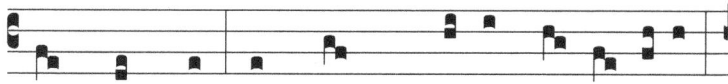

when they see How changed is our hu-mani- ty;

That flesh hath purged what flesh had stained, And

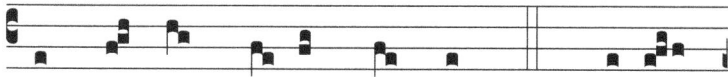

God, the Flesh of God, hath reigned. 5) O Christ,

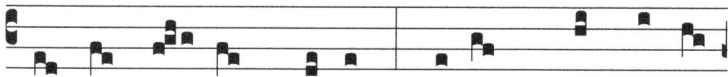

our joy, to   whom is given A throne o'er all the

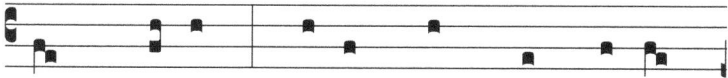

thrones of heaven, In thee, whose hand all things

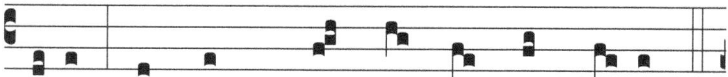

o- bey, The world's vain pleasures pass a- way.

6) So, sup-pliants here, we   seek to win Thy pardon

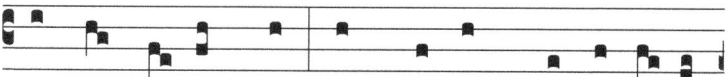

for thy people's sin, That, by thine all-prevailing

grace, Uplifted, we may seek thy face. 7) And when,

all heaven be- neath thee bowed, Thou com'st to

judgement throned in cloud, Then from our guilt

wash out the stain And give us our lost crowns a-

gain. A- men.

†95: Aeterne rex altissime

On the Ascension,
at First Nocturn.

Italy: Ascoli Piceno (13th–14th c.)

E–D

E - ter-nal Monarch, King most high, Whose

Anonymous (9th c.)
tr. Neale & Housman: 1–4 & 5–7 / 7

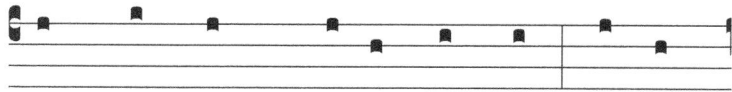

Blood hath brought re- demption nigh, By whom

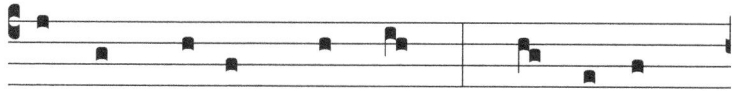

the death of Death was wrought, And conquering

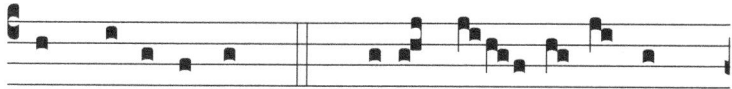

Grace's battle fought: 2) Ascending   to the throne

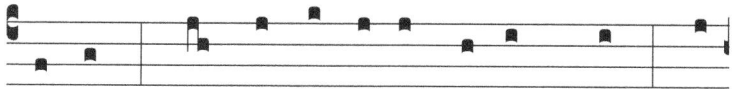

of might, And seated at the Fa- ther's right, All

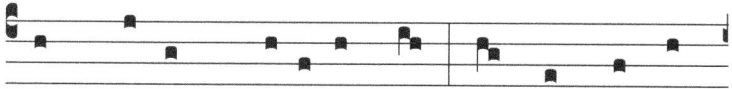

power in heaven is Je-su's own, That here his man-

hood had not known. 3) That so, in   na-ture's tri-

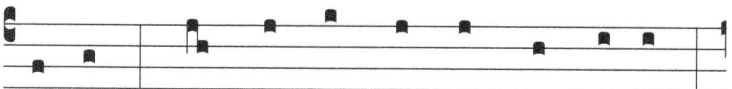

ple frame, Each heavenly and each earthly name,

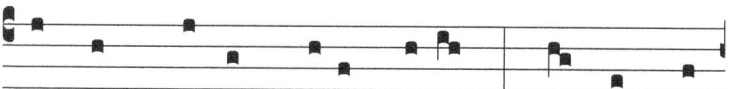

And things in Hell's a-byss abhorred, May bend the

knee and own him Lord. 4) Yea, An-gels   tremble

when they see How changed is our humani- ty;

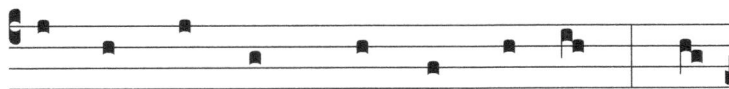

That flesh hath purged what flesh had stained, And

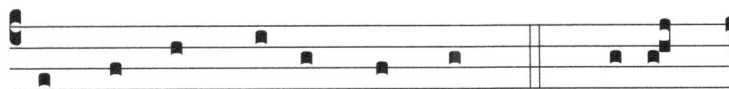

God, the Flesh of God, hath reigned. 5) O Christ,

our   joy, to whom is given A throne o'er all the

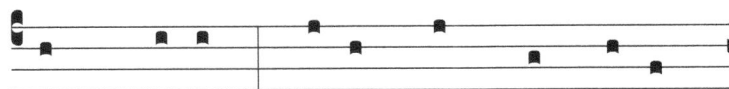

thrones of heaven, In thee, whose hand all things

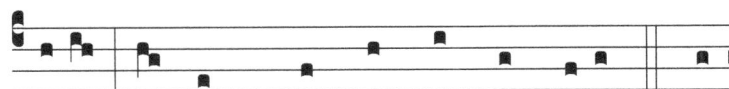

o-bey, The world's vain pleasures pass a-way. 6) So,

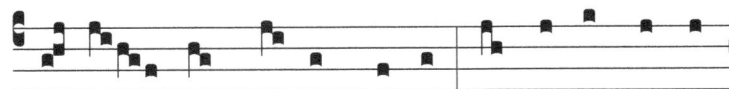

suppliants here, we seek to win Thy pardon for thy

people's sin, That, by thine all-prevailing grace, Up-

lifted, we may seek thy face. 7) And when, all

heaven be-neath thee bowed, Thou com'st to judge-

ment throned in cloud, Then from our guilt wash

out the stain And give us our lost crowns a-gain.

†96: Audi, benigne conditor

Italy: Verona (11th c.)

C–G

O Kind Crea-tor, bow thine ear To mark

Anonymous (9th c.)
tr. Thomas Alexander Lacey

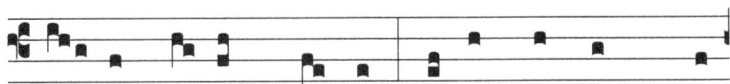

the cry, to know the tear Be-fore thy throne of

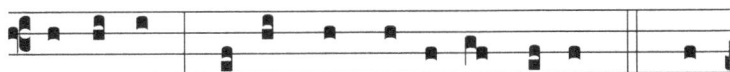

mercy spent In this thy ho-ly fast of Lent. 2) Our

hearts are o-pen, Lord, to thee: Thou knowest our

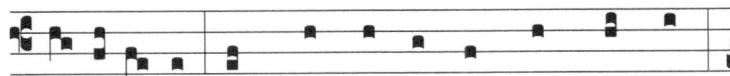

in-firmi-ty; Pour out on all who seek thy face

A-bundance of thy pardoning grace. 3) Our sins

are many, this we know; Spare us, good Lord,

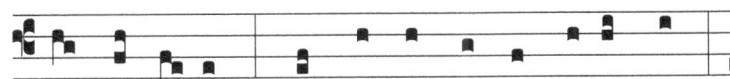

thy mercy show; And for the honour of thy name

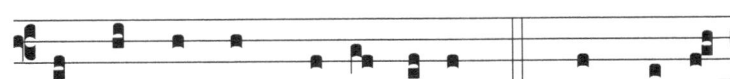

Our fainting souls to life re-claim. 4) Give us the

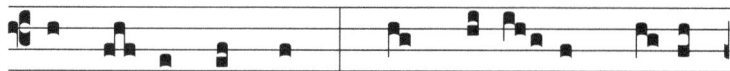

self-con-trol that springs From disci- pline of out-

ward things, That fasting inward se-cretly The soul

may purely dwell with thee. 5) We pray thee, Ho-

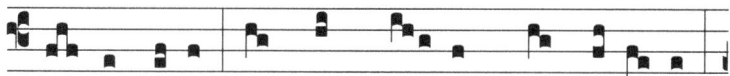

ly Trini- ty, One God, un- changing U-ni- ty,

That we from this our ab-stinence May reap the

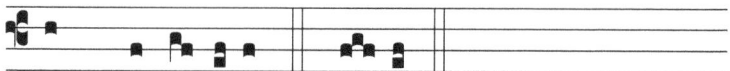

fruits of peni- tence. A- men.

†97: Audi, benigne conditor

At Second Vespers.

England: Worcester (ca. 1230)

D–C

O Kind Crea- tor, bow thine ear To mark the

cry, to know the tear Be-fore thy throne of mercy

spent In this thy ho-ly fast of Lent. 2) Our hearts

are o-pen, Lord, to thee: Thou knowest our in-fir-

mi-ty; Pour out on all who seek thy face A-bun-

dance of thy pardoning grace. 3) Our sins are man-

Anonymous (9th c.)
tr. Thomas Alexander Lacey

y,   this we know; Spare us, good Lord, thy mercy

show; And for the honour of thy name Our fainting

souls to   life re-claim. 4) Give us the self-con-trol

that springs From disci- pline of outward things,

That fasting inward se-cretly The soul may purely

dwell with thee. 5) We pray thee, Holy   Trini- ty,

One God, un-changing U-ni-ty, That we from this

our ab-sti-nence May reap the fruits of   peni- tence.

†98: Ave, maris stella

At a Nocturn.

Italy: Verona (11th c.)

A - ve, Star of O-cean, Child Di- vine who

barest, Mother, Ever-Vir-gin, Heaven's Portal fair-

est. 2) Taking that sweet A-ve Erst by Ga-briel spo-

ken, Eva's name re-versing, Be of peace the to-

ken. 3) Break the sinners' fetters, Light to blind re-

storing, All our ills dispel-ling, Eve- ry boon im-

Anonymous (9th c.)
tr. John Athelstan Laurie Riley

plor- ing. 4) Show thyself a   Mother In thy sup-

pli- ca-tion; He will hear who chose thee At   His

In-car-na- tion. 5) Maid all maids ex- celling, Pass-

ing meek and lowly, Win for sinners pardon, Make

us chaste and ho- ly. 6) As we onward journey

Aid our weak en- deavor, Till we gaze on Je- sus

And re-joice for-ev- er. 7) Fa-ther, Son, and Spirit

Three in One con-fessing, Give we e- qual glo-ry

E- qual praise and blessing.

†99: Ave, maris stella

Italy: Gaeta (12th c.)

C–C

A - ve, Star of O- cean, Child Di- vine who

barest, Mother, Ev- er-Virgin, Heaven's Portal fair-

est. 2) Taking that sweet A- ve Erst by Ga- briel

spoken, Eva's name re- versing, Be of peace the

to- ken. 3) Break the sinners' fet-ters, Light to blind

Anonymous (9th c.)
tr. John Athelstan Laurie Riley

re-storing, All our ills dispelling, Every boon im-

ploring. 4) Show thyself a Mother In thy suppli-

ca-tion; He will hear who chose thee At His In-

carna-tion. 5) Maid all maids ex-cel-ling, Passing

meek and lowly, Win for sin-ners pardon, Make

us chaste and ho-ly. 6) As we onward journey

Aid our weak endeavor, Till we gaze on Je-sus

And re-joice forev-er. 7) Fa-ther, Son, and Spirit

Three in One confessing, Give we e-   qual glory

E-qual praise and blessing.

†100: Ave, maris stella

At Compline.

Austria: Heiligenkreuz (12th–13th c.)

C–D

A - ve, Star of O-cean, Child Di-vine who bar-

est, Mother, Ever-Virgin, Heaven's Portal fair-est.

2) Taking that sweet A-ve   Erst by Gabriel spoken,

Eva's name re-versing, Be of peace the to- ken.

Anonymous (9th c.)
tr. John Athelstan Laurie Riley

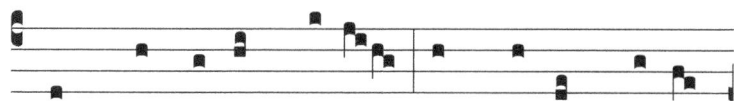

3) Break the sinners' fetters, Light to blind re-stor-

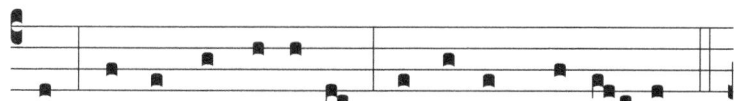

ing, All our ills dispelling, Every boon implor-ing.

4) Show thyself a Mother In thy supplica-tion; He

will hear who chose thee At His In-carna- tion.

5) Maid all maids ex-celling, Passing meek and low-

ly, Win for sinners pardon, Make us chaste and

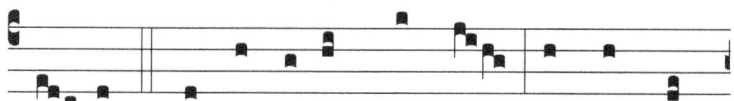

ho- ly. 6) As we onward journey Aid our weak

endeavor, Till we gaze on Je-sus And re-joice forev- er. 7) Fa-ther, Son, and Spirit Three in One

confessing, Give we e-qual glory E-qual praise and

blessing.

†101: Ave, maris stella

On the Assumption of Saint Mary.

France: Bayeux (ca. 1234)

C–C

A - ve, Star of O-cean, Child Di-vine who bar-

est, Mother, Ever-Vir-gin, Heaven's Portal fairest.

2) Taking that sweet A-ve Erst by Gabriel spoken,

Anonymous (9th c.)
tr. John Athelstan Laurie Riley

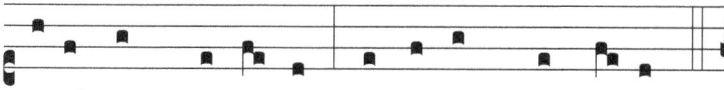

Eva's name re-versing, Be of peace the to-ken.

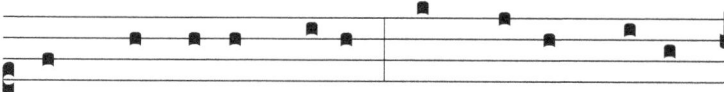

3) Break the sinners' fetters, Light to blind re-stor-

ing, All our ills dispel-ling, Every boon imploring.

4) Show thyself a Mother In thy supplica-tion; He

will hear who chose thee At His In-carna-tion.

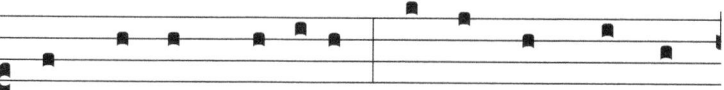

5) Maid all maids ex-celling, Passing meek and low-

ly, Win for sinners pardon, Make us chaste and ho-

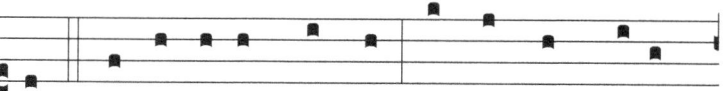

ly. 6) As we onward journey Aid our weak endeav-

or, Till we gaze on Je-sus And re-joice forev-er.

7) Fa-ther, Son, and Spirit Three in One confessing,

Give we e-qual glo-ry E-qual praise and blessing.

†102: Ave, maris stella

A song for the Blessed Virgin when her office is celebrated on Saturdays in the monastery.
For the Blessed Virgin at Vespers.

France: Paris (ca. 1255)

F–G

A - ve, Star of O-cean, Child Di-vine who

bar- est, Mother, Ever-Vir-gin, Heaven's Por-

tal fair-est. 2) Taking that sweet A-ve Erst by

Anonymous (9th c.)
tr. John Athelstan Laurie Riley

Gabriel spo- ken, Eva's name re- versing,   Be

of peace the to- ken. 3) Break the sinners' fet-

ters, Light to blind re-stor-ing, All our ills dispel-

ling,   Every boon implor-ing. 4) Show thyself a

Mother   In thy supplica- tion; He will hear who

chose thee   At His In-carna- tion. 5) Maid all

maids ex-celling, Passing meek and low-ly, Win for

sinners pardon,   Make us chaste and ho- ly.

6) As we onward journey   Aid our weak endeav-or,

Till we gaze on Je- sus   And re-joice forev-

er. 7) Fa-ther, Son, and Spirit   Three in One con-

fess-ing, Give we e-qual glo-ry   E-qual praise

and blessing.

†103: Ave, maris stella

On the Purification of Blessed Mary
at Compline.

Switzerland: Fribourg (14th c.)

G–E

A - ve, Star of O-cean, Child Di-vine who bar-

Anonymous (9th c.)
tr. John Athelstan Laurie Riley

P: 1a, R, 1b, R, 2a, R, 2b, R, etc.
R2 after 2a and 2b only

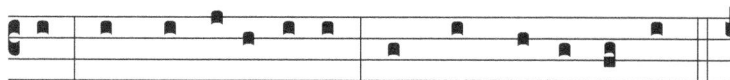

est, Mother, Ever-Virgin, Heaven's Portal fairest.

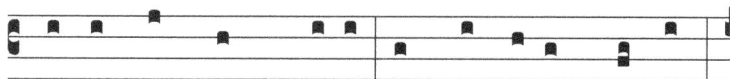

2) Taking that sweet A-ve Erst by Gabriel spoken,

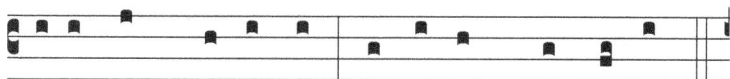

Eva's name re-versing, Be of peace the to-ken.

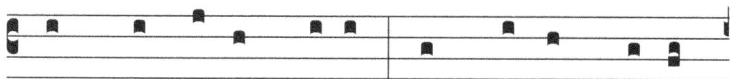

3) Break the sinners' fetters, Light to blind re-stor-

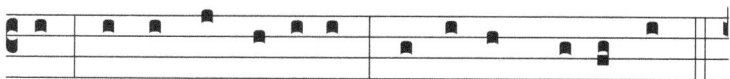

ing, All our ills dispelling, Every boon imploring.

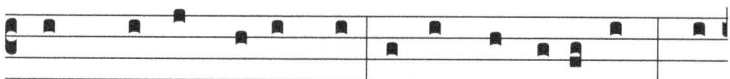

4) Show thyself a Mother In thy supplica-tion; He

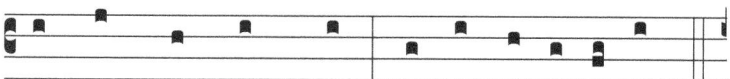

will hear who chose thee At His In-carna-tion.

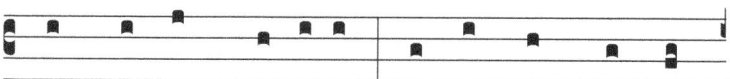

5) Maid all maids ex-celling, Passing meek and low-

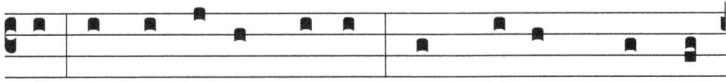

ly, Win for sinners pardon, Make us chaste and ho-

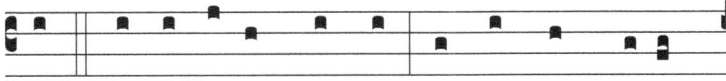

ly. 6) As we onward journey Aid our weak endeav-

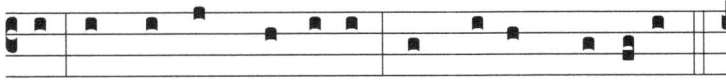

or, Till we gaze on Je-sus And re-joice forever.

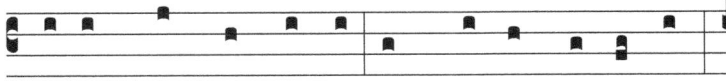

7) Fa-ther, Son, and Spirit Three in One confessing,

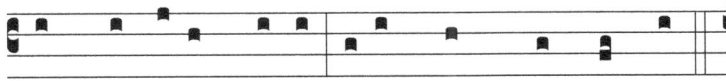

Give we e-qual glory E-qual praise and blessing.

A-men, A-men, A-men, A-men, A-men, A-men.

R1) Holy Mari-a, Holy, most ho-ly, Mari-a.

R2) Holy Mari-a, Holy, most ho-ly, Mari-a.

†104: Ave, maris stella

On the Assumption of Blessed Mary
at a Nocturn.

France: Normandy (14th–15th c.)

C–D

A - ve, Star of O- cean, Child Di-vine who

barest, Mother, Ever-Vir-gin, Heaven's Portal fair-

est. 2) Taking that sweet A- ve Erst by Gabriel

spoken, Eva's name re-versing, Be of peace the to-

ken. 3) Break the sinners' fet- ters, Light to blind re-

storing, All our ills dispel-ling, Every boon implor-

ing. 4) Show thyself a Mother In thy supplica-tion;

Anonymous (9th c.)
tr. John Athelstan Laurie Riley

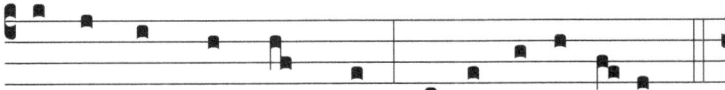

He will hear who chose thee At His In-carna-tion.

5) Maid all maids ex-cel- ling, Passing meek and low-

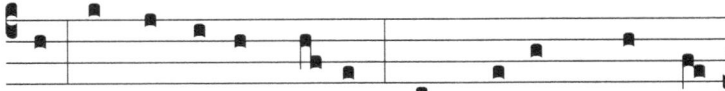

ly, Win for sinners pardon, Make us chaste and ho-

ly. 6) As we onward journey Aid our weak endeav-

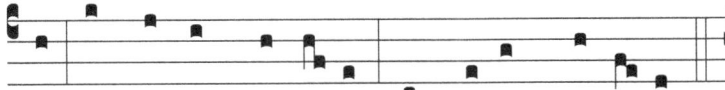

or, Till we gaze on Je-sus And re-joice forev-er.

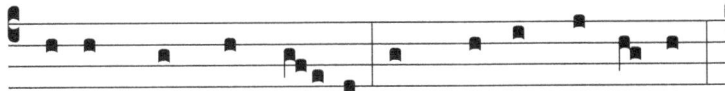

7) Fa-ther, Son, and Spir-it Three in One confessing,

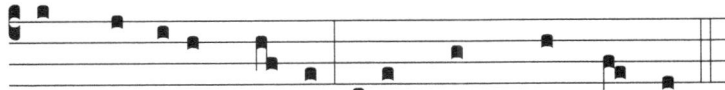

Give we e-qual glo-ry E-qual praise and blessing.

†105: Ave, maris stella

At Vespers.

Austria: Klosterneuburg (1336)

E–F

A - ve, Star of O- cean, Child Di- vine who

barest, Mother, Ever-Virgin, Heaven's Portal fair-

est. 2) Taking that sweet A-ve Erst by Ga-briel spo-

ken, Eva's name re-versing, Be of peace the to-

ken. 3) Break the sin-ners' fetters, Light to blind

re- storing, All our ills dis-pelling, Every boon

im-ploring. 4) Show thyself a Mother In thy sup-

Anonymous (9th c.)
tr. John Athelstan Laurie Riley

(1) iv:5

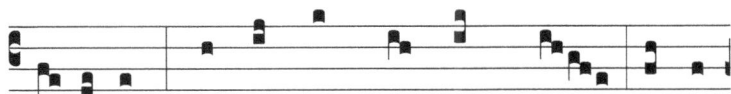

pli-ca-tion; He will hear who chose thee   At His

In-carna-tion. 5) Maid all maids ex-celling, Passing

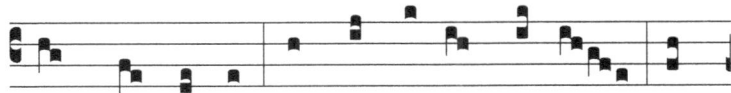

meek and lowly, Win for sinners pardon,   Make

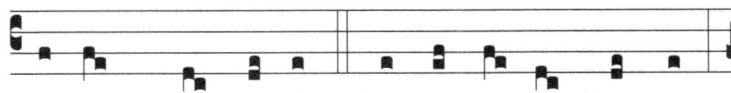

us chaste and ho-ly. 6) As we on-ward journey

Aid our weak en-deavor, Till we gaze on Je-sus

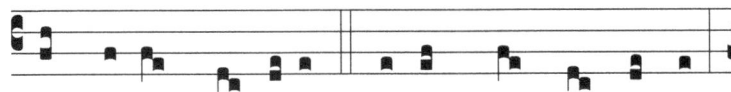

And re-joice for-ever. 7) Fa-ther, Son, and Spirit

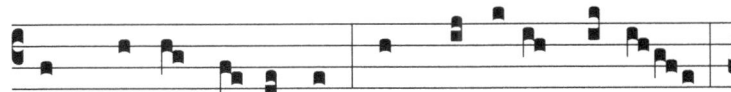

Three in One confessing, Give we e-qual glory

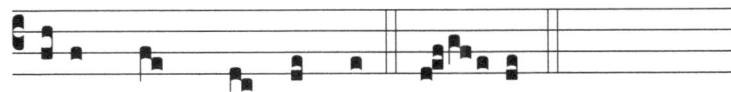

E-qual praise and blessing. A-   men.

308

†106: Beata nobis gaudia

On the holy day of Pentecost.

Germany: Kempten (ca. 1000)

F–F

B lest season! which with gladness fraught, A-

gain the circling year hath brought, When bright

o'er each disci-ple's head, The Spirit Para- clete

was shed. 2) The lambent flames with flickering ray,

The shape of tongue-like forms display; That el-o-

quent their speech may be, And fervent they in

chari- ty. 3) God in all languages they praise, The

Anonymous (9th c.)
tr. John David Chambers

Gentiles listen in a-maze, And mock, as if new wine

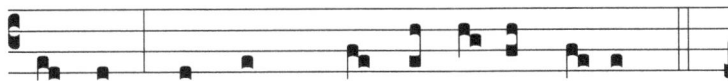

had fired The breasts His Spirit had in- spired.

4) 'Tis here all mystic figures meet; The Paschal days

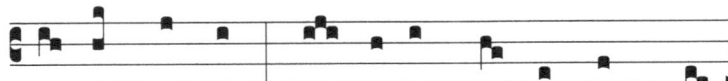

are now complete; That sa-cred number which set

free The debtor, by the law's de-cree. 5) O God of

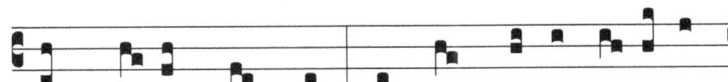

love! be-fore Thee now Thy flock in suppli-ca-tion

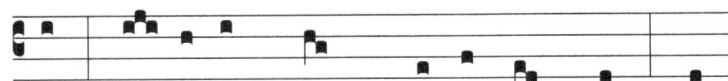

bow; On us from Heaven, in plenteous store, The

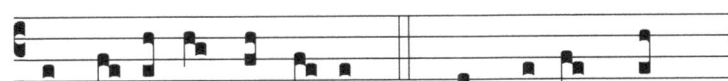

graces of Thy Spirit pour. 6) And as their breasts,

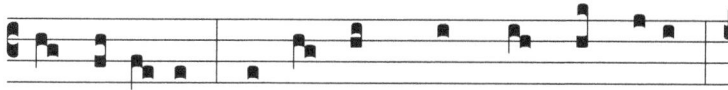

this festal tide, By Thy sweet gifts were sancti-fied;

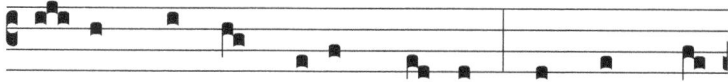

Do Thou our sins, O Lord! for-give, And grant us

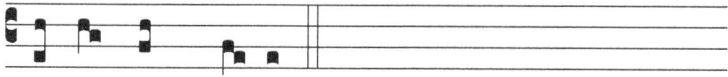

in Thy peace to live.

†107: Beata nobis gaudia

On Pentecost at Vespers.

France: Nevers (12th c.)

A–B

Blest season! which with gladness fraught,

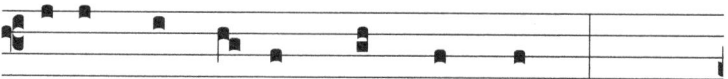

A- gain the cir- cling year hath brought, When

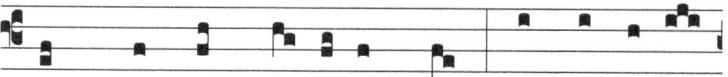

bright o'er each dis-ci-ple's head, The Spirit Par-

Anonymous (9th c.)
tr. John David Chambers

a- clete was shed. 2) The lambent flames with flick-

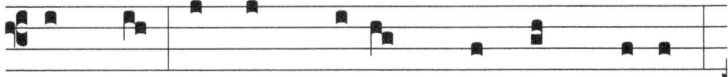

ering ray, The shape of tongue-like forms display;

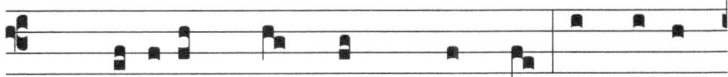

That el-o-quent their speech may be, And fervent

they in chari- ty. 3) God in all languages they

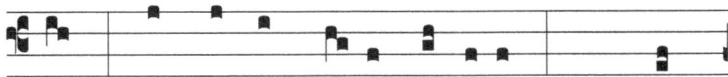

praise, The Gentiles lis-ten in a-maze, And mock,

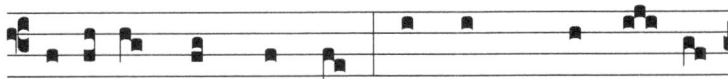

as if new wine had fired The breasts His Spir-it

had in-spired. 4) 'Tis here all mystic figures meet;

The Paschal days are now complete; That sa-cred

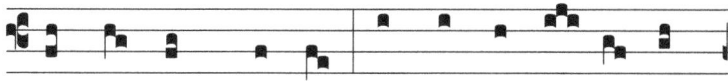

number which set free The debtor, by   the law's

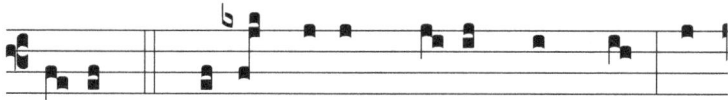

de-cree. 5) O God of love! be-fore Thee now Thy

flock in supplica-tion bow; On us from Heaven, in

plenteous store, The graces of   Thy Spirit pour.

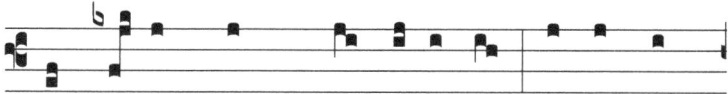

6) And as their breasts, this festal tide, By Thy sweet

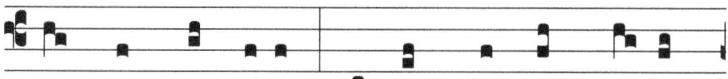

gifts were sancti-fied; Do Thou our sins, O   Lord!

forgive, And grant us in   Thy peace to live.

†108: Beata nobis gaudia

On Pentecost at Nocturns.

Central or southern Italy (ca. 1267)

C–C

B lest season! which with gladness fraught, A-

gain the circling year hath brought, When bright

o'er each disci- ple's head, The Spirit Para- clete

was shed. 2) The lambent flames with flickering ray,

The shape of tongue-like forms display; That el-

o- quent their speech may be, And fervent they

in chari- ty. 3) God in all languages they praise,

Anonymous (9th c.)
tr. John David Chambers

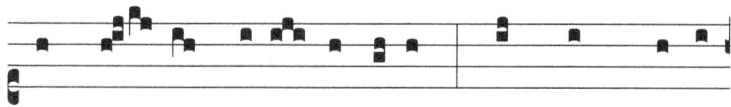

The Gen- tiles listen in a-maze, And mock, as if

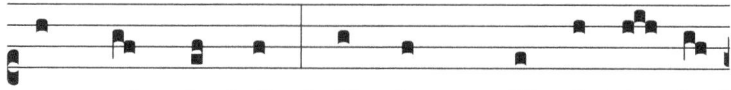

new wine had fired The breasts His Spirit had

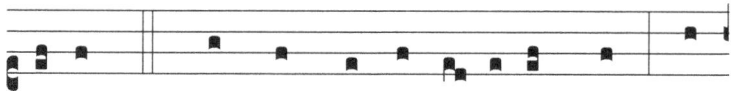

in-spired. 4) 'Tis here all mystic figures meet; The

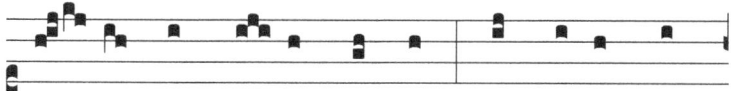

Pas- chal days are now complete; That sa-cred num-

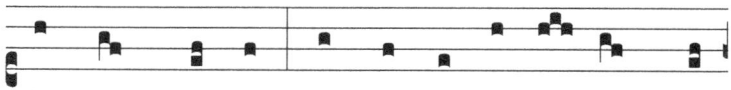

ber which set free The debtor, by the law's de-

cree. 5) O God of love! be-fore Thee now Thy flock

in suppli- ca-tion bow; On us from Heaven, in plen-

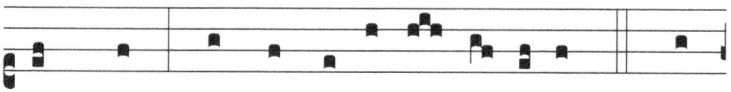

teous store, The graces of Thy Spirit pour. 6) And

as their breasts, this festal tide, By Thy sweet gifts

were sancti-fied; Do Thou our sins, O Lord! forgive,

And grant us in Thy peace to live.

†109: Beata nobis gaudia

On Pentecost at Vespers.

France: Paris (ca. 1255)

F–E

Blest season! which with glad-ness fraught,

A-gain the cir-cling year hath brought, When bright

o'er each disci- ple's head, The Spirit Para- clete

was shed. 2) The lambent flames with flickering ray,

Anonymous (9th c.)
tr. John David Chambers

The shape of tongue-like forms dis-play; That el-o-

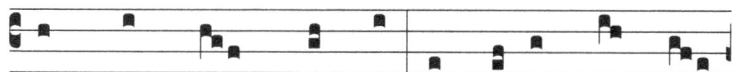

quent their speech may be, And fervent they in

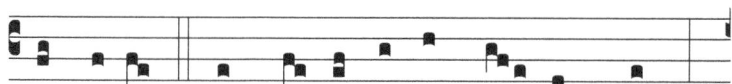

chari- ty. 3) God in all languages   they praise,

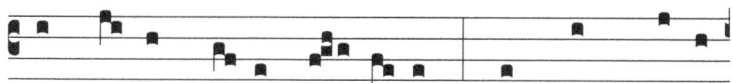

The Gentiles lis-ten in   a- maze, And mock, as if

new wine had fired The breasts His Spirit   had in-

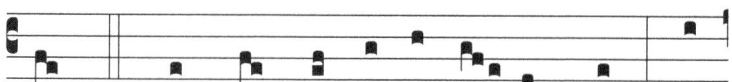

spired. 4) 'Tis here all mystic fig- ures meet; The

Paschal days are now complete; That sa-cred num-

ber which set free The debtor, by the law's de-cree. 5) O God of love! be-fore Thee now Thy flock

in supplica- tion bow; On us from Heaven, in plen-

teous store, The graces of Thy Spirit pour. 6) And

as their breasts, this fes- tal tide, By Thy sweet gifts

were sanc-ti- fied; Do Thou our sins, O Lord! for-

give, And grant us in Thy peace to live.

†110: Beata nobis gaudia

On the vigil of Pentecost
at Vespers.

France: Châlons-en-Champagne (1300–1350)

D–C

Blest season! which with gladness fraught, A-

gain the circling year hath brought, When bright

o'er each disci- ple's head, The Spirit Para- clete was

shed. 2) The lambent flames with flickering ray, The

shape of tongue-like forms display; That el- o-quent

their speech may be, And fervent they in chari-

Anonymous (9th c.)
tr. John David Chambers

ty. 3) God in all languages they praise, The Gen-

tiles listen in a-maze, And mock, as if new wine

had fired The breasts His Spirit had in-spired. 4) 'Tis

here all mystic figures meet; The Paschal days are

now complete; That sa-cred number which set free

The debtor, by the law's de-cree. 5) O God of love!

be-fore Thee now Thy flock in supplica-tion bow;

On us from Heaven, in plenteous store, The graces of Thy Spirit pour. 6) And as their breasts, this

festal tide, By Thy sweet gifts were sancti-fied; Do

Thou our sins, O Lord! for-give, And grant us in

Thy peace to live.

†111: Beata nobis gaudia

For the Holy Spirit
at Lauds.

Czech Republic: Prague (1300–1350)

D–E

Blest sea-son! which with gladness fraught,

A-gain the circling year hath brought, When bright

o'er each dis-ci- ple's head, The Spirit Para- clete

was shed. 2) The lambent flames with flickering ray,

The shape of tongue-like forms dis-play; That el-

o- quent their speech may be, And fervent they

in chari- ty. 3) God in all languages they praise,

Anonymous (9th c.)
tr. John David Chambers

(1) iii:3–4, iv:3, (2) iv:3

The Gentiles listen in a- maze, And mock, as if

new wine had fired The breasts His Spirit had in-

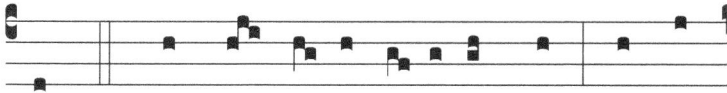

spired. 4) 'Tis here all mystic figures meet; The Pas-

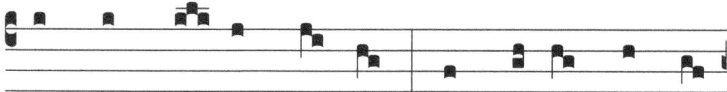

chal days are now complete; That sa-cred number

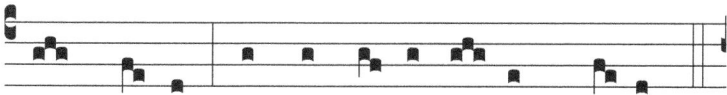

which set free The debtor, by the law's de-cree.

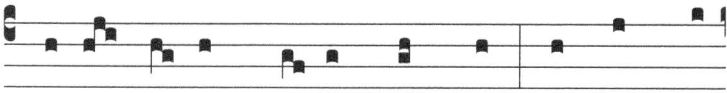

5) O God of love! be-fore Thee now Thy flock in

suppli- ca-tion bow; On us from Heaven, in plen-

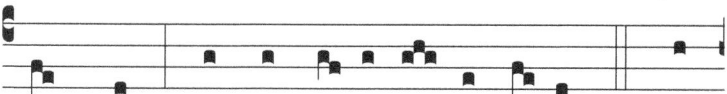

teous store, The graces of Thy Spirit pour. 6) And

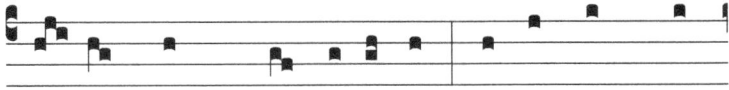

as their breasts, this festal tide, By Thy sweet gifts

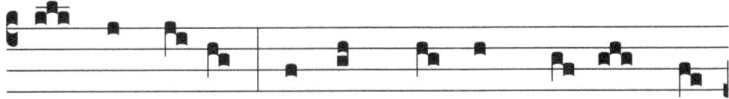

were sancti- fied; Do Thou our sins, O Lord! for-

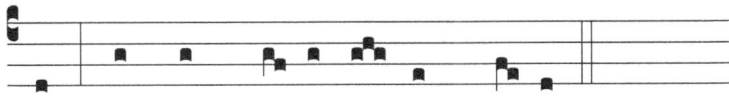

give, And grant us in Thy peace to live.

†112: Beata nobis gaudia

At Lauds, at Compline.

Austria: Klosterneuburg (1336)

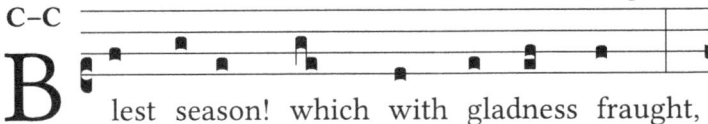

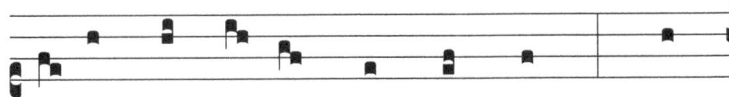

C–C

B lest season! which with gladness fraught,

A- gain the cir- cling year hath brought, When

bright o'er each disci-ple's head, The Spirit Para-

Anonymous (9th c.)
tr. John David Chambers

clete was shed. 2) The lambent flames with flick-

ering ray, The shape of tongue-like forms display;

That el- o- quent their speech may be, And fer-

vent they in chari- ty. 3) God in all languages they

praise, The Gentiles lis-ten in a-maze, And mock,

as if new wine had fired The breasts His Spirit

had in-spired. 4) 'Tis here all mystic figures meet;

The Paschal days are now complete; That sa-cred

number which set free The debtor, by the law's de-

cree. 5) O God of love! be-fore Thee now Thy flock

in suppli-ca-tion bow; On us from Heaven, in plen-

teous store, The graces of Thy Spirit pour. 6) And

as their breasts, this festal tide, By Thy sweet gifts

were sancti-fied; Do Thou our sins, O Lord! for-give,

And grant us in Thy peace to live. A- men.

†113: Nunc, sancte nobis Spiritus

At Terce.

France: Fécamp (12th–13th c.)

C–A

Come, Holy Ghost, who ever One Reignest

with Fa-ther and with Son, It is the hour, our

souls possess With Thy full flood of ho-li-ness.

2) Let flesh, and heart, and lips, and mind, Sound forth

our witness to mankind; And love light up our

mortal frame, Till others catch the living flame.

Anonymous (9th c.)
tr. John Henry Newman

†114: Nunc, sancte nobis Spiritus

France: Fécamp (12th–13th c.)

D–D

Come, Ho- ly Ghost, who ev- er One

Reignest with Fa-ther and with Son, It is the hour,

our souls possess With Thy full flood of ho- li-

ness. 2) Let flesh, and heart, and lips, and mind,

Sound forth our witness to mankind; And love

light up our mortal frame, Till others catch the

liv- ing flame.

Anonymous (9th c.)
tr. John Henry Newman

†115: Nunc, sancte nobis Spiritus

England (12th–13th c.)

C—C

Come, Holy Ghost, who ev-er   One Reignest

with Fa-ther and with Son, It is the hour, our souls

pos- sess With Thy full flood of ho-li-   ness. 2) Let

flesh, and heart, and lips, and mind, Sound forth

our witness to man- kind; And love light up our

mortal   frame, Till others catch the living   flame.

Anonymous (9th c.)
tr. John Henry Newman

†116: Nunc, sancte nobis Spiritus

At Terce with three lessons.

England: Worcester (ca. 1230)

D–D

Come, Holy Ghost, who ever One Reignest

with Fa-ther and with Son, It is the hour, our

souls possess With Thy full flood of ho-li-ness.

2) Let flesh, and heart, and lips, and mind, Sound forth

our witness to mankind; And love light up our

mortal frame, Till others catch the living flame.

Anonymous (9th c.)
tr. John Henry Newman

†117: Nunc, sancte nobis Spiritus

At the beginning of Advent, and the day of
Saint Thomas the apostle.

England: Worcester (ca. 1230)

D–E

Come, Holy Ghost, who ever One Reignest

with Fa-ther and with Son, It is the hour, our

souls possess With Thy full flood of ho-li-ness.

2) Let flesh, and heart, and lips, and mind, Sound forth

our witness to mankind; And love light up our mor-

tal frame, Till others catch the liv-ing flame.

Anonymous (9th c.)
tr. John Henry Newman

†118: Nunc, sancte nobis Spiritus

Sundays during the year except on solemn feasts
at Terce.

England: Worcester (ca. 1230)

C–D

Come, Ho- ly Ghost, who ever One Reignest

with Fa- ther and with Son, It is the hour, our

souls possess With Thy full flood of ho- li-

ness. 2) Let flesh, and heart, and lips, and mind,

Sound forth our wit- ness to mankind; And love

light up our mor- tal frame, Till others catch the

liv- ing flame.

Anonymous (9th c.)
tr. John Henry Newman

†119: Nunc, sancte nobis Spiritus

On the commemoration of Saints Oswald and Wulfstan
with twelve lessons.

England: Worcester (ca. 1230)

G–D

Come, Holy Ghost, who ever One Reignest

with Fa-ther and with Son, It is the hour, our souls

possess With Thy full flood of ho-li-ness. 2) Let

flesh, and heart, and lips, and mind, Sound forth our

witness to mankind; And love light up our mortal

frame, Till others catch the living flame.

Anonymous (9th c.)
tr. John Henry Newman

†120: Nunc, sancte nobis Spiritus

England: Worcester (ca. 1230)

G–G

Come, Ho- ly Ghost, who ev- er One

Reignest with Fa-ther and with Son, It is the

hour, our souls possess With Thy full flood of

ho- li-ness. 2) Let flesh, and heart, and lips,

and mind, Sound forth our witness to mankind;

And love light up our mortal frame, Till others

catch the liv- ing flame.

Anonymous (9th c.)
tr. John Henry Newman

†121: Nunc, sancte nobis Spiritus

At Terce on Sundays.

France: Châlons-en-Champagne (1309)

D–D

C ome, Holy Ghost, who ever One Reignest

with Fa-ther and with Son, It is the hour, our souls

possess With Thy full flood of ho- li- ness. 2) Let

flesh, and heart, and lips, and mind, Sound forth our

witness to mankind; And love light up our mortal

frame, Till others catch the living flame.

Anonymous (9th c.)
tr. John Henry Newman

†122: Nunc, sancte nobis Spiritus

At Terce on feasts with 9 lessons, and during
the octave of solemnities and on
the octave of solemnities.

France: Châlons-en-Champagne (1309)

C–B

Come, Holy Ghost, who ever One Reignest

with Fa-ther and with Son, It is the hour, our souls

possess With Thy full flood of ho-li-ness. 2) Let

flesh, and heart, and lips, and mind, Sound forth our

witness to mankind; And love light up our mortal

frame, Till others catch the living flame.

Anonymous (9th c.)
tr. John Henry Newman

†123: Nunc, sancte nobis Spiritus

At Terce.

Austria: Klosterneuburg (1336)

Come, Holy Ghost, who ever One Reignest

with Fa-ther and with Son, It is the hour, our souls

pos-sess With Thy full flood of ho- li- ness.

2) Let flesh, and heart, and lips, and mind, Sound forth

our witness to man-kind; And love light up our

mortal frame, Till oth- ers catch the liv- ing flame.

Anonymous (9th c.)
tr. John Henry Newman

(1) ii:7

†124: Nunc, sancte nobis Spiritus

On ferias at Terce.

Austria: Sankt Florian (15th c.)

E–G

Come, Holy Ghost, who ever One Reignest

with Fa-ther and with Son, It is the hour, our souls

possess With Thy full flood of ho- li- ness. 2) Let

flesh, and heart, and lips, and mind, Sound forth our

witness to mankind; And love light up our mortal

frame, Till others catch the living flame.

Anonymous (9th c.)
tr. John Henry Newman

†125: Aeterna caeli gloria

At Lauds.

Italy: Verona (11th c.)

D–B

E - ternal Glory of the sky, Blest hope of frail

humani- ty, The Fa-ther's Sole-begotten One,

Yet born a spotless Virgin's Son! 2) Uplift us with

Thine arm of might, And let our hearts rise pure

and bright: And ar-dent in God's praises, pay

The thanks we owe Him every day. 3) The Day-

star's rays are glittering clear, And tell that Day

Anonymous (9th–10th c.)
tr. John Mason Neale

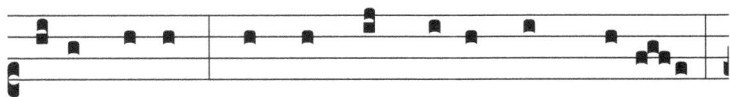

it-self is near: The shadows of the night depart:

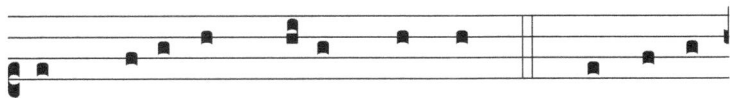

Thou, Holy Light, il-lume the heart! 4) Within our

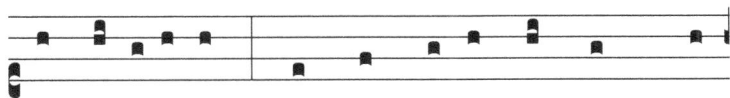

senses ever dwell, And worldly darkness thence ex-

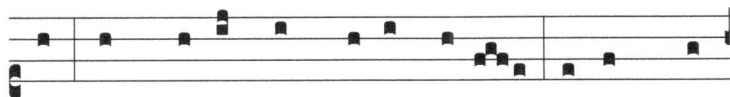

pel: Long as the days of life endure, Preserve our

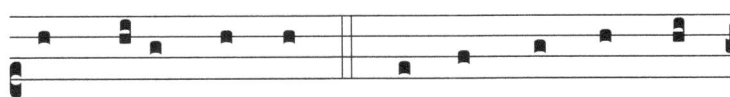

souls devout and pure: 5) The Faith that first must

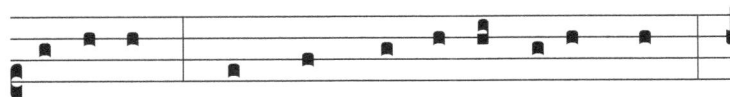

be possess'd, Root deep within our inmost breast:

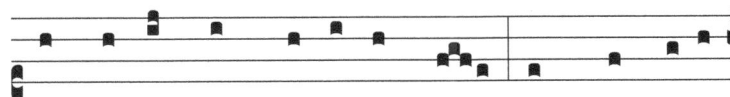

And joyous Hope in second place, Then Chari- ty,

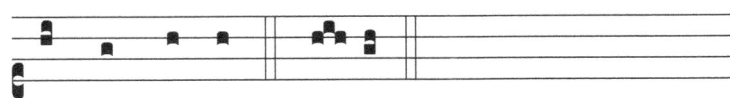

Thy greatest grace. A- men.

†126: Caeli Deus sanctissime

At Vespers.

Italy: Verona (11th c.)

D–A

O God, Whose hand hath spread the sky

And all its shining hosts on high, And painting

it with fiery light, Made it so beauteous and so

bright: 2) Thou, when the Wednesday was begun,

Didst frame the circle of the Sun, And set the Moon

for or-dered change, And planets for their wider

range: 3) To night and day, by certain line, Their

Anonymous (9th–10th c.)
tr. John Mason Neale

(1) ii:4

varying bounds Thou didst as-sign; And gav'st a

signal, known and meet, For months begun and

months complete: 4) Enlighten Thou the hearts of

men: Polluted souls make pure a-gain: Unloose the

bands of guilt within: Remove the burden of our sin.

†127: Christe, redemptor omnium

At a Nocturn.

Italy: Verona (11th c.)

B–A

O Christ, Redeemer of our race, Thou

Brightness of the Fa-ther's Face, Of Him and with

Anonymous (9th–10th c.)
tr. Henry Williams Baker

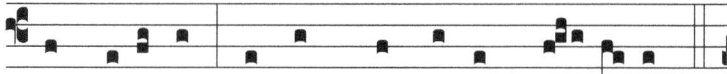

Him ever One, Ere times and seasons had be-gun;

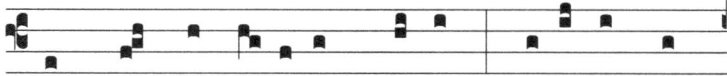

2) Thou that art very Light of Light, Unfailing Hope

in sin's dark night, Hear Thou the prayers Thy peo-

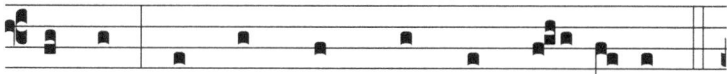

ple pray The wide world o'er, this blessed day.

3) Remember, Lord of Life and Grace, How once, to

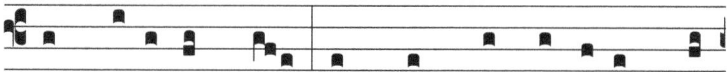

save a ru-ined race, Thou didst our very flesh as-

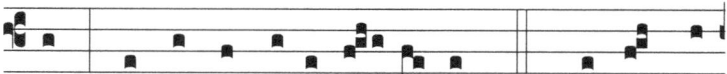

sume In Mary's unde-fil- ed womb. 4) To-day, as

year by year its light Sheds o'er the world a ra-

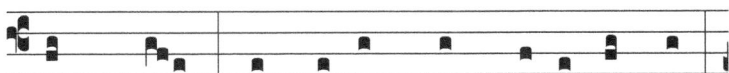

diance bright, One precious truth is echoed on,

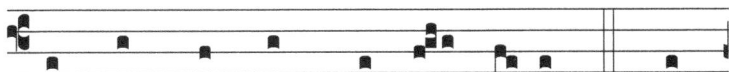

"'Tis Thou hast saved us, Thou a- lone." 5) Thou

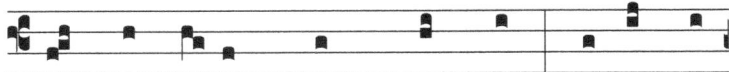

from the Fa-ther's Throne didst come To call His

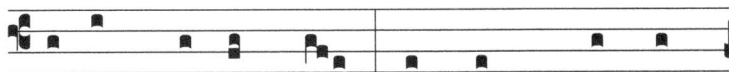

banished children home; And heaven, and earth,

and sea and shore His Love Who sent Thee here

a- dore. 6) And gladsome too are we to-day,

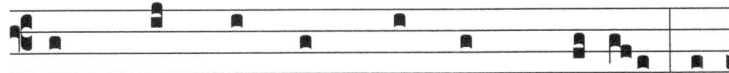

Whose guilt Thy Blood has washed a-way; Re-

deemed, the new-made song we sing; It is the

Birthday of our King. A- men.

344

†128: Christe, redemptor omnium

*On the Nativity of the Lord
at First Nocturn.*

Switzerland: Lausanne (13th c.)

D–D

O Christ, Redeemer of our race, Thou

Brightness of the Fa- ther's Face, Of Him and

with Him ever One, Ere times and sea- sons had

be- gun; 2) Thou that art very Light of Light,

Un- failing Hope in sin's dark night, Hear Thou

the prayers Thy people pray The wide world o'er,

Anonymous (9th–10th c.)
tr. Henry Williams Baker

this blessed day. 3) Remember, Lord of Life and

Grace, How once, to save a ru-ined race, Thou

didst our very flesh as-sume In Mary's un-de-

fil-ed womb. 4) To-day, as year by year its light

Sheds o'er the world a ra-diance bright, One pre-

cious truth is echoed on, "'Tis Thou hast saved us,

Thou a-lone." 5) Thou from the Fa-ther's Throne

didst come To call His ban-ished chil-dren home;

And heaven, and earth, and sea and shore His Love

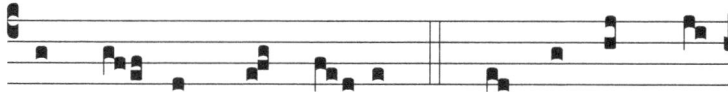

Who sent Thee here a-   dore. 6) And gladsome too

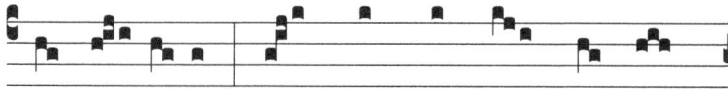

are we   to-day, Whose guilt Thy Blood has washed

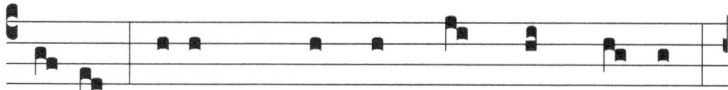

a- way; Redeemed, the new-made song we sing;

It is the Birthday of our King.

†129: Christe, redemptor omnium

At Matins.

England: Worcester (ca. 1230)

D–D

O Christ, Redeemer of our race, Thou

Anonymous (9th–10th c.)
tr. Henry Williams Baker

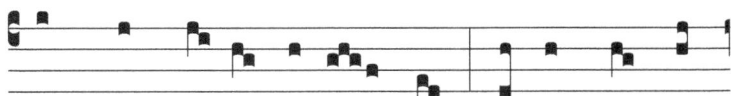

Brightness of the Fa-ther's Face, Of Him and with

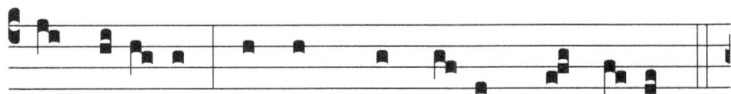

Him ever One, Ere times and seasons had be-gun;

2) Thou that art very Light of Light, Un- failing

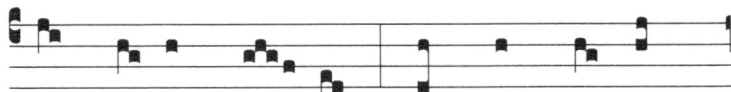

Hope in sin's dark night, Hear Thou the prayers

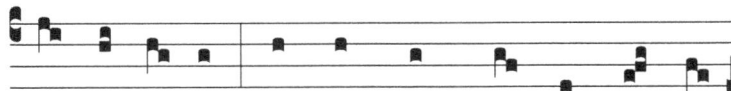

Thy people pray The wide world o'er, this blessed

day. 3) Re- member, Lord of Life and Grace, How

once, to save a ru-ined race, Thou didst our very

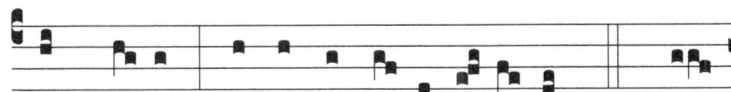

flesh as- sume In Mary's un-de-fil-ed womb. 4) To-

day, as year by year its light Sheds o'er the world

a ra-diance bright, One precious truth is echoed

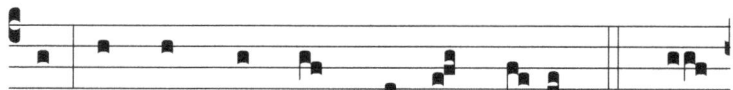

on, "'Tis Thou hast saved us, Thou a- lone." 5) Thou

from the Fa-ther's Throne didst come To call His

banished children home; And heaven, and earth, and

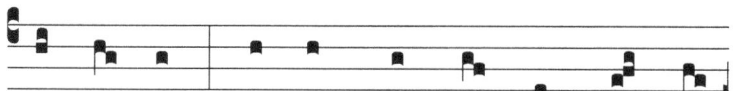

sea and shore His Love Who sent Thee here a-

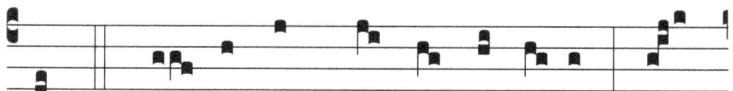

dore. 6) And gladsome too are we to-day, Whose

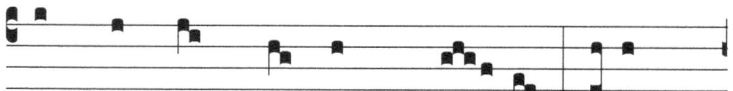

guilt Thy Blood has washed a- way; Redeemed,

the new-made song we sing; It is the Birthday of

our King.

†130: Christe, redemptor omnium

On the Nativity of the Lord
at Nocturns.

Switzerland: Engelberg (ca. 1400)

C–B

O Christ, Re- deemer of our race, Thou

Brightness of the Fa-ther's Face, Of Him and with

Him ever One, Ere times and seasons had begun;

2) Thou that art very Light of Light, Unfailing Hope

Anonymous (9th–10th c.)
tr. Henry Williams Baker

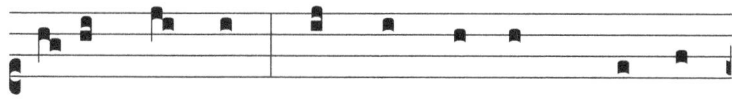

in sin's dark night, Hear Thou the prayers Thy peo-

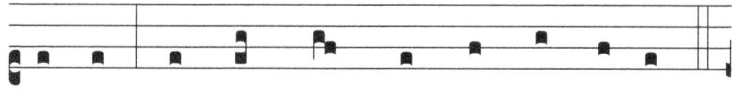

ple pray The wide world o'er, this blessed day.

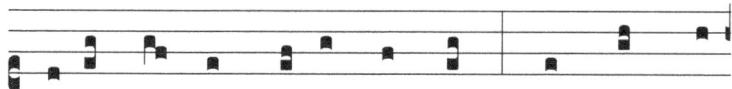

3) Remember, Lord of Life and Grace, How once, to

save a ru-ined race, Thou didst our very flesh as-

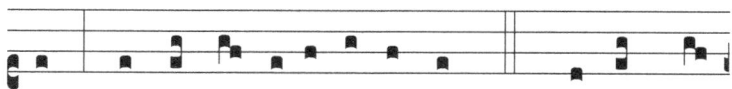

sume In Mary's unde-fil-ed womb. 4) To-day, as

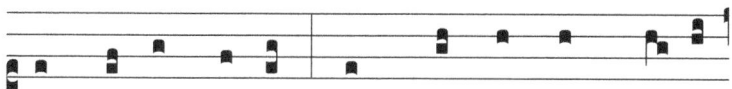

year by year its light Sheds o'er the world a ra-

diance bright, One precious truth is echoed on, "'Tis

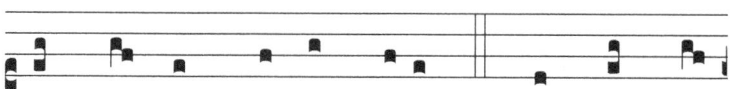

Thou hast saved us, Thou a- lone." 5) Thou from the

Fa-ther's Throne didst come To call His banished

children home; And heaven, and earth, and sea and

shore His Love Who sent Thee here a-dore. 6) And

gladsome too are we to-day, Whose guilt Thy Blood

has washed a- way; Redeemed, the new-made song

we sing; It is the Birthday of our King.

†131: Conditor alme siderum

During the Advent of the Lord
at Vespers.

Germany: Kempten (ca. 1000)

C–A

F air Framer of the stars so bright, Thou of

be- lieving hearts the light, Thou blessed Christ,

Redeemer dear, Vouchsafe our humble prayers to

hear. 2) In sov'reign pity Thou didst see The sin-

ner's coming miser-y; Thou didst the healing med-

'cine give, That so a dy-ing world might live.

3) And, like a bridegroom from his bower, Thou didst,

Anonymous (9th–10th c.)
tr. Alfred Edersheim

sel: 1–4, 6–7

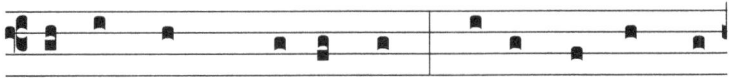

in our world's vesper- hour, A- mid its quickly

deepening gloom, Come from the Virgin-Mother's

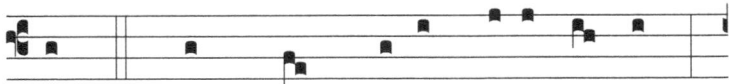

womb. 4) Whose power di-vine upon Thy throne

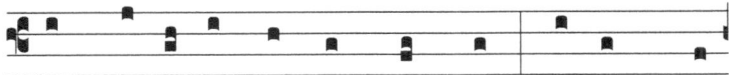

Shall every bending knee once own; All things in

earth and heaven high Acknowledge Thy suprem-

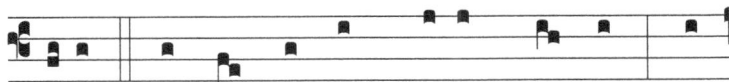

a- cy. 5) The sun, his wings of light who folds, The

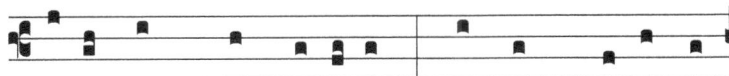

pallid moon, who vigil holds, The sheen of yonder

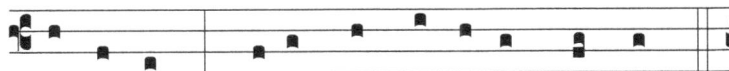

starry band— O- bey Thy sover- eign command.

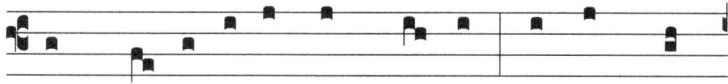

6) Thou, Ho-ly Je-su, when we call, Oh hear, Thou

coming Judge of all, And from the treach'rous en-

'my's dart To us Thy safety, Lord, impart! 7) Now

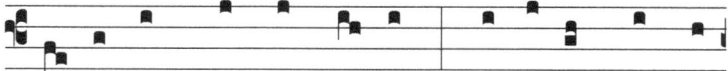

glo-ry, laud, and loudest praise To Fa-ther and to

Son we raise, And to the Holy Para- clete, As ev-

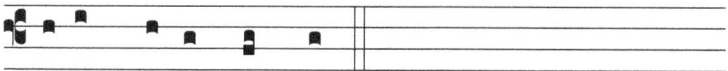

ermore is due and meet.

†132: Conditor alme siderum

Sundays during the Advent of the Lord.

Italy: Verona (11th c.)

F air Framer of the stars so bright, Thou of

be- lieving hearts the light, Thou blessed Christ,

Redeemer dear, Vouchsafe our humble prayers to

hear. 2) In sov'reign pit-y Thou didst see The sin-

ner's coming miser-y; Thou didst the healing med-

'cine give, That so a dy-ing world might live.

3) And, like a bridegroom from his bower, Thou didst,

Anonymous (9th–10th c.)
tr. Alfred Edersheim

sel: 1–4, 6–7

in our world's vesper- hour, A- mid its quickly

deepening gloom, Come from the Virgin-Mother's

womb. 4) Whose power di- vine upon Thy throne

Shall eve- ry bending knee once own; All things in

earth and heaven high Acknowledge Thy su-prem-

a- cy. 5) The sun, his wings of light who folds, The

pal- lid moon, who vig-il holds, The sheen of yon-

der starry band— O-bey Thy sover- eign command.

6) Thou, Holy Je- su, when we call, Oh hear, Thou

coming Judge of all, And from the treach'rous en-

'my's dart To us Thy safety, Lord, impart! 7) Now

glory, laud, and loudest praise To Fa- ther and to

Son we raise, And to the Ho-ly Para- clete, As ev-

ermore is due and meet. A- men.

†133: Conditor alme siderum

Sundays in the Advent of the Lord
at Vespers.

France: Nevers (12th c.)

C–D

Fair Framer of the stars so bright, Thou of

be- lieving hearts the light, Thou blessed Christ,

Redeemer dear, Vouchsafe our humble prayers to

hear. 2) In sov'reign pity Thou didst see The sin-

ner's coming miser-y; Thou didst the heal-ing med-

'cine give, That so a dy- ing world might live.

3) And, like a bridegroom from his bower, Thou didst,

Anonymous (9th–10th c.)
tr. Alfred Edersheim

(2–7) ii:4, iii:3
sel: 1–4, 6–7

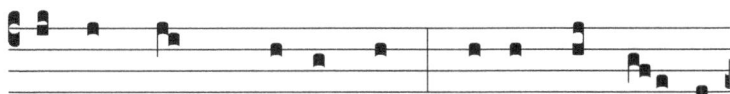

in our world's vesper- hour, A- mid its quickly

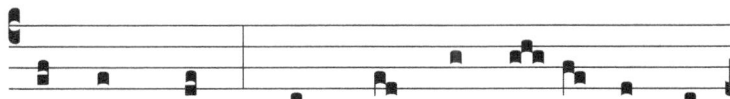

deepening gloom, Come from the Vir-gin-Mother's

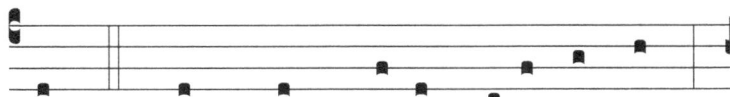

womb. 4) Whose power di-vine upon Thy throne

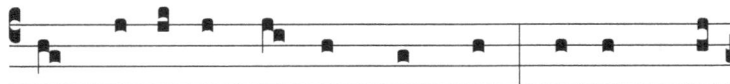

Shall every bending knee once own; All things in

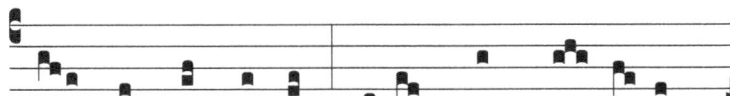

earth and heaven high Acknowledge Thy su-prem-

a- cy. 5) The sun, his wings of light who folds, The

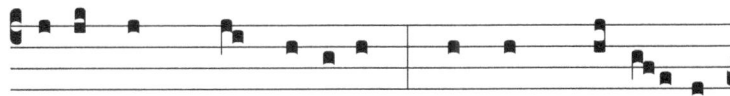

pallid moon, who vigil holds, The sheen of yon-der

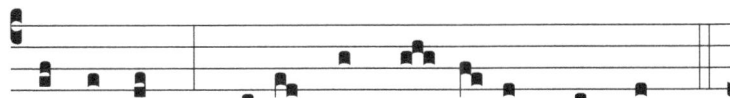

starry band— O-bey Thy sov-er- eign command.

6) Thou, Holy Je-su, when we call, Oh hear, Thou

coming Judge of all, And from the treach'rous en-

'my's dart To us Thy safe-ty, Lord, impart! 7) Now

glory, laud, and loudest praise To Fa-ther and to

Son we raise, And to the Ho- ly Para-clete, As ev-

ermore is due and meet.

†134: Deus, tuorum militum

France: Moissac (ca. 1000)

C–A

O f all Thy warrior Saints, O Lord! The por-

tion, crown, and great re-ward, As we Thy Martyr's

praises chant, Forgiveness to our er-rors grant.

2) From earth and its de-lu-sive joys, Its hurtful blan-

dishments and toys, As transient all, he turned a-

way, And reached the heavenly realms of Day.

3) By him the painful course was run, The shame en-

Anonymous (9th–10th c.)
tr. John David Chambers

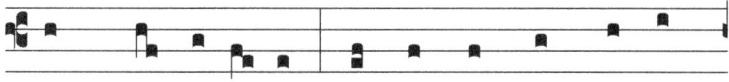

dured, the glory won; For Thy dear sake his blood

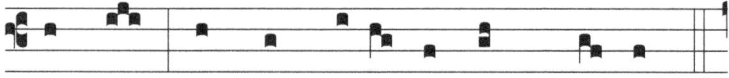

was shed, And gifts e- ter- nal crown his head.

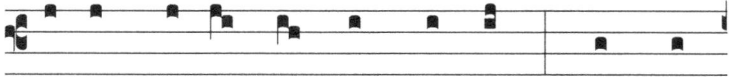

4) To Thee we therefore make our prayer, Most mer-

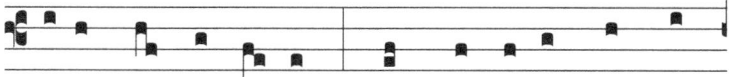

ci-ful! Thy people spare; That we, in this Thy Mar-

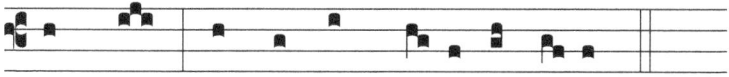

tyr's Feast, May joy from every sin re- leased.

†135: Deus, tuorum militum

One martyr.

France: Nevers (12th c.)

C–D

O f all Thy warrior Saints, O Lord! The por-

tion, crown, and great reward, As we Thy Martyr's

praises chant, Forgiveness to our er-rors grant.

2) From earth and its de-lu-sive joys, Its hurtful blan-

dishments and toys, As transient all, he turned a-

way, And reached the heavenly realms of Day.

3) By him the painful course was run, The shame en-

Anonymous (9th–10th c.)   (1) ii:7, (2–4) iv:2
tr. John David Chambers

dured, the glory won; For Thy dear sake his blood

was shed, And gifts e- ternal crown his head.

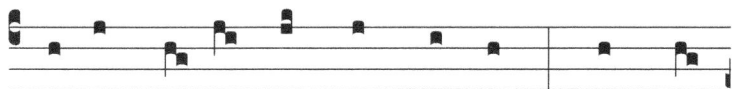

4) To Thee we therefore make our prayer, Most mer-

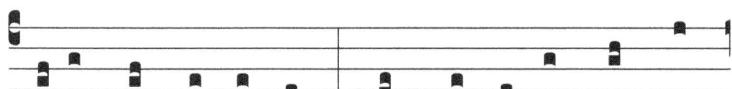

ci-ful! Thy people spare; That we, in this Thy Mar-

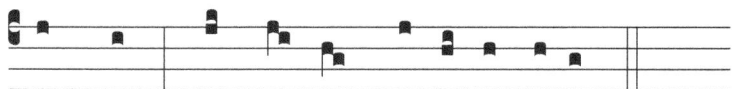

tyr's Feast, May joy from every sin re-leased.

†136: Deus, tuorum militum

For one martyr.

Austria: Heiligenkreuz (12th–13th c.)

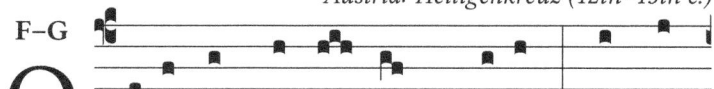

F–G

O f all Thy warrior Saints, O Lord! The por-

Anonymous (9th–10th c.)
tr. John David Chambers

tion, crown, and great re- ward, As we Thy Mar-

tyr's praises chant, Forgiveness to our er- rors

grant. 2) From earth and its de- lu- sive joys, Its

hurtful blandishments and toys, As transient all, he

turned a- way, And reached the heavenly realms

of Day. 3) By him the painful course was run,

The shame endured, the glory won; For Thy dear

sake his blood was shed, And gifts e- ternal crown

his head. 4) To Thee we therefore make our prayer,

Most merci-ful! Thy people spare; That we, in this

Thy Martyr's Feast, May joy from every sin re-

leased.

†137: Deus, tuorum militum

On the vigil of one martyr
at Vespers and at Nocturns.

Southern Italy (13th c.)

C–B

Of all Thy warrior Saints, O Lord! The por-

tion, crown, and great reward, As we Thy Martyr's

Anonymous (9th–10th c.)
tr. John David Chambers

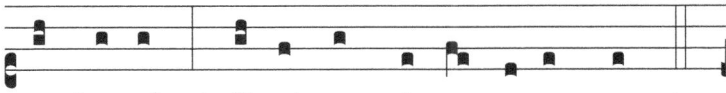

praises chant, Forgiveness to our er-rors grant.

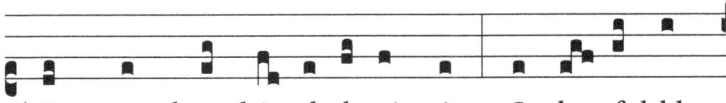

2) From earth and its de-lu-sive joys, Its hurtful blan-

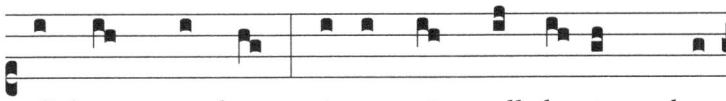

dishments and toys, As transient all, he turned a-

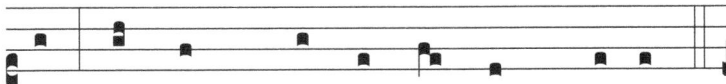

way, And reached the heavenly realms of Day.

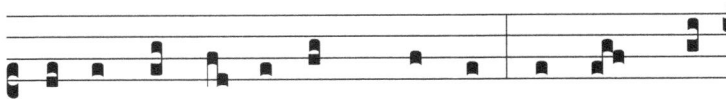

3) By him the painful course was run, The shame en-

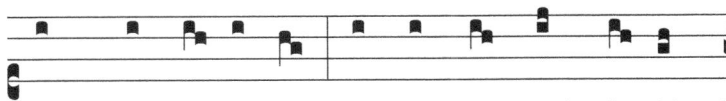

dured, the glo-ry won; For Thy dear sake his blood

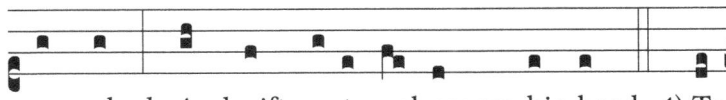

was shed, And gifts e- ternal crown his head. 4) To

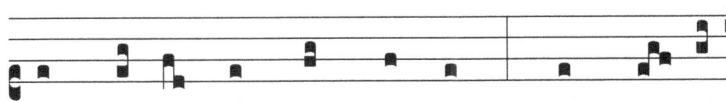

Thee we therefore make our prayer, Most mer-ci-ful! Thy people spare; That we, in this Thy Mar-

tyr's Feast, May joy from every sin re-leased.

†138: Ex more docti mystico

At a Nocturn.

Italy: Verona (11th c.)

C–A

L et us, the scholars of Christ's school, Trained

in the Church's mystic rule, Keep the known fast,

or-dained of old, The ten days' cir-clet four times

told. 2) The Law and Prophets, in their day, Pro-

longed to us this Lental way, Which Christ hath

Anonymous (9th–10th c.)
tr. William John Blew

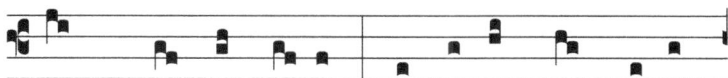

blessed and sancti- fied, Maker and King of time

and tide. 3) Be thriftier then, and more subdued,

Our use of speech, sleep, drink, and food; Scant

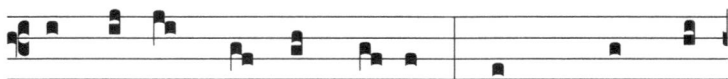

jest be ours, and straiter ward; Christ's watchers,

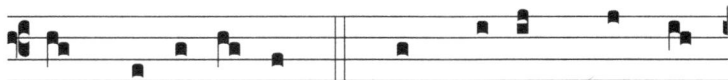

stand we on our guard. 4) Shun we things foul that,

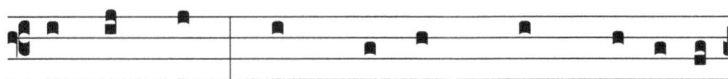

dragging down Men's wandering minds, in ru-in

drown; Nor to the crafty   foe give place, With ty-

rant yoke and thraldom base. 5) In prayer all pros-

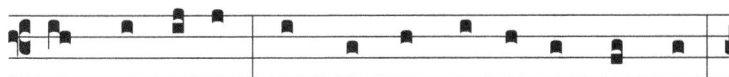

trate let us fall, And cry for mercy one and all;

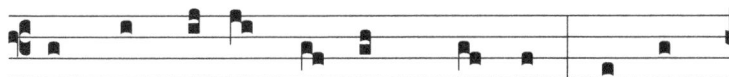

And wail be-fore our Judge, and seek His veng-

ing wrath to bend and break. 6) Our deeds of ill

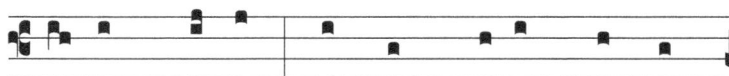

do wrong to Thee, And cross, O Lord, Thy clem-

ency; Then pour on us, Thou God of grace, For-

giveness from Thy ho-ly place. 7) Remember, Lord,

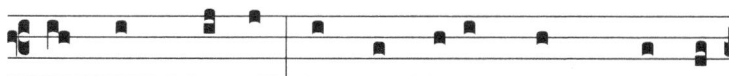

that Thine we are, Thy handi-work though frailty

mar; Then give not to an-other's claim, We pray,

the honour of Thy name. 8) The ills that we have

done undo, In-crease the good for which we sue;

Whence we may please and honour Thee, Here, and

through all e- terni- ty. A- men.

†139: Iam Christus astra ascenderat

At a Nocturn.

France: Nevers (12th c.)

C–B

Now Christ beyond the stars is gone, Un-

to the throne from which He came, Soon to be-

stow the Fa-ther's Boon, The Spirit's Unction and

Anonymous (9th–10th c.)   sel: 1, 3–4
tr. John Wallace

His Flame. 2) The revo- lu-tion of the sphere, With

sevenfold seven- times mystic round, Brought on

the day of all the year Which most in blessings

doth a- bound. 3) 'Tis now the third hour of the

day, A mighty sound the air now rends, Brings tid-

ings to the Twelve who pray, That God the Ho-

ly Ghost de- scends. 4) So is He then the glow-

ing Fire Of the E- ter- nal Fa- ther's Beams; He

comes their faithful hearts t'inspire, To fill them

with His fervent streams. 5) Which inward ar-dour

now they burn, Urged by the Ho-ly Spirit's Grace;

To speak in di-verse tongues they learn, The Al-

mighty's wondrous works they praise. 6) The Na-

tions in a- mazement stand, Roman, Barbar-i- an,

and Greek; Each hears the tongue of his own land

Whilst the in- spired A- postles speak. 7) Then Juda's faithless people rave A-gainst the Twelve, and

dare to call Them drunk with wine, who seek to

save The souls of men from sinful thrall. 8) But Pe-

ter speaks, and clearly shows The meaning of these

wondrous signs, Confutes the slanders of their foes

Condemned by Jo-el's mystic lines.

†140: Iam Christus astra ascenderat

At Vespers.

Italy: Gaeta (12th c.)

C–A

Now Christ beyond the stars is gone, Unto

the throne from which He came, Soon to be-stow

the Fa-ther's Boon, The Spirit's Unction and His

Flame. 2) The rev- o- lu-tion of the sphere, With

sevenfold seven-times mystic round, Brought on

the day of all the year Which most in blessings

doth a- bound. 3) 'Tis now the third hour of the

Anonymous (9th–10th c.)
tr. John Wallace

sel: 1, 3–4

day, A mighty sound the air now rends, Brings

tidings to the Twelve who pray, That God the Ho-

ly Ghost de-scends. 4) So is He then the glowing

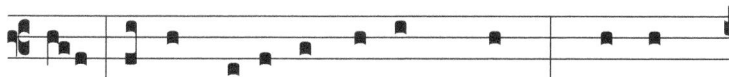

Fire Of the E- ternal Fa-ther's Beams; He comes

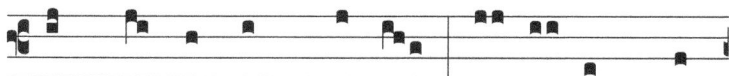

their faithful hearts t'inspire, To fill them with

His fervent streams. 5) Which in-ward ar-dour now

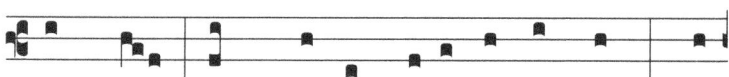

they burn, Urged by the Holy Spirit's Grace; To

speak in di- verse tongues they learn, The Almight-

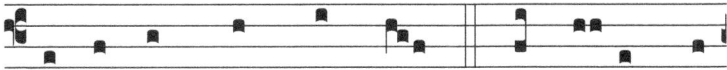

y's wondrous works they praise. 6) The Na- tions in

a-mazement stand, Roman, Barbari- an, and Greek;

Each hears the tongue of his own land Whilst the

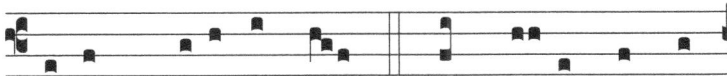

in-spired A-postles speak. 7) Then Ju- da's faithless

people rave A-gainst the Twelve, and dare to call

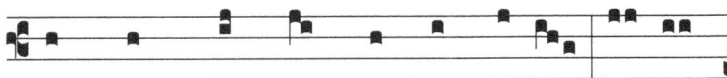

Them drunk with wine, who seek to save The souls

of men from sinful thrall. 8) But Pe- ter speaks,

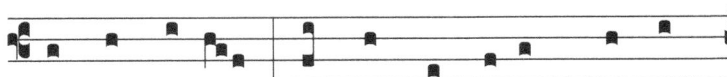

and clearly shows The meaning of these wondrous

signs, Confutes the slanders of their foes Con-

demned by Jo-el's mystic lines.

†141: Iam Christus astra ascenderat

On Pentecost at Vespers.

Austria: Heiligenkreuz (12th–13th c.)

F–E

Now Christ beyond the stars is gone, Unto

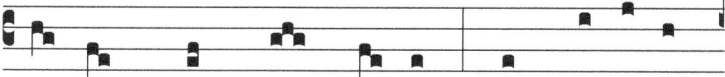

the throne from which He came, Soon to be-stow

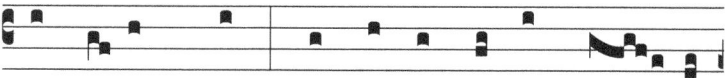

the Fa-ther's Boon, The Spirit's Unction and His

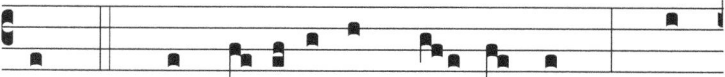

Flame. 2) The revo- lu- tion of the sphere, With

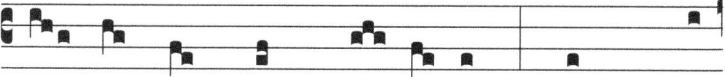

sevenfold seven-times mys-tic round, Brought on

Anonymous (9th–10th c.)
tr. John Wallace

sel: 1, 3–4

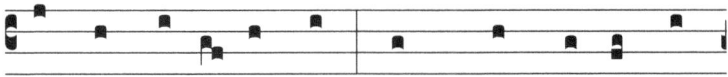

the day of all the year Which most in blessings

doth a-bound. 3) 'Tis now the third hour of   the

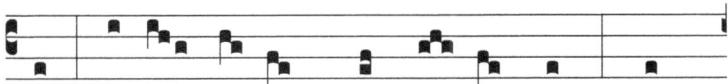

day, A mighty   sound the air now rends, Brings

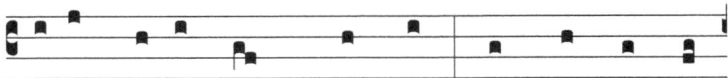

tidings to the Twelve who pray, That God the Ho-

ly Ghost de-scends. 4) So is He then the glowing

Fire Of the E- ter-nal Fa- ther's Beams; He comes

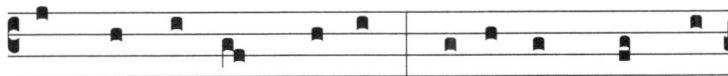

their faithful hearts t'inspire, To fill them with His

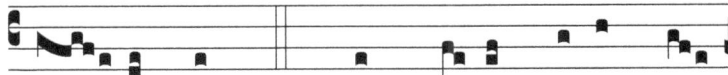

fer-   vent streams. 5) Which in-ward ar-dour now

they burn, Urged by the Ho-ly Spir-it's Grace; To

speak in di-verse tongues they learn, The Almight-

y's wondrous works they praise. 6) The Na-tions in

a-mazement stand, Roman, Barbar-i- an, and Greek;

Each hears the tongue of his own land Whilst the

in-spired A-pos- tles speak. 7) Then Ju-da's faith-

less peo-ple rave A-gainst the Twelve, and dare to

call Them drunk with wine, who seek to save The

souls of men from sin- ful thrall. 8) But Pe- ter

speaks, and clearly shows The meaning of these

wondrous signs, Confutes the slanders of their foes

Condemned by Jo-el's mys- tic lines.

†142: Iam Christus astra ascenderat

On Pentecost at a Nocturn.

Southern Italy (13th c.)

F–D

Now Christ beyond the stars is gone, Un-

to the throne from which He came, Soon to be-

stow the Fa-ther's Boon, The Spirit's Unction and

Anonymous (9th–10th c.)
tr. John Wallace

sel: 1, 3–4

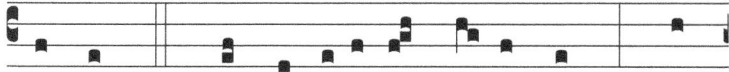

His Flame. 2) The revo- lu-tion of the sphere, With

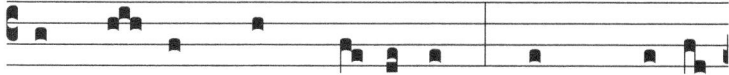

sevenfold seven-times mystic round, Brought on the

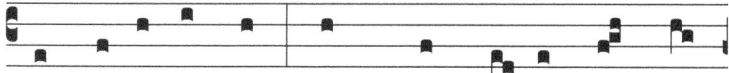

day of all the year Which most in blessings doth

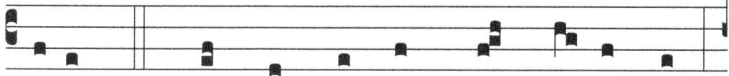

a- bound. 3) 'Tis now the third hour of the day,

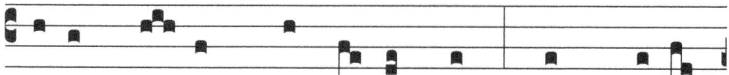

A mighty   sound the air now rends, Brings tidings

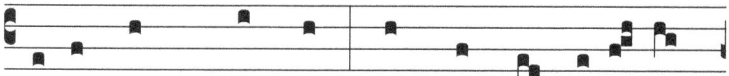

to the Twelve who pray, That God the Holy Ghost

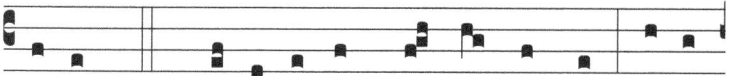

de-scends. 4) So is He then the glowing Fire Of the

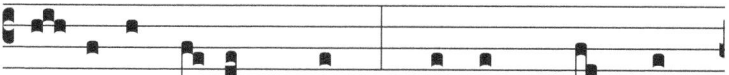

E-   ternal Fa- ther's Beams; He comes their faith-

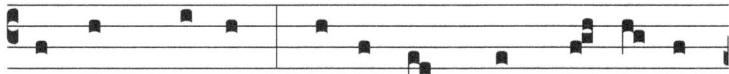

ful hearts t'inspire, To fill them with His fer-vent

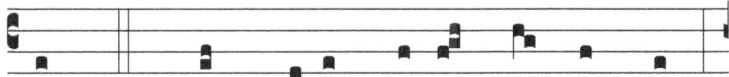

streams. 5) Which inward ar-dour now they burn,

Urged by the Holy Spirit's Grace; To speak in di-

verse tongues they learn, The Almighty's wondrous

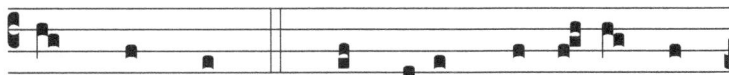

works they praise. 6) The Nations in a- mazement

stand, Roman, Bar-bari- an, and Greek; Each hears

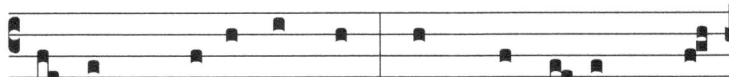

the tongue of his own land Whilst the in-spired A-

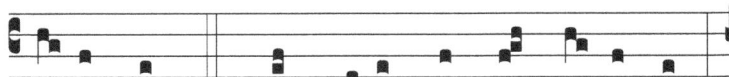

postles speak. 7) Then Juda's faithless people rave

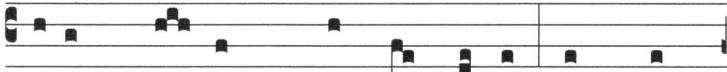

A-gainst the Twelve, and dare to call Them drunk

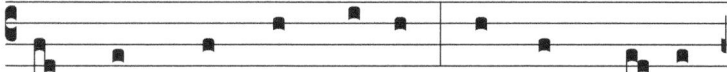

with wine, who seek to save The souls of men

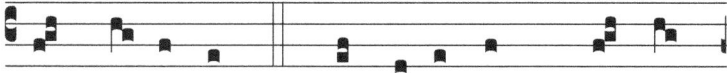

from sin-ful thrall. 8) But Pe-ter speaks, and clear-

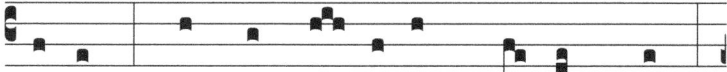

ly shows The meaning of these wondrous signs,

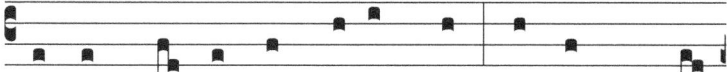

Confutes the slanders of their foes Condemned by

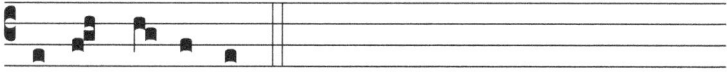

Jo-el's mystic lines.

†143: Iesu, corona virginum

For virgins.

Austria: Heiligenkreuz (12th–13th c.)

D–E

Je- su, the Vir- gins' Crown, do Thou Ac-

cept us, as in prayer we bow; Born of that Virgin,

whom a- lone The Mother and the Maid we own.

2) A- mongst the lil- ies Thou dost feed, With Vir-

gin choirs ac-companied; With glory decked, the

spotless brides Whose bridal gifts Thy love pro-

vides. 3) They, whereso- e'er Thy footsteps bend,

Anonymous (9th–10th c.)
tr. John Mason Neale

(musical notation)

With hymns and praises still at- tend; In blessed

(musical notation)

troops they follow Thee, With dance, and song, and

(musical notation)

melo- dy. 4) We   pray Thee therefore to be- stow

(musical notation)

Upon our senses here be-low Thy grace, that so we

(musical notation)

may en-dure From taint of all corruption pure.

†144: Iesu, corona virginum

On the nativity of one virgin
at Vespers and at Lauds.

Germany: Lehel (1227–1235)

D–A

(musical notation)

J e- su, the Virgins' Crown, do Thou Accept us,

Anonymous (9th–10th c.)
tr. John Mason Neale

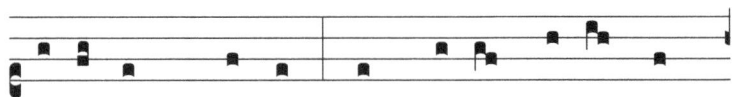

as in prayer we bow; Born of that Virgin, whom

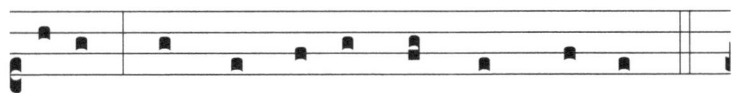

a- lone The Mother and the Maid we own.

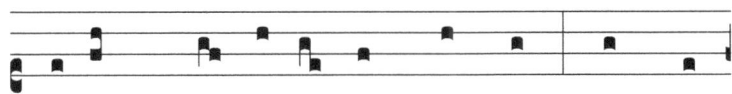

2) A- mongst the lil- ies Thou dost feed, With Vir-

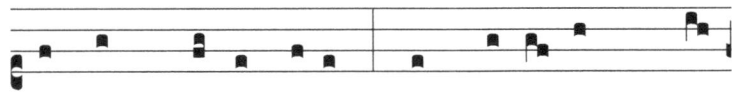

gin choirs ac- companied; With glory decked, the

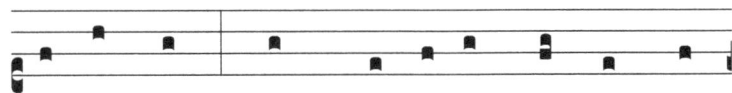

spotless brides Whose bridal gifts Thy love pro-

vides. 3) They, whereso- e'er Thy footsteps bend,

With hymns and praises still at- tend; In blessed

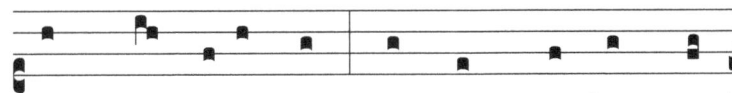

troops they follow Thee, With dance, and song, and

melo-dy. 4) We pray Thee therefore to be-stow Up-

on our senses here be-low Thy grace, that so we

may endure From taint of all corruption pure.

†145: Iesu, corona virginum

At Lauds.

England: Worcester (ca. 1230)

C–A

Je- su, the Virgins' Crown, do   Thou Accept

us, as in prayer we bow; Born of that Vir- gin,

whom a- lone The Mother and the Maid we own.

2) A-mongst the lil-ies Thou dost feed, With Virgin

Anonymous (9th–10th c.)
tr. John Mason Neale

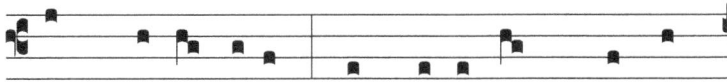

choirs ac-companied; With glory decked, the spot-

less brides Whose bridal gifts Thy love provides.

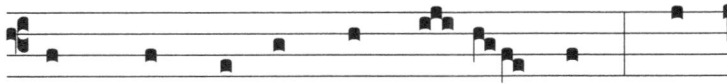

3) They, whereso- e'er Thy footsteps bend, With

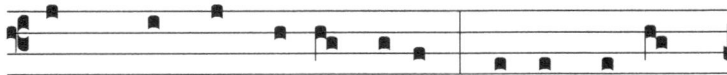

hymns and praises still at-tend; In blessed troops

they follow Thee, With dance, and song, and mel-

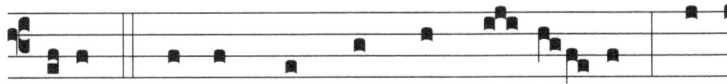

o-dy. 4) We pray Thee therefore to be- stow Up-

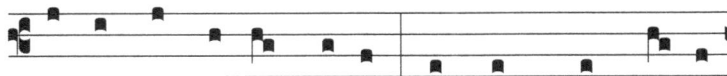

on our senses here be-low Thy grace, that so we

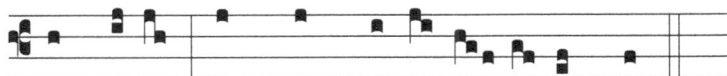

may endure From taint of all cor- ruption pure.

†146: Iesu, corona virginum

For virgins.

Austria: Klosterneuburg (1336)

A–A

J e- su, the Vir-gins' Crown, do Thou Accept

us, as in prayer we bow; Born of that Virgin,

whom a- lone The Mother and the Maid we own.

2) A-mongst the lil- ies Thou dost feed, With Vir-

gin choirs ac- companied; With glory decked, the

spotless brides Whose bridal gifts Thy love pro-

vides. 3) They, whereso-e'er Thy footsteps bend,

Anonymous (9th–10th c.)
tr. John Mason Neale

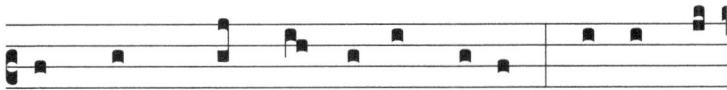

With hymns and praises still at-tend; In blessed

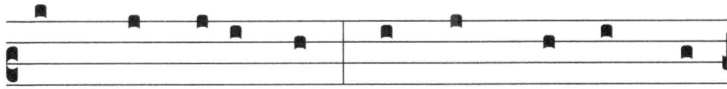

troops they follow Thee, With dance, and song, and

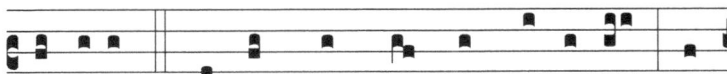

melo-dy. 4) We pray Thee therefore to be-stow Up-

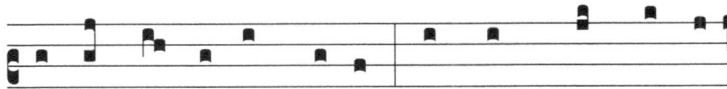

on our senses here be-low Thy grace, that so we

may endure From taint of all corruption pure.

†147: Iesu, corona virginum

On feasts for virgins.

Switzerland: Engelberg (1372)

C–F

Je-su, the Virgins' Crown, do Thou Accept us,

Anonymous (9th–10th c.)
tr. John Mason Neale

as in prayer we bow; Born of that Virgin, whom

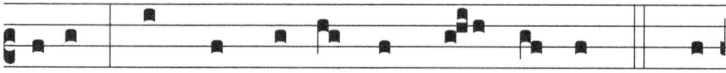

a- lone The Mother and the Maid we own. 2) A-

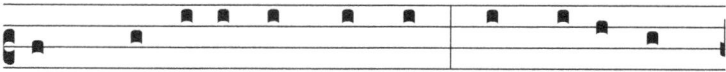

mongst the lil-ies Thou dost feed, With Virgin choirs

ac- com- panied; With glory decked, the spotless

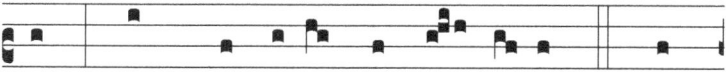

brides Whose bridal gifts Thy love provides. 3) They,

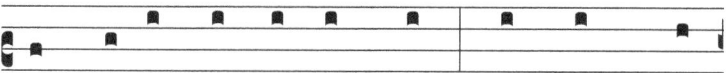

whereso-e'er Thy footsteps bend, With hymns and

praises still at-tend; In blessed troops they follow

Thee, With dance, and song, and mel- o- dy.

4) We pray Thee therefore to be-stow Upon our sens-

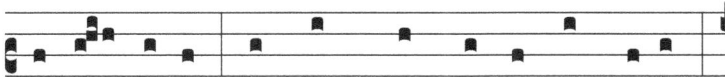

es here be-low Thy grace, that so we may endure

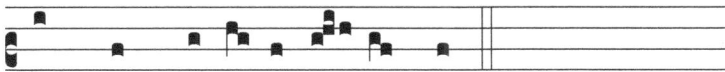

From taint of all corrup-tion pure.

†148: Iesu, nostra redemptio

At Compline.

Italy: Verona (11th c.)

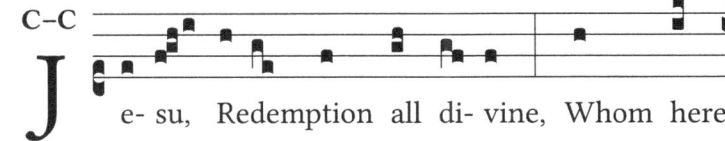

Je- su, Redemption all di- vine, Whom here

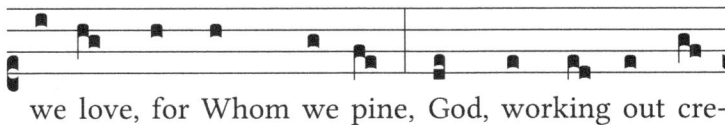

we love, for Whom we pine, God, working out cre-

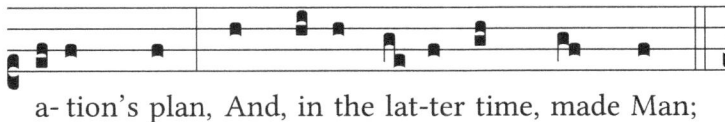

a- tion's plan, And, in the lat-ter time, made Man;

Anonymous (9th–10th c.)
tr. John Mason Neale

(3) iii:6–7

2) What love of Thine was that, which led To take

our woes upon Thy Head, And pangs and cruel

death to bear, To ransom us from death's de-spair!

3) To Thee Hell's gate gave ready way, Demanding

there his captive prey: And now, in pomp and vic-

tor's pride, Thou sittest at the Fa-ther's side. 4) Let

ver-y mercy force Thee still To spare us, conquering

all our ill; And, granting that we ask on high With

Thine Own Face to satis- fy. 5) Be Thou our Joy and

Thou our Guard, Who art to be our great Reward:

Our glory and our boast in Thee For ever and for

ever be! A- men.

†149: Iesu, nostra redemptio

The Ascension of the Lord at Vespers.

France: Nevers (12th c.)

G–A

Je- su, Re-demption all di-vine, Whom here we

love, for Whom we pine, God, working out cre-a-

Anonymous (9th–10th c.)
tr. John Mason Neale

tion's plan, And, in the lat-ter time, made Man;

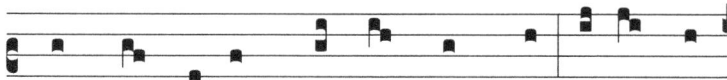

2) What love of Thine was that, which led To take our

woes upon Thy Head, And pangs and cruel death

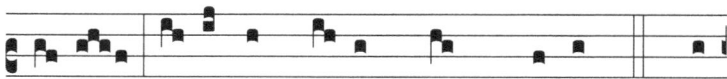

to bear, To ransom us from death's de-spair! 3) To

Thee Hell's gate gave ready way, Demanding there

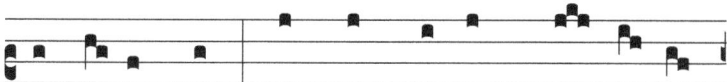

his captive prey: And now, in pomp and vic-tor's

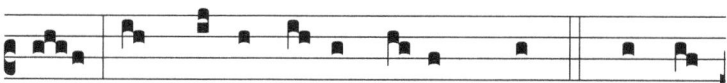

pride, Thou sittest at the Fa-ther's side. 4) Let ver-

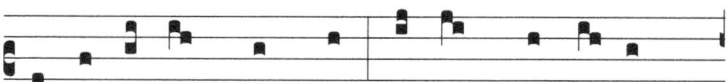

y mercy force Thee still To spare us, conquering

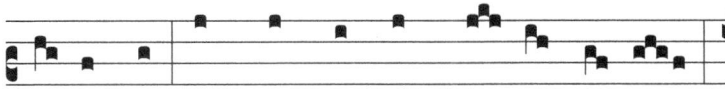

all our ill; And, granting that we ask on high

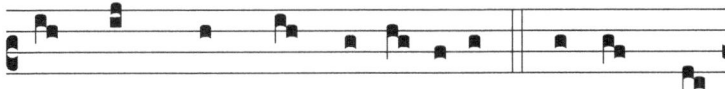

With Thine Own Face to sat-is-fy. 5) Be Thou our

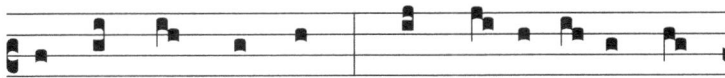

Joy and Thou our Guard, Who art to be our great

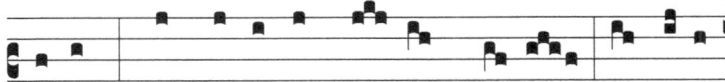

Reward: Our glory and our boast in Thee For ever

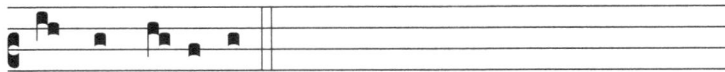

and for ev-er be!

†150: Iesu, nostra redemptio

At Compline.

Austria: Heiligenkreuz (12th–13th c.)

D–D

Je- su, Re-demption all di-vine, Whom here

Anonymous (9th–10th c.)
tr. John Mason Neale

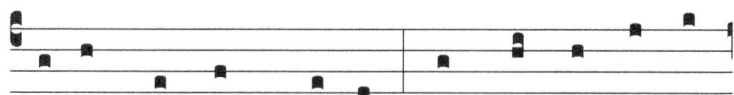

we love, for Whom we pine, God, working out cre-

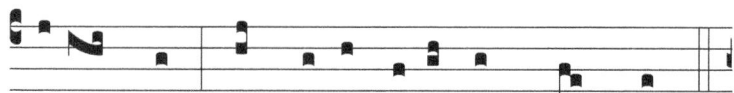

a- tion's plan, And, in the latter time, made Man;

2) What love of Thine was that, which led To take our

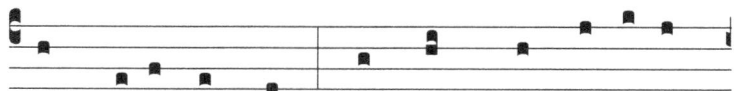

woes upon Thy Head, And pangs and cruel death

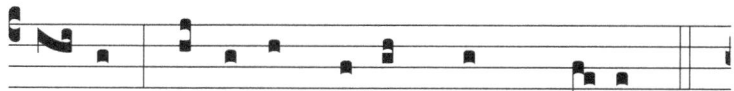

to   bear, To ransom us from death's de- spair!

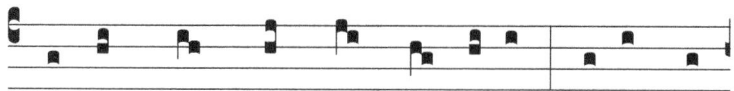

3) To Thee Hell's gate gave ready way, Demanding

there his captive prey: And now, in pomp and vic-

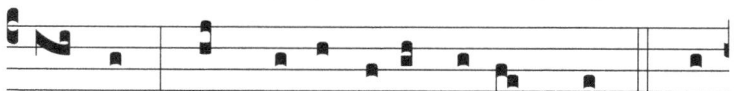

tor's pride, Thou sittest at the Fa-ther's side. 4) Let

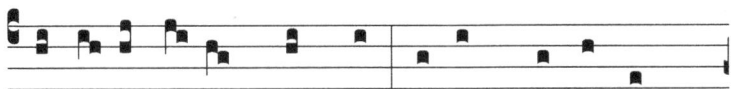

very mercy force Thee still To spare us, conquering

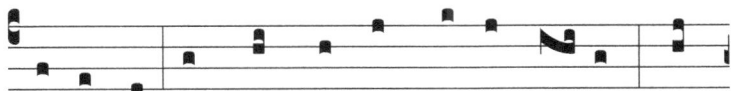

all our ill; And, granting that we ask on high With

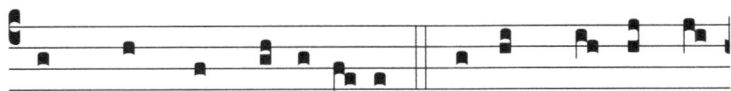

Thine Own Face to satis- fy. 5) Be Thou our Joy and

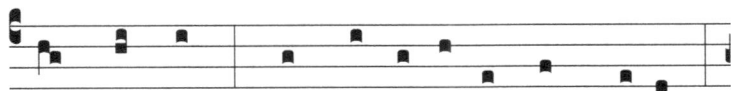

Thou our Guard, Who art to be our great Reward:

Our glory and our boast in Thee For ever and for

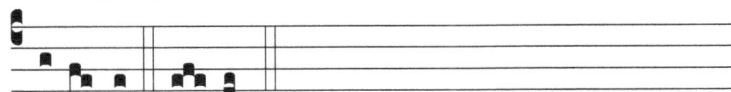

ever be! A- men.

†151: Iesu, nostra redemptio

On the Ascension of the Lord
at Lauds.

France: Bayeux (ca. 1234)

Je- su, Re- demption all di- vine, Whom

here we love, for Whom we pine, God, work-

ing out cre- a- tion's plan, And, in the lat- ter

time, made Man; 2) What love of Thine was that,

which led To take our woes upon Thy Head,

And pangs and cruel death to bear, To ransom

us from death's de- spair! 3) To Thee Hell's

Anonymous (9th–10th c.)
tr. John Mason Neale

gate gave ready way, Demanding there his cap-

tive prey: And now, in pomp and victor's pride,

Thou sittest at the Fa-ther's side. 4) Let ver-

y mercy force Thee still To spare us, con-

quering all our ill; And, granting that we ask

on high With Thine Own Face to satis- fy.

5) Be Thou our Joy and Thou our Guard, Who art

to be our great Re- ward: Our glory and our

boast in Thee For ever and for ever be!

†152: Iesu, redemptor omnium

For one confessor.

France: Moissac (ca. 1000)

D–C

Je-su, Redeemer Thou of all, Thy prelates' last-

ing coro-nal; Hear us, and of Thy gentleness This

day our voice, O Je-su, bless: 2) This day—when glo-

rious he be-came, Confessor of Thy Holy Name;

This day—whereon Thy flock's true fold Delights his

Anonymous (9th–10th c.)
tr. William John Blew

yearly feast to hold. 3) Who putting far a-way from

him This world's frail gauds, as faint and dim; Joy-

ous, with angels of the sky, Now feeds on joys that

never die. 4) Vouchsafe us, then, of Thy great grace,

The treadings of his steps to trace; Hear Thou the

prayer Thy servants pray, And wash their stain of

guilt a-way.

†153: Iesu, redemptor omnium

One confessor.

France: Nevers (12th c.)

F–F

J e- su, Redeemer Thou of all, Thy prelates' last-

ing coro- nal; Hear us, and of Thy gentleness This

day our voice, O   Je-su, bless: 2) This day—when

glorious he be-came, Confessor of Thy Holy Name;

This day—whereon Thy flock's true fold Delights his

yearly feast to hold. 3) Who putting far a- way from

him This world's frail gauds, as faint and dim; Joy-

Anonymous (9th–10th c.)
tr. William John Blew

ous, with angels of the sky, Now feeds on joys that

never die. 4) Vouchsafe us, then, of Thy great grace,

The treadings of his steps to trace; Hear Thou the

prayer Thy servants pray, And wash their stain of

guilt a-way.

†154: Iesu, redemptor omnium

One confessor at Lauds.

Switzerland: Lausanne (13th c.)

F–D

Je-su, Redeemer Thou of all, Thy prelates'

lasting coro- nal; Hear us, and of Thy gentleness

Anonymous (9th–10th c.)
tr. William John Blew

This day our voice, O Je-su, bless: 2) This day—-

when glorious he be-came, Confes-sor of Thy Ho-

ly Name; This day—whereon Thy flock's true fold

Delights his yearly feast to hold. 3) Who put- ting

far a- way from him This world's frail gauds, as

faint and dim; Joyous, with angels of the sky,

Now feeds on joys that never die. 4) Vouchsafe us,

then, of Thy great grace, The treadings of his steps

to trace; Hear Thou the prayer Thy servants pray,

And wash their stain of guilt a-way.

†155: Iesu, redemptor omnium

For confessors at Nocturns.

Germany: Rüdnitz (1325–1375)

C–B

Je- su, Re-deemer Thou of all, Thy prelates'

last-ing coro-nal; Hear us, and of Thy gentleness

This day our voice, O Je- su, bless: 2) This day—-

when glorious he be-came, Confessor of Thy Ho-

ly Name; This day—whereon Thy flock's true fold

Anonymous (9th–10th c.)
tr. William John Blew

Delights his yearly   feast to hold. 3) Who putting

far a-   way from him This world's frail gauds, as

faint and dim; Joyous, with angels of the sky, Now

feeds on joys that never die. 4) Vouchsafe us, then,

of   Thy great grace, The treadings of   his steps

to trace; Hear Thou the prayer Thy servants pray,

And wash their stain of   guilt a-way.

†156: Immense caeli conditor

At Vespers.

Germany: Kempten (ca. 1000)

C–A

O great Crea- tor of the sky, Who would-

est not the floods on high With earthly waters to

confound, But mad'st the firmament their bound;

2) The floods a- bove Thou didst or- dain: The floods

be- low Thou didst re- strain: That moisture might

at-temper heat, Lest the parch'd earth should ru- in

meet. 3) Up-on our souls, good Lord, be-stow The

Anonymous (9th–10th c.)
tr. John Mason Neale

410

gift of grace in endless flow: Lest some re-new'd

de-ceit or wile Of former sin should us beguile.

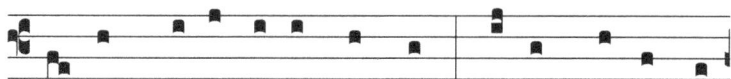

4) Let Faith discover heav'nly light: So shall its ray di-

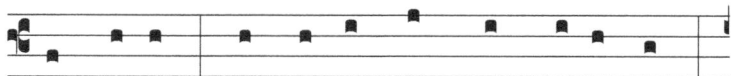

rect us right: And let this Faith each er-ror chase:

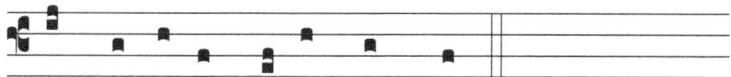

And never give to falsehood place.

†157: Lucis creator optime

Sundays at Vespers.

Germany: Kempten (ca. 1000)

E–C

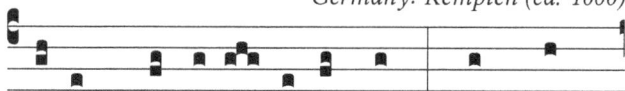

O Blest Crea- tor of the light, Who mak'st

Anonymous (9th–10th c.)
tr. John Mason Neale

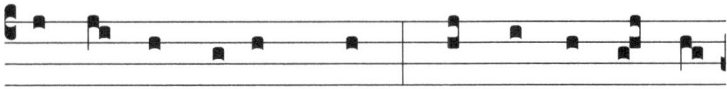

the day with ra-diance bright, And o'er the forming

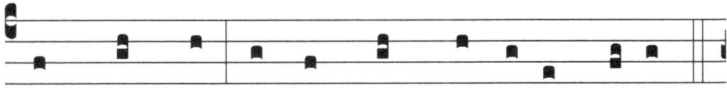

world didst call The light from Chaos first of all:

2) Whose wisdom join'd in meet ar-ray The morn and

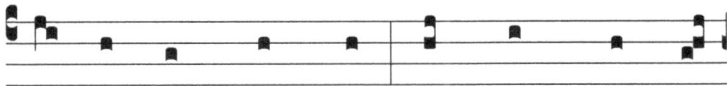

eve, and nam'd them Day; Night comes with all

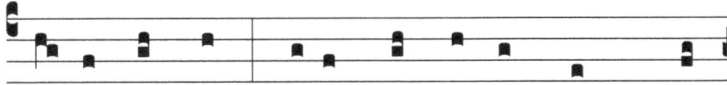

its darkling fears; Regard thy people's prayers and

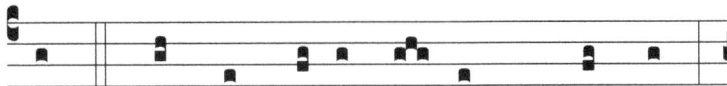

tears. 3) Lest, sunk in sin, and whelm'd with strife,

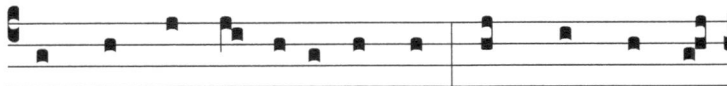

They lose the gift of endless life; While thinking but

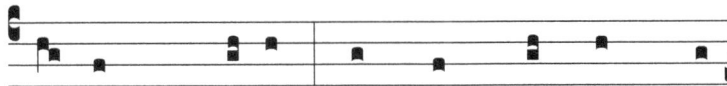

the thoughts of time, They weave new chains of

woe and crime. 4) But grant them grace that they

may strain The heav'nly gate and prize to gain;

Each harmful lure a- side to cast, And purge a-way

each er-ror past.

†158: Lucis creator optime

*On Sundays until the beginning of Lent
at Vespers.*

Italy: Piacenza (ca. 1200)

C–A

O Blest Crea- tor of the light, Who mak'st

the day with ra-diance bright, And o'er the forming

Anonymous (9th–10th c.)
tr. John Mason Neale

world didst call The light from Chaos first of all:

2) Whose wisdom join'd in meet ar-ray The morn and

eve, and nam'd them Day; Night comes with all

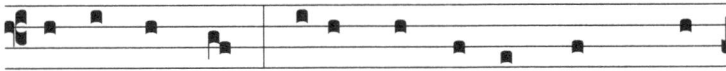

its darkling fears; Regard thy people's prayers and

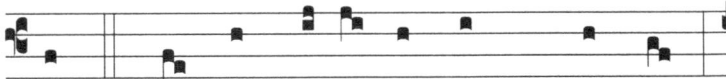

tears. 3) Lest, sunk in sin, and whelm'd with strife,

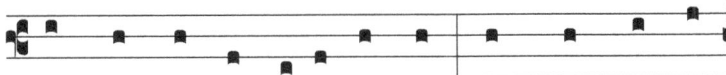

They lose the gift of endless life; While thinking but

the thoughts of time, They weave new chains of

woe and crime. 4) But grant them grace that they

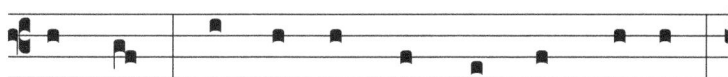

may strain The heav'nly gate and prize to gain;

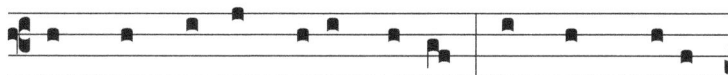

Each harmful lure a- side to cast, And purge a-way

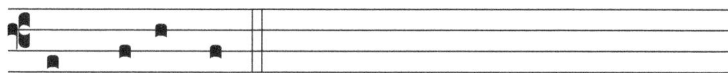

each er-ror past.

†159: Lucis creator optime

All Sundays after Trinity until Advent, and after the octave of the Epiphany until Lent at Vespers.

England: Worcester (ca. 1230)

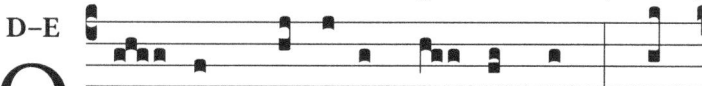

D–E

O Blest Crea- tor of the light, Who

mak'st the day with ra-diance bright, And o'er the

forming world didst call The light from Chaos first

Anonymous (9th–10th c.)
tr. John Mason Neale

of all: 2) Whose wisdom join'd in meet ar-ray

The morn and eve, and nam'd them Day; Night

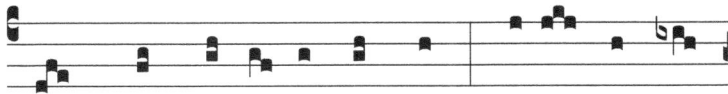

comes with all its darkling fears; Regard thy peo-

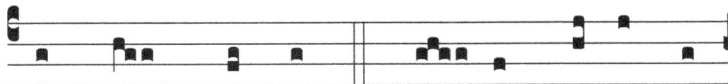

ple's prayers and tears. 3) Lest, sunk in sin, and

whelm'd with strife, They lose the gift of endless

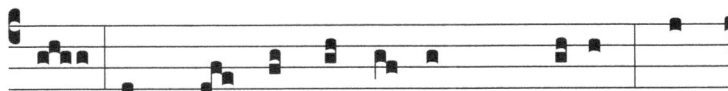

life; While thinking but the thoughts of time, They

weave new chains of woe and crime. 4) But grant

them grace that they may strain The heav'nly gate

and prize to gain; Each harmful lure a- side to

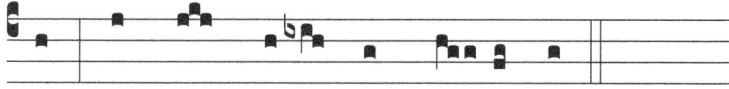

cast, And purge a- way each er- ror past.

†160: Lucis creator optime

France: Clermont-Ferránd (14th c.)

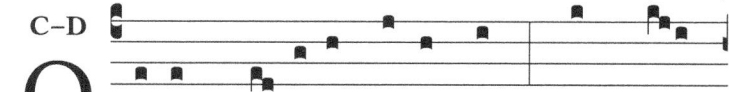

C–D

O Blest Crea- tor of the light, Who mak'st

the day with ra- diance bright, And o'er the form-

ing world didst call The light from Chaos first

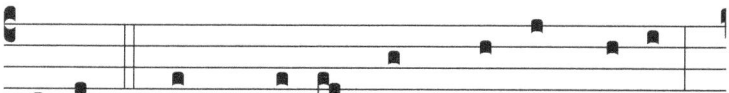

of all: 2) Whose wisdom join'd in meet ar-ray

Anonymous (9th–10th c.)
tr. John Mason Neale

The morn and eve, and nam'd them Day; Night

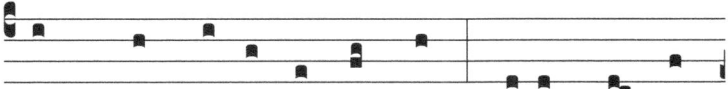

comes with all its darkling fears; Regard thy peo-

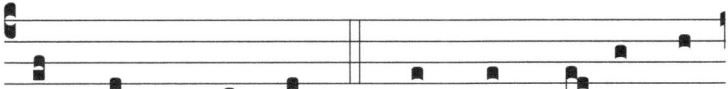

ple's prayers and tears. 3) Lest, sunk in sin, and

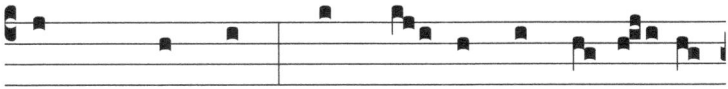

whelm'd with strife, They lose the gift of end-less

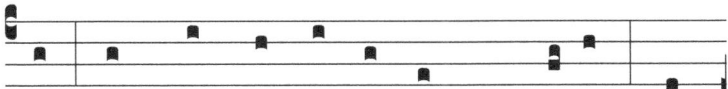

life; While thinking but the thoughts of time, They

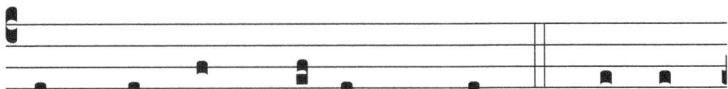

weave new chains of woe and crime. 4) But grant

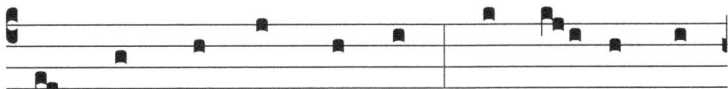

them grace that they may strain The heav-'nly gate

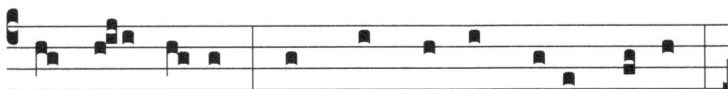

and prize to gain; Each harmful lure a- side to cast,

And purge a- way each er-ror past.

†161: Magnae Deus potentiae

At Vespers.

Italy: Verona (11th c.)

D–A

A l- mighty God, Who from the flood Didst

bring to light a twofold brood: Part in the firma-

ment to fly, And part in o- cean depths to lie:

2) Appointing fishes in the sea, And fowls in o- pen

air to be: That each, by or-i- gin the same, Its sep-

arate dwelling-place might claim: 3) Grant that Thy

Anonymous (9th–10th c.)
tr. John Mason Neale

(1) ii:4

servants, by the tide Of Blood and Water puri-fied,

No guilty fall from Thee may know, Nor death e-

ternal undergo. 4) Let none de-spair through sin's

distress; Be none puffed up with boastfulness: That

contrite hearts be not dismayed, Nor haughty souls

in ru-in laid.

†162: Primo dierum omnium

From the feast of Saint Michael until Advent,
and after the octave of the Epiphany until the first Sunday of Lent
at Matins.

England: Worcester (ca. 1230)

C–B

First Day of days! wherein ar-rayed In light

and beauty, Earth was made; And life to give us,

from the dead Victo-rious our Crea- tor sped!

2) Let us with joyful hearts a- rise, And chasing slum-

ber from our eyes, Right ear-ly seek The Lord of

Grace, As erst the Prophet sought His Face; 3) That

He may hearken to our prayer, Stretch forth His

Anonymous (9th–10th c.)
tr. John David Chambers

arm with kindly care, And eve-ry past of-fence

for-given, Restore us to our homes in   Heaven;

4) And as on this His sa-cred Day, We here our

thankful homage pay Of praise and prayer, each

peaceful hour May o'er us amply, blessings shower.

†163: Quem terra pontus aethera

On the feast of the Purification
at Matins.

France: Paris (ca. 1255)

C–C

The God whom earth, and sea, and sky,

Anonymous (9th–10th c.)   sel: 1–2, 4–5
tr. Neale & Dearmer: 1–2, 4–5 & 6–8 / 8

A- dore, and laud, and magni- fy; Who o'er their

three- fold fabric reigns, The Virgin's spotless

womb contains. 2) The God whose will by moon

and sun And all things in due course is done,

Is borne upon a Maiden's breast, By fullest heav-

enly grace possesst. 4) How blest that Moth-er, in

whose shrine The great Ar-tif- i- cer Di- vine,

Whose hand contains the earth and sky, Vouchsafed,

as in his ark, to lie! 5) Blest, in the mes- sage

Gabriel brought; Blest, by the work the Spirit

wrought; From whom the Great Desire of earth

Took human flesh and human birth. 6) O Glorious

Maid, exalted far Beyond the light of burning star,

From him who made thee thou hast won Grace to

be Mother of his Son. 7) That which was lost in

hapless Eve Thy ho- ly Sci- on did re- trieve: The

tear-worn sons of Adam's race Through thee have

seen the heavenly place. 8) Thou wast the gate of

heaven's high Lord, The door through which the

light hath poured. Christians re-joice, for through

a   Maid To all mankind is   life conveyed!

†164: Quem terra pontus aethera

On the Purification of Blessed Mary
at Lauds.

France: Normandy (14th–15th c.)

D–C

T he God whom earth, and sea, and sky, A-

Anonymous (9th–10th c.)   sel: 1–2, 4–5
tr. Neale & Dearmer: 1–2, 4–5 & 6–8 / 8

dore, and laud, and magni- fy; Who o'er their

threefold fabric reigns, The Vir- gin's spotless

womb contains. 2) The God whose will by moon

and sun And all things in due course is done,

Is borne upon a Maiden's breast, By full-est heav-

enly grace possesst. 4) How blest that Mother, in

whose shrine The great Ar-tif- i- cer Di- vine,

Whose hand contains the earth and sky, Vouchsafed,

as in his ark, to lie! 5) Blest, in the message Gabriel

brought; Blest, by   the work the Spirit   wrought;

From whom the Great Desire of   earth Took hu-

man flesh and hu-man birth. 6) O Glorious Maid, ex-

alted   far Beyond the light of burning   star, From

him who made thee thou hast won Grace to   be

Mother of his Son. 7) That which was lost in hap-

less Eve Thy ho- ly Sci- on did re-   trieve: The

tear-worn sons of Adam's race Through thee have

seen the heavenly place. 8) Thou wast the gate of

heaven's high Lord, The door through which the

light hath poured. Christians re-joice, for through

a Maid To all mankind is life conveyed!

†165: Quem terra pontus aethera

On the Purification of Blessed Mary
at Lauds.

France: Normandy (14th–15th c.)

D–A

The God whom earth, and sea, and sky, A-

Anonymous (9th–10th c.) sel: 1–2, 4–5
tr. Neale & Dearmer: 1–2, 4–5 & 6–8 / 8

dore, and laud, and magni-fy; Who o'er their three-

fold fabric reigns, The Virgin's spotless womb con-

tains. 2) The God whose will by moon and sun

And all things in due course is done, Is borne upon

a Maiden's breast, By fullest heavenly grace pos-

sesst. 4) How blest that Mother, in whose shrine

The great Ar-tif-i- cer Di-vine, Whose hand contains

the earth and sky, Vouchsafed, as in his ark, to

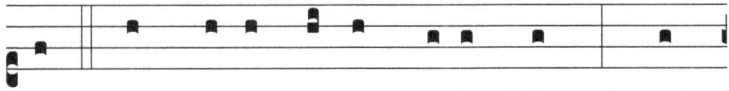

lie! 5) Blest, in the message Gabriel brought; Blest,

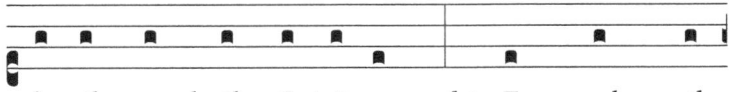

by the work the Spirit wrought; From whom the

Great Desire of earth Took human flesh and hu-

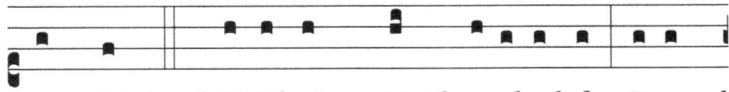

man birth. 6) O Glorious Maid, exalted far Beyond

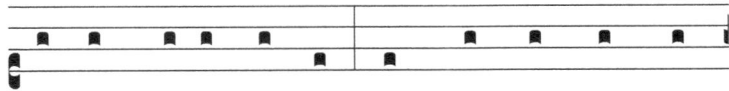

the light of burning star, From him who made thee

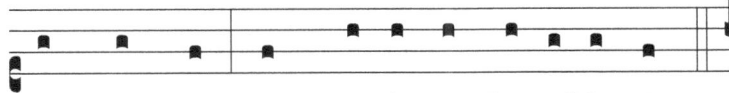

thou hast won Grace to be Mother of his Son.

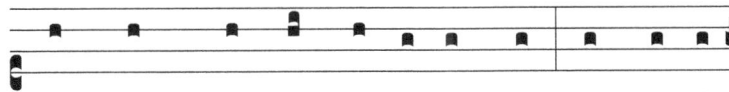

7) That which was lost in hapless Eve Thy ho-ly

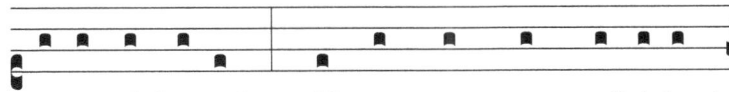

Scion did re-trieve: The tear-worn sons of Adam's

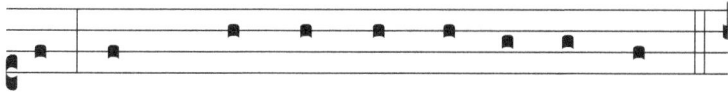

race Through thee have seen the heavenly place.

8) Thou wast the gate of heaven's high Lord, The door

through which the light hath poured. Christians re-

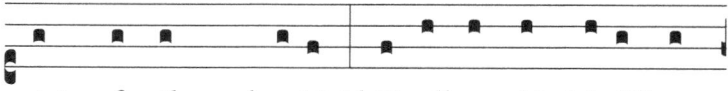

joice, for through a Maid To all mankind is life con-

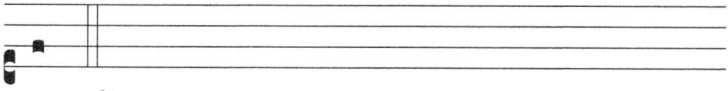

veyed!

†166: Quem terra pontus aethera

Germany: Hegau (1439–1442)

D–E

The God whom earth, and sea, and sky, A-

dore, and laud, and magni- fy; Who o'er their

threefold fabric reigns, The Vir-gin's spotless womb

contains. 2) The God whose will by moon and

sun And all things in due course is done, Is

borne upon a Maiden's breast, By full-est heavenly

grace possesst. 4) How blest that Mother, in whose

Anonymous (9th–10th c.)   sel: 1–2, 4–5
tr. Neale & Dearmer: 1–2, 4–5 & 6–8 / 8

shrine The great Ar- tif- i- cer Di- vine, Whose

hand contains the earth and sky, Vouchsafed, as

in his ark, to lie! 5) Blest, in the message Gabriel

brought; Blest, by the work the Spirit   wrought;

From whom the Great Desire of earth Took hu-man

flesh and human birth. 6) O Glorious Maid, ex- alt-

ed far Beyond the light of burning star, From him

who made thee thou hast won Grace to be Mother of his Son. 7) That which was lost in hapless

Eve Thy ho-ly Sci-on did re- trieve: The tear-worn

sons of Adam's race Through thee have seen the

heavenly place. 8) Thou wast the gate of heaven's

high Lord, The door through which the light hath

poured. Christians re-joice, for through a Maid To

all mankind is life conveyed!

434

†167: Rerum Deus tenax vigor

Switzerland: Einsiedeln (1100–1150)

E–A

O Thou true life of all that live! Who dost,

unmoved, all motion sway; Who dost the morn and

evening give, And through its changes guide the

day: 2) Thy light upon our evening pour,— So may

our souls no sunset see; But death to us an o-pen

door To an e- ternal morning be.

Anonymous (9th–10th c.)
tr. Edward Caswall

†168: Rerum Deus tenax vigor

At None.

France: Nevers (12th c.)

C–A

O Thou true life of all that live! Who dost,

unmoved, all motion sway; Who dost the morn and

evening give, And through its changes guide the

day: 2) Thy light upon our evening pour,— So may

our souls no sunset see; But death to us an o-pen

door To an e- ternal morning be.

Anonymous (9th–10th c.)
tr. Edward Caswall

†169: Rerum Deus tenax vigor

At None
on third doubles.

France: Châlons-en-Champagne (1309)

C–A

O Thou true life of all that live! Who dost,

unmoved, all motion sway; Who dost the morn and

evening give, And through its changes guide the

day: 2) Thy light upon our evening pour,— So may

our souls no sunset see; But death to us an o-pen

door To an e- ter-nal morning be.

Anonymous (9th–10th c.)
tr. Edward Caswall

†170: Rerum Deus tenax vigor

At None.

Austria: Klosterneuburg (1336)

D–C

O Thou true life of all that live! Who dost,

unmoved, all motion sway; Who dost the morn and

evening give, And through its changes guide the

day: 2) Thy light upon our evening pour,— So may

our souls no sunset see; But death to us an o-pen

door To an e- ter-nal morning be.

Anonymous (9th–10th c.)
tr. Edward Caswall

† 171: Rex gloriose martyrum

Italy: Verona (11th c.)

All Glorious King of Martyrs Thou! Crown of

Confessors here be-low! Whom, casting earthly

joys a- way, Thou guidest to ce-lestial Day, 2) O

quickly lend a gracious ear And listen to our sup-

pliant prayer! As we their sa-cred triumphs chant

Forgiveness to our er-rors grant. 3) In Martyrs' Vic-

tor, Thou art e'er In Thy Confessors prone to spare;

Anonymous (9th–10th c.)
tr. John David Chambers

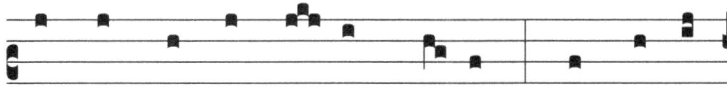

e'er now our guilty pride o'erthrow And all Thy

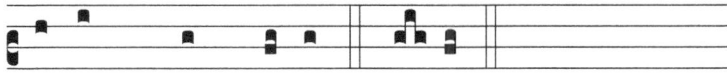

pardoning grace be-stow! A- men.

†172: Rex gloriose martyrum

Several martyrs.

France: Nevers (12th c.)

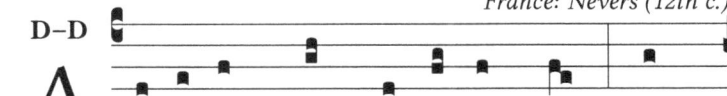

All Glorious King of Martyrs Thou! Crown

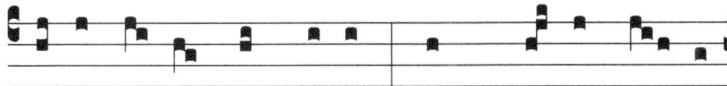

of Confes-sors here be-low! Whom, casting earthly

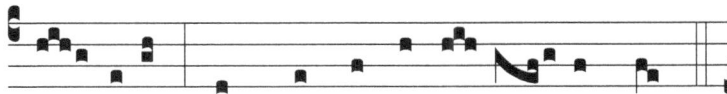

joys a-way, Thou guidest to ce- les- tial Day,

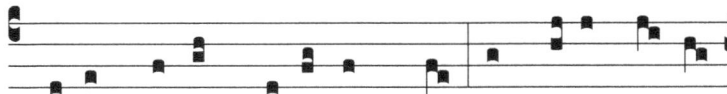

2) O quickly lend a gracious ear And listen to our

Anonymous (9th–10th c.)
tr. John David Chambers

suppliant prayer! As we their sa- cred tri- umphs

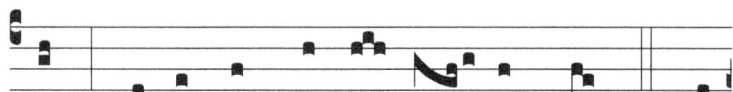

chant Forgiveness to our er- rors grant. 3) In

Martyrs' Victor, Thou art e'er In Thy Confes-sors

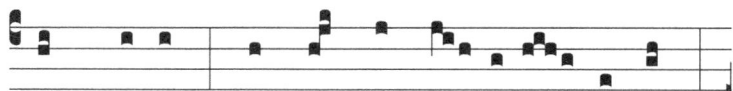

prone to spare; e'er now our guilty pride o'erthrow

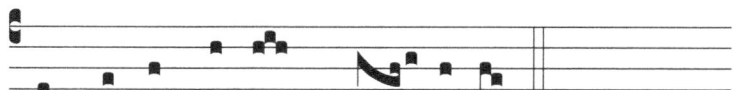

And all Thy pardoning grace be-stow!

†173: Rex gloriose martyrum

Several martyrs.

France: Nevers (12th c.)

C–A

A ll Glorious King of Martyrs Thou! Crown

Anonymous (9th–10th c.)   (1) iii:4, (2–3) iii:7
tr. John David Chambers

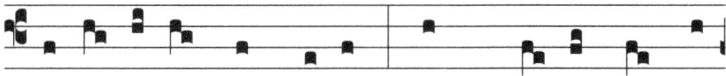

of Confessors here be-low! Whom, casting earthly

joys a-way, Thou guidest to ce-lestial Day, 2) O

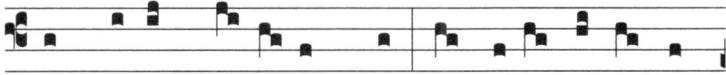

quickly lend a   gracious ear And listen to our sup-

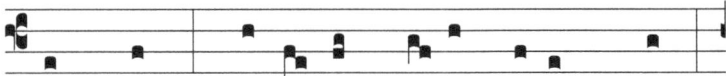

pliant prayer! As we their sa-cred triumphs chant

Forgiveness to our er-rors grant. 3) In Martyrs'

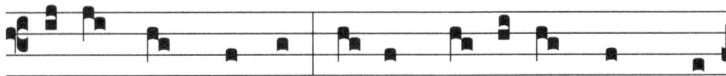

Victor, Thou art e'er In Thy Confessors prone to

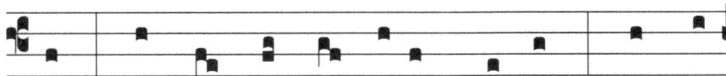

spare; e'er now our guilty pride o'erthrow And all

Thy pardoning grace be-stow!

†174: Rex gloriose martyrum

For several martyrs.

Germany: Fritzlar (1334)

D–D

All Glorious King of Martyrs Thou! Crown

of Confessors here be-low! Whom, casting earthly

joys a- way, Thou guidest to ce- les-tial Day, 2) O

quickly lend a gracious ear And listen to our sup-

pliant prayer! As we their sa-cred triumphs chant

Forgiveness to our er- rors grant. 3) In Martyrs' Vic-

tor, Thou art e'er In Thy Confessors prone to spare;

Anonymous (9th–10th c.)
tr. John David Chambers

e'er now our guilty pride o'erthrow And all Thy

pardoning grace be-stow!

†175: Telluris ingens conditor

At Vespers.

Italy: Verona (11th c.)

D–A

Thou mighty Maker of earth's frame, Who

gavest land and sea their name, Hast swept the wa-

ters to their bound, And fixed for aye the solid

ground. 2) That soon upspringing should be seen

The herb with blossoms gold and green, And fruit

Anonymous (9th–10th c.)
tr. Samuel Willoughby Duffield

(1) ii:4

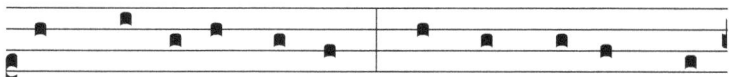

which ripely hangeth there, And grass to which the

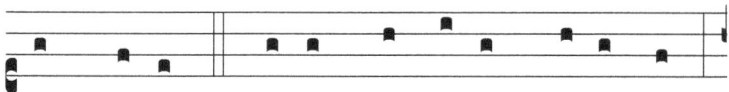

herds re-pair. 3) Re-lieve the sorrows of the soul!

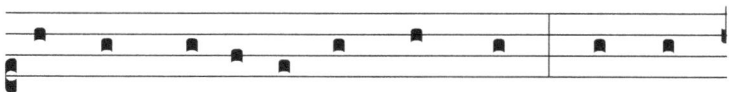

Our wounded spirits make thou whole, That tears

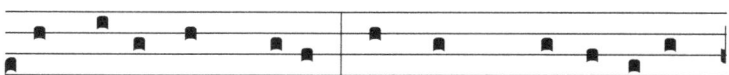

may sinful deeds al-lay, And cleanse all baser lusts

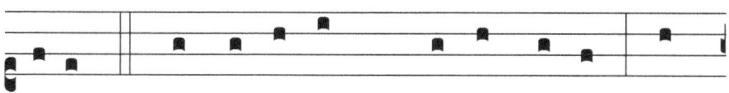

a-way. 4) Let us be swayed by thy de-cree, From

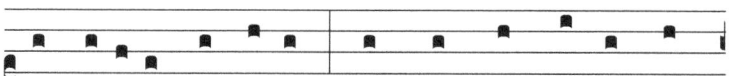

many e-vils set us free; With goodness fill the wait-

ing heart, And keep all fear of death a-part!

†176: Agnoscat omne saeculum

On the Nativity of the Lord
at Nocturns.

Germany: Kempten (ca. 1000)

F–F

Let every age and na-tion own That life's re-

ward at length is shewn; The Foe's hard yoke is

cast a- way, Redemption hath appeared to-day.

2) I- sa-iah's strains ful-filment meet, And in the Vir-

gin are complete: The Angel's tongue hath called

her blest: The Holy Ghost hath filled her breast.

3) The Virgin Mary hath conceived By that true

Anonymous (999)
tr. John Mason Neale

sel: 1–3, 7

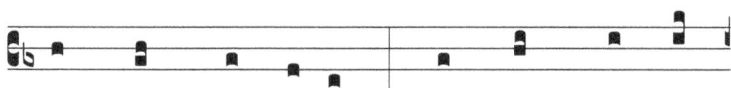

word which she be-lieved; And Whom the wide

world cannot hold, A spotless maiden's arms en-

fold. 4) Now buds the flower of Jesse's root; Now

Aaron's rod puts out its fruit; She sees her off-

spring rise to view, The Mother, yet the Virgin

too. 5) He, by Whose Hand the Light was made,

Deigns in a manger to be laid; He with His Fa-

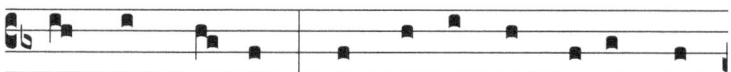

ther made the skies, And by His Mother swaddled

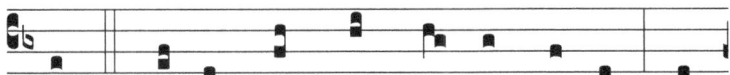

lies. 6) He that once gave the Law to men, And

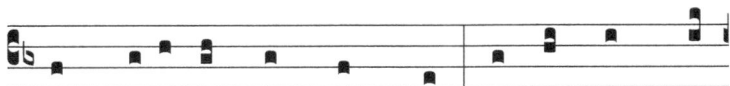

wrote it in Commandments Ten, Himself man's na-

ture deigns to share, The fetters of the Law to

wear. 7) Now the Old Adam's sinful stain Doth the

New Adam cleanse a-gain; And what the first by

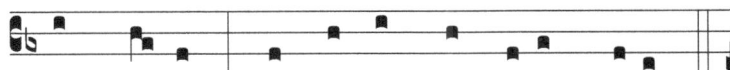

pride o'erthrew This lowliest One uprears a-new.

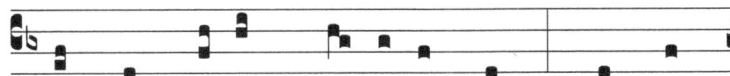

8) Now light is come, Sal-va-tion shewn, And night

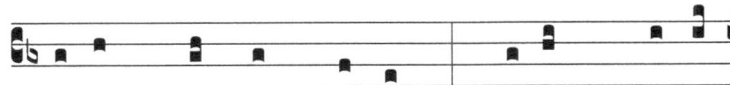

re-pelled, and Death o'erthrown; Approach, ye na-

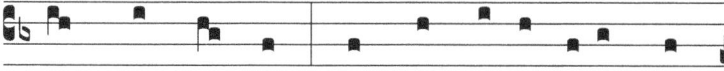

tions! own this morn, That God of Mary hath been

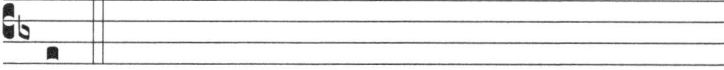

born.

†177: Agnoscat omne saeculum

At Terce.

Italy: Verona (11th c.)

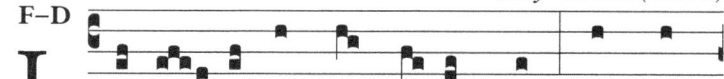

F–D

Let eve- ry age and na-tion own That life's

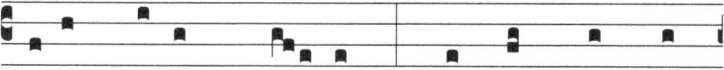

reward at length is shewn; The Foe's hard yoke

is cast a-way, Redemption hath ap-peared to-day.

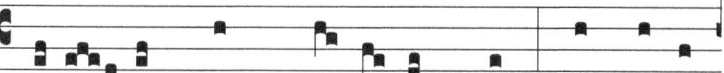

2) I- sa- iah's strains ful-fil-ment meet, And in the

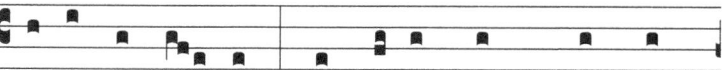

Virgin are com-plete: The Angel's tongue hath called

Anonymous (999)
tr. John Mason Neale

(8) iv:7
sel: 1–3, 7

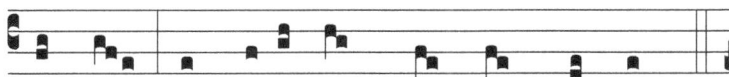

her blest: The Holy Ghost hath filled her breast.

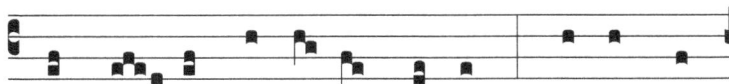

3) The Vir- gin Mary hath conceived By that true

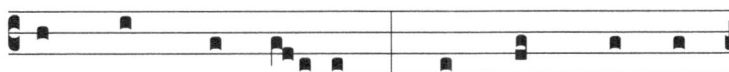

word which she be- lieved; And Whom the wide

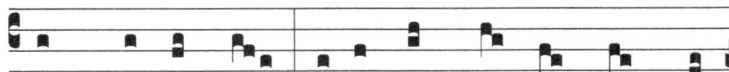

world cannot hold, A spotless maiden's arms en-

fold. 4) Now buds the flower of Jes-se's root; Now

Aaron's rod puts out its fruit; She sees her off-

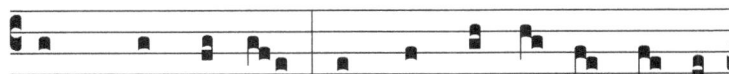

spring rise to view, The Mother, yet the Vir- gin

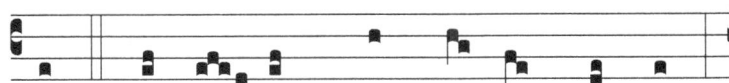

too. 5) He, by Whose Hand the Light was made,

Deigns in a manger to be   laid; He with His Fa-

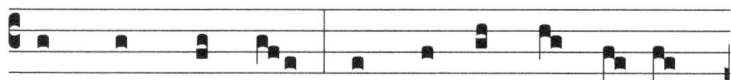

ther made the skies, And by His Mother swad-

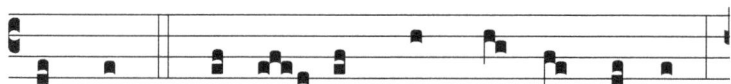

dled lies. 6) He that once gave the Law to men,

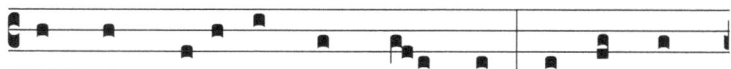

And wrote it in Commandments Ten, Himself man's

na-ture deigns to share, The fetters of the Law to

wear. 7) Now the Old Adam's sin-ful stain Doth the

New Adam cleanse a-   gain; And what the first by

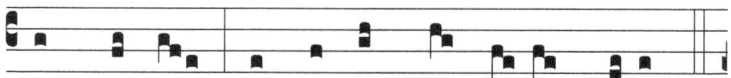

pride o'erthrew This lowliest One up-rears a-new.

8) Now light is come, Sal-va-tion shewn, And night

re-pelled, and Death o'er-thrown; Approach, ye na-

tions! own this morn, That God of Mary   hath been

born.

†178: A Patre unigenitus

At Compline.

Italy: Verona (11th c.)

D–D

S ent down by God to this world's frame, The

Only Son through Mary came: And hallow'd by his

Cross the wave, To give new life, and man to save.

Anonymous (ca. 1026)
tr. John Mason Neale: 1–5 / 6

2) From highest heav'n he came on earth; He took the

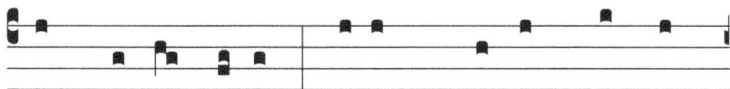

form of man at birth: Redeem'd by death the world

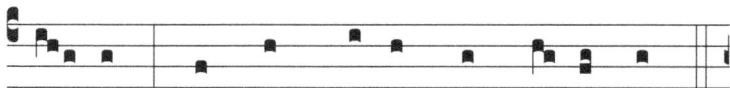

he   made, And gives us joys that cannot fade.

3) Glide on, thou glorious Sun, and bring The gift of

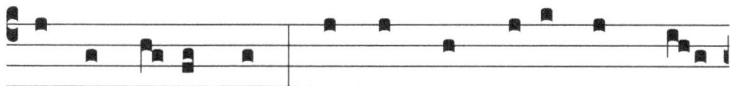

healing on thy wing: The clearness of thy light dis-

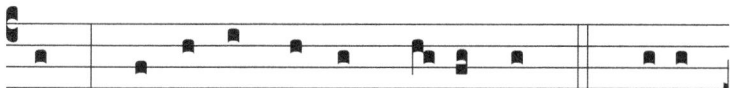

pense, To all thy people's ev- 'ry sense. 4) A-bide

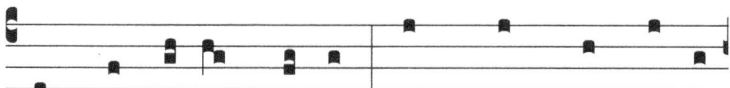

with us, O Lord, to-day, Chase night and all its

shades a-way: The stains of ev-'ry sin re- move,

And give us healing of thy love. 5) We, knowing

thou didst come of yore, Be-lieve thou shalt re-turn

once more: The glorious flock of thine e- lect

With thy de-fending shield protect.

†179: A Patre unigenitus

At Lauds.

France: Nevers (12th c.)

D–C

S ent down by God to this world's frame, The

Only Son through Mary came: And hallow'd by

Anonymous (ca. 1026)
tr. John Mason Neale: 1–5 / 6

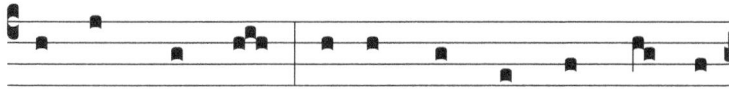

his Cross the wave, To give new life, and man to

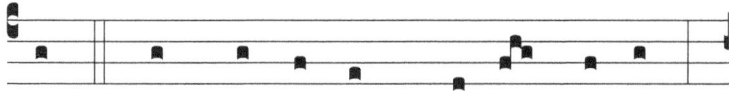

save. 2) From highest heav'n he came on earth;

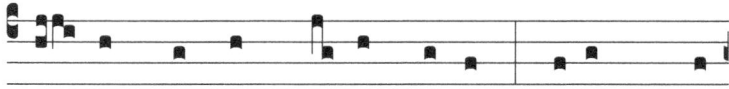

He took the form of man at birth: Redeem'd by

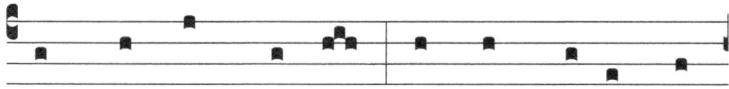

death the world he made, And gives us joys that

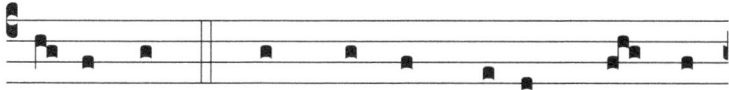

cannot fade. 3) Glide on, thou glorious Sun, and

bring The gift of healing on thy wing: The clear-

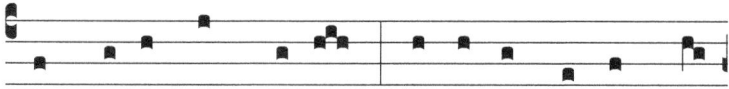

ness of thy light dispense, To all thy people's ev-

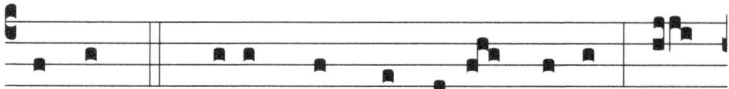

'ry sense. 4) A-bide with us, O Lord, to-day, Chase

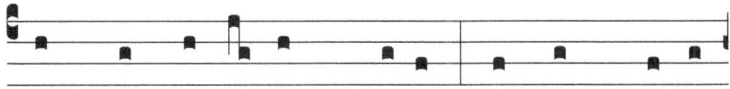

night and all its shades a-way: The stains of ev-

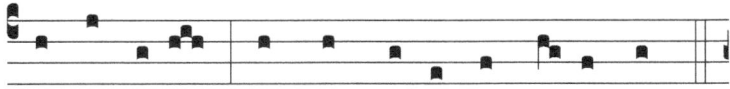

'ry sin remove, And give us healing of thy love.

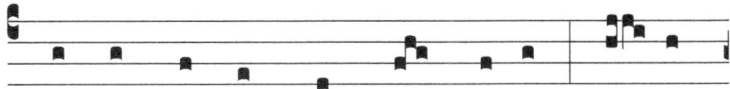

5) We, knowing thou didst come of yore, Be- lieve

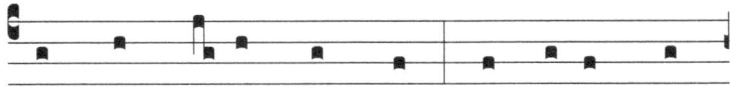

thou shalt re- turn once more: The glorious flock

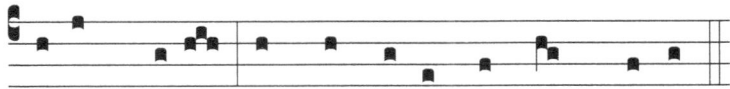

of thine e- lect With thy de-fending shield protect.

†180: Iam, Christe, sol iustitiae

Italy: Verona (11th c.)

E–C

O Christ! Thou Sun of Jus- tice! come

Anonymous (1000–1075)
tr. John David Chambers

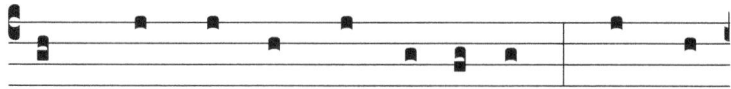

Pierce with Thy rays our mental gloom With vir-

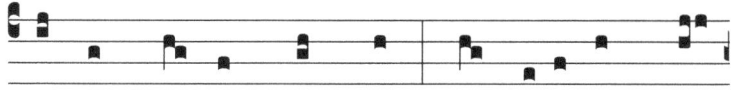

tue light our souls once more, And unto Earth Thy

Day re-store! 2) Thy time ac-cepta-ble is here;

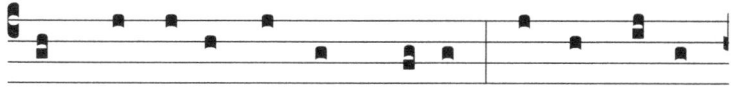

Make our re-pentant hearts sincere; Convert us with

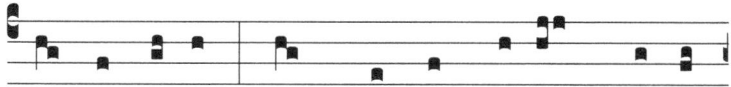

Thy kindly care, Whom Thy long-suffering mercies

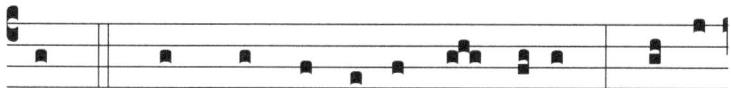

spare. 3) Grant that for all our deep of-fence, We of-

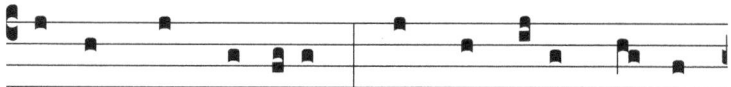

fer Thee meet peni- tence; That Thy benign and sov-

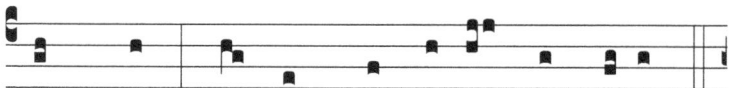

ereign grace May these our heinous sins ef-face.

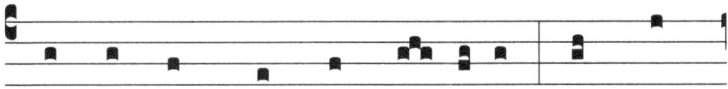

4) Thy Day draws near, that Day of bliss When teem-

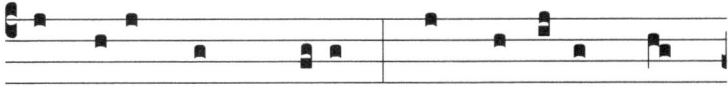

ing Nature blooms a- fresh; May we re-joice there-

in, O Lord! To Thy sweet fa-vour then re-stored.

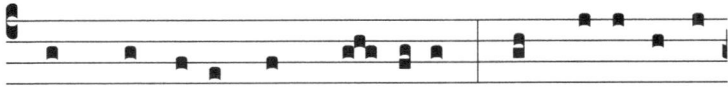

5) Kind Trini- ty! Thee ev- ermore The U-ni- versal

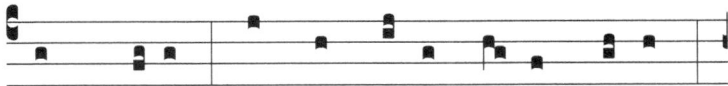

worlds a- dore; And new create, by Thee forgiven,

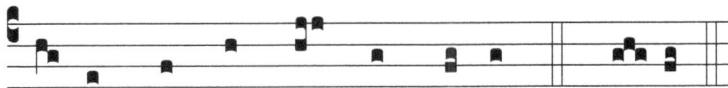

We raise this new-made song to Heaven! A- men.

†181: Qua Christus hora sitiit

At Sext.

Switzerland: Engelberg (ca. 1400)

E–A

This Hour when Christ our Lord a- thirst, Was

lifted on The Cross ac-curst, May He, as we His

praise express Give us the thirst of Righteousness.

2) And hunger which of Him create He with Himself

shall sa- ti- ate; Whereof e- nough to have is sin,

And more to crave shall Glory win. 3) O may The

Holy Ghost in-spire With gracious gifts our hymn-

Anonymous (1000–1075)
tr. John David Chambers

ing choir; Each carnal appe-tite to chill, And luke-

warm hearts with fervour fill.

†182: Optatus votis omnium

On the Ascension of the Lord.

Italy: Gaeta (12th c.)

F–E

A t length the long'd-for joy is given, The sa-

cred day begins to shine, When Christ our God, our

Hope di-vine, Ascends the ra-diant steep of heaven.

2) Ascending where He used to be, The Lord re- sumes

His ancient throne; The heavenly realms with joys

Anonymous (11th c.)
tr. Elizabeth Rundle Charles

sel: 1, 3–7

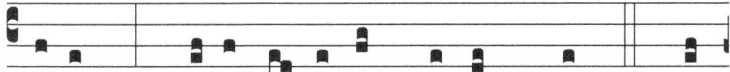

unknown, Only-be-gotten, welcome Thee. 3) The

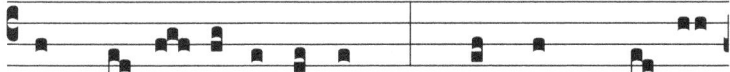

mighty vic-to-ry is wrought, The prince of this

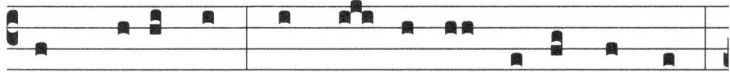

world li-eth low; The Son of God presenteth now

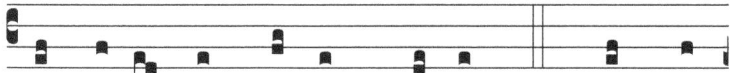

The human flesh in which He fought. 4) High o'er

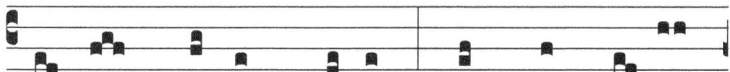

the clouds He comes to reign, Gives hope to those

who in Him trust; The Par-a-dise which Adam lost

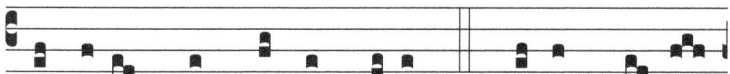

He o-pens wide to man a-gain. 5) O mighty joy

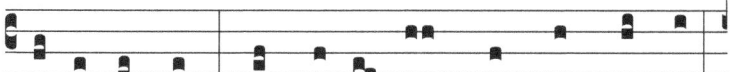

to all our race! The Virgin-born, who bore for us

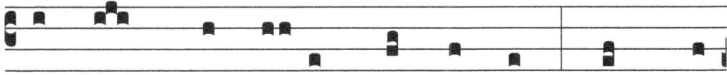

The stripes, the spitting, and the cross, Takes on

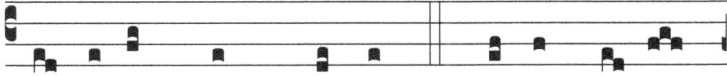

the Fa-ther's throne His place. 6) To Thee let cease-

less praises rise, Champion of our salva-tion Thou,

Bearing Thy hu-man body now In the high palace

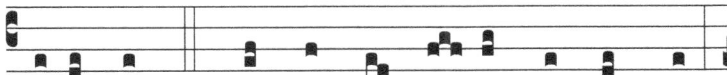

of the skies. 7) One common joy this day shall fill

The hearts of an- gels and of men; To them that

Thou art come a- gain, To us that Thou art with us

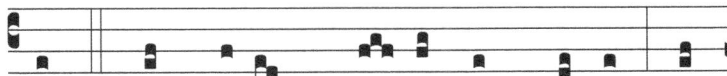

still. 8) Now, following in the steps He trod, 'Tis

462

ours to look for Christ from heaven, And so to

live that it be given To rise with Him at last to God.

†183: Optatus votis omnium

On the Ascension
of the Lord.

Austria: Heiligenkreuz (12th–13th c.)

C–C

A t length the long'd-for joy is given, The

sa- cred day begins to shine, When Christ our

God, our Hope di-vine, Ascends the ra- diant steep

of heaven. 2) As-cending where He used to be,

Anonymous (11th c.)
tr. Elizabeth Rundle Charles

sel: 1, 3–7

The Lord re-sumes His ancient throne; The heav-

enly realms with joys unknown, Only- be- got-

ten, welcome Thee. 3) The mighty vic- to-ry is

wrought, The prince of this world li-eth low; The

Son of God present- eth now The hu- man flesh

in which He fought. 4) High o'er the clouds He

comes to reign, Gives hope to those who in Him

trust; The Para- dise which Ad- am lost He o-pens wide to man a-gain. 5) O mighty joy to all

our race! The Vir-gin-born, who bore for us   The

stripes, the spit-ting, and   the cross, Takes on   the

Fa- ther's throne His place. 6) To Thee let cease-

less praises rise, Champion of our salva-tion Thou,

Bearing Thy hu- man bod- y now In the high pal-

ace of the skies. 7) One common joy this day shall

fill The hearts of an-gels and of men; To them that

Thou art come a-gain, To us   that Thou art with us

still. 8) Now, fol-lowing in   the steps He trod, 'Tis

ours to look for Christ from heaven, And so to live

that it   be given To rise with Him at last to God.

†184: O quanta qualia sunt illa sabbata

For the Book of Wisdom,
Saturday at Vespers.

Switzerland: Rheinau (12th c.)

C–D

How great, of what de-gree, In Heaven's

courts on high Shall those blest Sabbaths be Which

Peter Abelard (ca. 1131)
tr. Gerard Moultrie

they keep joy- ously! Prize for the brave is there,

Rest for the weary thrall, When ever everywhere

God shall be all in all. 2) Truly Je-ru-sa-lem,

Vi-sion of ho- ly peace, Gives peace with joy to

them— Joy which shall nev- er cease; Where full

frui- tion shall Than the wish swifter be, Nor can

de-sire forestall The bright re- al-i- ty. 3) What

king, what courts are these, What palace-hall is

this, Af-ter life's toil what ease Fills full the cup

of bliss? Souls, those de-lights which share, You on-

ly mirror can How vast the glory there, Passing

the thoughts of man. 4) Ours be it, lamp in hand,

To a-wait ea- gerly Thy call to seek the land

Of our last home with thee; And to Je-ru-sa-lem

Wait we with hearts in-tent Thy leave at length to

come From our long banish- ment. 5) When cares

our path which throng Vanish, and sore distress,

We shall sing Si-on's song In peace and hap- pi-

ness: Endlessly, joyously, Shall the blest people,

Lord, Give praise and thanks to thee For thine own

great re- ward. 6) Sabbath there follows not Sab-

bath: of all the blest One Sabbath is the lot,

One endless Sab- bath-rest: Ceaseless the songs of

praise Rising full-voiced to thee, Which we and angels sing In that high ju-bi- lee. 7) Lord of the eter-

nal land, Praise to thy Name we sing, From whom,

and through whom, and In whom is eve- ry-thing:

"From whom"—the Fa-ther is; "Through whom"—the

Only Son; "In whom"—the Spirit. This Worship we,

Three in One.

†185: Verbum supernum prodiens

On the solemnity of
the Body and Blood of the Lord.

Italy: Milan (12th c.)

G–A

The Word supernal forth proceeds, Nor leaves

the right hand of His Sire, To exe- cute His loft-

y deeds With life's sad e- ven drawing nigher.

2) By His disci- ple unto death Unto His ene- mies

be- trayed, He first the sus- te- nance of breath

Himself to His disci- ples made. 3) To whom He

Thomas Aquinas (1264)
tr. Athanasius Diedrich Wackerbarth

div: 1–4; 5–6

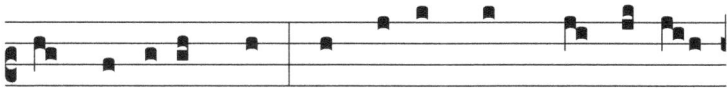

gave in ei-ther kind The sa-cred flesh, the pretious

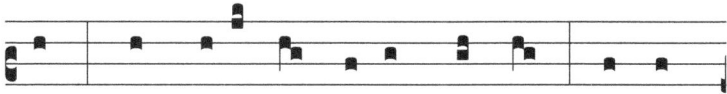

blood, That unto man of both combined He might

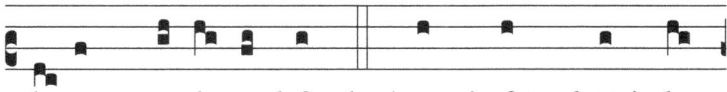

be-come ce-les-tial food. 4) Man's friend He's born

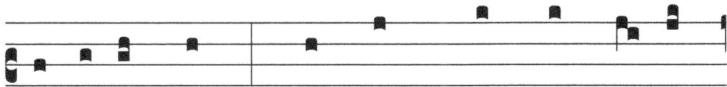

in human guise,— And dwells with him his food

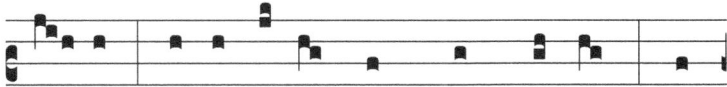

to be,— As his re-demption's price He dies,— And

reigns his crown of majes-ty. 5) O! Victim of Salva-

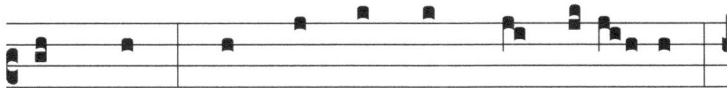

tion's cause, Who Heaven's gates hast o-pen laid,

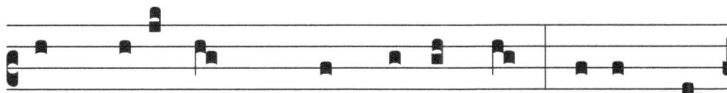

While o-verwhelm'd with hostile wars, Af-ford us

strength and grant us aid. 6) To great Je-ho-vah, one

and three, Be ever-lasting glory   given: A life of

endless bliss may He A-ward us in the realms of

Heaven.

†186: Verbum supernum prodiens

For the Body of Christ.

Poland: Środa Śląska (15th c.)

D–E

he Word su- pernal forth proceeds, Nor

leaves the right hand of His Sire, To exe- cute His

Thomas Aquinas (1264)   div: 1–4; 5–6
tr. Athanasius Diedrich Wackerbarth

lofty deeds With life's sad e-ven drawing nigher.

2) By His dis-ci-ple un-to death Unto His ene-mies

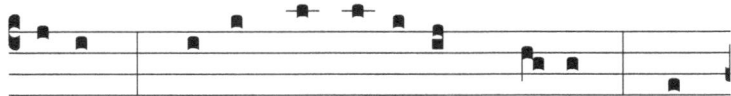

be-trayed, He first the suste-nance of breath Him-

self to His dis-ci-ples made. 3) To whom He

gave in ei-ther kind The sa-cred flesh, the pretious

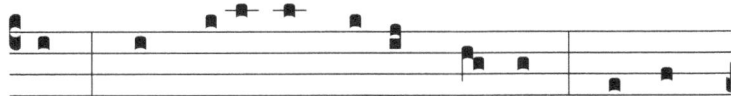

blood, That unto man of both combined He might

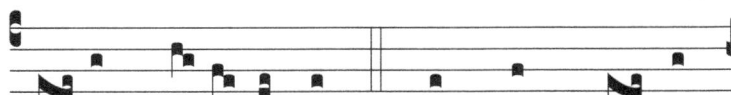

be-come ce-les-tial food. 4) Man's friend He's born

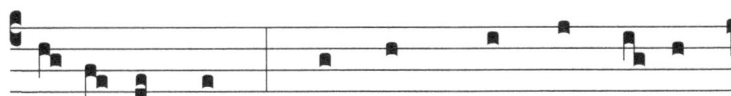

in hu-man guise,— And dwells with him his food

to be,— As his re-demption's price He dies,— And

reigns his crown of majes-ty. 5) O! Victim of Sal-

va- tion's cause, Who Heaven's gates hast o- pen

laid, While o-verwhelm'd with hostile wars, Af-ford

us strength and grant us aid. 6) To great Je- hovah,

one and three, Be ever-lasting glory given: A life

of endless bliss may He A-ward us in the realms

of Heaven.

†187: Verbum supernum prodiens

At a Nocturn.

Germany: Schäftlarn (1462)

The Word supernal forth proceeds, Nor leaves

the right hand of His Sire, To ex-e-cute His lofty

deeds With life's sad e- ven drawing nigher. 2) By

His disci- ple un- to death Un-to His en-e- mies

be-trayed, He first the suste-nance of breath Him-

self to His dis-ci- ples made. 3) To whom He gave

in ei- ther kind The sa- cred flesh, the pre-tious

Thomas Aquinas (1264)
tr. Athanasius Diedrich Wackerbarth

div: 1–4; 5–6

blood, That un-to man of both combined He might

be-come ce- les- tial food. 4) Man's friend He's born

in hu- man guise,— And dwells with him his food

to be,— As his re-demption's price He dies,— And

reigns his crown of maj- es-ty. 5) O! Vic-tim of

Sal-va- tion's cause, Who Heaven's gates hast o-

pen laid, While o- verwhelm'd with hostile wars,

Af-ford us strength and grant us aid. 6) To great Je-ho-vah, one and three, Be ev- er-lasting glo-ry

given: A life of endless bliss may He A-ward us

in the realms of Heaven.

Further Information on the Hymnal

Methodology

554 translations from various sources were collected for the 56 poems. The majority of these translations were found using *A Dictionary of Hymnology* by John Julian and *The Latin Hymn-Writers and their Hymns* by Samuel Duffield. One translation was selected for each poem, paying attention to several criteria. First, the content of the translation needed to match that of the original. A word-for-word translation was not necessary, but corresponding stanzas needed to be close in meaning. Second, the meter of the translation needed to match that of the original. This is important for aligning the melody to the words. All of the poems in this hymnal have translations with matching meters except *Mediae noctis tempus est* (see "Notes on the Poems and Melodies"). Third, the style of writing needed to be consistent between the selected translations. Other aspects considered were how many of the stanzas were translated, whether the lines of the poem could be understood clearly when sung, whether the translation had been altered by others, whether metaphors and imagery in the original were maintained in the translation, whether an unaltered form of the Latin text was used when writing the translation, what rhyme scheme was used, and finally, how

the choice of words contributed to the overall quality of the translation.

For each poem, all available melodies in *HA* were selected, and then the selection was narrowed down in the following way. First, melodies that were only found in sources after 1500 were removed. In *HA*, similar melodies are grouped by number into families. The variants within a family are indicated by another number after the decimal. For example, melody 501.1 and melody 501.2 are both in the 501 family. If a poem had several melody variants in the same family, the variant from the earliest source was chosen. The melodies were then checked for duplication. If a melody was duplicated, the poem with the least number of melodies was selected to be used with that melody. If there was a tie, the variant from the earlier source was chosen, and if there was still a tie, the older poem was chosen. The result was that no melodies for the selected poems were lost, each poem kept some of its associated melodies, and none of these melodies were reused with other poems. There was one exception: if there was only one melody associated with a poem, the melody was kept, regardless of duplication. In the end, only 3 melodies from *HA* were reused: 142, 145, and 702. A consequence of this process is that a selected melody may not be the earliest record of the melody in *HA* (though it is the earliest for that particular poem). For example, melody 8 used with *Deus, creator omnium* from Heiligenkreuz, Stiftsbibliothek 20 has an earlier variant in Verona, Biblioteca Capitolare CIX (102), but the melody there is used with a different poem, *Iesu, redemptor omnium*.

The dates for each poem were taken from *OHLH*, if they were listed there. If not, dates in *The Canterbury Dictionary of Hymnology* were used. If no dates were given there either, the dates of the earliest manuscript containing the poem were used, as recorded in the final table of Jullien's "Les sources de la tradition ancienne des quatorze 'Hymnes' attribuées à saint Ambroise de Milan". Most of the places and dates of the archives containing the melodies were found in *HA*. In the few cases where this information was missing, sources such as *Berliner Repertorium* and *Biblioteca Apostolica Vaticana* were consulted. Note that the place where the archive is held is not necessarily the same as the place or region associated with the archive. For example, London, British Museum Add. 34209 is from Milan. The authors listed for the poems were taken from *OHLH*, and authors prefixed with phrases like "attributed to" and "traditionally ascribed to" were simply labelled as anonymous.

Modifications

Most of the poems are written in iambic dimeter, which, in Latin prosody, has 4 iambs per line. The remaining poems are written in trochaic tetrameter catalectic, trochaic dimeter brachycatalectic, octosyllabic verse, paired hexasyllabic cola, and elegiac couplets (dactylic hexameter and pentameter). All, except for the last, have a fixed number of syllables per line, which allows the same melody to be reused for multiple stanzas. Poems written in elegiac couplets are more problematic because the syllable count for each couplet is not constant. To fit the couplets to a repeated melody, certain notes need to be added or removed. For these particular hymns, I first examined how the melody in *HA* was modified between couplets in the Latin and then applied the same techniques to the English. In fact, there are only two such poems in this hymnal: *Crux benedicta nitet* and *Gloria, laus, et honor.*

Not all stanzas to the poems are present in manuscripts.

481

In many cases, only one stanza is present, and it is not necessarily the first. On the other hand, some manuscripts have additional stanzas. A doxology, for example, is commonly added to the end of a poem. To determine the original form and content of each poem, I relied on the information presented in *OHLH*. In the cases where the stanza numbers in *HA* did not match those given in *OHLH*, I decided to move the melodic alterations to other stanzas. For example, if *HA* listed a melodic alteration in stanza 9, but the poem in *OHLH* only had 8 stanzas, I moved the alteration from the 9th stanza to the 8th. In these and similar cases, I gave priority to changes between the first and second stanzas, followed by changes between the penultimate and last stanzas in an attempt to preserve the musical structure of the hymn. These adjustments on the whole are quite rare but are, nevertheless, listed in "Notes on the Poems and Melodies".

Melodic alterations given in *HA* are included with two exceptions. Stäblein mentions that a few of the alterations are probably mistakes in the manuscripts, and I omitted these. In other cases, where the poem does not adhere strictly to the meter, the alterations appear to be made to accommodate extra syllables in the poem's lines. For example, in melody 26.2 for *Illluminans altissimus*, a note at (1) ii:5 is repeated to accommodate the extra syllable in the line: *micantium astrorum globos*. Since these changes are specific to the Latin, it did not seem relevant to include them in this hymnal. Though, as mentioned in the introduction, it may be helpful to apply this same technique to certain English contractions which are awkward to sing on a single note.

Stäblein lists three special neumes present in some of the manuscripts: the franculus, the quilisma, and the liquescent neume. Initially, I intended to include these in the scores. However, I was unable to find any satisfactory answers on what these neumes actually mean. David Hiley, musicologist at the University of Regensburg, gives some idea of the confusion surrounding these neumes. On the oriscus, supposedly a component of the franculus, he writes,

> "[It has] been suggested that some special vocal delivery was involved. Wagner believed that a non-diatonic pitch was involved. ... Cardine believed its significance was rhythmic, directing rhythmic weight to the succeeding note, which is very often lower. Whether this rhythmic nuance is sufficient justification for the use of a special sign is debatable" (*Western* 359).

Writers do not even agree on the symbol to which the franculus refers. On the virga strata, Hiley comments, "This sign has also been called the franculus, but Huglo questions the correctness of this identification" (*Western* 36). Information on the quilisma was equally unconvincing: "Aurelian of Réôme (fl? 840–50) spoke of it as a trembling and rising sound and most modern writers have not ventured beyond this. Tack suggested that it concerns a method of voice production no longer practised" (Hiley, "Quilisma"). On liquescent neumes, Leo Treitler describes André Mocquereau's theory as "problematic on all sides" (393). Hiley writes,

> "The manner of performance of liquescent signs is not entirely clear. A passing-note of some sort seems to be involved, ... Comparisons between sources indicate that the use of liquescent signs was inconsistent, ... no two scribes would put them in exactly the same places, ..." (*Western* 357).

After going back and forth on the matter, I finally decided to omit these special neumes from the scores.

Notes on the Poems and Melodies

Over the centuries, the words in some of these poems were changed. Two books which were widely used that contain revised forms of the poems are the Roman Breviary of 1632 and the Paris Breviary of 1736. Some of these revisions are slight, changing only one or two words, while other revisions are substantial enough that the revised forms could be considered different poems altogether. To complicate matters, some poems share the same name but are not the same poems. And finally, some poems that are, in fact, the same have different names because they do not all begin on the first stanza. Such details are listed below.

The birth and death dates of the translators are taken from *WorldCat Identities*. Stäblein is abbreviated with an S, and sources for the melodies are marked with brackets to differentiate them from the archive dates. Mistakes in the melody numbers in *HA* have been corrected by comparing a second set of numbers with the information in the "Kritischer Bericht". These are pointed out in the individual melodies.

Aeterne rerum conditor

This poem is by Ambrose of Milan (ca. 334–397). It consists of 8 stanzas of 4 lines in iambic dimeter. All 8 stanzas are translated by Herbert Kynaston (1809–1878). See further Walsh viii, 2–5, 383–384; Kynaston 138–140.

†1 is melody 143.3 from Kempten, Germany and is found in Zürich, Zentralbibliothek, Rh 83 (ca. 1000) [S 251].

†2 is melody 701 from Verona, Italy and is found in Verona, Biblioteca Capitolare CIX (102) (11th c.) [S 358, 600].

†3 is melody 588 from Rheinau, Switzerland and is found in Zürich, Zentralbibliothek, Rh 21 and 22 (1459) [S 323].

Deus, creator omnium

This poem is by Ambrose of Milan (ca. 334–397). It consists of 8 stanzas of 4 lines in iambic dimeter and was sometimes divided into a separate hymn at stanza 5: *Ut cum profunda clauserit*. All 8 stanzas are translated by John David Chambers (1805–1893). See further Walsh viii, 10–13, 386–387; Chambers I: 55–56.

†4 is melody 52.4 from Kempten, Germany and is found in Zürich, Zentralbibliothek, Rh 83 (ca. 1000) [S 254].

†5 is melody 501.2 from Verona, Italy and is found in Verona, Biblioteca Capitolare CIX (102) (11th c.) [S 361, 364, 600].

†6 is melody 229 from Laon, France and is found in Laon, Bibliothèque Com. 263 (1100–1150) [S 144].

†7 is melody 8.2 from Heiligenkreuz, Austria and is found in Heiligenkreuz, Stiftsbibliothek 20 (12th–13th c.) [S 28, 515].

†8 is melody 502 from Klosterneuburg, Austria and is found in Klosterneuburg, Stiftsbibliothek 1000 (1336) [S 214, 567].

Hic est dies verus Dei

This poem is by Ambrose of Milan (ca. 334–397). It consists of 8 stanzas of 4 lines in iambic dimeter. All 8 stanzas are translated by George Ratcliffe Woodward (1848–1934). See further Walsh viii, 26–29, 394–395; Woodward 96.

†9 is melody 117.3 from Gaeta, Italy and is found in Roma, Biblioteca Casanatense 1574 (12th c.) [S 418].

†10 is melody 17.2 from Heiligenkreuz, Austria and is found in Heiligenkreuz, Stiftsbibliothek 20 (12th–13th c.). This melody was often used for *Veni, creator Spiritus*, though the melody predates that poem [S 27, 35, 515; Hornby, "Veni"].

†11 is melody 5.3 from Einsiedeln, Switzerland and is found in Einsiedeln, Stiftsbibliothek 336 (1225–1275) [S 278].

Iam surgit hora tertia

This poem is by Ambrose of Milan (ca. 334–397). It consists of 8 stanzas of 4 lines in iambic dimeter. All 8 stanzas are translated by William John Copeland (1804–1885). See further Walsh viii, 8–11, 385–386; Copeland 145–147.

†12 is melody 6.2 from Heiligenkreuz, Austria and is found in Heiligenkreuz, Stiftsbibliothek 20 (12th–13th c.) [S 35, 518].

Illuminans altissimus

This poem is by Ambrose of Milan (ca. 334–397). It consists of 8 stanzas of 4 lines in iambic dimeter. All 8 stanzas are translated by William John Copeland (1804–1885). See further Walsh viii, 391–392; Copeland 170–172.

> †13 is melody 703 from Verona, Italy and is found in Verona, Biblioteca Capitolare CIX (102) (11th c.) [S 365, 372, 601].
>
> †14 is melody 26.2 from Heiligenkreuz, Austria and is found in Heiligenkreuz, Stiftsbibliothek 20 (12th–13th c.). I removed the extra note at (1) ii5, which was inserted to accommodate the extra syllable in the Latin text [S 31, 516].

Intende, qui regis Israel

This poem is by Ambrose of Milan (ca. 334–397). It consists of 8 stanzas of 4 lines in iambic dimeter. Stanza 1 is omitted in many sources, and the poem is more often referred to by the first line of the second stanza, *Veni, redemptor gentium.* Stanzas 2–8 out of 8 are translated by John Mason Neale (1818–1866). See further Walsh viii, 387–389; Julian 1211–1212; Neale, *The Words* 34–36.

> †15 is melody 138 from Nevers, France and is found in Paris, Bibliothèque Nationale n. a. lat. 1235 (12th c.) [S 80, 540].
>
> †16 is melody 503.2 from Einsiedeln, Switzerland and is found in Einsiedeln, Stiftsbibliothek 336 (1225–1275) [S 273].

†17 is melody 406 from Worcester, England and is found in Worcester, Cathedral Library F 160 (ca. 1230) [S 177].

†18 is melody 597 from Dürnstein, Austria and is found in Sankt Florian, Stiftsbibliothek XI 407 (15th c.) [S 328].

Splendor paternae gloriae

This poem is by Ambrose of Milan (ca. 334–397). It consists of 8 stanzas of 4 lines in iambic dimeter. All 8 stanzas are translated by Robert Seymour Bridges (1844–1930). See further Walsh viii, 384–385; Bridges 29.

†19 is melody 2.4 from Kempten, Germany and is found in Zürich, Zentralbibliothek, Rh 83 (ca. 1000). I removed the extra note at (1) iv5, which was inserted to accommodate the extra syllable in the Latin text [S 253].

†20 is melody 3.2 from Heiligenkreuz, Austria and is found in Heiligenkreuz, Stiftsbibliothek 20 (12th–13th c.) [S 26].

†21 is melody 749 from Lehel, Germany and is found in München, Fransician abbey of St. Anna s. n. (1227–1235) [S 441].

†22 is melody 268 from Le Mans, France and is found in Paris, Bibliothèque Sainte-Geneviève 112 (1450–1500) [S 163].

Ales diei nuntius

This poem is by Prudentius (348–410). It consists of 25 stanzas of 4 lines in iambic dimeter. All 25 stanzas are translated by

Robert Martin Pope (1865-1944). See further Walsh ix, 54–61, 403–407; Pope 6–13.

†23 is melody 702 from Verona, Italy and is found in Verona, Biblioteca Capitolare CIX (102) (11th c.) [S 362, 363, 600].

Nox et tenebrae et nubila

This poem is by Prudentius (348–410). It consists of 28 stanzas of 4 lines in iambic dimeter and was sometimes divided into a separate hymn at stanza 7: *Sol ecce surgit igneus,* though this line was modified to *Lux ecce surgit aurea.* All 28 stanzas are translated by Robert Martin Pope (1865-1944). See further Walsh ix, 62–71, 408–412; Pope 14–21.

†24 is melody 540 from Einsiedeln, Switzerland and is found in Einsiedeln, Stiftsbibliothek 336 (1225–1275) [S 279].

†25 is melody 578 from Engelberg, Switzerland and is found in Engelberg, Stiftsbibliothek 8 (ca. 1400) [S 318].

Aeterna Christi munera

This poem is by an anonymous author and was written between 390 and 423. It consists of 8 stanzas of 4 lines in iambic dimeter. The Roman Breviary of 1632 contains another form of the poem called *Christo profusum sanguinem.* A different but related poem, *Aeterna Christi apostolorum,* is found in numerous breviaries. All 8 stanzas are translated by John Mason Neale (1818–1866), though they were taken from two separate translations. See further Walsh 42–45, 400; Julian 24–25; Neale, *The Words* 96–97; Ramsey 4.

†26 is melody 115.1 from Moissac, France and is found in Roma, Biblioteca Apostolica Vaticana Ross. 205 (ca. 1000). I removed the extra note at ii4, which was inserted to accommodate the extra syllable in the Latin text [S 60].

†27 is melody 127.3 from Verona, Italy and is found in Verona, Biblioteca Capitolare CIX (102) (11th c.) [S 395, 403, 605].

A solis ortus cardine

This poem is by Sedulius (fl. 425–450). It consists of 23 stanzas of 4 lines in iambic dimeter and was sometimes divided into a separate hymn at stanza 8: *Hostis Herodes impie.* It is an acrostic, with each successive stanza beginning on the next letter of the alphabet. The Roman Breviary of 1632 contains another form of the second part called *Crudelis Herodes, Deum.* A different poem shares the same first line but has *semitam* in place of *limitem* in line 2; another has *Annam* in place of *Christum* in line 3. Stanzas 1–9, 11, and 13 out of 23 are translated by John Mason Neale (1818–1866). See further Walsh 86–93; Julian 4–5; Neale, *The Words* 39–40; S 665; Springer.

†28 is melody 505.2 from Kempten, Germany and is found in Zürich, Zentralbibliothek, Rh 83 (ca. 1000) [S 256].

†29 is melody 227 from Laon, France and is found in Laon, Bibliothèque Com. 263 (1100–1150) [S 143, 556].

†30 is melody 538 from Einsiedeln, Switzerland and is found in Einsiedeln, Stiftsbibliothek 336 (1100–1150) [S 276].

†31 is melody 36.2 from Gaeta, Italy and is found in Roma, Biblioteca Casanatense 1574 (12th c.) [S 413].

†32 is melody 721 from Gaeta, Italy and is found in Roma, Biblioteca Casanatense 1574 (12th c.) [S 410].

†33 is melody 409 from Worcester, England and is found in Worcester, Cathedral Library F 160 (ca. 1230) [S 180].

†34 is melody 254 from Clermont-Ferránd, France and is found in Clermont-Ferránd, Bibliothèque Municipale et Universitaire 74 (14th c.) [S 156].

Mediae noctis tempus est

This poem is by an anonymous author and was written between 475 and 525. It consists of 14 stanzas of 4 lines in octosyllabic verse. Some sources have *tempore* in place of *tempus est*. All 14 stanzas are translated by Edward Caswall (1814–1878). The translation does not quite preserve the meter and is missing one syllable per line. It is also missing the 14th stanza, which is a general doxology; I used a doxology with matching meter from another of Caswall's translations. See further Walsh 120–125, 430–432; Caswall 78, 235–237; S 673.

†35 is melody 761 from central or southern Italy and is found in Berlin, Staatsbibliothek Hamilton 688 (ca. 1267). Because the meter does not quite match, I combined neumes 6 and 7 on each line [S 448].

Crux benedicta nitet

This poem is by Venantius Fortunatus (ca. 535–610) and was written around 567. It consists of 9 elegiac couplets in dactylic hexameter and pentameter. All 9 couplets are translated by John Mason Neale (1818–1866). See further Walsh xi, 104–107, 424–426; Thompson 238.

†36 is melody 1009 from Ravenna, Italy and is found in Padova, Biblioteca Capitolare A 47 (12th c.). This hymn was used as a processional. The refrain was repeated after each line of the poem. Stäblein writes that it is not clear what part of couplet 1 served as the refrain. He also gives a different order in which the couplets were sung: 1, 2, 5, 6, 7, 4. Regarding melodic alterations, see "Further Information on the Hymnal" [S 483, 617].

Pange, lingua

This poem is by Venantius Fortunatus (ca. 535–610) and was written around 567. It consists of 10 stanzas of 3 lines in trochaic tetrameter catalectic and was sometimes divided into a separate hymn at stanza 6: *Lustra sex qui iam peracta* or stanza 8: *Crux fidelis, inter omnes.* Several other poems share the same name; probably the most familiar is the one by Thomas Aquinas, written for the Office and Mass of Corpus Christi in 1264. The one used in this hymnal is distinguished from Aquinas's and others by the end of its first line: *proelium certaminis.* All 10 stanzas are translated by Hamilton Montgomerie MacGill (1807–1880). See further Walsh xi, 96–101, 422–426, 498; Julian 880–881; MacGill 36–37; S 675.

†37 is melody 101 from Moissac, France and is found in Roma, Biblioteca Apostolica Vaticana Ross. 205 (ca. 1000) [S 52].

†38 is melody 102 from Moissac, France and is found in

Roma, Biblioteca Apostolica Vaticana Ross. 205 (ca. 1000) [S 52].

†39 is melody 56.5 from Verona, Italy and is found in Verona, Biblioteca Capitolare CIX (102) (11th c.) [S 385, 604].

†40 is melody 724 from Gaeta, Italy and is found in Roma, Biblioteca Casanatense 1574 (12th c.) [S 417].

†41 is melody 1007 from Paris, France and is found in Roma, Biblioteca Casanatense 1695 (12th–13th c.). This hymn was used as a processional. The 8th stanza acted as a refrain; it was sung first and then repeated after each stanza. Stanza 5 is omitted in the manuscript [S 481, 616].

†42 is melody 769 from southern Italy and is found in Bari, San Nicola s. n. (13th c.) [S 452].

†43 is melody 623 from Rüdnitz, Germany and is found in Praha, Knihovna pražské metropolitní kapituly, Sveti Vid Cim. 7 (1325–1375) [S 342].

†44 is melody 140.2 from Klosterneuburg, Austria and is found in Klosterneuburg, Stiftsbibliothek 1000 (1336) [S 227, 572].

Vexilla regis prodeunt

This poem is by Venantius Fortunatus (ca. 535–610) and was written around 567. It consists of 8 stanzas of 4 lines in iambic dimeter. Several other poems share the same first line; the one used in this hymnal is distinguished from those by its second line: *fulget crucis mysterium*. All 8 stanzas are translated by Elizabeth Rundle Charles (1828–1896). See further Walsh xi, 100–103, 424–425; Charles 131–132; S 679.

†45 is melody 32.6 from Kempten, Germany and is found

in Zürich, Zentralbibliothek, Rh 83 (ca. 1000) [S 257].

Iam lucis orto sidere

This poem is by an anonymous author from the 8th century. It consists of 4 stanzas of 4 lines in iambic dimeter. A different poem shares the same first line but has *dignare* instead of *Deum* in line 2. All 4 stanzas are translated by Alan Gordon McDougall (1895–1964). See further Walsh 112–113; Boynton, "Medieval"; Britt 33–34; Julian 577–578; S 671.

†46 is melody 125 from Limoges, France and is found in Paris, Bibliothèque Nationale lat. 777 (11th c.) [S 67].

†47 is melody 134.5 from Einsiedeln, Switzerland and is found in Einsiedeln, Stiftsbibliothek 336 (1100–1150) [S 266].

†48 is melody 225 from Laon, France and is found in Laon, Bibliothèque Com. 263 (1100–1150) [S 142].

†49 is melody 226 from Laon, France and is found in Laon, Bibliothèque Com. 263 (1100–1150) [S 142].

†50 is melody 533 from Einsiedeln, Switzerland and is found in Einsiedeln, Stiftsbibliothek 336 (1100–1150) [S 265].

†51 is melody 59.2 from Nevers, France and is found in Paris, Bibliothèque Nationale n. a. lat. 1235 (12th c.) [S 71].

†52 is melody 65.2 from Nevers, France and is found in Paris, Bibliothèque Nationale n. a. lat. 1235 (12th c.) [S 73].

†53 is melody 129 from Nevers, France and is found in Paris, Bibliothèque Nationale n. a. lat. 1235 (12th c.) [S 73].

†54 is melody 130.1 from Nevers, France and is found in

Paris, Bibliothèque Nationale n. a. lat. 1235 (12th c.)
[S 73].

†55 is melody 132 from Nevers, France and is found in
Paris, Bibliothèque Nationale n. a. lat. 1235 (12th c.)
[S 75].

†56 is melody 249 from Fécamp, France and is found in
Rouen, Bibliothèque de la Ville 248 (12th–13th c.)
[S 154].

†57 is melody 275 from Fécamp, France and is found in
Rouen, Bibliothèque de la Ville 248 (12th–13th c.)
[S 167].

†58 is melody 768 from southern Italy and is found in
Bari, San Nicola s. n. (13th c.) [S 451].

†59 is melody 401 from Worcester, England and is found
in Worcester, Cathedral Library F 160 (ca. 1230)
[S 170, 172].

†60 is melody 427 from Worcester, England and is found in
Worcester, Cathedral Library F 160 (ca. 1230) [S 203].

†61 is melody 185 from Paris, France and is found in
Roma, Santa Sabina, Archivum Generale Ordinis
Predicatorum s. n. (ca. 1255) [S 121, 697; Wagner 328].

†62 is melody 237 from Angers, France and is found in
Angers, Bibliothèque de la Ville 113 (105) (14th–15th
c.) [S 148].

†63 is melody 526 from Klosterneuburg, Austria and is
found in Klosterneuburg, Stiftsbibliothek 1000 (1336)
[S 245].

Rector potens, verax Deus

This poem is by an anonymous author from the 8th century.
It consists of 2 stanzas of 4 lines in iambic dimeter. Both of the

stanzas are translated by John David Chambers (1805–1893). See further Walsh 144–145; Boynton, "Medieval"; Chambers I: 37.

†64 is melody 238 from Angers, France and is found in Angers, Bibliothèque de la Ville 113 (105) (14th–15th c.) [S 148].

†65 is melody 216 from Châlons-en-Champagne, France and is found in Paris, Bibliothèque Nationale lat. 1269 (1309) [S 137].

†66 is melody 265 from Paris, France and is found in Paris, Bibliothèque Mazarine 344 (1350–1400) [S 162].

†67 is melody 577 from Engelberg, Switzerland and is found in Engelberg, Stiftsbibliothek 8 (ca. 1400) [S 317].

†68 is melody 270 from Paris, France and is found in Paris, Bibliothèque de l' Arsenal 114 (1471) [S 164].

Te lucis ante terminum

This poem is by an anonymous author from the 8th century. It consists of 2 stanzas of 4 lines in iambic dimeter. Sometimes 3 stanzas are given, but the third is not part of the original poem. Both of the stanzas are translated by John William Hewett (1824–1886). See further Walsh 110–111, 426–427; Boynton, "Medieval"; Hewett 14–15.

†69 is melody 529 from Kempten, Germany and is found in Zürich, Zentralbibliothek, Rh 83 (ca. 1000) [S 254].

†70 is melody 534 from Einsiedeln, Switzerland and is found in Einsiedeln, Stiftsbibliothek 336 (1100–1150) [S 269].

†71 is melody 135 from Nevers, France and is found in Paris, Bibliothèque Nationale n. a. lat. 1235 (12th c.)

[S 78].

†72 is melody 136.1 from Nevers, France and is found in Paris, Bibliothèque Nationale n. a. lat. 1235 (12th c.). Stäblein lists (3) i:1,4 and ii:2 as alterations; because Walsh lists only 2 stanzas, I moved the changes in stanza 3 to 2 [S 79, 539].

†73 is melody 10.2 from Heiligenkreuz, Austria and is found in Heiligenkreuz, Stiftsbibliothek 20 (12th–13th c.) [S 28, 515].

†74 is melody 747 from Rome, Italy and is found in Roma, Biblioteca Capitolare San Pietro B 79 (1200–1250). Stäblein lists (1) ii:1 and (3) i:6 as alterations; because Walsh lists only 2 stanzas, I moved the change in stanza 3 to 2 [S 440, 609; "Arch.Cap."].

†75 is melody 625 from Rüdnitz, Germany and is found in Praha, Knihovna pražské metropolitní kapituly, Sveti Vid Cim. 7 (1325–1375) [S 343].

†76 is melody 601 from Sankt Lambrecht, Austria and is found in Graz, Universitätsbibliothek 387 (1350–1400) [S 330].

†77 is melody 602 from Vorau, Austria and is found in Vorau, Stiftsbibliothek 252 (ca. 1458) [S 331].

Aurora lucis rutilat

This poem is by an anonymous author from the 8th or 9th century. It consists of 11 stanzas of 4 lines in iambic dimeter and was sometimes divided into separate hymns at stanzas 5: *Tristes erant apostoli* or 6: *Sermone blando angelus* and 9: *Claro paschali gaudio*. The Roman Breviary of 1632 contains another form of the poem called *Aurora caelum purpurat*. All 11 stanzas are translated by John Mason Neale (1818–1866). See further Walsh 124–129; Boynton, "Medieval"; Julian 94–96; Neale, *The Words* 67–69.

†78 is melody 544 from Einsiedeln, Switzerland and is found in Einsiedeln, Stiftsbibliothek 336 (1100–1150) [S 287].

†79 is melody 723 from Gaeta, Italy and is found in Roma, Biblioteca Casanatense 1574 (12th c.) [S 412, 419, 607].

†80 is melody 763 from central or southern Italy and is found in Berlin, Staatsbibliothek Hamilton 688 (ca. 1267) [S 449].

†81 is melody 180 from Lausanne, Switzerland and is found in Lausanne, Bibliothèque Cantonale et Universitaire V 1184 (13th c.) [S 118].

†82 is melody 770 from southern Italy and is found in Bari, San Nicola s. n. (13th c.) [S 452].

†83 is melody 574 from Engelberg, Switzerland and is found in Engelberg, Stiftsbibliothek 314 (1372) [S 316].

Dei fide, qua vivimus

This poem is by an anonymous author from the 8th or 9th century. It consists of 3 stanzas of 4 lines in iambic dimeter. All 3 stanzas are translated by John David Chambers (1805–1893). See further Walsh 134–135; Boynton, "Medieval"; Chambers I: 131–132.

†84 is melody 413.3 from Verona, Italy and is found in Verona, Biblioteca Capitolare CIX (102) (11th c.) [S 381, 603].

†85 is melody 255 from Clermont-Ferránd, France and is found in Clermont-Ferránd, Bibliothèque Municipale et Universitaire 74 (14th c.) [S 157].

Gloria, laus, et honor

This poem is by Theodulf of Orléans (ca. 750–821) and was written around 818. It consists of 78 elegiac couplets in dactylic hexameter and pentameter. Couplets 1–7 out of 39 are translated by John Mason Neale (1818–1866). See further Walsh xiv, 254–257, 471–472; Neale, *Mediæval* 22–24.

> †86 is melody 1011b from Benevento, Italy and is found in Benevento, Biblioteca Capitolare VI 38 (11th c.). This hymn was used as a processional. The first couplet acted as a refrain and was repeated after each couplet. Stäblein also lists couplets 8–12, 17. The melody does not align very well with the meter of the poem, and words are even split over phrases, suggesting that a pre-existing melody was adapted for use with the poem. The rubric mistakenly attributes the poem to Juvencus (4th c.). Regarding melodic alterations, see "Further Information on the Hymnal" [S 485, 618; Gajard 249].
>
> †87 is melody 1011a from Regensburg, Germany and is found in Regensburg, Staatliche und Kreisbibliothek Lit. 19 (14th c.). This hymn was used as a processional. For the processional pattern, Stäblein lists 1, 1b/2a, 1, 3, 1b, etc. (which is probably a mistake). Regarding melodic alterations, see "Further Information on the Hymnal" [S 484].

Consors paterni luminis

This poem is by an anonymous author and cited by Gottschalk of Orbais (ca. 803–869). It consists of 4 stanzas of 4 lines in iambic dimeter. All 4 stanzas are translated by Edward Caswall (1814–1878). See further Walsh 150–151; Boynton, "Gottschalk"; Caswall 12.

†88 is melody 142.4 from Kempten, Germany and is found in Zürich, Zentralbibliothek, Rh 83 (ca. 1000) [S 250, 253].

O lux beata Trinitas

This poem is by an anonymous author and cited by Gottschalk of Orbais (ca. 803–869). It consists of 2 stanzas of 4 lines in iambic dimeter. The Roman Breviary of 1632 contains another form of the poem called *Iam sol recedit igneus*. A different poem shares the same first line but has *tres* instead of *et principalis* in line 2. Both of the stanzas are translated by William Drummond (1585–1649). See further Walsh 168–169; Boynton, "Gottschalk"; Julian 842–843; S 674; Ward 227.

†89 is melody 22.5 from Kempten, Germany and is found in Zürich, Zentralbibliothek, Rh 83 (ca. 1000) [S 252].

†90 is melody 535.1 from Einsiedeln, Switzerland and is found in Einsiedeln, Stiftsbibliothek 336 (1100–1150) [S 271].

Somno refectis artubus

This poem is by an anonymous author and cited by Gottschalk of Orbais (ca. 803–869). It consists of 4 stanzas of 4 lines in iambic dimeter. All 4 stanzas are translated by John Wallace (1838–1896). John Wallace changed his first name to Wilfrid after he entered the Benedictine order. See further Walsh 152–153; Boynton, "Gottschalk"; Britt 371; Wallace 43–44.

†91 is melody 267 from Le Mans, France and is found in Paris, Bibliothèque Sainte-Geneviève 112 (1450–1500) [S 163].

Summae Deus clementiae

This poem is by an anonymous author and cited by Gottschalk of Orbais (ca. 803–869). It consists of 4 stanzas of 4 lines in iambic dimeter. The Roman Breviary of 1632 contains another form of the poem called *Summae Parens clementiae*. A different poem shares the same first line but has *infunde* instead of *mundique* in line 2. All 4 stanzas are translated by John David Chambers (1805–1893). See further Walsh 148–149; Boynton, "Gottschalk"; Chambers I: 31; Julian 1101; S 678.

†92 is melody 142.7 from Verona, Italy and is found in Verona, Biblioteca Capitolare CIX (102) (11th c.). Stäblein lists (1) i:1–4 and (2,5) i:4–5 as alterations; because Walsh lists only 4 stanzas, I moved the change in stanza 5 to 4 [S 358, 363, 599–600].

Tu, Trinitatis unitas

This poem is by an anonymous author and cited by Gottschalk of Orbais (ca. 803–869). It consists of 5 stanzas of 4 lines in iambic dimeter. though the final stanza may not be part of the original poem. All 5 stanzas are translated by John David Chambers (1805–1893). See further Walsh 246–249, 469–470; Boynton, "Gottschalk"; Chambers I: 27; Julian 1187–1188.

†93 is melody 142.7 from Verona, Italy and is found in Verona, Biblioteca Capitolare CIX (102) (11th c.). Stäblein lists (6) i:4–5 as an alteration; because Walsh

lists only 5 stanzas, I moved the change in stanza 6 to
5 [S 358, 363, 599–600].

Aeterne rex altissime

This poem is by an anonymous author from the 9th century.
It consists of 7 stanzas of 4 lines in iambic dimeter and
was sometimes divided into a separate hymn at stanza 5:
Tu, Christe, nostrum gaudium. A different poem shares the
same first line but has *reddens* instead of *redemptor* in line
2. Stanzas 1–4 out of 7 are translated by John Mason Neale
(1818–1866) and the remaining 3 stanzas are translated by
Laurence Housman (1865–1959). See further Walsh 178–181;
Birkbeck et al. 118; Julian 26–27; S 664; Watson, "Aeterne".

   †94 is melody 62.4 (mistakenly labelled 61.4) from Verona,
       Italy and is found in Verona, Biblioteca Capitolare
       CIX (102) (11th c.) [S 370, 390, 601].
   †95 is melody 800 from Ascoli Piceno, Italy and is found
       in Roma, Biblioteca Apostolica Vaticana Regin. lat.
       2050 (13th–14th c.) [S 470; Cuthbert, 225].

Audi, benigne conditor

This poem is by an anonymous author from the 9th century. It
consists of 5 stanzas of 4 lines in iambic dimeter. All 5 stanzas
are translated by Thomas Alexander Lacey (1853–1931). See
further Walsh 174–177; Birkbeck et al. 56; Hornby, "Audi".

   †96 is melody 55.6 from Verona, Italy and is found in
       Verona, Biblioteca Capitolare CIX (102) (11th c.)
       [S 381, 603].

†97 is melody 411.1 from Worcester, England and is found
in Worcester, Cathedral Library F 160 (ca. 1230)
[S 185].

Ave, maris stella

This poem is by an anonymous author from the 9th century.
It consists of 7 stanzas of 4 lines in trochaic dimeter brachycatalectic. All 7 stanzas are translated by John Athelstan
Laurie Riley (1858–1945). See further Walsh 200–203; Britt
317–318; Hornby, "Ave".

†98 is melody 149.5 from Verona, Italy and is found in
Verona, Biblioteca Capitolare CIX (102) (11th c.)
[S 375].

†99 is melody 737 from Gaeta, Italy and is found in Roma,
Biblioteca Casanatense 1574 (12th c.) [S 428].

†100 is melody 67.1 from Heiligenkreuz, Austria and is
found in Heiligenkreuz, Stiftsbibliothek 20 (12th–13th
c.) [S 40].

†101 is melody 174 from Bayeux, France and is found in
Paris, Bibliothèque de l' Arsenal 279 (ca. 1234) [S 115].

†102 is melody 191 from Paris, France and is found in
Roma, Santa Sabina, Archivum Generale Ordinis
Predicatorum s. n. (ca. 1255) [S 124, 553].

†103 is melody 1031 from Fribourg, Switzerland and is
found in Freiburg (Schweiz), Kantons- und
Universitätsbibliothek L 322 (14th c.). This hymn was
used as a processional. The refrain, a later addition to
the hymn, was repeated after every two lines of the
poem. The refrain reads, *Sancta Maria / sancta et
sancta Maria*, and I translated this as *Holy Maria /
Holy, most holy, Maria*. The refrain for the second

504

stanza is slightly altered, and I included it as R2 in the score [S 500, 624].

†104 is melody 208 from Normandy, France and is found in Paris, Bibliothèque Sainte-Geneviève 113 (14th–15th c.) [S 133].

†105 is melody 507.1 from Klosterneuburg, Austria and is found in Klosterneuburg, Stiftsbibliothek 1000 (1336) [S 222, 570].

Beata nobis gaudia

This poem is by an anonymous author from the 9th century. It consists of 6 stanzas of 4 lines in iambic dimeter. A different poem shares the same first line but has *commendant* in place of *anni* in line 2; another has *dant* in the same place. All 6 stanzas are translated by John David Chambers (1805–1893). See further Walsh 188–191; Chambers I: 212; S 665; Watson, "Beata".

†106 is melody 530.1 from Kempten, Germany and is found in Zürich, Zentralbibliothek, Rh 83 (ca. 1000) [S 258].

†107 is melody 64.2 from Nevers, France and is found in Paris, Bibliothèque Nationale n. a. lat. 1235 (12th c.) [S 76, 94].

†108 is melody 764 from central or southern Italy and is found in Berlin, Staatsbibliothek Hamilton 688 (ca. 1267) [S 449].

†109 is melody 186 from Paris, France and is found in Roma, Santa Sabina, Archivum Generale Ordinis Predicatorum s. n. (ca. 1255) [S 122].

†110 is melody 235 from Châlons-en-Champagne, France and is found in Berlin, Staatsbibliothek Mus. ms. 40612 (1300–1350) [S 146].

†111 is melody 618 from Prague, Czech Republic and is found in Praha, Univerzitní knihovna XII E 15c (1300–1350) [S 339, 594].

†112 is melody 514.1 from Klosterneuburg, Austria and is found in Klosterneuburg, Stiftsbibliothek 1000 (1336) [S 232, 574].

Nunc, sancte nobis Spiritus

This poem is by an anonymous author from the 9th century. It consists of 2 stanzas of 4 lines in iambic dimeter. Both of the stanzas are translated by John Henry Newman (1801-1890). See further Walsh 242–243; Newman 219; Watson, "Nunc".

†113 is melody 175 from Fécamp, France and is found in Rouen, Bibliothèque de la Ville 248 (12th–13th c.) [S 115].

†114 is melody 251 from Fécamp, France and is found in Rouen, Bibliothèque de la Ville 248 (12th–13th c.) [S 155].

†115 is melody 432 from England and is found in Oxford, Corpus Christi College N. 134 (12th–13th c.) [S 207; "GB-Occ"].

†116 is melody 128.2 from Worcester, England and is found in Worcester, Cathedral Library F 160 (ca. 1230) [S 179].

†117 is melody 402.1 from Worcester, England and is found in Worcester, Cathedral Library F 160 (ca. 1230) [S 171, 173, 560].

†118 is melody 403 from Worcester, England and is found in Worcester, Cathedral Library F 160 (ca. 1230) [S 173].

†119 is melody 404 from Worcester, England and is found in Worcester, Cathedral Library F 160 (ca. 1230) [S 174].

†120 is melody 428 from Worcester, England and is found in
Worcester, Cathedral Library F 160 (ca. 1230) [S 204].

†121 is melody 214 from Châlons-en-Champagne, France
and is found in Paris, Bibliothèque Nationale lat. 1269
(1309) [S 136].

†122 is melody 215 from Châlons-en-Champagne, France
and is found in Paris, Bibliothèque Nationale lat. 1269
(1309) [S 137].

†123 is melody 131.3 from Klosterneuburg, Austria and is
found in Klosterneuburg, Stiftsbibliothek 1000 (1336)
[S 246, 577].

†124 is melody 596 from Sankt Florian, Austria and is
found in Sankt Florian, Stiftsbibliothek XI 410 (15th c.)
[S 328].

Aeterna caeli gloria

This poem is by an anonymous author and is found in Paris,
Bibliothèque Nationale, lat. 1327 (9th–10th c.). It consists of 5
stanzas of 4 lines in iambic dimeter. It is an acrostic, with each
successive line beginning on the next letter of the alphabet.
All 5 stanzas are translated by John Mason Neale (1818–1866).
See further Walsh 154–155; Jullien 168–169; Neale, *The Words*
28–29.

†125 is melody 702 from Verona, Italy and is found in
Verona, Biblioteca Capitolare CIX (102) (11th c.)
[S 362, 363, 600].

Caeli Deus sanctissime

This poem is by an anonymous author and is found in Paris, Bibliothèque Nationale, lat. 1327 (9th–10th c.). It consists of 4 stanzas of 4 lines in iambic dimeter. All 4 stanzas are translated by John Mason Neale (1818–1866). See further Walsh 162–163; Julian 241; Jullien 168–169; Neale, *The Words* 25–26.

†126 is melody 145.6 (mistakenly labelled 145.7) from Verona, Italy and is found in Verona, Biblioteca Capitolare CIX (102) (11th c.) [S 362, 363, 600].

Christe, redemptor omnium

This poem is by an anonymous author and is found in Paris, Bibliothèque Nationale, lat. 1327 (9th–10th c.). It consists of 6 stanzas of 4 lines in iambic dimeter. The Roman Breviary of 1632 and the Paris Breviary of 1736 contain other forms of the poem, and both begin with *Iesu, redemptor omnium*. Confusingly, neither of these is the same *Iesu, redemptor omnium* included in this hymnal. A different poem shares the same first line but has *conserva* in place of *ex patre* in line 2; another has *victor* in the same place. All 6 stanzas are translated by Henry Williams Baker (1821–1877). See further Walsh 170–173; Biggs 53–54; Julian 228–230; Jullien 170–171; S 666; *Iesu, redemptor omnium* (below).

†127 is melody 704 from Verona, Italy and is found in Verona, Biblioteca Capitolare CIX (102) (11th c.) [S 366, 601].

†128 is melody 177 from Lausanne, Switzerland and is found in Lausanne, Bibliothèque Cantonale et Universitaire V 1184 (13th c.) [S 117].

†129 is melody 407 from Worcester, England and is found in Worcester, Cathedral Library F 160 (ca. 1230) [S 177].

†130 is melody 579 from Engelberg, Switzerland and is found in Engelberg, Stiftsbibliothek 8 (ca. 1400) [S 318].

Conditor alme siderum

This poem is by an anonymous author and is found in Paris, Bibliothèque Nationale, lat. 1327 (9th–10th c.). It consists of 7 stanzas of 4 lines in iambic dimeter. The Roman Breviary of 1632 contains another form of the poem called *Creator alme siderum*. A different poem shares the same first line but has *o Iesu* in place of *aeterna lux* in line 2. All 7 stanzas are translated by Alfred Edersheim (1825–1889). See further Walsh 166–169; Edersheim 33–34; Julian 257–258; Jullien 170–171; S 667.

†131 is melody 23.5 from Kempten, Germany and is found in Zürich, Zentralbibliothek, Rh 83 (ca. 1000) [S 255, 580].

†132 is melody 19.3 from Verona, Italy and is found in Verona, Biblioteca Capitolare CIX (102) (11th c.) [S 364].

†133 is melody 4.3 from Nevers, France and is found in Paris, Bibliothèque Nationale n. a. lat. 1235 (12th c.). Stäblein lists (2) ii:4 and iii:3 as alterations and notes that only stanzas 1 and 2 are present in the manuscript; because of this and because Walsh lists 7 stanzas, I extended the changes in stanza 2 to include 2–7 [S 70, 529].

Deus, tuorum militum

This poem is by an anonymous author and is found in Paris, Bibliothèque Nationale, lat. 1327 (9th–10th c.). It consists of 4 stanzas of 4 lines in iambic dimeter. Several other poems share the same first line; the one used in this hymnal is distinguished from those by its second line: *sors et corona, praemium*. All 4 stanzas are translated by John David Chambers (1805–1893). See further Walsh 192–193; Chambers II: 12–13; Jullien 188–189; S 667.

†134 is melody 118 from Moissac, France and is found in Roma, Biblioteca Apostolica Vaticana Ross. 205 (ca. 1000) [S 61].

†135 is melody 150.1 from Nevers, France and is found in Paris, Bibliothèque Nationale n. a. lat. 1235 (12th c.) [S 91, 100, 542].

†136 is melody 57 from Heiligenkreuz, Austria and is found in Heiligenkreuz, Stiftsbibliothek 20 (12th–13th c.) [S 34, 44].

†137 is melody 778 from southern Italy and is found in Bari, San Nicola s. n. (13th c.) [S 457].

Ex more docti mystico

This poem is by an anonymous author and is found in Paris, Bibliothèque Nationale, lat. 1327 (9th–10th c.). It consists of 8 stanzas of 4 lines in iambic dimeter. The Paris Breviary of 1736 contains another form of the poem called *Quod lex adumbravit vetus*. All 8 stanzas are translated by William John Blew (1808–1894). See further Walsh 172–175; Blew, 1–2 in sec. "Lent"; Julian 359; Jullien 170–171.

†138 is melody 412.4 from Verona, Italy and is found in
      Verona, Biblioteca Capitolare CIX (102) (11th c.)
      [S 379, 603].

Iam Christus astra ascenderat

This poem is by an anonymous author and is found in Paris,
Bibliothèque Nationale, lat. 1327 (9th–10th c.). It consists of
8 stanzas of 4 lines in iambic dimeter and was sometimes divided into a separate hymn at stanza 5: *Impleta gaudent vis-
cera.* All 8 stanzas are translated by John Wallace (1838–1896).
John Wallace changed his first name to Wilfrid after he entered the Benedictine order. See further Walsh 184–187; Britt
371; Jullien 174–175; Wallace 11–12.

†139 is melody 133 from Nevers, France and is found in
      Paris, Bibliothèque Nationale n. a. lat. 1235 (12th c.)
      [S 75, 94, 538].
†140 is melody 727 from Gaeta, Italy and is found in Roma,
      Biblioteca Casanatense 1574 (12th c.). I removed the
      extra note at i5, which was inserted to accommodate
      the extra syllable in the Latin text [S 421].
†141 is melody 63 from Heiligenkreuz, Austria and is found
      in Heiligenkreuz, Stiftsbibliothek 20 (12th–13th c.). I
      removed the extra 3 notes at (1) i1, which were
      inserted to accommodate the extra syllable in the
      Latin text [S 38, 518].
†142 is melody 772 from southern Italy and is found in
      Bari, San Nicola s. n. (13th c.). I removed the extra
      note at i5, which was inserted to accommodate the
      extra syllable in the Latin text [S 453].

Iesu, corona virginum

This poem is by an anonymous author and is found in Paris, Bibliothèque Nationale, lat. 1327 (9th–10th c.). It consists of 4 stanzas of 4 lines in iambic dimeter. A different poem shares the same first line but has *perpes* instead of *quem* in line 2. All 4 stanzas are translated by John Mason Neale (1818–1866). See further Walsh 194–195; Jullien 188–189; Neale, *The Words* 102; S 671.

†143 is melody 24.2 from Heiligenkreuz, Austria and is found in Heiligenkreuz, Stiftsbibliothek 20 (12th–13th c.) [S 41, 44].

†144 is melody 750 from Lehel, Germany and is found in München, Fransician abbey of St. Anna s. n. (1227–1235) [S 442].

†145 is melody 426 from Worcester, England and is found in Worcester, Cathedral Library F 160 (ca. 1230) [S 203].

†146 is melody 525 from Klosterneuburg, Austria and is found in Klosterneuburg, Stiftsbibliothek 1000 (1336) [S 244].

†147 is melody 570 from Engelberg, Switzerland and is found in Engelberg, Stiftsbibliothek 314 (1372) [S 313].

Iesu, nostra redemptio

This poem is by an anonymous author and is found in Paris, Bibliothèque Nationale, lat. 1327 (9th–10th c.). It consists of 5 stanzas of 4 lines in iambic dimeter. The Roman Breviary of 1632 contains another form of the poem called *Salutis humanae Sator*. A different poem shares the same first line but has *adstantum* instead of *amor* in line 2; another has *pro* in the same place. All 5 stanzas are translated by John Mason Neale (1818–1866). See further Walsh 176–179; Julian 592–593; Jullien 174–175; Neale, *The Words* 80–81; S 671.

†148 is melody 513.3 from Verona, Italy and is found in Verona, Biblioteca Capitolare CIX (102) (11th c.) [S 372, 390, 602].

†149 is melody 16.3 from Nevers, France and is found in Paris, Bibliothèque Nationale n. a. lat. 1235 (12th c.) [S 87, 93].

†150 is melody 61 from Heiligenkreuz, Austria and is found in Heiligenkreuz, Stiftsbibliothek 20 (12th–13th c.) [S 37, 518].

†151 is melody 168 from Bayeux, France and is found in Paris, Bibliothèque de l' Arsenal 279 (ca. 1234) [S 112].

Iesu, redemptor omnium

This poem is by an anonymous author and is found in Paris, Bibliothèque Nationale, lat. 1327 (9th–10th c.). It consists of 4 stanzas of 4 lines in iambic dimeter. A different poem shares the same first line but has *quem* instead of *perpes* in line 2; another has *qui morte* in the same place. All 4 stanzas are translated by William John Blew (1808–1894). See further Walsh 196–197; Blew, 12 in sec. "Holy Days"; Jullien 188–189; S 671; *Christe, redemptor omnium* (above).

†152 is melody 119 from Moissac, France and is found in Roma, Biblioteca Apostolica Vaticana Ross. 205 (ca. 1000). Stäblein mentions that the neumes in the manuscript are difficult to read for this melody [S 62, 527].

†153 is melody 71.4 from Nevers, France and is found in Paris, Bibliothèque Nationale n. a. lat. 1235 (12th c.)

[S 104].

†154 is melody 182 from Lausanne, Switzerland and is found in Lausanne, Bibliothèque Cantonale et Universitaire V 1184 (13th c.) [S 119].

†155 is melody 624 from Rüdnitz, Germany and is found in Praha, Knihovna pražské metropolitní kapituly, Sveti Vid Cim. 7 (1325–1375) [S 342].

Immense caeli conditor

This poem is by an anonymous author and is found in Turin, Biblioteca Nazionale, 1106 (G.V.38) (9th–10th c.). It consists of 4 stanzas of 4 lines in iambic dimeter. All 4 stanzas are translated by John Mason Neale (1818–1866). See further Walsh 158–159; Jullien 168–169; Neale, *The Words* 21–22.

†156 is melody 145.4 from Kempten, Germany and is found in Zürich, Zentralbibliothek, Rh 83 (ca. 1000) [S 253].

Lucis creator optime

This poem is by an anonymous author and is found in Turin, Biblioteca Nazionale, 1106 (G.V.38) (9th–10th c.). It consists of 4 stanzas of 4 lines in iambic dimeter. All 4 stanzas are translated by John Mason Neale (1818–1866). See further Walsh 156–157; Jullien 168–169; Neale, *The Words* 15-16.

†157 is melody 528.1 from Kempten, Germany and is found in Zürich, Zentralbibliothek, Rh 83 (ca. 1000) [S 252].

†158 is melody 743 from Piacenza, Italy and is found in Piacenza, Biblioteca Capitolare 65 (ca. 1200) [S 438].

†159 is melody 155.2 from Worcester, England and is found in Worcester, Cathedral Library F 160 (ca. 1230)

[S 182].

†160 is melody 253 from Clermont-Ferránd, France and is found in Clermont-Ferránd, Bibliothèque Municipale et Universitaire 74 (14th c.) [S 156].

Magnae Deus potentiae

This poem is by an anonymous author and is found in Paris, Bibliothèque Nationale, lat. 1327 (9th–10th c.). It consists of 4 stanzas of 4 lines in iambic dimeter. All 4 stanzas are translated by John Mason Neale (1818–1866). See further Walsh 164–165; Jullien 168–169; Neale, *The Words* 27.

†161 is melody 145.6 (mistakenly labelled 145.7) from Verona, Italy and is found in Verona, Biblioteca Capitolare CIX (102) (11th c.) [S 362, 363, 600].

Primo dierum omnium

This poem is by an anonymous author and is found in Turin, Biblioteca Nazionale, 1106 (G.V.38) (9th–10th c.). It consists of 4 stanzas of 4 lines in iambic dimeter. Some sources have 4 additional stanzas, the first of which begins with *Iam nunc, paterna claritas*. The Roman Breviary of 1632 contains another form of the poem called *Primo die, quo Trinitas*. All 4 stanzas are translated by John David Chambers (1805–1893). See further Walsh 146–147, 438–439; Chambers I: 1–2; Julian 912–913; Jullien 168–169.

†162 is melody 410 from Worcester, England and is found in Worcester, Cathedral Library F 160 (ca. 1230) [S 181].

Quem terra pontus aethera

This poem is by an anonymous author and is found in Paris, Bibliothèque Nationale, lat. 1327 (9th–10th c.). It consists of 8 stanzas of 4 lines in iambic dimeter and was sometimes divided into a separate hymn at stanza 6: *O gloriosa femina*. The Roman Breviary of 1632 contains another form of the poem called *Quem terra, pontus, sidera*. A different poem shares the same first line but has *Agnes* instead of *trinam* in line 3. Stanzas 1–2 and 4–5 out of 8 are translated by John Mason Neale (1818–1866) and the last 3 stanzas are translated by Percy Dearmer (1867–1936). See further Walsh 198–201; Birkbeck et al. 180–181; Julian 944–945; Jullien 180–181; S 676.

†163　is melody 187 from Paris, France and is found in Roma, Santa Sabina, Archivum Generale Ordinis Predicatorum s. n. (ca. 1255) [S 122].

†164　is melody 205 from Normandy, France and is found in Paris, Bibliothèque Sainte-Geneviève 113 (14th–15th c.) [S 131].

†165　is melody 206 from Normandy, France and is found in Paris, Bibliothèque Sainte-Geneviève 113 (14th–15th c.) [S 132].

†166　is melody 646 from Hegau, Germany and is found in Karlsruhe, St. Blasien 77 (1439–1442) [S 356; "Karlsruhe"].

Rerum Deus tenax vigor

This poem is by an anonymous author and is found in Turin, Biblioteca Nazionale, 1106 (G.V.38) (9th–10th c.). It consists of 2 stanzas of 4 lines in iambic dimeter. Both of the stanzas are

translated by Edward Caswall (1814–1878). See further Walsh
144–147; Caswall 8; Jullien 168–169.

†167 is melody 51.4 from Einsiedeln, Switzerland and is
      found in Einsiedeln, Stiftsbibliothek 336 (1100–1150)
      [S 268].

†168 is melody 7.2 from Nevers, France and is found in
      Paris, Bibliothèque Nationale n. a. lat. 1235 (12th c.)
      [S 77, 78].

†169 is melody 217 from Châlons-en-Champagne, France
      and is found in Paris, Bibliothèque Nationale lat. 1269
      (1309) [S 138].

†170 is melody 527 from Klosterneuburg, Austria and is
      found in Klosterneuburg, Stiftsbibliothek 1000 (1336)
      [S 246].

Rex gloriose martyrum

This poem is by an anonymous author and is found in Paris,
Bibliothèque Nationale, lat. 1327 (9th–10th c.). It consists of 3
stanzas of 4 lines in iambic dimeter. A different poem shares
the same first line but has *remunerator* instead of *corona* in
line 2. All 3 stanzas are translated by John David Chambers
(1805–1893). See further Walsh 190–191; Jullien 188–189;
Chambers I: 99; S 677.

†171 is melody 719 from Verona, Italy and is found in
      Verona, Biblioteca Capitolare CIX (102) (11th c.)
      [S 404, 606].

†172 is melody 53.2 from Nevers, France and is found in
      Paris, Bibliothèque Nationale n. a. lat. 1235 (12th c.)
      [S 81, 103, 540].

†173 is melody 158.1 from Nevers, France and is found in
      Paris, Bibliothèque Nationale n. a. lat. 1235 (12th c.).

Stäblein lists (1) iii:4 and (2) iii:7 as alterations but likely means (3) iii:4 and (4) iii:7, since only stanzas 3 and 4 are listed as being present in the manuscript; because of this and because Walsh lists 3 stanzas, I maintained the change in stanza 1 and extended the change in stanza 2 to include 2 and 3 [S 101, 546–547].

†174 is melody 559 from Fritzlar, Germany and is found in Kassel, Landesbibliothek theol. 2° 96 (1334) [S 307].

Telluris ingens conditor

This poem is by an anonymous author and is found in Turin, Biblioteca Nazionale, 1106 (G.V.38) (9th–10th c.). It consists of 4 stanzas of 4 lines in iambic dimeter. The Roman Breviary of 1632 contains another form of the poem called *Telluris alme conditor*. All 4 stanzas are translated by Samuel Willoughby Duffield (1843–1887). See further Walsh 160–161; Duffield 354–355; Julian 1136–1137; Jullien 168–169.

†175 is melody 145.6 (mistakenly labelled 145.7) from Verona, Italy and is found in Verona, Biblioteca Capitolare CIX (102) (11th c.) [S 362, 363, 600].

Agnoscat omne saeculum

This poem is by an anonymous author and is found in Boulogne, Bibliothèque Municipale, 20 (999). It consists of 8 stanzas of 4 lines in iambic dimeter and was sometimes divided into separate hymns at stanzas 3: *Maria ventre concepit*, 5: *Praesepe poni pertulit*, and 7: *Adam vetus quod polluit*. All 8 stanzas are translated by John Mason Neale

(1818–1866). See further Walsh 234–237; Jullien 170–171; Neale, *The Words* 42–44.

†176 is melody 405.3 from Kempten, Germany and is found in Zürich, Zentralbibliothek, Rh 83 (ca. 1000) [S 255].

†177 is melody 705.1 from Verona, Italy and is found in Verona, Biblioteca Capitolare CIX (102) (11th c.). Stäblein lists (9) iv:7 as an alteration; because Walsh lists only 8 stanzas, I moved the change in stanza 9 to 8 [S 367, 601].

A Patre unigenitus

This poem is by an anonymous author and is found in Zürich, Zentralbibliothek, Rheinau 83 (ca. 1026). It consists of 6 stanzas of 4 lines in iambic dimeter. It is an acrostic, with each successive line beginning on the next letter of the alphabet. The poem beginning *A Patre unigenite* is identical to this one with a few exceptions. Stanzas 1–5 out of 6 are translated by John Mason Neale (1818–1866). See further Walsh 248–251; Blume 146; Jullien 170–171; Lawson 114.

†178 is melody 1.4 (mistakenly labelled 1.5) from Verona, Italy and is found in Verona, Biblioteca Capitolare CIX (102) (11th c.) [S 360, 366, 600].

†179 is melody 14.3 from Nevers, France and is found in Paris, Bibliothèque Nationale n. a. lat. 1235 (12th c.) [S 81].

Iam, Christe, sol iustitiae

This poem is by an anonymous author and is found in Paris, Bibliothèque Nationale, lat. 103 (1000–1075). It consists of 5 stanzas of 4 lines in iambic dimeter. The Roman Breviary of 1632 contains another form of the poem called *O sol salutis, intimis*. All 5 stanzas are translated by John David Chambers (1805–1893). See further Walsh 244–247; Chambers I: 129–130; Julian 576; Jullien 170–171.

†180 is melody 148.2 from Verona, Italy and is found in Verona, Biblioteca Capitolare CIX (102) (11th c.) [S 380, 603].

Qua Christus hora sitiit

This poem is by an anonymous author and is found in Paris, Bibliothèque Nationale, lat. 103 (1000–1075). It consists of 3 stanzas of 4 lines in iambic dimeter. All 3 stanzas are translated by John David Chambers (1805–1893). See further Walsh 242–245; Chambers I: 132; Jullien 172–173.

†181 is melody 580 from Engelberg, Switzerland and is found in Engelberg, Stiftsbibliothek 8 (ca. 1400) [S 319].

Optatus votis omnium

This poem is by an anonymous author and is found in Amiens, Bibliothèque Municipale, 131 (11th c.). It consists of 8 stanzas of 4 lines in iambic dimeter. A different poem shares the same first line but has *venit* instead of *sacratus* in line 2. All 8 stanzas are translated by Elizabeth Rundle Charles (1828–1896). See further Walsh 182–185; Charles 104–105; Jullien 174–175; S 674.

†182 is melody 116.6 from Gaeta, Italy and is found in

Roma, Biblioteca Casanatense 1574 (12th c.) [S 410,
419, 607].

†183 is melody 60 from Heiligenkreuz, Austria and is found
in Heiligenkreuz, Stiftsbibliothek 20 (12th–13th c.)
[S 36].

O quanta qualia sunt illa sabbata

This poem is by Peter Abelard (1079–1142) and was written
around 1131. It consists of 7 stanzas of 4 lines in paired hexasyllabic cola. All 7 stanzas are translated by Gerard Moultrie
(1829–1885). The order of stanzas in Moultrie's translation
do not agree with the order in *OHLH*; I changed the order so
that the poem matches what is in *OHLH*. See further Walsh
276–279; Moultrie 343–345; Wulstan, *Paraclete*.

†184 is melody 590 from Rheinau, Switzerland and is found
in Zürich, Zentralbibliothek, Rh 18 (12th c.). The
variant used in this collection is listed in the
"Kritischer Bericht" of *HA*. Wulstan writes that the
original melody was in Major instead of Dorian,
though I left it as it is written in *HA* [S 324, 592;
Wulstan, "O Quanta"].

Verbum supernum prodiens

This poem is by Thomas Aquinas (1225–1274) and was written
in 1264. It consists of 6 stanzas of 4 lines in iambic dimeter
and was sometimes divided into a separate hymn at stanza
5: *O salutaris hostia*. Several other poems share the same
first line; the one used in this hymnal is distinguished from
those by its second line: *nec Patris linquens dexteram*. All 6

stanzas are translated by Athanasius Diedrich Wackerbarth (1813–1884). See further Walsh 360–363, 496–498; S 679; Wackerbarth 8–11.

†185 is melody 13.1 from Milan, Italy and is found in London, British Museum Add. 34209 (12th c.). Note that the melody predates the poem [S 7, 10, 506–507].

†186 is melody 628 from Środa Śląska, Poland and is found in Wrocław, Biblioteka Kapitulna, Cod. 58 (15th c.). The old name for this archive is Diözesanarchiv, Ms. 58 [S 344, 595, 691; Kornrumpf].

†187 is melody 636 from Schäftlarn, Germany and is found in München, Bayerische Staatsbibliothek Clm 17009 (1462) [S 350].

Pronouncing the Titles

The following is provided to help with the pronunciation of the Latin titles. Say "a" as in "father", "e" as in "red", "i" as in "feet", "o" as in "for", "u" as in "moon", "g" as in "golf", and "r" as a rolled sound. Pronounce each vowel as above even if two are next to each other. See further Solesmes, xxxvj–xxxix.

A Patre unigenitus:	A Pa-tre u-ni-je-ni-tus
A solis ortus cardine:	A so-lis or-tus kar-di-ne
Aeterna caeli gloria:	E-ter-na che-li glo-ri-a
Aeterna Christi munera:	E-ter-na Kris-ti mu-ne-ra
Aeterne rerum conditor:	E-ter-ne re-rum kon-di-tor
Aeterne rex altissime:	E-ter-ne reks al-tis-si-me
Agnoscat omne saeculum:	A-nyos-kat om-ne se-ku-lum
Ales diei nuntius:	A-les di-e-i nun-ti-us
Audi, benigne conditor:	Au-di, be-ni-nye kon-di-tor
Aurora lucis rutilat:	Au-ro-ra lu-chis ru-ti-lat
Ave, maris stella:	A-ve, ma-ris stel-la
Beata nobis gaudia:	Be-a-ta no-bis gau-di-a
Caeli Deus sanctissime:	Che-li De-us sank-tis-si-me
Christe, redemptor omnium:	Kris-te, red-emp-tor om-ni-um
Conditor alme siderum:	Con-di-tor al-me si-de-rum
Consors paterni luminis:	Con-sors pa-ter-ni lu-mi-nis
Crux benedicta nitet:	Cruks be-ne-dik-ta ni-tet
Dei fide, qua vivimus:	De-i fi-de, qua vi-vi-mus
Deus, creator omnium:	De-us, kre-a-tor om-ni-um
Deus, tuorum militum:	De-us, tu-o-rum mi-li-tum
Ex more docti mystico:	Eks mo-re dok-ti mis-ti-ko

Gloria, laus, et honor:	Glo-ri-a, laus, et o-nor
Hic est dies verus Dei:	Ik est di-es ve-rus De-i
Iam, Christe, sol iustitiae:	Yam, Kris-te, sol yus-ti-ti-e
Iam Christus astra	Yam Kris-tus as-tra
ascenderat:	a-shen-de-rat
Iam lucis orto sidere:	Yam lu-chis or-to si-de-re
Iam surgit hora tertia:	Yam sur-jit o-ra ter-ti-a
Iesu, corona virginum:	Ye-su, ko-ro-na vir-ji-num
Iesu, nostra redemptio:	Ye-su, nos-tra red-emp-ti-o
Iesu, redemptor omnium:	Ye-su, red-emp-tor om-ni-um
Illuminans altissimus:	Il-lu-mi-nans al-tis-si-mus
Immense caeli conditor:	Im-men-se che-li kon-di-tor
Intende, qui regis Israel:	In-ten-de, qui re-jis Is-ra-el
Lucis creator optime:	Lu-chis kre-a-tor op-ti-me
Magnae Deus potentiae:	Ma-nye De-us pot-en-ti-e
Mediae noctis tempus est:	Me-di-e nok-tis tem-pus est
Nox et tenebrae et nubila:	Noks et te-ne-bre et nu-bi-la
Nunc, sancte nobis Spiritus:	Nunk, sank-te no-bis Spi-ri-tus
O lux beata Trinitas:	O luks be-a-ta Tri-ni-tas
O quanta qualia	O quan-ta qua-li-a
sunt illa sabbata:	sunt il-la sab-ba-ta
Optatus votis omnium:	Op-ta-tus vo-tis om-ni-um
Pange, lingua:	Pan-je, lin-gua
Primo dierum omnium:	Pri-mo di-e-rum om-ni-um
Qua Christus hora sitiit:	Qua Kris-tus o-ra si-ti-it
Quem terra pontus aethera:	Quem ter-ra pon-tus e-te-ra
Rector potens, verax Deus:	Rek-tor pot-ens, ve-raks De-us
Rerum Deus tenax vigor:	Re-rum De-us te-naks vi-gor
Rex gloriose martyrum:	Reks glo-ri-o-se mar-ti-rum
Somno refectis artubus:	Som-no re-fek-tis ar-tu-bus
Splendor paternae gloriae:	Splen-dor pa-ter-ne glo-ri-e
Summae Deus clementiae:	Sum-me De-us kle-men-ti-e
Te lucis ante terminum:	Te lu-chis an-te ter-mi-num
Telluris ingens conditor:	Tel-lu-ris in-jens kon-di-tor
Tu, Trinitatis unitas:	Tu, Tri-ni-ta-tis u-ni-tas
Verbum supernum prodiens:	Ver-bum su-per-num prod-i-ens
Vexilla regis prodeunt:	Ve-ksil-la re-jis prod-e-unt

Reading Square Notation

The music for the hymns is written in square notation. This notation developed during the Middle Ages and is essentially an early form of modern music notation. The particular form of square notation used in this hymnal has very few symbols. Below is a constructed example with the essential features.

T his is a sample that con-veys how to read

square no-ta-tion. It's not hard.

Probably the most important difference between square notation and modern notation is that there are no measures. There are bar lines, but they do not mark off a set number of beats. Instead, bar lines mark the end of phrases and are typically where the singer pauses to take a breath. Different bar lines are used in this hymnal, but these differences are simply to highlight the structure of the poems.

Two clefs are used: the Do clef and the Fa clef. Technically, they denote relative pitches, but I prefer to assume Do is C and Fa is F. Then, I simply transpose up or down, depending on the ranges of the singers. In the example, the Do clef is shown at the very beginning and denotes that C is on the 3rd line from the bottom. Thus, the first four notes are C, B, A, A, and C. The Do clef is also at the beginning of the second system. The Fa clef is shown after the first double bar and denotes that F is on the top line (where E used to be). The clefs can be moved up or down on the staff; very often, the Do clef is on the top line, making the top line C and the bottom line D. Notice there are only 4 staff lines.

The notes (also called neumes) all have roughly the same duration, regardless of how much horizontal space is between them on the page. Each syllable is sung to one neumatic element, which may be a single note or several closely spaced notes. In the example, "read" is sung to one note, whereas "how" is sung to 6 notes. Notes are aligned with the syllables, and in this hymnal, the first note of a neumatic element aligns with the first letter of the syllable. If notes are stacked vertically, the lower one is sung first. "It's" in the example is sung on A and then B-flat. A stem or other vertical line attached to a note does not have a function like it does in modern music and is written simply to mark certain note combinations. If a syllable has two consecutive notes that are the same pitch, such as "is" in the example, that syllable is held twice as long. "That" is sung on A and then D, but A is held twice as long as D. A downward sloping bar represents two notes; where the bar begins and ends on the staff determines these notes. "Con" is sung C, B, C, and "square" is sung D, A, C (held), B. At the end of each system, a guide note, called a custos, is written. This note is not sung and is there only to prepare the singer for the next note. Notice that "square" begins on D, which is indicated by the custos on the previous system. See further Solesmes, xj–xxxv.

Rubrics for the Poems and Hymns

The rubrics below are taken from *OHLH*, *HA*, or *Cantus Index*.

A Patre unigenitus

>At Compline. †178
>At Lauds. †179
>Christmas.
>Epiphany.
>First Vespers on the feast of the Baptism of the Lord.

A solis ortus cardine

>At Lauds. †31, †32
>Christmas Day.
>Lauds from the Nativity to the Epiphany: stanzas 1–7.
>On the Epiphany. †28
>On the vigil of the Nativity of the Lord. †29
>Vespers from the Epiphany to the Baptism of Our Lord:
> stanzas 8–9, 11, 13.
>Within the octave of the Epiphany with three lessons.
> †33

Aeterna caeli gloria

>At Lauds. †125
>Friday at Lauds.

Aeterna Christi munera

>At a Nocturn. †27
>Common of apostles.
>On the nativity of apostles. †26

Aeterne rerum conditor

> At Lauds. †1, †2
> Nocturnal Hymn.
> Second Nocturn.
> Sundays, Ferial Office.

Aeterne rex altissime

> Ascension Thursday.
> At Lauds. †94
> Office of Readings on the feast of the Ascension.
> On the Ascension, at First Nocturn. †95

Agnoscat omne saeculum

> At Terce. †177
> Christmas Day.
> Feast of Christmas.
> On the Nativity of the Lord at Nocturns. †176
> Second Vespers on the feast of the Annunciation:
>   stanzas 1–3, 7.

Ales diei nuntius

> At Lauds. †23
> Daily Office: stanzas 1–2, 21, 25.
> Private Meditation.
> Reading and Recitation.

Audi, benigne conditor

> At Second Vespers. †97
> First Sunday of Lent.
> Lent, various hours.
> Vespers from Ash Wednesday until the end of Week 5 in
>   Lent.

Aurora lucis rutilat

> At First Nocturn. †81
> At Lauds. †79
> Eastertide.
> Lauds on Easter Sunday: stanzas 1–4.
> Octave of Easter.

On Sundays at Lauds. †80
Saturday in the octave of Pascha at Lauds. †82

Ave, maris stella

A song for the Blessed Virgin when her office is
celebrated on Saturdays in the monastery. For the
Blessed Virgin at Vespers. †102
Annunciation of Mary (Lady Day).
At a Nocturn. †98
At Compline. †100
At Vespers. †105
On the Assumption of Blessed Mary at a Nocturn. †104
On the Assumption of Saint Mary. †101
On the Purification of Blessed Mary at Compline. †103
Second Vespers on the Common of the Blessed Virgin
Mary.

Beata nobis gaudia

At Lauds, at Compline. †112
For the Holy Spirit at Lauds. †111
Lauds on Whit Sunday.
On Pentecost at Nocturns. †108
On Pentecost at Vespers. †107, †109
On the holy day of Pentecost. †106
On the vigil of Pentecost at Vespers. †110
Pentecost.
Pentecost Sunday (Whitsunday).

Caeli Deus sanctissime

At Vespers. †126
Wednesday Vespers.

Christe, redemptor omnium

At a Nocturn. †127
At Matins. †129
Christmas Day.
Christmas Day, various times.
Christmas Day, Vespers.
On the Nativity of the Lord at First Nocturn. †128

On the Nativity of the Lord at Nocturns. †130

Conditor alme siderum

>Advent.
>During the Advent of the Lord at Vespers. †131
>First Sunday of Advent.
>Sundays during the Advent of the Lord. †132
>Sundays in the Advent of the Lord at Vespers. †133
>Vespers.

Consors paterni luminis

>Feria 3 at Nocturns. †88
>Nocturns on Tuesdays.
>Office of Readings on Tuesday when held during the night or early morning.

Crux benedicta nitet

>Holy Cross Day (Exaltation of the Cross).
>On the Exaltation of the Holy Cross. †36

Dei fide, qua vivimus

>At Terce. †84
>During Lent. †85
>Terce in Lent.

Deus, creator omnium

>At Vespers. †7
>Evening Hymn.
>Saturday in the octave of Pentecost. †6
>Saturdays at Vespers. †4, †8
>Sundays, Ferial Office.

Deus, tuorum militum

>Common of one martyr.
>For one martyr. †136
>On the vigil of one martyr at Vespers and at Nocturns. †137
>One martyr. †135
>Vespers on the feast of the Common of a single martyr.

Ex more docti mystico

> At a Nocturn. †138
> First Sunday of Lent.
> Lent, various days and hours.
> Office of Readings on Sunday: stanzas 1–4.

Gloria, laus, et honor

> At the station. †87
> Palm Sunday.
> Processional on Palm Sunday: stanzas 1–6.
> The verses composed in praise of Christ by the presbyter Juvencus *[sic]*. They are sung when they have returned and are approaching the main doors of the church. †86

Hic est dies verus Dei

> On Pascha until the Ascension except on holy feasts. †10
> On the Resurrection of the Lord. †9
> Third Sunday after Easter.

Iam, Christe, sol iustitiae

> Lent.
> Weekdays of Lent at Lauds.

Iam Christus astra ascenderat

> At a Nocturn. †139
> At Vespers. †140
> On Pentecost at a Nocturn. †142
> On Pentecost at Vespers. †141
> Pentecost at Terce, Sext, and None.
> Pentecost Sunday (Whitsunday).

Iam lucis orto sidere

> At Prime. †51, †52, †53, †54, †55, †56, †58, †63
> First Sunday after the octave of the Epiphany at Prime. †61
> Lauds on Thursdays.
> On the Epiphany at Prime. †49

On feasts with nine lessons. †62
On the vigil of the Epiphany at Prime. †48
Prime.
Sundays in Advent at Prime, and on the day of Saint
    Paul the apostle. †59

Iam surgit hora tertia

At Terce during the whole week. †12
Palm Sunday.
Terce.

Iesu, corona virginum

At Lauds. †145
Common of several virgins.
Common of virgins.
For virgins. †143, †146
On feasts for virgins. †147
On the nativity of one virgin at Vespers and at Lauds.
    †144
Second Vespers in the Common of virgins.

Iesu, nostra redemptio

Ascension Thursday.
At Compline. †148, †150
First Vespers of Ascension Thursday.
Holy Week.
Nocturns at Easter.
On the Ascension of the Lord at Lauds. †151
The Ascension of the Lord at Vespers. †149

Iesu, redemptor omnium

Fifth Sunday of Lent (Passion Sunday).
For confessors at Nocturns. †155
For one confessor. †152
Office of Readings on the feast of the Common of more
    than one Saint.
One confessor. †153
One confessor at Lauds. †154

Illuminans altissimus

> At Lauds. †13
> Baptism of Christ.
> Epiphany.
> Holy Epiphany.
> On the Epiphany of the Lord. †14

Immense caeli conditor

> At Vespers. †156
> Vespers on Monday.

Intende, qui regis Israel

> First Sunday of Advent.
> Nativity of the Lord.
> On the Nativity of the Lord at Vespers. †15
> Vigil of the Nativity at Vespers. †17

Lucis creator optime

> All Sundays after Trinity until Advent, and after the
>   octave of the Epiphany until Lent at Vespers. †159
> On Sundays until the beginning of Lent at Vespers. †158
> Sunday Vespers.
> Sundays at Vespers. †157
> Sundays, Ferial Office.

Magnae Deus potentiae

> At Vespers. †161
> Thursday Vespers.

Mediae noctis tempus est

> First Nocturn (midnight).
> Sunday Office of Readings in Week 2: stanzas 1–6, 13.
> Third and fourth Sundays in Lent at Nocturns. †35

Nox et tenebrae et nubila

> Contemplation at the hour of the morning office.
> On the Nativity of the Lord at Nocturns. †25

Nunc, sancte nobis Spiritus

> At Terce. †113, †123

At Terce on feasts with 9 lessons, and during the octave
of solemnities and on the octave of solemnities. †122
At Terce on Sundays. †121
At Terce with three lessons. †116
At the beginning of Advent, and the day of Saint Thomas
the apostle. †117
On ferias at Terce. †124
On the commemoration of Saints Oswald and Wulfstan
with twelve lessons. †119
Sundays during the year except on solemn feasts at
Terce. †118
Sundays, Ferial Office.
Terce in Advent.

O lux beata Trinitas

At Vespers. †89
Second Vespers on Sundays in Week 2.
Trinity Sunday.

O quanta qualia sunt illa sabbata

Day Hymn.
For the Book of Wisdom, Saturday at Vespers. †184
Vespers on Saturdays.

Optatus votis omnium

Ascension Thursday.
Lauds on the feast of the Ascension: stanzas 1, 3–7.
On the Ascension of the Lord. †182, †183

Pange, lingua

At a Nocturn. †39, †44
Fifth Sunday of Lent (Passion Sunday).
For the Passion of the Lord. †37
Lauds from Sunday to Friday in Holy Week:
stanzas 7–10.
Office of Readings from Sunday to Friday in Holy Week:
stanzas 1–4, 6.
On the Passion of the Lord at a Nocturn. †43
Saturday on the Passion of the Lord at Lauds. †42

Sunday on the Passion of the Lord at Vespers and at
Nocturns. †40

Primo dierum omnium

From the feast of Saint Michael until Advent, and after
the octave of the Epiphany until the first Sunday of
Lent at Matins. †162
Sunday Nocturns.
Sundays, Ferial Office.

Qua Christus hora sitiit

At Sext. †181
Sext in Lent.

Quem terra pontus aethera

Assumption of Mary.
Office of Readings int he Common of the Blessed Virgin
Mary: stanzas 1–2, 4–5.
On the feast of the Purification at Matins. †163
On the Purification of Blessed Mary at Lauds. †164,
†165

Rector potens, verax Deus

At Sext. †64, †67
At Sext on thirds and all doubles. †65
Sext between Christmas and Epiphany.
Sundays, Ferial Office.

Rerum Deus tenax vigor

At None. †168, †170
At None on third doubles. †169
None between Christmas and Epiphany.
Sundays, Ferial Office.

Rex gloriose martyrum

At Lauds. †171
Common of several martyrs.
For several martyrs. †174
Office of Readings when more than one martyr is being
celebrated.

536

Several martyrs. †172, †173

Somno refectis artubus

Feria 2 at Matins. †91
Monday Nocturns.
Office of Readings on Monday of Week 1 when
conducted at night or at first light.

Splendor paternae gloriae

At Lauds. †19, †20, †21
Feria 2 at Lauds. †22
Matins, between dawn and sunrise.

Summae Deus clementiae

Nocturns on Saturdays.
Office of Readings on Saturdays in Week 1 when the
Office of Readings is said at night or at break of day.
Saturday at Nocturns. †92
Saturdays, Ferial Office.

Te lucis ante terminum

At Compline. †69, †71, †72, †74
Compline.
For Saint Lambert. †76
Ordinary days at Compline. †73
Saturdays at Compline. †75
Sundays, Ferial Office.

Telluris ingens conditor

At Vespers. †175
Tuesday Vespers.

Tu, Trinitatis unitas

Feria 6 at Nocturns. †93
Nocturns.
Office of Readings on Fridays in Week 1.

Verbum supernum prodiens

At a Nocturn. †187
Benediction of the Blessed Sacrament: stanzas 5–6.

Corpus Christi at Lauds.
For the Body of Christ. †186
On the solemnity of the Body and Blood of the Lord.
    †185

Vexilla regis prodeunt

Fifth Sunday of Lent (Passion Sunday).
For the Passion of the Lord. †45
Vespers in Holy Week: stanzas 1, 3, 5–6, 8.

Liturgical Themes

Advent

> Conditor alme siderum | Iam lucis orto sidere |
> Intende, qui regis Israel | Nunc, sancte nobis Spiritus

Annunciation

> Agnoscat omne saeculum | Ave, maris stella

Apostles

> Aeterna Christi munera

Ascension

> Aeterne rex altissime | Iesu, nostra redemptio |
> Optatus votis omnium

Assumption

> Ave, maris stella | Quem terra pontus aethera

Baptism of Christ

> A Patre unigenitus | A solis ortus cardine |
> Illuminans altissimus

Benediction of the Blessed Sacrament

> Verbum supernum prodiens

Christmas

> A Patre unigenitus | Agnoscat omne saeculum |
> Christe, redemptor omnium | Intende, qui regis Israel |
> Nox et tenebrae et nubila | Rector potens, verax Deus |
> Rerum Deus tenax vigor

Confessors

> Iesu, redemptor omnium

Corpus Christi

> Verbum supernum prodiens

Easter

> Aurora lucis rutilat | Hic est dies verus Dei |
> Iesu, nostra redemptio

Epiphany

> A Patre unigenitus | A solis ortus cardine |
> Iam lucis orto sidere | Illuminans altissimus

General

> All poems *except:*
> Crux benedicta nitet | Deus, tuorum militum |
> Gloria, laus, et honor | Hic est dies verus Dei |
> Iam, Christe, sol iustitiae | Iesu, redemptor omnium |
> Intende, qui regis Israel | Optatus votis omnium |
> Quem terra pontus aethera | Vexilla regis prodeunt

Holy Cross

> Crux benedicta nitet

Holy Week

> Iesu, nostra redemptio | Pange, lingua |
> Vexilla regis prodeunt

Lent

> Audi, benigne conditor | Dei fide, qua vivimus |
> Ex more docti mystico | Iam, Christe, sol iustitiae |
> Mediae noctis tempus est | Primo dierum omnium |
> Qua Christus hora sitiit

Martyrs

> Deus, tuorum militum | Rex gloriose martyrum

Palm Sunday

> Gloria, laus, et honor | Iam surgit hora tertia

Passion Sunday

    Iesu, redemptor omnium | Pange, lingua |
    Vexilla regis prodeunt

Pentecost

    Beata nobis gaudia | Deus, creator omnium |
    Iam Christus astra ascenderat

Purification

    Ave, maris stella | Quem terra pontus aethera

Mary

    Ave, maris stella | Quem terra pontus aethera

Saints

    Iam lucis orto sidere: Saint Paul |
    Iesu, redemptor omnium |
    Nunc, sancte nobis Spiritus:
        Saint Thomas, Saint Oswald, Saint Wulfstan |
    Primo dierum omnium: Saint Michael |
    Te lucis ante terminum: Saint Lambert

Trinity Sunday

    O lux beata Trinitas

Virgins

    Iesu, corona virginum

Sequential Hymn List

†1–†3:	Aeterne rerum conditor
†4–†8:	Deus, creator omnium
†9–†11:	Hic est dies verus Dei
†12:	Iam surgit hora tertia
†13–†14:	Illuminans altissimus
†15–†18:	Intende, qui regis Israel
†19–†22:	Splendor paternae gloriae
†23:	Ales diei nuntius
†24–†25:	Nox et tenebrae et nubila
†26–†27:	Aeterna Christi munera
†28–†34:	A solis ortus cardine
†35:	Mediae noctis tempus est
†36:	Crux benedicta nitet
†37–†44:	Pange, lingua
†45:	Vexilla regis prodeunt
†46–†63:	Iam lucis orto sidere
†64–†68:	Rector potens, verax Deus
†69–†77:	Te lucis ante terminum
†78–†83:	Aurora lucis rutilat
†84–†85:	Dei fide, qua vivimus
†86–†87:	Gloria, laus, et honor
†88:	Consors paterni luminis
†89–†90:	O lux beata Trinitas
†91:	Somno refectis artubus
†92:	Summae Deus clementiae
†93:	Tu, Trinitatis unitas
†94–†95:	Aeterne rex altissime

†96–†97:	Audi, benigne conditor
†98–†105:	Ave, maris stella
†106–†112:	Beata nobis gaudia
†113–†124:	Nunc, sancte nobis Spiritus
†125:	Aeterna caeli gloria
†126:	Caeli Deus sanctissime
†127–†130:	Christe, redemptor omnium
†131–†133:	Conditor alme siderum
†134–†137:	Deus, tuorum militum
†138:	Ex more docti mystico
†139–†142:	Iam Christus astra ascenderat
†143–†147:	Iesu, corona virginum
†148–†151:	Iesu, nostra redemptio
†152–†155:	Iesu, redemptor omnium
†156:	Immense caeli conditor
†157–†160:	Lucis creator optime
†161:	Magnae Deus potentiae
†162:	Primo dierum omnium
†163–†166:	Quem terra pontus aethera
†167–†170:	Rerum Deus tenax vigor
†171–†174:	Rex gloriose martyrum
†175:	Telluris ingens conditor
†176–†177:	Agnoscat omne saeculum
†178–†179:	A Patre unigenitus
†180:	Iam, Christe, sol iustitiae
†181:	Qua Christus hora sitiit
†182–†183:	Optatus votis omnium
†184:	O quanta qualia sunt illa sabbata
†185–†187:	Verbum supernum prodiens

Alphabetical Hymn List

A Patre unigenitus	†178–†179
A solis ortus cardine	†28–†34
Aeterna caeli gloria	†125
Aeterna Christi munera	†26–†27
Aeterne rerum conditor	†1–†3
Aeterne rex altissime	†94–†95
Agnoscat omne saeculum	†176–†177
Ales diei nuntius	†23
Audi, benigne conditor	†96–†97
Aurora lucis rutilat	†78–†83
Ave, maris stella	†98–†105
Beata nobis gaudia	†106–†112
Caeli Deus sanctissime	†126
Christe, redemptor omnium	†127–†130
Conditor alme siderum	†131–†133
Consors paterni luminis	†88
Crux benedicta nitet	†36
Dei fide, qua vivimus	†84–†85
Deus, creator omnium	†4–†8
Deus, tuorum militum	†134–†137
Ex more docti mystico	†138
Gloria, laus, et honor	†86–†87
Hic est dies verus Dei	†9–†11
Iam, Christe, sol iustitiae	†180
Iam Christus astra ascenderat	†139–†142
Iam lucis orto sidere	†46–†63
Iam surgit hora tertia	†12

Iesu, corona virginum	†143–†147
Iesu, nostra redemptio	†148–†151
Iesu, redemptor omnium	†152–†155
Illuminans altissimus	†13–†14
Immense caeli conditor	†156
Intende, qui regis Israel	†15–†18
Lucis creator optime	†157–†160
Magnae Deus potentiae	†161
Mediae noctis tempus est	†35
Nox et tenebrae et nubila	†24–†25
Nunc, sancte nobis Spiritus	†113–†124
O lux beata Trinitas	†89–†90
O quanta qualia sunt illa sabbata	†184
Optatus votis omnium	†182–†183
Pange, lingua	†37–†44
Primo dierum omnium	†162
Qua Christus hora sitiit	†181
Quem terra pontus aethera	†163–†166
Rector potens, verax Deus	†64–†68
Rerum Deus tenax vigor	†167–†170
Rex gloriose martyrum	†171–†174
Somno refectis artubus	†91
Splendor paternae gloriae	†19–†22
Summae Deus clementiae	†92
Te lucis ante terminum	†69–†77
Telluris ingens conditor	†175
Tu, Trinitatis unitas	†93
Verbum supernum prodiens	†185–†187
Vexilla regis prodeunt	†45

Works Cited

Poems and Melodies

Stäblein, Bruno. *Die mittelalterlichen Hymnenmelodien des Abendlandes.* Bärenreiter, 1956. Monumenta Monodica Medii Aevi, vol. 1.

Walsh, Peter G. and Christopher Husch, editors. *One Hundred Latin Hymns: Ambrose to Aquinas.* Harvard UP, 2012.

Translations

Biggs, Louis Coutier, editor. *Hymns Ancient and Modern.* Novello, 1867.

Birkbeck, W. J., et al, editors. *The English Hymnal.* Oxford UP, 1906.

Blew, William John and Henry John Gauntlett, editors. *The Church Hymn and Tune Book.* Francis and John Rivington, 1852.

Bridges, Robert and H. Ellis Wooldridge, editors. *The Yattendon Hymnal.* Oxford UP, 1899.

Britt, Matthew, editor. *The Hymns of the Breviary and Missal.* Benziger Brothers, 1922.

Caswall, Edward, translator. *Hymns and Poems.* 2nd ed., Burns and Oates, 1873.

Chambers, John David, translator. *Lauda Syon.* J. Masters, 1866. 2 parts.

Charles, Elizabeth Rundle. *The Voice of Christian Life in Song.* Robert Carter, 1859.

Copeland, William John, translator. *Hymns for the Week, and Hymns for the Seasons.* W. J. Cleaver, 1848.

Duffield, Samuel Willoughby. *The Latin Hymn-Writers and Their Hymns.* Edited by R. E. Thompson, Funk and Wagnalls, 1889.

Edersheim, Alfred, translator. *The Jubilee Rhythm of St. Bernard of Clairvaux on the Name of Jesus, and Other Hymns.* James Nisbet, 1847.

Hewett, John William, translator. *Verses by a Country Curate.* T. Wayte, 1859.

Kynaston, Herbert. *Occasional Hymns.* R. Clay, Son, and Taylor, 1862.

Lawson, Mary Sackville, editor. *Collected Hymns, Sequences, and Carols of John Mason Neale.* Hodder and Stoughton, 1914.

MacGill, Hamilton, M., translator. *Songs of the Christian Creed and Life.* Basil Montagu Pickering, 1876.

Moultrie, Gerard. *Hymns and Lyrics for the Seasons and Saints' Days of the Church.* Joseph Masters, 1867.

Neale, John Mason, translator. *Mediæval Hymns and Sequences.* Joseph Masters, 1851.

———, translator. *The Words of the Hymnal Noted.* J. Alfred Novello, 1885.

Newman, John Henry. *Verses on Various Occasions.* Burns and Oates, 1868.

Pope, R. Martin, translator. *The Hymns of Prudentius.* J. M. Dent, 1905.

Thompson, Henry. *History of Roman Literature.* John Joseph Griffin, 1852.

Wackerbarth, Athanasius Diedrich, translator. *Lyra Ecclesiastica.* J. Bohn, 1842.

Wallace, John, translator. *Hymns of the Church.* Burns and Oates, 1874.

Ward, William. C., editor. *The Poems of William Drummond of Hawthornden.* Vol. 2, Lawrence and Bullen, 1894.

Woodward, G. R., editor. *Songs of Syon.* Schott, 1905.

Additional Information

"Arch.Cap.S.Pietro.B.79". *Manuscripts Catalogue.* Biblioteca Apostolica Vaticana, www.mss.vatlib.it/guii/console?service=shortDetail&id=228815. Accessed Feb. 20, 2020.

Blume, Clemens, editor. *Repertorium Repertorii: Kritischer Wegweiser Durch U. Chevalier's Repertorium Hymnologicum.* O. R. Reisland, 1901.

Boynton, Susan, et al. "Medieval Hymns and Hymnals". *The Canterbury Dictionary of Hymnology,* www.hymnology.co.uk/m/medieval-hymns-and-hymnals. Accessed Feb. 20, 2020.

———. "Gottschalk of Orbais". *The Canterbury Dictionary of Hymnology,* www.hymnology.co.uk/g/gottschalk-of-orbais. Accessed Feb. 20, 2020.

Caldwell, John, et al. "Latin Hymns". *The Canterbury Dictionary of Hymnology,* www.hymnology.co.uk/l/latin-hymns. Accessed Feb. 20, 2020.

Cuthbert, Michael Scott and Sasha Zamler-Carhart. "International Style and Medieval Italian Music: A Flemish Motet in the Ascoli Piceno/Montefortino Fragment". *Fama e Publica Vox nel Medioevo,* edited by Isa Lori Sanfilippo and Antonio Rigon, Istituto storico italiano per il Medioevo, 2011, pp. 213–227.

Gajard, Joseph. *Les Principaux Manuscrits de Chant: Grégorien, Ambrosien, Mozarabe, Gallican, Publiés en Fac-similés Phototypiques.* Vol. 14, Desclée, 1931.

"GB-Occ MS 134: Corpus Christi College, Oxford, United Kingdom". *The Digital Image Archive of Medieval Music,* Répertoire Internationale des Sources Musicales, Jan. 23, 2017, www.diamm.ac.uk/sources/553/#/.

Hiley, David. "Quilisma". *Grove Music Online.* 2001, Oxford UP, doi.org/10.1093/gmo/9781561592630.article.22699.

———. *Western Plainchant: A Handbook.* Clarendon Press, 1995.

Hornby, Emma and J. R. Watson. "Audi, Benigne Conditor". *The Canterbury Dictionary of Hymnology,*

www.hymnology.co.uk/a/audi,-benigne-conditor. Accessed
Feb. 20, 2020.

———. "Ave Maris Stella". *The Canterbury Dictionary of
Hymnology*, www.hymnology.co.uk/a/ave-maris-stella.
Accessed Feb. 20, 2020.

———. "Veni Creator Spiritus". *The Canterbury Dictionary of
Hymnology*, www.hymnology.co.uk/v/veni-creator-spiritus.
Accessed Feb. 20, 2020.

Julian, John, editor. *A Dictionary of Hymnology*. Revised ed., J.
Murray, 1915. 2 vols.

Jullien, Marie-Hélèn. "Les Sources de la Tradition Ancienne des
Quatorze 'Hymnes' Attribuées à Saint Ambroise de Milan".
Revue d'Histoire des Textes, bulletin no. 19 (1989), 1990, pp.
57–189, doi.org/10.3406/rht.1990.1339.

"Karlsruhe, Badische Landesbibliothek, Cod. St. Blasien 77".
Berliner Repertorium. Humboldt-Universität zu Berline,
repertorium.sprachen.hu-berlin.de/repertorium/browse/manus
cript/8782?_bc=S2.S50.S12. Accessed Feb. 20, 2020.

Koláček, Jan and Debra Lacoste. *Cantus Index*, Feb. 20, 2020,
cantusindex.org.

Kornrumpf, Gisela and Jürgen Wolf. "Breslau / Wrocław, Dombibl.
(Biblioteka Kapitulna), Cod. 58 [früher Diözesanarchiv, Ms.
58]". *Handschriftencensus: Eine Bestandsaufnahme der
handschriftlichen Überlieferung Deutschsprachiger Texte des
Mittelalters*. Philipps-Universität Marburg, Dec. 2018,
www.handschriftencensus.de/12712.

Ramsey, Boniface, translator. *The Sermons of St. Maximus of Turin*.
Newman Press, 1989. Ancient Christian Writers.

Solesmes, editors. *The Liber Usualis*. Desclée, 1961.

Springer, Carl P. E. "Sedulius". *The Canterbury Dictionary of
Hymnology*, www.hymnology.co.uk/s/sedulius. Accessed Feb.
20, 2020.

Treitler, Leo. *With Voice and Pen: Coming to Know Medieval Song
and How It Was Made*. Vol. 2, Oxford UP, 2003.

Wagner, Peter. *Einführung in die Gregorianischen Melodien:
Neumenkunde, Paläographie des Liturgischen Gesanges*. 2nd ed.,
Breitkopf and Härtel, 1912.

Watson, J. R. and Emma Hornby. "Aeterne Rex Altissime". *The Canterbury Dictionary of Hymnology*, www.hymnology.co.uk/a/aeterne-rex-altissime. Accessed Feb. 20, 2020.

———. "Beata Nobis Gaudia". *The Canterbury Dictionary of Hymnology*, www.hymnology.co.uk/b/beata-nobis-gaudia. Accessed Feb. 20, 2020.

———. "Nunc Sancte Nobis Spiritus". *The Canterbury Dictionary of Hymnology*, www.hymnology.co.uk/n/nunc-sancte-nobis-spiritus. Accessed Feb. 20, 2020.

WorldCat Identities. OCLC, Inc., worldcat.org/identities/.

Wulstan, David. "O Quanta Qualia Sunt Illa Sabbata". *The Canterbury Dictionary of Hymnology*, www.hymnology.co.uk/o/o-quanta-qualia-sunt-illa-sabbata. Accessed Feb. 20, 2020.

———. "Paraclete Hymnal". *The Canterbury Dictionary of Hymnology*, www.hymnology.co.uk/p/paraclete-hymnal. Accessed Feb. 20, 2020.

Bibliography

Research

Barrow, Julia, et al. "A Checklist of the Manuscripts Containing the Writings of Peter Abelard and Heloise and Other Works Closely Associated With Abelard and His School". *Revue d'Histoire des Textes*, bulletin no. 14–15 (1984–1985), 1986, pp. 183–302, doi.org/10.3406/rht.1986.1278.

Bell, Nicolas. "Byzantine Music and Musical Manuscripts". *Greek Manuscripts*, British Library, www.bl.uk/greek-manuscripts/articles/byzantine-music-and-musical-manuscripts. Accessed Feb. 20, 2020.

Berten, Oliver, editor. *GregoBase: A Database of Gregorian Scores*, Feb. 20, 2020, gregobase.selapa.net/.

Chenu, Marie-Dominique. "St. Thomas Aquinas: Italian Christian Theologian and Philosopher". *Encyclopædia Britannica*, Mar. 3, 2020, www.britannica.com/biography/Saint-Thomas-Aquinas.

"Detailed Record for Additional 37517". Catalogue of Illuminated Manuscripts. The British Library, www.bl.uk/catalogues/illuminatedmanuscripts/record.asp?MSID=8710. Accessed Feb. 20, 2020.

Dunkle, Brian P. *Enchantment and Creed in the Hymns of Ambrose of Milan*. Oxford UP, 2016.

Gueranger, Prosper. *The Liturgical Year: The Time After Pentecost*. Translated by Laurence Shepherd, James Duffy and Sons, 1879. 2 vols.

Haberl, Franz Xavier. *Kirchenmusikalisches Jahrbuch: Zwanzigster Jahrgang*. Friedrich Pustet, 1907.

Handschin, J. "Noch Eine Stimmtauschmässige Hymnenkomposition". *Acta Musicologica*, vol. 7, fasc. 2, Apr. – Jun. 1935, pp. 70–71, www.jstor.org/stable/931562.

Koláček, Jan. *Global Chant Database*, Nov. 2, 2009, www.globalchant.org/about.php.

"Liquescent". *Grove Music Online*. 2001, Oxford UP, doi.org/10.1093/gmo/9781561592630.article.16740.

Martin, Michael. "Hymni". *Thesaurus Precum Latinarum*. 2020, www.preces-latinae.org/thesaurus/Hymni.html.

Milfull, Inge. "Canterbury Hymnal". *The Canterbury Dictionary of Hymnology*, www.hymnology.co.uk/c/canterbury-hymnal. Accessed Feb. 20, 2020.

———. "Winchester Hymnal". *The Canterbury Dictionary of Hymnology*, www.hymnology.co.uk/w/winchester-hymnal. Accessed Feb. 20, 2020.

Mocquereau, André. *Les Principaux Manuscrits de Chant: Grégorien, Ambrosien, Mozarabe, Gallican, Publiés en Fac-similés Phototypiques*. Vol. 12, Desclée, 1922.

"Oriscus". *Grove Music Online*. 2001, Oxford UP, doi.org/10.1093/gmo/9781561592630.article.20467.

Palmer, G. H. and Francis Burgess, editors. *The Plainchant Gradual*. Revised 2nd ed., S. Mary's Press, 1965. 4 parts.

Parrish, Carl. *The Notation of Medieval Music*. Pendragon Press, 1978.

Sievers, Eduard, editor. *Die Murbacher Hymnen*. Booksellers of the Orphanage in Halle, 1874.

Solesmes, editors. *The Gregorian Missal for Sundays*. Desclée: 1990.

Stevenson, J., editor. *The Latin Hymns of the Anglo-Saxon Church, With an Interlinear Anglo-Saxon Gloss*. George Andrews, 1851.

Thornton, R. *St. Ambrose: His Life, Times, and Teaching*. Pott and Young, 1879.

"Virga Strata [Gutturalis, Franculus]". *Grove Music Online*. 2001, Oxford UP, doi.org/10.1093/gmo/9781561592630.article.52896.

Wackernagel, Philipp. *Das Deutsche Kirchenlied von der Ältesten Zeit*. Vol. 2, B. O. Leubner, 1867.

Wagner, Peter. *Einführung in die Gregorianischen Melodien: Gregorianische Formenlehre, Eine Choralische Stilkunde.* Breitkopf and Härtel, 1921.

Walpole, A. S., editor. *Early Latin Hymns.* Cambridge UP, 1922.

Weinmann, Carl. *Hymnarium Parisiense: Das Hymnar der Zisterzienser-Abtei Pairis im Elsass.* Friedrich Pustet, 1904.

Wieland, Gernot Rudolf, editor. *The Canterbury Hymnal: Edited From British Library MS. Additional 37517.* Pontifical Institute of Mediaeval Studies, 1982.

Unused Translations

A Collection of Anthems, Psalms and Hymns Sung at the Holy Trinity Church, Kingston Upon Hull. W. Rawson, 1803.

Adams, Nehemiah, editor. *Church Pastorals: Hymns and Tunes for Public and Social Worship.* Ticknor and Fields, 1864.

Alexander, William Lindsay, editor. *A Selection of Hymns for Public Worship in Christian Churches.* Adams and Charles Black, 1865.

Alford, Henry, editor. *Psalms and Hymns Adapted to the Sundays and Holydays.* Francis and John Rivington, 1844.

Anderson, Robert, editor. *The Works of the British Poets.* Vol. 4, John and Arthur Arch, 1795.

Anketell, John, translator. *Gospel and Epistle Hymns for the Christian Year.* Church Record Company, 1889.

Athanasius and Other Poems. Joseph Masters, 1858.

Bagshawe, Edward G, translator. *Breviary Hymns and Missal Sequences.* Art and Book Company, 1900.

Banks, James. *Nugæ: The Solace of Rare Leisure.* Robert Hardwicke, 1854.

Benedict, Erastus C, translator. *The Hymn of Hildebert and Other Mediæval Hymns.* Enlarged ed., Anson D. F. Randolph, 1868.

Blount, Walter Kirkham, translator. *Compleat Office of the Holy Week.* Matthew Turner, 1687.

Boggs, Edward B., editor. *The American Church Review.* Vol. 28, Trübner, 1876.

Bonar, H. N., editor. *Hymns by Horatius Bonar.* Henry Frowde, 1904.

Bonar, Horatius. *Hymns of Faith and Hope.* James Nisbet, 1861.

Brady and Tate, editors. *A Supplement to the New Version of Psalms.* 3rd ed., Daniel Brown, 1702.

Brown-Borthwick, Robert. *Select Hymns for Church and Home.* Edmonston and Douglas, 1871.

Burton, Edward, editor. *Three Primers Put Forth in the Reign of Henry VIII.* Oxford UP, 1834.

Byrnes, Aquinas, editor. *The Hymns of the Dominican Missal and Breviary.* B. Herder Book Company, 1943.

Catholic Hours, or the Family Prayer-Book. 5th ed., T. Jones, 1845.

Chandler, John, translator. *The Hymns of the Primitive Church.* John W. Parker, 1837.

Clay, William Keatinge, editor. *Private Prayers Put Forth by Authority During the Reign of Queen Elizabeth.* Cambridge UP, 1851.

Connelly, Joseph. *Hymns of the Roman Liturgy.* 1954.

Cosin, J. *A Collection of Private Devotions.* 11th ed., J. G. and F. Rivington, 1838.

Crippen, T. G., translator. *Ancient Hymns and Poems, Chiefly From the Latin.* Hodder and Stoughton, 1868.

Devotions, for the Use of the Liverpool Congregation. Vol. 2, G. Woods, 1783.

Doane, William Croswell, editor. *The Life and Writings of George Washington Doane.* Vol. 1, D. Appleton, 1860.

Eddis, Edward Wilton. *Hymns for the Use of the Churches.* 2nd ed., Strangeways and Walden, 1871.

Faber, Frederick W. *Jesus and Mary.* James Burns, 1849.

Florio, Caryl, editor. *Children's Hymns, With Tunes.* Biglow and Main, 1885.

Gurney, Alfred, editor. *Hymns From the Ancient English Service Books, Together With Sequences From Various Sources.* 1882.

Hall, Charles Cuthbert and Sigismond Lasar, editors. *Evangelical Hymnal With Tunes.* A. S. Barnes, 1880.

Heber, Reginald. *Hymns, Written and Adapted to the Weekly Church Service of the Year.* John Murray, 1827.

Housman, Henry, editor. *John Ellerton: Being a Collection of His Writings on Hymnology*. E. and J. B. Young: 1896.

Hymns Ancient and Modern. Revised ed., William Clowes, 1904.

Hymns and Anthems Adjusted to the Church Services Throughout the Christian Year. Hope, 1851.

Irons, William J. *Psalms and Hymns for the Church*. J. T. Hayes, 1883.

Johnston, J. A. *The English Hymnal*. John Henry Parker, 1852.

Keble, J. *Miscellaneous Poems*. 2nd ed., James Parker, 1869.

Kynaston, Herbert. *Miscellaneous Poetry*. B. Fellowes, 1841.

Lyons, editor. *The Catholic Psalmist*. Translated by Thomas J. Potter, 3rd ed., James Duffy, 1859.

Mant, Richard, translator. *Ancient Hymns From the Roman Breviary*. J. G. and F. Rivington, 1837.

McDougall, Alan G., translator. *Pange Lingua: Breviary Hymns of Old Uses With an English Rendering*. Burns and Oats, 1916.

Mercer, William, editor. *The Church Psalter and Hymn Book*. Music arranged by John Goss, James Nisbet, 1864.

Monk, William Henry, editor. *Hymns Ancient and Modern*. Complete ed., William Clowes, 1875.

Morgan, David T., translator. *Hymns of the Latin Church*. 1871.

Moultrie, Gerard. *Cantica Sanctorum or Hymns for the Black Letter Saints' Days*. St. Giles, 1880.

Nelson, et al., editors. *The Sarum Hymnal*. Brown and W. P. Aylward, 1868.

Newton, Wilberforce, editor. *Voices From a Busy Life or Selections From the Poetical Works of the Late Edward A. Washburn*. Anson D. F. Randolph, 1918.

Noyes, George Rapall and George Reuben Potter, editors. *Hymns Attributed to John Dryden*. University of California Berkeley Press, 1937.

Oxenham, Henry Nutcombe. *The Sentence of Kaïres, and Other Poems*. 2nd ed., Longmans and Green, 1867.

Palmer, G. H., editor. *The Hymner*. 1904.

Palmer, W. *Short Poems and Hymns, the Latter Mostly Translations*. I. Shrimpton, 1845.

Putnam, Alfred P. *Singers and Songs of the Liberal Faith.* Roberts Brothers, 1875.

Russell, Arthur T. *Psalms and Hymns, Partly Original, Partly Selected for the Use of the Church of England.* John Deighton, 1851.

Schaff, Philip, editor. *Christ in Song: Hymns of Immanuel Selected From All Ages With Notes.* Sampson Low, Son, and Marston, 1870.

Shipley, Orby, editor. *Annus Sanctus: Hymns of the Church for the Ecclesiastical Year.* Burns and Oates, 1884.

———, editor. *Lyra Eucharistica: Hymns and Verses on the Holy Communion.* 2nd ed., Longmans, Green, Longman, Roberts, and Green, 1864.

———, editor. *Lyra Messianica: Hymns and Verses on the Life of Christ.* Longmans, Green, Longman, Roberts, and Green, 1864.

———, editor. *Lyra Mystica: Hymns and Verses on Sacred Subjects, Ancient and Modern.* Longmans, Green, Longman, Roberts, and Green, 1865.

Singleton, Robert Corbet and Edwin George Monk, editors. *The Anglican Hymn Book.* 1st and 2nd eds. Novello and Ewer, 1868 and 1871.

Skinner, James, editor. *The Daily Service Hymnal.* Rivingtons, 1863.

Stuart, John Patrick Crighton (Marquess of Bute), translator. *The Roman Breviary.* Vol 2, William Blackwood, 1879.

Sullivan, Arthur, editor. *Church Hymns With Tunes.* E. and J. B. Young, 1885.

The Hymnal Noted, With Appendix Revised and Greatly Enlarged and Supplement. 10th ed., J. Masters, 1889.

The People's Hymnal. 6th ed., J. Masters, 1877.

Waddell, Helen, translator. *Mediæval Latin Lyrics.* Henry Holt, 1948.

Walton, Henry Baskerville, editor. *The First Book of Common Prayer of Edward VI and the Ordinal of 1549 Together With the Order of the Communion, 1548.* Rivingtons, 1869.

Whytehead, Thomas. *Poems.* J. G. F. and J. Rivington, 1842.

Williams, Isaac. *Hymns on the Catechism.* James Burns, 1843.

———. *Hymns Translated From the Parisian Breviary.* J. G. F. and J. Rivington, 1839.

———. *Thoughts in Past Years.* D. Appleton, 1841.

Williams, J., translator. *Ancient Hymns of Holy Church.* Henry S. Parsons, 1845.

Wither, George. *The Hymnes and Songs of the Church.* 1623.

Woodford, J. R., translator. *Hymns, Arranged for the Sundays and Holy-Days of the Church of England.* Joseph Masters, 1855.

Woodman, Clarence E. *A Manual of Prayers for the Use of the Catholic Laity.* Burns and Oates, 1889.

Woodward, G. R, editor. *The Cowley Carol Book for Christmas, Easter, and Ascension-Tide.* Revised ed., A. R. Mowbray, 1922.